n
7/7/06

Families And People With Mental Retardation And Quality Of Life: International Perspectives

Families And People With Mental Retardation And Quality Of Life: International Perspectives

Edited by

Ann Turnbull,

Ivan Brown,

and H. Rutherford Turnbull III

David L. Braddock

Editor, AAMR Books and Monographs

AAMR

American Association on Mental Retardation

Published by
American Association on Mental Retardation
444 North Capitol Street, NW
Suite 846
Washington, DC 20001-1512

The points of view expressed herein are those of the authors and do not necessarily represent the official policy or opinion of the American Association on Mental Retardation. Publication does not imply endorsement by the editor, the Association, or its individual members.

Printed in the United States of America

ISBN: 0-940898-87-X

Contributors

Nehama Baum
Center for Health Promotion
University of Toronto
Toronto, Canada

Gwen Beegle
Beach Center on Families and
    Disabilities
University of Kansas
Lawrence, Kansas

Martha Blue-Banning
Beach Center on Families and
    Disabilities
University of Kansas
Lawrence, Kansas

Nancy Breitenbach
Formerly of Inclusion International
Paris, France

Ivan Brown
Centre of Excellence for Child
    Welfare
University of Toronto
Toronto, Ontario, Canada

Roy I. Brown
Center for Health Promotion
University of Toronto
Toronto, Canada
Flinders University
Adelaide, South Australia, Australia
University of Calgary
Calgary, Alberta, Canada
University of Victoria
Victoria, British Columbia, Canada

Ruth Davey
School of Special Education and
    Disability Studies
Flinders University
Adelaide, South Australia, Australia

Corine Frankland
Beach Center on Families and
    Disabilities
University of Kansas
Lawrence, Kansas

Barry Isaacs
Center for Health Promotion
University of Toronto
Toronto, Canada

Stephanie Jones
Applied Research Unit
Psychological Medicine
University of Wales College of
    Medicine
Cardiff, Wales, United Kingdom

Jean Judes
Tel-Hai Academic College
Upper Galilee, Israel

Batya Krauss
Tel-Hai Academic College
Upper Galilee, Israel

Margaret Kyrkou
School of Special Education and
    Disability Studies
Flinders University
Adelaide, South Australia, Australia

Lisa Mische Lawson
Beach Center on Families and
    Disabilities
University of Kansas
Lawrence, Kansas

Janet Marquis
Beach Center on Families and
    Disabilities
University of Kansas
Lawrence, Kansas

Barbara McCormick
Center for Health Promotion
University of Toronto
Toronto, Canada

Shimshon M. Neikrug
Tel-Hai Academic College
Upper Galilee, Israel

Louise Lord Nelson
Beach Center on Families and
    Disabilities
University of Kansas
Lawrence, Kansas

JiYeon Park
Beach Center on Families and
    Disabilities
University of Kansas
Lawrence, Kansas

Trevor R. Parmenter
Centre for Developmental
    Disability Studies
Royal Rehabilitation Centre Sydney
University of Sydney
Ryde, New South Wales, Australia

Denise Poston
Beach Center on Families and
    Disabilities
University of Kansas
Lawrence, Kansas

Rebecca Renwick
Center for Health Promotion
University of Toronto
Toronto, Canada

Dana Roth
Tel-Hai Academic College
Upper Galilee, Israel

Robert L. Schalock
Hastings College
Hastings, Nebraska

Jo Shearer
School of Special Education and
    Disability Studies
Flinders University
Adelaide, South Australia, Australia

Julia Shearn
Applied Research Unit
Psychological Medicine
University of Wales College of
    Medicine
Cardiff, Wales, United Kingdom

Matt Stowe
Beach Center on Families and
    Disabilities
University of Kansas
Lawrence, Kansas

Jean Ann Summers
Beach Center on Families and
    Disabilities
University of Kansas
Lawrence, Kansas

Stuart Todd
Applied Research Unit
Psychological Medicine
University of Wales College of
    Medicine
Cardiff, Wales, United Kingdom

Ann Turnbull
Beach Center on Families and
    Disabilities
University of Kansas
Lawrence, Kansas
H. Rutherford Turnbull III
Beach Center on Families and
    Disabilities
University of Kansas
Lawrence, Kansas

Table Of Contents

List Of Tables xi
List Of Figures xiii
Preface
       Rud Turnbull, Ann Turnbull, and Ivan Brown xv

Part 1 Foundations Of Family Quality Of Life
Chapter 1: **Family Quality Of Life As An Area Of Study**
       Ivan Brown and Roy I. Brown 3
Chapter 2: **Moving From Individual To Family Quality Of Life**
       As A Research Topic
       Robert L. Schalock 11
Chapter 3: **Concepts For Beginning Study In Family**
       Quality Of Life
       Ivan Brown and Roy I. Brown 25

Part 2 Family Quality Of Life Inquiry in Five Countries
Chapter 4: **Enhancing Quality Of Life Of Families Of Children**
       And Youth With Disabilities In The United States
       Ann Turnbull, Rud Turnbull, Denise Poston, Gwen Beegle,
       Martha Blue-Banning, Corine Frankland, Lisa Mische
       Lawson, Louise Lord Nelson, Janet Marquis, Ji Yeon Park,
       Matt Stowe, and Jean Ann Summers 51
Chapter 5: **Family Quality Of Life In Wales**
       Stuart Todd, Pauline Young, Julia Shearn,
       and Stephanie Jones 103
Chapter 6: **Family Quality Of Life In Israel**
       Shimshon M. Neikrug, Jean Judes, Dana Roth,
       and Batya Krauss 151
Chapter 7: **Family Quality Of Life In Canada**
       Ivan Brown, Barry Isaacs, Barbara McCormack,
       Nehama Baum, and Rebecca Renwick 185
Chapter 8: **Family Quality Of Life In Australia**
       Roy Brown, Ruth Davey, Jo Shearer,
       and Margaret Kyrkou 223

Part 3 Implications for Policies and Practices

Chapter 9: **Family Quality Of Life: Implications For Policy**
Trevor R. Parmenter 265

Chapter 10: **Family Quality Of Life: Implications
For Family Support**
Nancy Breitenbach 299

Epilogue
Rud Turnbull, Ann Turnbull, and Ivan Brown 321

Tables

Table 2.1   Core Quality Of Life Domains And Indicators 15

Table 2.2   Family Quality Of Life Measurement And
              Application Principles 18

Table 4.1   Poston Family Needs In Three Service System Strands 62

Table 4.2   Overview Of Studies To Develop Measurement Tools 70

Table 4.3   Core Concepts Of Disability Policy 71

Table 4.4   Illustrative Core Concepts As They Relate To The
              Poston's Family Quality Of Life 74

Table 4.5   Domains And Indicators Of Interpersonal Partnerships 77

Table 4.6   Family Quality Of Life Domains, Indicators,
              And Poston Family Examples 81

Table 6.1   Percentage Of Identified Special-Needs Children Who
              Receive Various Special Services 159

Table 6.2   Percentage Of Special-Needs Children Not Receiving
              Required Services For Three Age Groups 160

Table 7.1   Number Of Families Reporting Family
              Relationship Activities 203

Table 7.2   Number Of Families Reporting Degrees Of Practical
              And Emotional Support 204

Table 7.3   Number Of Families Reporting Use
              Of Seven Types Of Services 206

Table 7.4   Number Of Families Reporting Degrees Of Spiritual
              And Cultural Support 208

Table 8.1   Conceptualization Of Quality Of Life 253

Table 8.2   Principles Of Quality Of Life 253

Table 8.3   Examples Of Key Family Quality Of Life Indicators 253

Table 8.4   Examples Of Critical Components In Family
              Quality Of Life 254

Figures

Figure 2.1   Methodological Pluralism Model 16

Figure 4.1   Old Paradigm: Emphasis On "Fixing" The Individual 59

Figure 4.2   New Paradigm: Emphasis On "Fixing" The System 60

Figure 4.3   Continuum Of Family Participation In Research 66

Figure 4.4   New Paradigm Analytical Framework For
Enhancing Family Quality Of Life .67

Figure 4.5   Original And Revised Partnership Models 80

Figure 4.6   Steps In Constructing Family Partnership And Family
Quality Of Life Scales, Indices, And Matrices 84

Figure 4.7   Structural Model For Explanatory Research 85

Figure 7.1   Attainment In Nine Areas Of Family Life For 28 Parents
Of Children With Intellectual Disabilities 212

Figure 7.2   Opportunities In Nine Areas Of Family Life For 28
Parents Of Children With Intellectual Disabilities 213

Figure 7.3   Initiative In Nine Areas Of Family Life For 28 Parents
Of Children With Intellectual Disabilities 214

Figure 7.4   Satisfaction In Nine Areas Of Family Life For 28
Parents Of Children With Intellectual Disabilities 215

Figure 9.1   A Dynamic Model Of Social Capital 288

Preface

The Unusualness Of This Book

There was a time when the mantra "Nothing about us without us" was novel and radical. Novel in that it was new; radical in that it challenged the status quo. Today, and in this book, that mantra—that postmodern, consumer-grounded premise—finds a different expression. Instead of being a rallying cry for the "self-advocacy" movement, it is the premise of this book: Nothing about family quality of life without the voice of the families. That is one of the unusual features of this book: It gives voice to the families whose quality of life is under discussion.

Another unusual feature is that the book places the families' voices on the same platform, and at the same height, as the voices of two other powerful groups: researchers and policy leaders. Here, then, is a tripartite perspective on family quality of life: families, researchers, and policy leaders join in writing this book.

More than these features, however, this book is unique in yet another way. It is international. Here are chapters that are emblematic of the family quality of life issues as they arise in Canada, Israel, Australia, the United Kingdom (Wales), and the United States of America. These are preceded by three chapters that provide a foundation for understanding the evolution in inquiry from a focus on individual quality of life to family quality of life, as well as an overview of basic concepts related to family quality of life. The book concludes with broad-stroke chapters focusing on policy, research directions, and perspectives about research, programs, and policy.

Four Common Themes

With all this, one might well ask: Are there any common themes? What unifies the text? Or is there disjunction and disconnection throughout? The answer is that there are unifying themes. They fall into four categories: research, family-centered programs, policy, and family voices.

Acknowledgment And Gratitude

A few words about the source of this book are appropriate. It arises from a symposium organized and sponsored by the Beach Center on Families and Disability, the University of Kansas (Ann and Rud Turnbull, codirectors, Anette Lundsgaarde, assistant director), with cosponsorship by the Centre for Health Promotion, University of Toronto (Ivan Brown, director), and the Inter-American Children's Institute, a specialized organ of the Organization of American States (Alejandro Bonasso, director general).

The symposium was held in late July and early August 2000, in conjunction with the 11th World Congress of the International Association for the Scientific Study of Intellectual Disabilities, in Seattle, Washington, U.S.A.

The symposium honored Maria Eloisa Garcia Etchegoyhen de Lorenzo, a pioneer (in her role as director of the mental retardation unit of the Inter-American Children's Institute and in other roles) in international forums for the quality of life of families affected by disability.

Eloisa's commitment to families is best evidenced by her own words:

> We have a common faith; we are committed to improve the quality
> of life of those who in silent ways are the testimony of our capacity
> for giving creatively and with love.

Similarly, Eloisa's inspiring presence remained throughout the symposium, proof of her faith:

> Life goes through us, it enriches us and keeps on going indefinitely.
> Each one of us can work to change a part of life's events. The sum
> of those actions will provide the ingredients for writing the history
> of this generation.

Enriching the symposium by their memories of Eloisa were two of her and Juan Carlos' children, Isabella Lorenzo-Hubert and Marcos Lorenzo; commentary by Alejandro Bonasso of the Inter-American Children's Institute and Graziella Reyes, consul general of Uruguay for the U.S.A./Midwest Region, both of whom were Eloisa's friends; and a special citation and greeting from the president of Uruguay, Dr. Jorge Batlle, also one of Eloisa's friends.

The symposium would not have been possible without the significant and long-term support of Marianna Kistler Beach and Ross Beach, of Hays and Lawrence, Kansas, U.S.A., who were close friends of Eloisa's. Indeed, Mrs. Beach served three terms as president of the Institute's Directing Council and has been the person most responsible for connecting Eloisa, the Turnbulls, the Beach Center, and the Inter-American Children's Institute to each other and for inspiring them to sponsor this symposium in Eloisa's honor.

Likewise, support for the symposium came from the Kansas University Endowment Association (James B. Martin, president); the National Institute for Disability and Rehabilitation Research, U.S. Department of Education (Roseann Rafferty, Project Officer); various units of the University of Kansas; and the Center for International Rehabilitation Research

Information and Exchange, the University of Buffalo, New York, U.S.A. (John Stone, project director, and Kathleen Pipitone, project coordinator).

We are grateful to all who made this book possible and who have launched this new line of inquiry and policy reform.

Rud Turnbull

Ann Turnbull

Ivan Brown

Part 1

FOUNDATIONS OF FAMILY QUALITY OF LIFE

The three chapters in Part 1 provide a context for studying family quality of life from the perspectives of current knowledge derived from research on individual quality of life and the emerging research area of family quality of life.

Chapter 1

Family Quality Of Life As An Area Of Study

Ivan Brown
University of Toronto
Toronto, Ontario, Canada

Roy I. Brown
Flinders University
Adelaide, South Australia, Australia

This book represents an introduction to family quality of life as an area of study. It arises from collaboration among scholars, family members, policy makers, and service providers from several countries over the past 3 years. One significant outcome of this collaboration was the Eloisa de Lorenzo Symposium on Family Quality of Life, held in Seattle, Washington, U.S.A., July 30 to August 1, 2000, and sponsored by the Beach Center for Studies in Family and Disability at the University of Kansas (U.S.A.). This symposium offered a unique opportunity for scholars to bring forward work they were beginning to undertake in family quality of life, and for scholars, family members, policy makers, and service providers to present and discuss important conceptual and practical ideas to the emerging area of family quality of life study. The contents of this book reflect the expanded thinking of the principal presenters at the symposium.

Focus Of The Book

The focus of this book is on quality of life within families that have at least one member with an intellectual disability, often referred to as *mental retardation* in the United States and elsewhere, *developmental disabilities* in Canada and other countries, and *learning disabilities* in the United Kingdom. These terms relate to the presence of cognitive and social impairments, which may be accompanied by emotional difficulties. Some individuals concerned also experience other and allied disabilities (e.g., seizure disorder). Disabilities arise from both genetic and environmental factors, and often genetic and/or environmental factors interact in complex ways to contribute to an individual's disabilities (for a full explanation of causes of and contributing factors to intellectual disabilities, see Percy & Brown, 1999).

Why Study Family Quality Of Life?

The main purpose for undertaking study in the area of family quality of life is to work toward ensuring that families have resources available and feel supported in their efforts to have all family members lead lives that are effective and fulfilling. At the same time, it is recognized that study in the area of family quality of life within the context of intellectual disability will have strong application to all families, with or without a member with disabilities.

Families have always been important to people with intellectual disabilities. For centuries, families were the main caregivers and supporters, and it has only been within the past two centuries that options outside the family have been available. Due to policy and practice changes of recent years in promoting community living, however, families are once again playing a more central role in supporting people with intellectual disabilities than has been the case for many earlier decades of this century. An increasing proportion of children and adults, particularly those with severe disabilities, is being supported at home since most of the institutions in the Western world have been closed. Associated with this is a higher survival rate among people with severe and profound disabilities, many of whom are now living well into their adult years.

There is renewed interest on the part of policy makers in (a) providing support to families so that they can help themselves, (b) assuring that families have a number of options available to them from which to choose the types of supports they need, and (c) ensuring that families are empowered to make choices that are best for them and for their sons or daughters with disabilities. These interests have resulted in initiatives that feature family-centered approaches. Family-centered approaches stress what is best for families and are based on the principle that families' lives are best when the unique voices of families and each of their members are encouraged and responded to, when their unique abilities are developed, and when their unique needs are supported. Initial efforts to put family-centered approaches into practice have taken the form in most higher-income countries of trying to find ways for families, services, and policy makers to work together in partnership (A. Turnbull & R. Turnbull, 1996). In this sense, the current renewed focus on families is very timely indeed.

There is growing recognition of how a family member with an intellectual disability affects a family. Considerable work has been directed toward stress within such families (e.g., Baxter, Cummins, & Yiolitis, 2000; Glidden & Floyd, 1997; Minnes, Nachshen, & Woodford, 1999), and some work has been completed on the need for services (e.g., Hayden & Goldman, 1996; Smith, Tobin, & Fullmer, 1995a), family coping (e.g., Mickelson,

Wroble, & Helgeson, 1999), planning for the future (e.g., Bigby, 2000; Clark & Susa, 2000), concerns of elderly parents (e.g., McCallion & Tobin, 1995; Smith, Tobin, & Fullmer, 1995b), effects on siblings (e.g., Eisenberg, Baker, & Blacher, 1998; Senel & Akkoek, 1995; Stoneman & Berman, 1993), working with families (e.g., Bromley, 1998; Munro, 1999), and other aspects of family life.

One striking aspect of this literature is how little of it focuses on the positive effects of having a son or daughter with an intellectual disability. Indeed, for the past several decades, the literature has referred to the beliefs and attitudes of parents of children with intellectual disabilities primarily by describing a wide range of negative feelings. This emphasis may have resulted from the belief, held throughout most of the 20th century, that it was best to remove children with intellectual disabilities from their families and society.

There have been exceptions in the literature to emphasizing the negative aspects of having a child with an intellectual disability. The writing of Hannam (1975), a parent who had a child with Down syndrome, provided a vivid and frank account of some of the issues facing family members. Even now, however, many of his recommendations have not put been put into effect. Other exceptions to negative expression of disability within families were contained in two collections of parent perspectives that described family joys and challenges in a context of current policy, service, and academic advancement (A. Turnbull & R. Turnbull, 1978; R. Turnbull & A. Turnbull, 1985). Similarly, Lawrence, Brown, Mills, and Estay (1993) looked at the quality of life of adults with Down syndrome and provided commentary from parents and others on relationships within the family. Much of this reporting is positive, with many comments on the changing perceptions of parents as their children grow and face adulthood. More recently, Renwick, Brown, and Raphael (1998) asked 38 sets of parents of children with intellectual disabilities how their lives had been enriched, and these authors reported a number of positive effects described by parents. There is no doubt that having a son or daughter with an intellectual disability is difficult in many ways and presents unique challenges, but there is equally no doubt that the presence of intellectual disability within a family frequently gives family members reason to believe their lives have been enriched.

It is interesting that the work on positive effects of having a son or daughter with a disability has arisen almost exclusively from literature that emphasizes families' own perspectives and that gives family members an opportunity to have a voice. But, besides those referred to above, there has been only a rather thin trickle of reports to date that represent the voice of family members about the quality of family life as a whole (e.g., Crutcher, 1990; Ficker Terrill, 1996; Knox et al., 1995; McPhail, 1996; A. Turnbull & Ruef, 1997). Thus the infrequent emphasis on the positive effects of intellectual disability in families may result primarily from a body of literature that has not solicited the perspective of family members as frequently as it might have. The nature and severity of a disability may also be critically important in this regard. Further, it must be recognized that it is only during the last quarter of the 20th century that most people with intellectual disability remained under parental supervision.

Even most of the quality of life literature in the field of intellectual disabilities that reflects perceptions focuses on individuals with disabilities themselves, rather than the rest of the family. In fact, the importance of the perceptions of families and individual family members—including grandparents and other "extended" family members—of the quality of their own lives and the lives of the family members with disabilities is only beginning to be clearly recognized (e.g., Gath & McCarthy, 1996; Hayes, 1996; McKenzie, 1999).

Researchers and practitioners have not stressed the family perspective perhaps in part because the emphasis of services in most higher-income countries has changed rather quickly, over the past three decades, from institutional care to community living to family inclusion; this change is still underway. The change within service delivery to an emphasis on family inclusion will, no doubt, have both beneficial and detrimental effects on the quality of family life. There is now a fairly strong belief in many quarters that people with intellectual disabilities have better lives and are better served within their own families. This belief has even resulted in the term *service* often being replaced by the term *support.*

Yet there are dangers to moving fully to supporting individuals with intellectual disabilities within family contexts, rather than providing service to them as individuals: Such action may become mission-oriented and overlook its detrimental effects; the values associated with it may be too closely connected to providing services based on principles of cost-efficiency, a process often referred to as economic rationalization (Brown, 1999); and families differ considerably in their ability to seek out services and provide effective and stimulating family environments (Clarke & Clarke, 2000). These and other dangers associated with current and emerging service delivery philosophy represent another strong reason for careful examination of the quality of life within a family, including an exploration of what contributes to family quality of life and to what degree it can be enhanced. As this book unfolds, therefore, the reader will see that contributors examine both the beneficial and detrimental effects of having a family member with an intellectual disability on family quality of life.

Moving Forward

Family Quality of Life and International Perspectives introduces us to the study of family quality of life. In part 1 the context for studying family quality of life is set out from the perspective of current knowledge about quality of life and of family advocacy. Part 2 presents the work of teams of parents, practitioners, and researchers from each of five countries—the United States, the United Kingdom, Israel, Canada, and Australia. The chapters here place families within the context of the customs and sociopolitical trends of their own countries, in an effort to provide the basis of a broad understanding of the close relationship between environment and family quality of life. They also provide details of the lives of families to illustrate the complex nature of family quality of life, by featuring the stories, ideas, and research findings from each country research team—made up of both family members and experts in disability, family life, and quality of life. These chapters also begin to identify some of the factors that are crucial to experiencing a high level of family quality of life. Finally, part 3 synthesizes some of the ideas presented in the preceding chapters and outlines implications for future work related to family quality of life for policy development and practice.

As editors and authors of *Family Quality of Life and International Perspectives*, we have compiled the material with the intention of introducing family quality of life as a focus of study and research. In doing so, we have made every attempt to pay particular attention to making such study and research relevant to the lives of families who have family members with intellectual disabilities by placing our analyses within the context of family stories. But it is also our belief that focused study in family quality of life, when applied, will be of considerable benefit to these families.

References

Baxter, C., Cummins, R. A., & Yiolitis, L. (2000). Parental stress attributed to family members with and without disability: A longitudinal study. *Journal of Intellectual & Developmental Disabilities, 25,* 105–118.

Bigby, C. (2000). Models of parental planning. In M. Janicki & E. Ansello (Eds.), <u>Community supports for aging adults with lifelong disabilities</u> (pp. 81–95). Baltimore: Paul H. Brookes.

Bromley, J. (1998). Working with families. In E. Emerson & C. Hatton (Eds.), *Clinical psychology and people with intellectual disabilities* (pp. 247–264). The Wiley series in clinical psychology. Chichester, UK: American Ethnological Press.

Brown, I. (1999). Embracing quality of life in times of spending restrain. *Journal of Intellectual & Developmental Disabilities, 24,* 299–308.

Clark, P. G., & Susa, C. B. (2000). Promoting personal, familial, and organizational change through futures planning. In M. Janicki & E. Ansello (Eds.), *Community supports for aging adults with lifelong disabilities* (pp. 121–136). Baltimore: Paul H. Brookes.

Clarke, A. M., & Clarke, A. D. B. (2000). *Early experience in the life path.* London: Jessica Kingsley.

Crutcher, D. (1990). Quality of life versus quality of life judgments: A parent's perspective. In R. Schalock (Ed.), *Quality of life: Perspectives and issues* (pp. 17–22). Washington, DC: American Association on Mental Retardation.

Eisenberg, L., Baker, B., & Blacher, J. (1998). Siblings of children with mental retardation living at home or in residential placement. *Journal of Child Psychology & Psychiatry & Allied Disciplines, 39,* 355–363.

Ficker Terrill, C. (1996). Quality: A parent's perspective. In R. Schalock (Ed.), *Quality of life: Vol. 1. Conceptualization and measurement* (pp. 33–36). Washington, DC: American Association on Mental Retardation.

Gath, A., & McCarthy, J. (1996). Families and siblings: A response to recent research. In B. Stratford & P. Gunn (Eds.), *New approaches to Down syndrome* (pp. 361–368). London: Cassell.

Glidden, L., & Floyd, F. (1997). Disaggregating parental depression and family stress in assessing families of children with developmental disabilities: A multisample analysis. *American Journal on Mental Retardation, 102,* 250–266.

Hannam, C. (1975). *Parents and mentally handicapped children.* Harmondsworth, UK: Penguin Books.

Hayden, M., & Goldman, J. (1996). Families of adults with mental retardation: Stress levels and need for services. *Social Work, 41,* 657–667.

Hayes, A. (1996). Family life in community context. In B. Stratford & P. Gunn (Eds.), *New approaches to Down syndrome* (pp. 369–404). London: Cassell.

Knox, M., Parmenter, T. R., Atkinson, N., Kearney, B., Mattock, D., & Yazbeck, M. (1995). *If only they would listen to us.* Sydney, Australia: Macquarie University, School of Education, Unit for Community Integration Studies.

Lawrence, P. L., Brown, R. I., Mills, J., & Estay, I. (1993). *Adults with Down syndrome: Together we can do it.* Toronto: Captus Press & Canadian Down Syndrome Society.

McCallion, P., & Tobin, S. (1995). Social workers' perceptions of older parents caring at home for sons and daughters with developmental disabilities. *Mental Retardation, 33,* 153–162.

McKenzie, S. (1999). Using quality of life as the focus for investigating the lives of people who have children with disabilities. *International Journal of Practical Approaches to Disability, 23*(2), 9–16.

McPhail, E. (1996). A parent's perspective. In R. Renwick, I. Brown, & M. Nagler (Eds.), *Quality of life in health promotion and rehabilitation: Conceptual approaches, issues, and applications* (pp. 279–289). Thousand Oaks, CA: Sage.

Mickelson, K., Wroble, M., & Helgeson, V. (1999). "Why my child?": Parental attributions for children's special needs. *Journal of Applied Social Psychology, 29,* 1263–1292.

Minnes, P., Nachshen. J., & Woodford, L. (1999). The role of families. In I. Brown & M. Percy (Eds.), *Developmental disabilities in Ontario* (pp. 157–172). Toronto: Front Porch.

Munro, D. (1999). Understanding and helping "difficult" families. In I. Brown & M. Percy (Eds.), *Developmental disabilities in Ontario* (pp. 173–180). Toronto: Front Porch.

Percy, M., & Brown, I. (1999). Causes and contributing factors, and approaches to intervention. In I. Brown & M. Percy (Eds.), *Developmental disabilities in Ontario* (pp. 223–251). Toronto: Front Porch.

Renwick, R., Brown, I., & Raphael, D. (1998). *The family quality of life project: Final report to the Ontario Ministry of Community and Social Services.* Toronto: University of Toronto, Centre for Health Promotion, Quality of Life Research Unit.

Senel, H., & Akkoek, F. (1995). Stress levels and attitudes of normal siblings of children with disabilities. *International Journal for the Advancement of Counselling, 18*(2), 61–68.

Smith, G., Tobin, S., & Fullmer, E. (1995a). Assisting older families of adults with lifelong disabilities. In G. Smith, S. Tobin, & E. Fullmer

(Eds.), *Strengthening aging families: Diversity in practice and policy* (pp. 80–98). Thousand Oaks, CA: Sage.

Smith, G., Tobin, S., & Fullmer, E. (1995b). Elderly mothers caring at home for offspring with mental retardation: A model of permanency planning. *American Journal on Mental Retardation, 99,* 487–499.

Stoneman, Z., & Berman, P. (Eds.). (1993). *The effects of mental retardation, disability, and illness on sibling relationships: Research issues and challenges.* Baltimore: Paul H. Brookes.

Turnbull, A., & Ruef, M. (1997). Family perspectives on inclusive lifestyle issues for people with problem behavior. *Exceptional Children, 63,* 211–227.

Turnbull, A., & Turnbull, R. (Eds.). (1978). *Parents speak out: Growing with a handicapped child.* Columbus, OH: C. E. Merrill.

Turnbull, A., & Turnbull, R. (1996). *Families, professionals, and exceptionality: A special partnership.* Upper Saddle River, NJ: Merrill.

Turnbull, R., & Turnbull, A. (Eds.). (1985). *Parents speak out: Then and now.* Columbus, OH: C. E. Merrill.

Chapter 2

Moving From Individual To Family Quality Of Life As A Research Topic

Robert L. Schalock
Hastings College
Hastings, Nebraska

Introduction And Overview

We have learned a great deal about the conceptualization, measurement, and application of the quality of life concept from the significant work over the past two decades on individual quality of life. Only relatively recently has a major effort been made to understand the domains of family quality of life and identify core indicators for each. Because the emerging work on family quality of life is being influenced and shaped significantly by the work done on individual quality of life, the major purpose of this chapter is to discuss the natural progression of the research interests in quality of life from a focus on the individual to include that of the family. The chapter is based on the following four premises:

- The concept of quality of life is a social construct that is impacting program development and service delivery in the areas of education, health care, intellectual disabilities, and mental health.
- The concept of quality of life is being used as the criterion for assessing the effectiveness of services to people with disabilities and their families.
- The pursuit of quality is apparent at three levels of today's human service programs: individuals and families who desire a life of quality, providers who want to deliver a quality product, and evaluators who assess quality outcomes.
- Our views of family quality of life are currently influenced to a considerable extent by the extensive work that has been done on the concept of individual quality of life.

My task in this chapter is to accomplish three goals. First, to provide the context for the remaining sections of the chapter, I will discuss briefly the history and importance of the concept of quality of life. Second, I will summarize five current individual-referenced quality of life research approaches. Third, I will characterize the emerging nature of research on family quality of life. I conclude the chapter with a brief discussion of the relevance of both the concept of quality of life and quality of life research to families and their enhanced well-being.

History And Importance

During the 1980s the field of intellectual disabilities–mental retardation embraced the concept of quality of life (QOL) as both a sensitizing notion and an overarching principle for service delivery. Why? Because the concept captured the changing vision of people with disabilities, provided a common language for individuals across disciplines and functional statuses, and was consistent with the larger "quality revolution." As discussed in this section, the history and recent work on individual quality of life establishes the context for the emerging family quality of life agenda and allows us to understand better the research themes and trends that are discussed in later chapters.

QOL Captured The Changing Vision

Over the past two decades, there has been a significant change in the way we view people with disabilities (e.g., Edgerton, 1996). This transformed vision of what constitutes the life possibilities of people with intellectual disabilities is reflected in terms that are familiar to the reader: self-determination, equity, and inclusion. As a term and concept, *quality of life* became during the 1980s a *social construct* that captured this changing vision and thus became the vehicle through which consumer-referenced equity, empowerment, and increased life satisfaction could be achieved. It was also consistent with the individualization and person-centered focus rapidly emerging in the field. Additionally, the assumption of most was that if adequate and appropriate supports were available, the person's quality of life would be enhanced significantly.

QOL Provided A Common Language

The past two decades have been exciting times to be in this field, for during these years the field has changed significantly, trying to adjust to the major upheavals caused by normalization, deinstitutionalization, and mainstreaming. As important as these movements were, they were more process- than outcome-oriented and failed to provide a clearly articulated goal for the people involved. The concept of quality of life thus became attractive as a universal principle that provides a common goal across environments and people. Thus the statement "to enhance one's quality of life" has become our goal. This *sensitizing notion* goes beyond the processes of systems change, to the outcomes of those processes. The desire for a life of quality is characteristic of everyone, and thus a common language has been born.

QOL Was Consistent With The Quality Revolution

One "product" of the quality revolution is a "new way of thinking" guided largely in the field of intellectual disabilities by the concept of quality of life, which has become the *unifying theme* around which programmatic changes and "the new way of thinking" are organized. This new way of thinking stresses person-centered planning, the supports model, quality enhancement techniques, and individual-referenced quality outcomes (Schalock, 1999, 2000). More specifically, this new quality-of-life-oriented thinking has resulted in: (a) service providers reorganizing resources around individuals rather than rearranging people in program slots; (b) consumers and service providers embracing the supports paradigm; (c) program evaluation shifting its focus to individual-referenced outcomes used to improve organizational efficiency and enhance services and supports; and (d) management styles focusing on learning organizations, reengineered corporations, entrepreneurship, and continuous quality improvement.

Thus the concept of quality of life has become a *social construct* that has challenged us to improve and enhance a person's and family's perceived quality of life, a *sensitizing notion* that has given us a sense of reference and guidance from the individual's perspective, focusing on the person, the family, and the environment, and a *unifying theme* that has provided us with a systematic or organizing framework to focus on the multidimensionality of the concept. Its importance is reflected in the following five quality of life conceptualization principles promulgated by the Special Interest Research Group on Quality of Life of the International Association for the Scientific Study of Intellectual Disabilities (Schalock et al., 2002).

1. Quality of life is composed of those same factors and relationships for people with intellectual disabilities and their families that are important to those without disabilities.
2. A life of quality is experienced when a person's or family's needs are met and when they have the opportunity to pursue life enrichment in major life settings.
3. Quality of life has both subjective and objective components; but it is primarily the perception of the individual or family that reflects the quality of life they experience.
4. A life of quality is based on individual needs, choices, and control.
5. Quality of life is a multidimensional construct influenced by personal and environmental factors such as intimate relationships, family life, friendships, work, neighborhood, city or town of residence, housing, education, health, standard of living, and the state of one's nation.

Research Approaches

It is beyond the scope of this chapter to discuss in detail the various approaches that have historically been used to study the concept of quality of life. Refer to Schalock (1996, 1997, 2000) and Schalock and Verdugo (2002) for a detailed review of the five approaches discussed in this section. If the considerable recent research in individual quality of life is any guide, future research approaches to family quality of life will involve the following five specific strategies: (a) a focus on the multidimensional nature of quality of life: (b) the use of methodological pluralism; (c) a focus on personal (i.e., family) outcomes; (d) the inclusion of individuals with disabilities and their families in the research endeavor; and (e) the use of multivariate research designs.

A Focus On The Multidimensional Nature

There is increasing agreement that quality of life is a multidimensional concept that precludes reducing it to a single "thing" of which the person may have considerable, some, or none. Current and ongoing research in this area (e.g., Cummins, 1997; Felce & Perry, 1997; Hughes & Hwang, 1996; Schalock, 1996) has identified a number of individual-referenced core quality of life domains. Common to this research are the eight core domains summarized in Table 2.1: emotional well-being, interpersonal relationships, material well-being, personal development, physical well-being, self-determination, social inclusion, and rights. The core indicators associated with each core domains, also shown in Table 2.1, are based on those found in the international literature on individual quality of life (Schalock & Verdugo, 2002).

Use Of Methodological Pluralism

Most individual-referenced quality of life research and evaluation use a combination of qualitative (i.e., "subjective") and quantitative (i.e., "objective") measurement strategies as a basis for determining quality-of-life-related outcomes. Objective indicators generally refer to external, environmentally based conditions such as health, social welfare, friendships, standard of living, education, public safety, housing, neighborhood, and leisure. These indicators may be defined as a statistic of direct normative interest that facilitates concise, comprehensive, and balanced judgments about the conditions of major aspects of either society or one's life (Andrews & Withey, 1976). Subjective indicators focus on a person's subjective reactions to life experiences and are usually measured from one of two perspectives: psychological well-being or personal satisfaction. An example of the first perspective is the work of Flanagan (1982), who identified five general domains of quality of life: physical and material well-being; relations with others; social, community, and civic activities; personal development and fulfillment; and recreation. The second perspective underlies the work of

Heal and his associates (Heal, Rubin, & Park, 1995), who measure the individual's satisfaction with factors such as home and community, friends, leisure activities, self-control, and social support and safety.

Table 2.1
Core Quality Of Life Domains And Indicators

Core Domain	Core Indictors
1. Physical well-being	Health
	Activities of daily living
	Health care
	Leisure
2. Emotional well-being	Contentment
	Self-concept
	Lack of stress
3. Interpersonal relations	Interactions
	Relationships
	Supports (emotional, physical, feedback)
4. Social inclusion	Community integration and participation
	Community roles
	Social supports
5. Personal development	Education
	Personal competence
	Performance
6. Material well-being	Financial status
	Employment
	Housing
7. Self-determination	Autonomy and personal control
	Goals and personal values
	Choices
8. Rights	Human (respect, dignity, equality)
	Legal (citizenship, access, due process)

The use of both quantitative and qualitative measures is consistent with the methodological pluralism model shown in Figure 2.1 (Schalock, 2001). As depicted in the center of Figure 2.1, the model's three components include standards, focus, and outcomes. The model's *standards* reflect two perspectives on accountability: performance versus value; its *focus* reflects an emphasis on the organization (agency or service) or the individual (client/consumer/customer); and its *outcomes* denote measurable results that are captured in a number of individualized individual- or organization-referenced performance or value indicators. In reference to the individual:

- *Individual performance* outcomes include physical status and material well-being. These outcomes are best obtained by conducting *functional assessments* of the individual's adaptive behavior and role status. Specific measures include rating scales, observation, objective behavioral measures, and status indicators (e.g., education, living, and employment status).
- *Individual value outcomes* include emotional well-being, personal development, self-determination, interpersonal relations, social inclusion, and rights. These outcomes are best obtained by using *personal appraisal* strategies such as personal interviews, surveys, or focus groups.

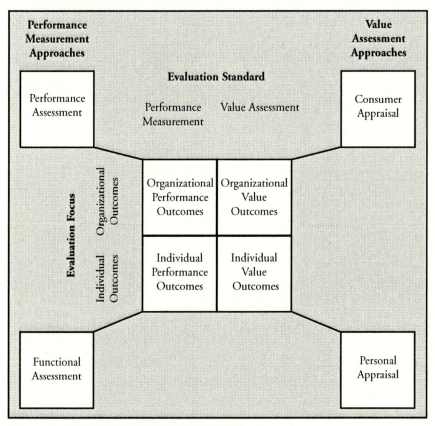

Figure 2.1 **Methodological pluralism model.**

There are a number of advantages to the Methodological Pluralism Model shown in Figure 2.1. First, it guides and clarifies the quality of life assessment process, as the outcome categories are the core quality of life domains. Second, all measurements and assessments are focused on agreed-upon outcomes related to the person (or the organization, in reference to customer satisfaction surveys, which represent a valued organization outcome). Third, it allows researchers and evaluators to meet the following objectives of using mixed-method evaluation (Schalock, 2001): triangulation (i.e., the determination of correspondence of results across measurement approaches); complementarity (i.e., the use of qualitative and quantitative methods to measure the overlapping, but distinct, facets of the outcomes); and initiation (i.e., the recasting of questions or results from one strategy with questions or results from a contrasting strategy).

A Focus On Personal Outcomes

As discussed by Gardner and Nudler (1997), we are experiencing a redefinition of quality in terms of outcomes for people rather than program compliance or product focus. As stated by these authors, "In the service sector, the definition of quality begins with the perception of the recipient of services rather than with the provider or the content of the service alone" (p. 135). Furthermore, as stated by Albrecht (1992), "In the customer value paradigm, the primary focus of measurement is on outcomes" (p. 41).

The focus on measuring personal (or, more generically, quality) outcomes is reflected in the work of the Accreditation Council on Services for People With Disabilities (Gardner & Nudler, 1997; Accreditation Council, 1995) and that of the Maryland Ask Me! Project (Bonham et al., in press). In reference to the Council, performance-based measures are those related to choice, social inclusion, relationships, rights, dignity and respect, health, environment, security, and satisfaction. In reference to the Ask Me! Project, which is a consumer-directed quality of life assessment and program-improvement project, the outcome categories are the eight core quality of life dimensions listed in Table 2.1.

Focusing on personal (i.e., quality) outcomes involves two additional aspects of the work on individual-referenced quality of life. First, one cannot separate the person from his or her environment, and thus the measurement and application of quality of life outcomes typically involves the use of a *system's perspective* that includes understanding behavior and outcomes from the perspective of the person and family (the microsystem), the community including human services and service or support programs (the mesosystem), and the society or larger culture (the macrosystem). Each of these levels impacts one's quality of life and each can be the focus of quality enhancement techniques. Second, measurement and application principles are essential to follow as one attempts to measure one's perceived quality of life and apply those findings to either program enhancement or systems-level change. Table 2.2 summarizes five key measurement and application principles stemming from the international consensus process (Schalock et. al., 2002).

Table 2.2
Family Quality Of Life Measurement And Application Principles

Measurement Principles

1. Quality of life measures the degree to which families have meaningful life experiences that they value.
2. Quality of life measurement enables families to move toward a meaningful life they enjoy and value.
3. Quality of life measures the degree to which life's domains contribute to a full and interconnected life.
4. Quality of life measurement is undertaken within the context of environments that are important to families: where they live, work, and play.
5. Quality of life measurement for families is based upon both common human experiences and unique, individual family experiences.

Application Principles

1. The primary purpose for applying the concept of quality of life is to enhance the family's well-being.
2. Quality of life needs to be applied in light of the family's cultural and ethnic heritage.
3. The aims of any quality-of-life-oriented program should be to collaborate for change at the personal, family, program, community, and national levels.
4. Quality of life applications should enhance the degree of family control and opportunities exerted in relation to their activities, interventions, and environments.
5. Quality of life should occupy a prominent role in gathering evidence, especially in identifying the significant predictors of a life of quality and the impact of targeting resources to maximize positive effects.

Including People With Disabilities And Their Families In The Research

Participatory action research (PAR), an emerging approach to problem solving and social change, is particularly suited to issues of quality of life. As discussed by Whitney-Thomas (1997), PAR relies on the involvement of stakeholders who can either identify subjective elements in their lives that warrant change or understand the social contexts in which change occurs. Individuals with disabilities and their families can contribute to our collective understanding of how quality of life can be conceptualized, what a life of quality looks like, and ways to improve outcomes. Participation in research, policy formulation, and practice should also involve those affected. Three key PAR concepts relate to this chapter: (a) PAR is an approach to problem solving, not a research design; (b) PAR involves stakeholder participation; and (c) PAR is a call to action. The reader will find further elaboration of these three key concepts in subsequent chapters.

Use Of Multivariate Research Designs

One of the biggest research stumbling blocks has been overcome by shifting our mindset regarding the research and statistical design used to study the quality of life concept. Specifically, we have seen a significant shift from a "between" to a "multivariate or within" approach. Historically, the study of quality of life was approached from a between-groups (or conditions) perspective; investigators sought to find factors, such as social economic status and large demographic population descriptors, that could discriminate between those persons or countries with a high and those with a lower quality of life. This "between mentality" spilled over to our early work on quality of life in subtle ways, as reflected in the attitude expressed by some that "we need to have different measures or quality of life indices for those who are higher functioning (or for families without a member with a disability) than for those who are nonverbal or lower functioning (or for families with a member who has a disability)."

Shifting to a multivariate research design has a number of research and policy implications. First, it allows one to focus more on the correlates and predictors of a life of quality than on comparing quality of life scores or status. More specifically, one can use multivariate research designs to determine the relationship among a number of measured predictor variables and perceived quality of life (e.g., Schalock, Lemanowicz, Conroy, & Feinstein, 1994; Schalock & Faulkner, 1997; Schalock, Bontham, & Marchand, 2000). Second, once these significant predictors are identified, policy and programmatic changes can be made to enhance the family's quality of life through techniques and strategies such as those described in the next section. Third, multivariate research designs help us understand better the complexity of the concept of quality of life and the role that a number of contextual variables play in the perception of a life of quality. Finally, multivariate designs shift the focus of our interventions from personal and/or family characteristics to environmental factors as major sources of quality of life enhancement.

The Emergence Of Family Quality Of Life Research

There is a general agreement that a positive quality of life for families should be an appropriate outcome of public policy and services. By extension, a positive quality of life for families with children who have disabilities is regarded as "a useful indicator of outcomes of policy initiatives" (Bailey et al., 1998, p. 322). Indeed, improving quality of life for families may be the "only acceptable outcome" of policies and services (Osher, 1998, p. 232). However, until the efforts summarized in this volume, researchers and others have not been as successful in conceptualizing, much less measuring, family quality of life as they have been in doing so for individual quality of life (Bailey et al., 1998; Accreditation Council, 1995). It is within this context that the significant work (summarized in later chapters of this volume) being done in Canada, Israel, Australia, Wales, and the United States should be considered.

Since the study of quality of life began in the 1970s (Andrews & Withey, 1976; Campbell, Converse, & Rogers, 1976), researchers have agreed on two fundamental concepts: (a) that quality of life is a multidimensional construct with interrelated domains; and (b) that quality of life can include both subjective and objective aspects. The subjective aspect is usually tied to the importance of a particular domain to the family and to how the family members feel about life with respect to that domain. The value that a family places on a domain is also influenced by the family's experiences and culture. By contrast, the objective aspect is usually measured by things such as income, housing, or health data. Although the subjective indicators of a specific domain do not necessarily correlate with the objective indicator, it is useful to compare populations on the objective indicators as well as on the subjective indicators (Cummins, 1996, 1997).

Based on the work on individual quality of life summarized above, one would think that research on family quality of life with family members who have a disability would have been the next natural progression in our understanding of the concept, and in developing tools to measure it. Unfortunately, this progressive step was not taken seriously until of late. Prior to this volume, the limited work on family quality-of-life-related outcomes has focused on satisfaction, general family functioning, family stability, self-sufficiency, reduction in stress, employment, or increase in parenting skills (Anderson, Rivera, & Kutash, 1998; Bailey et al., 1998; Blacher, 2001; Frey, Greenberg, & Fewell, 1989; Flynt & Wood, 1989; Keogh, Bernheimer, Gallimore, & Weisner, 1998).

The work represented in subsequent chapters in this volume reflects at least four common themes that have emerged recently in family quality of life research:

1. It is important for families to have a clear understanding of the domains of well-being and the need for forward planning that links self-image and satisfaction. This importance is reflected in the current active and ongoing attempt to identify the core domains reflective of a family's quality of life.

2. Families with a member who has a disability are challenged not just by the disability and stigma associated therewith, but also by the lack of services and the costs of services.

3. Family quality of life relates to specific domains of living, is currently linked closely to core individual quality of life domains, and is impacted significantly by personal and social-cultural factors.

4. There is an implicit assumption throughout the concepts and work summarized in the subsequent chapters that our better understanding of the concept of family quality of life will result in a positive theoretical and conceptual framework within which to understand and develop family-centered approaches to support.

Conclusion

Based on the work on individual quality of life summarized in this chapter, I am convinced that in the next decade the concept of family quality of life will continue to emerge in response to the need for a positive theoretical and conceptual framework within which to understand and develop family-centered approaches of support. Although there are challenges related to the uniqueness of the concept to each family and the differential use and operationalization of the concept, the promise of an enhanced family quality of life will continue to change the way people think and approach public policy and service delivery systems. At its core, the concept of quality of life gives us (a) a sense of reference and guidance from the individual's and family's perspective, (b) an overriding principle to enhance people's well-being and collaborate for change at the societal level, and (c) a common language and systematic framework to guide our current and future endeavors.

The past two decades of research on individually referenced quality of life have seen considerable progress in both how we approach the concept and measurement of quality of life and how we understand the significant role and impact that the concept has played in the lives of people with intellectual disabilities or mental retardation and the systems with which they interact. Indeed, quality of life has extended beyond the person and has now impacted an entire service delivery system because of its power as a social construct, unifying notion, and integrating concept. My anticipation is that it will have similar effects on families, for, as Victor Hugo reminded us, some concepts are more powerful than all the armies of the world—an idea whose time has come.

References

Accreditation Council on Services for People With Disabilities. (1995). *Outcome measures for early childhood intervention services.* Towson, MD: Author.

Albrecht, K. A. (1992). *The only thing that matters: Bringing the power of the customer into the center of your business.* New York: Harper Business.

Anderson, J. A., Rivera, V. R., & Kutash, K. (1998). Measuring consumer satisfaction with children's mental health services. In, M. E. Kutash & A. Duchnowski (Eds.), *Outcomes for children and youth with emotional behavioral disorders and their families: Programs and evaluation best practices* (pp. 455–482). Austin, TX: Pro-Ed.

Andrews, E. R., & Withey, S. B. (1976). *Social indicators of well-being: Americans' perceptions of life quality.* New York: Plenum Press.

Bailey, D. B., McWilliam, R. A., Darkes, L. A., Hebbeler, K., Simeonsson, R. J., Spiker, D., & Wagner, M. (1998). Family outcomes in early intervention: A framework for program evaluation and efficacy research. *Exceptional Children, 64,* 313–328.

Blacher, J. (2001). Transition to adulthood: Mental retardation, families, and culture. *American Journal on Mental Retardation, 106,* 173–188.

Bonham, S. G., Basehart, S., Schalock, R. L., Marchand, C. B., Kirchner, N., & Rumenap, J. M. (in press). Consumer-based quality of life assessment: The Maryland Ask Me! Project. *Mental Retardation.*

Campbell, A., Converse, P. E., & Rogers, W. L. (1976). *The quality of American life: Perceptions, evaluation, and satisfaction.* New York: Russell Sage Foundation.

Cummins, R. A. (1996). The domains of life satisfaction: An attempt to order chaos. *Social Indicators Research, 38,* 303–328.

Cummins, R. A. (1997). Assessing quality of life. In R. I. Brown (Ed.), *Quality of life for people with disabilities: Models, research, and practice* (pp. 116–150). Cheltenham, UK: Stanley Thornes.

Edgerton, R. B. (1996). A longitudinal-ethnographic research perspective on quality of life. In R. L. Schalock (Ed.), *Quality of life: Vol. 1. Conceptualization and measurement* (pp. 83–90). Washington, DC: American Association on Mental Retardation.

Felce, D., & Perry, J. (1997). Quality of life: The scope of the term and its breath of measurement. In R. I. Brown (Ed.), *Quality of life for people with disabilities: Models, research, and practice* (pp. 56–70). Cheltenham, UK: Stanley Thornes.

Flanagan, J. C. (1982). Measurement of quality of life: Current state of the art. *Archives of Physical Medicine and Rehabilitation, 63,* 56–59.

Flynt, S. W., & Wood, T. A. (1989). Stress and coping of mothers of children with moderate mental retardation. *American Journal on Mental Retardation, 94,* 278–283.

Frey, K. S., Greenberg, M. T., & Fewell, R. R. (1989). Stress and coping among parents of handicapped children: A multidimensional approach. *American Journal on Mental Retardation, 94,* 240–249.

Gardner, J. F., & Nudler, S. (1997). Beyond compliance to responsiveness: Accreditation reconsidered. In R. L. Schalock (Ed.), *Quality of life: Vol. 2. Application to persons with disabilities* (pp. 135–148). Washington, DC: American Association on Mental Retardation.

Heal, L. W., Rubin, S. S., & Park, W. (1995). *Lifestyle Satisfaction Scale.* Champaign-Urbana: University of Illinois, Transition Research Institute.

Hughes, C., & Hwang, B. (1996). Attempts to conceptualize and measure quality of life. In R. L. Schalock (Ed.), *Quality of life: Vol. 1. Conceptualization and measurement* (pp. 51–62). Washington, DC: American Association on Mental Retardation.

Keogh, B. K., Bernheimer, L. P., Gallimore, R., & Weisner, T. S. (1998). Child and family outcomes over time: A longitudinal perspective on developmental delays. In M. Lewis & C. Feiring (Eds.), *Families, risk, and competence* (pp. 269–287). Mahwah, NJ: Lawrence Erlbaum.

Osher, T. W. (1998). Outcomes and accountability from a family perspective. *Journal of Behavioral Health Services and Research, 25,* 230–232.

Schalock, R. L. (1996). Reconsidering the conceptualization and measurement of quality of life. In R. L. Schalock (Ed.), *Quality of life: Vol. 1. Conceptualization and measurement* (pp. 123–139). Washington, DC: American Association on Mental Retardation.

Schalock, R. L. (Ed.). (1997). *Quality of life: Vol. 2. Application to persons with disabilities.* Washington, DC: American Association on Mental Retardation.

Schalock, R. L. (1999). A quest for quality: Achieving organizational outputs and personal outcomes. In J. Gardner & S. Nudger (Eds.), *Quality performance in human services* (pp. 55–80). Baltimore: Paul H. Brookes.

Schalock, R. L. (2000). Three decades of quality of life. In M. L. Wehmeyer & J. R. Patton (Eds.), *Mental retardation in the 21st century* (pp. 335–358). Austin, TX: Pro-Ed.

Schalock, R. L. (2001). *Outcome-based evaluation* (2nd ed.). New York: Kluwer Academic/Plenum.

Schalock, R. L., Brown, I., Brown, R., Cummins, R. A., Felce, D., Matikka, L., Keith, K., & Parmenter, T. (2002). Conceptualization, measurement, and application of quality of life for persons with intellectual disabilities:

Results of an international panel of experts. *Mental Retardation, 40 (6)*, 457-470.

Schalock, R. L., Bontham, G., & Marchand, C. (2000). Consumer-based quality of life assessment: A path model of perceived satisfaction. *Evaluation and Program Planning, 23,* 77–87.

Schalock, R. L., & Faulkner, E. H. (1997). Cross-validation of a contextual model of quality of life. *European Journal on Mental Disability, 4*(14), 18–27.

Schalock, R. L., Lemanowicz, J. A., Conroy, J. W., & Feinstein, C. S. (1994). A multivariate investigative study of the correlates of quality of life. *Journal on Developmental Disabilities, 3*(2), 59–73.

Schalock, R. L., & Verdugo, M. A. (2002). *A handbook on quality of life for human service practitioners.* Washington, DC: American Association on Mental Retardation.

Whitney-Thomas, J. (1997). Participatory action research as an approach to enhancing quality of life for individuals with disabilities. In R. L. Schalock (Ed.), *Quality of life: Vol. 2. Application to persons with disabilities* (pp. 181–198). Washington, DC: American Association on Mental Retardation.

Chapter 3

Concepts For Beginning Study In Family Quality Of Life

Ivan Brown
University of Toronto
Toronto, Ontario, Canada

Roy I. Brown
University of Adelaide
Adelaide, South Australia, Australia

This chapter puts forward key concepts for the study of family quality of life by beginning to explore the meaning of family quality of life under four subtopics: (a) the foundation of family quality of life, (b) its current spheres of interest, (c) its emerging conceptual and theoretical structures, and (d) its methods of inquiry. The key concepts introduced here emerge from a broad analysis of applicable literature and particularly from recent work by an international committee of researchers of the International Association for the Scientific Study of Intellectual Disabilities that sought to set out a consensus of international knowledge on quality of life conception, measurement, and application at the turn of the millennium (Schalock et al., in press).

The purpose of the chapter is to build upon the previous chapter by presenting some additional linkages between the body of knowledge about quality of life that has developed to date from theoretical considerations and research evidence and the newly emerging concept of family quality of life. Our intent is to present an overview or summary rather than a detailed account of quality of life. Concepts that we consider to be critical are introduced to help the reader think about the contents of subsequent chapters of this book and to begin the process of developing the conceptual context for family quality of life study.

Family Quality Of Life As A Concept

Family quality of life is a concept that has emerged recently from its parent concept, quality of life of people with intellectual disabilities. More specifically, it has emerged in response to the need for a positive theoretical and conceptual framework within which to understand and develop family-centered approaches to support. Though in its infancy, the concept of family quality of life is put forward in this chapter with the intention of providing a useful conceptual framework through which family-centered approaches that enhance family life can be explored and developed. In functioning as a conceptual framework in this way, family quality of life stands upon a basic support principle: Renewed service involvement with families in the lives of individuals with intellectual disabilities must strive to understand and improve family life as a whole. We believe this emerges clearly from the accounts of family quality of life in the five countries presented in this book.

Family quality of life is multifaceted to the extent that it might best be thought of as a broad, overarching term within which numerous other concepts are contained. Its broad, overarching nature suggests that it is sufficiently complex to constitute an area of study. This is an area of study that does not exist in isolation, however. Rather, it has its roots in, and continues to be informed by, a number of other areas of study. These provide the *foundation,* but family quality of life builds upon this foundation to set out its own *conceptual and theoretical structures,* its own *spheres of interest,* and its own set of *methods of inquiry.*

The Foundation Of Family Quality Of Life

Family has been a cornerstone of all human social structures since time immemorial. Our knowledge of the family, and the interrelationship between the family and other human and environmental structures, has developed within several fields such as philosophy, history, biology, and, more recently, sociology, anthropology, jurisprudence, and psychology. In particular, a considerable amount of work has been carried out in family systems, and much of this work is highly relevant to the study of family quality of life (for a full explanation of family systems research, see Turnbull & Turnbull, 2001).

The main functions of family have been stable across human cultures and over the millennia of human existence: to bring children into the world and to nurture them until they become independent, to provide a way in which physical and emotional attachments to others can be expressed, and to provide a basic network around which other social and physical structures can be built.

With these general functions in mind, family is typically seen as a formal arrangement of two or more adults with or without children, or an adult with a child or children. Every country has developed and uses a number of legal and quasilegal definitions of family, definitions that vary in scope and specificity with the purpose for which they are intended (e.g., child welfare and protection, family law, taxation, substitute decision making, and policies such as parental, compassionate, and other leaves). For the purposes of offering a preliminary meaning for family within the context of studying family quality of life and intellectual disability, family is taken to mean a formal arrangement where one, two, or more adults are the main providers of a home and community life for at least one person with an intellectual disability and perhaps for other children or adults as well. It should be recognized, however, that family may be described slightly differently in other chapters of this book, and that the meaning of family within the context of family quality of life will evolve as this area of study develops.

Understanding Enhancement Of Family Life

For families in lower-income countries, and to some extent in higher-income countries, fundamental, primary needs such as food, water, shelter, and clothing are not always being adequately met. Meeting such needs is an essential first step to maintaining or enhancing family quality of life, and thus this must remain within a family quality of life framework. In recent years, however, economic and social advancement has meant that basic needs are being met for increasing numbers of families. Such families often look for further ways to enhance the quality of their family life.

The further ways family quality of life can be enhanced for individual families and individual family members will be an area of considerable exploration over the next several years. For the present, however, it seems wise to begin by looking at those aspects of human endeavor that appear to have added quality to human cultures around the world over the centuries (Woodill, Renwick, Brown, & Raphael, 1994). From this view, family quality of life is not simply a Western, postindustrial concept with little application to low-income areas of the world. Instead, it is a concept that builds upon the many attributes of quality of life, though not labeled as such, that have been part of many societies for thousands of years.

These attributes can be found within domains of life that we have developed as part of our thought processes and as part of our cultural expression because they have proven important to human beings. This has occurred not merely by chance. As humans, we have a natural inclination to cope, to adapt, and to enhance our lives. We have indulged this inclination by developing innumerable practical ways to improve our daily lives and very sophisticated forms of science that have allowed us to observe, measure, and understand how our life conditions can be made better. In the process, we have developed and used huge numbers of ideas, tools and resources that have encouraged us to enhance our lives even further.

We have indulged this inclination, too, by developing forms of art that are also often very sophisticated. Literature, music, art, and theater have allowed us to transcend our daily experience, to hope, dream, imagine and create, and to express such experiences in words, actions, pictures, and other representations that enhance the quality of our daily lives (Warren, 1997). Leisure, fun, and humor are ways to play, to delight in our experiences, and to explore enjoyment and fulfillment of life in safe and alternate emotional environments. Philosophy has provided a way for us to look for a deeper and alternative meaning to life. Religious ideas and practices have equipped us to find meaning for being, to bond in a spiritual sense, and to share spiritual and ethereal experiences with others (Neufeldt & McGinley, 1997). Achievement in the arts has provided us both with a way to enhance the quality of our present lives and with encouragement to strive for even greater achievement. The individual quality of life literature has already drawn extensively from cultural expressions of ways of enhancing individual life.

In looking for sound ways to develop concepts for enhancing family life within a quality of life framework, it seems prudent to begin by examining the many expressions of practical development, scientific advancement, and artistic achievement within human cultures that apply to family life. It is probable that these expressions house, and will inform us about, the very attributes that enhance quality of life for families. It is also beneficial to maintain a quality of life perspective, because such a perspective sensitizes us to the values behind our various activities (Taylor, 1994) and provides a way for us to evaluate and summarize those activities that are most important to enhancing the lives of individuals, families, and communities (R. Brown, 1997a).

Current Spheres Of Interest

Areas of study evolve in ways that reflect the influence of events and characteristics of the times. Such influences guide the scope and focus of study. In doing so, spheres of interest emerge, spheres that do not represent the whole area of study but, rather, specific parts of it. Study in family quality of life begins because of the influence of a number of interrelated events and characteristics of our times. Such events and characteristics also influence how we perceive family quality of life and how quality of life can be improved for families. We suggest that the most important of these are

- the expectation that families will play a larger role in decision making and the care of their family member with an intellectual disability;
- the slowly developing recognition that families with a member who has an intellectual disability should attain quality living;
- concern for individual quality of life of family members, including the member with an intellectual disability;
- the increased survival of individuals with severe and multiple disabilities;

- the increased longevity of individuals with intellectual disabilities resulting in long-term family involvement.

These have led to or developed at the same time as:

- the perceived need by governments in high-income countries to contain spending on social programs;
- the growing trend in most high-income countries for public services to respond to the needs of individuals and individual families.

Family Involvement

Spheres of interest are also influenced by the values held by those who carry out study in an area. As study begins in the area of family quality of life, it is strongly influenced by two strong values: (a) work in this area should be carried out solely for the purpose of improving the lives of families that have a member with an intellectual disability, and (b) the voice of family members is an essential part of this work.

These interrelated events and characteristics of our times and values held by current investigators suggest that—at least initially—study in the area of family quality of life might take place in specific spheres:

- exploring and understanding what contributes to good family quality of life;
- considering the best methods for describing, assessing, and measuring family quality of life;
- identifying what supports, if any, are essential to a family for them to experience good family quality of life;
- advocating for, and helping to shape, public policy that provides supports needed by families for good quality of life;
- developing ways to understand what is important to individual families and how best to respond to their unique needs and wishes;
- exploring the extent to which families that have a member with an intellectual disability have a right to good quality of life, and developing strategies that support and enhance it;
- discerning ways to respect privacy and individual wishes, but, at the same time, ensuring that opportunities are available to families and individuals *who* remain hidden in poor conditions;
- exploring methods of intervention and support that are consistent with acceptable quality of life principles.

Emerging Conceptual And Theoretical Structures

Quality of life deals, in a lay sense, with the goodness of life, and *family quality of life* deals with the goodness of family life. The primary purpose of family quality of life study is to improve family quality of life. Family quality of life study seeks to understand and explain differences between what each family believes would be ideal and the reality of a family's own life. At times, and to the extent it can, this area of study seeks to measure the quality of family life so as to describe these differences. It seeks to put forward strategies to reduce those differences and to enable families to move their "reality" closer to the ideal. In making this effort, this area of study recognizes that families have different visions of the "ideal"; accordingly, the strategies to achieve families' "ideal" must vary.

As study in quality of life has evolved, there has been a move away from attempting to provide a single definition for the term. Instead, attention has moved toward describing and understanding the conditions that enhance and promote a "good" life (Schalock et al., in press). In defining the fledgling term *family quality of life,* it seems wise to follow what has been learned from the more general *quality of life* field and avoid attempts to provide a single definition. Rather, here let's turn to describing and understanding conditions that enhance and promote good family life.

Understanding Family Quality Of Life

The study of individual quality of life has not been without growing pains, doubts, and misunderstandings. The term itself has been the subject of helpful critical examination (e.g., Hatton, 1998; Taylor, 1994). Many definitions have been given (e.g., R. Brown, 2000a), but it appears that a precise definition is somewhat elusive and possibly undesirable at this stage since the concept is still under development. The quality of life literature has also struggled with how to describe the uniqueness of quality of life for individuals and how to aggregate quality of life information to describe groups. (These same struggles will be faced by those studying family quality of life.) Nevertheless, as the 20th century came to a close, an international consensus was emerging about the central conceptualizations, measurement approaches, and applications of quality of life (Schalock et al., in press). This consensus has led us to some degree of confidence in our understanding of individual quality of life, and allows us to describe the principles and concepts that are now generally accepted as contributing to quality of life. This understanding can, at least in part, be adopted by family quality of life.

In one sense, quality of life is a simple enough concept to understand at a general level (I. Brown, 1994). There are many aspects of family life that people everywhere—in all parts of the world and across the centuries—share and within which they strive to attain a satisfactory quality. As a general rule, families like to produce and raise children and mold them into the ways of the family and of the broader social context in which the family lives. Family members like to be healthy and have energy to be active both inside and outside the family. Family members like to produce and accomplish things, both individually and as a group. Families like to do things together: to explore and create; to play, laugh, and continuously seek out new ways to be amused; and to experience the environment in which they live. Families like their members to be closely connected to one another, to love, feel compassion, and care for one another. Families like to interact with other families. Families like to form part of and connect with what their culture has accomplished and carry on its traditions. Families like to transcend everyday experience, to dream, and to connect with powers that are greater than themselves. Families strive for stability in economic, psychological, and social terms. These important aspects of family quality of life appear to be experienced by most families to different degrees; they tend to be part of the human experience of family living. As family members see they cannot attain the things that they want, they are likely to sense dissatisfaction, reduced empowerment and self-image, increased stress, and in some cases dissension.

But one of the most interesting things about human life is that no two families are alike. Although families share many characteristics with other families, each is unique. Each family has its own set of things that it feels is important. Each unit has its own likes and dislikes, its own characteristics and habits, its own personal attitudes and values. In fact, it would be a very dull world indeed if each family was not just a little different from all others. Because of its uniqueness, each family has its own idea of what constitutes good family quality of life. Thus when we consider family quality of life, we need to consider aspects of family life that are highly valued by all families, tempered by the unique interests and values of individual families and individuals within families (I. Brown & Renwick, 1997).

Challenges For Understanding Family Quality Of Life

Three aspects of applying the general understanding of quality of life to specific individuals are very likely to present challenges for the understanding of family quality of life.

First, when the general meaning of the term *quality of life* is applied to the life of an individual or group, including a family, it takes on a unique meaning to that individual or group (i.e., no two families have precisely the same perspective on what "quality" means to them and to other families). Each family has a unique understanding of the term *quality of life*, as generalized to all families and in a more specific way as personalized to itself. A family uniquely blends these two meanings of family quality of life by referring to desired aspects of family life it shares with other families and aspects of family life that describe it alone.

Second, the term *quality of life* is used for different purposes and within differing groups, and thus its general meaning has been operationalized in different ways. The degree to which this is problematic may arise primarily from failure to describe adequately the context within which the term is being used (I. Brown, Renwick, & Nagler, 1996). This same problem is likely to occur in family quality of life study, and we will need to determine ways to address it.

Third, the very use of the term *quality of life* changes our perspective, a change that sometimes puts us at odds with the traditional perspective of families and people with intellectual disabilities. Taylor (1994) noted that the term sensitizes us, and R. Brown (1997a) argued that quality of life helps us to look at people from a nontraditional perspective. This different perspective results in a rotation of the prism that colors our professional views. It encourages us to see the individual with a disability from his or her own position. In terms of a family's quality of life, it helps us focus on the individual with a disability and other family members from their own positions within the family and community. It helps us to consider the impact of experiences on their lives and the family as a whole. Such a perspective is essential for developing person-centered and family-centered approaches to support (Renwick, Brown, & Raphael, 2000).

Critical Components Of Family Quality Of Life

Three critical components of individual quality of life (summarized by I. Brown, 1999a) appear to be a practical starting point for enumerating the critical components of family quality of life. Initially, then, it can be stated that families experience satisfactory family quality of life when they: (a) *attain* what families everywhere, and they in particular, strive for; (b) are *satisfied* with what families everywhere, and they in particular, have attained; and (c) feel *empowered* to live the lives they wish to live

Attainment And Satisfaction

When have families attained what they strive for? When are families satisfied with what they have attained? There is no absolute standard to determine this, for four reasons.

First, each family is different; its ideas of what it is striving for and when that has been attained and its ideas about what constitutes satisfaction are different from those of other families. There are also differences within families, as a family is a group of individuals who may not necessarily have common goals. Indeed, the extent of internal cohesiveness within a family may be an important aspect of that family's quality of life.

Second, because family quality of life is dynamic in nature, attainment is relevant only for the present time. Life will change, as will families' views on what they wish to attain and what will bring them satisfaction. New discrepancies may result (R. Brown, Bayer, & MacFarlane, 1989).

Third, there are degrees of attainment and of satisfaction. For example, a family may have attained a comfortable home, but not the home of its dreams, and a family may be satisfied enough, but not as satisfied as it really wishes to be. The concept of *threshold* is helpful to our understanding of degrees of attainment and happiness as a dichotomized way to describe which side of the fence the family is on: attained or not attained, satisfied or not satisfied. The idea here is that each family has a threshold, below which it does not consider itself to have attained what it strives for, and above which it does. Each family also has a threshold for being satisfied with its life, which may well be different from its threshold for attainment. For example, a family might have attained what it strives for but not have reached its threshold of satisfaction, or a family might be satisfied yet not have attained what it strives for.

Fourth, it appears that the relationship between attainment and satisfaction may be intrinsically unstable. Times of change, where new things are attained, can also be times of uncertainty, times of new possibilities and real options, and times to contrast the present situation with the past or with the attainments of others. Such times can result in greater uncertainly about satisfaction with life and, often, in lower degrees of contentment (R. Brown, Bayer, & Brown, 1992; James, 1997). Humans are very adaptable, though, and when discrepancies between reality and wishes occur, adjustments tend to take place within their individual or family systems, bringing them back to equilibrium (Cummins, 2000). Thus it is typically only extreme and nonadapted discrepancies that are likely to be apparent over time; these may require support and service assistance. An interesting question that remains, however, is why some people appear to cope in environments that are really unreasonable.

Empowerment

Empowerment is a third critical component of family quality of life. For families to have satisfactory quality of life, supports need to be in place so that the family can control life conditions and events. Empowerment refers to the degree to which families consider that (a) there are realistic life options available to them that they wish to pursue and (b) they feel both free to pursue those options and supported in doing so. In the quality of life literature, the availability of life options is sometimes referred to as opportunities, and the act of pursuing those options is sometimes referred to as making choices. The term *control* is sometimes used in quality of life literature as a close synonym of empowerment, referring to the freedom and ability to make choices from available options. Quality of life is very much concerned with personal control—both opportunities and choices. Work in the area of family quality of life must equally be concerned with family control—opportunities available to families and the choices families make. Empowerment within the family quality of life context further implies the need to consider the empowerment of each family member and the relationship among the types and degrees of empowerment of family members (R. Brown, Brown, & Bayer, 1994).

Improvement in empowerment does not necessarily lead to happiness or satisfaction, however, because of increased awareness. This is likely to be particularly true when disability clouds the issue. R. Brown, Bayer, and Brown (1992) made the case that when individuals with disabilities knew they had gained greater control of their environments, they became more dissatisfied because they realized that change had become a possibility. Quality of life had improved as personal controls had increased and choices had been met, but control and choices acted upon also represented examples of how life might be in other areas of their lives. Thus individuals became dissatisfied with aspects of life that they had not considered before. This same phenomenon is likely to arise when considering a family's quality of life, and it is important that families understand this. Further, those delivering services should be aware that as variables of comparison come into play, greater criticism of services may come about (see also James, 1997).

Still, it is essential to recognize, and wherever possible to support, family opportunities and choices. To ignore them is to impede family development. This is not to suggest that "everything a family says, goes," for choice has to take place within a developmental structure (R. Brown et al., 1994). Rather, family choice must be placed centrally when family programs are developed.

Conceptual Characteristics Of Family Quality Of Life

A number of conceptual characteristics that emerge from the body of knowledge on individual quality of life influence the expression of these three critical components of family quality of life. Seven such characteristics are described below.

Dynamic Nature

A family's perceived quality of life is ever changing because life and our outlook toward life are ever changing. Time moves forward and we move forward with it. Our own bodies alter season by season and year by year. Within families, new family members are introduced, and current members develop, grow older, and eventually die. At the same time, our knowledge, ideas, attitudes, and values develop and change. What is vitally important to us one year is sometimes not so important the next year. What we strive for with great enthusiasm when we are 25 is often replaced with different activities when we are 50, and again when we are 75. The need to look at quality of life as a dynamic concept has been stressed in the individual quality of life literature (e.g., Renwick & Brown, 1996), and there seems no reason to assume that it should not be equally stressed in the family quality of life literature.

Association With Lifespan

The association of family quality of life with *lifespan* is related to the dynamic nature of quality of life, which has also been well documented (R. Brown, 2000a). *Lifespan* implies the need to look at families and individuals across time, recognizing that each developmental period influences later development. Quality experiences in very early life have consequences for later development and adaption, not just of the individual but for the family as a working unit. Likewise, negative experiences within the family, such as high stress in the early years, are likely to impact later well-being. Thus it is important to ensure and recognize the influences that impact the family (e.g., the complex issue of premenstrual pain and health and psychological factors facing females who have a disability has been clearly described by Kyrkou, in Bottroff et al., in press). Not only do positive and negative experiences have later consequences for each family member, but also they have an overriding importance for the development of policy and service delivery (R. Brown et al., 1992; R. Brown et al., 1989).

But even these general influences are too simple, for positive experiences at any stage are likely to set up expectations for similar or other positive experiences at later stages, and, if these do not occur, disappointment, dissatisfaction, and disillusionment may follow. For example, a family that is excited and adapted to a child's elementary-school experience may have powerful responses if those same positive experiences do not carry over into secondary education. The fact that educational systems are developmental, and that notions of changes, such as inclusion with students in regular classroom settings, happen initially at preschool or elementary school but are still inadequately developed at the secondary-education level may have major implications for family quality of life. Inclusion, which has been seen as a separate concept from quality of life, is in reality embedded in both individual and family quality of life, not just in terms of school inclusion but also inclusion within the wider community (see R. Brown & Shearer, 1999).

The concept of lifespan also emphasizes all phases of a person's life. In the field of intellectual disabilities, work in individual quality of life to date has primarily concerned younger and middle-aged adults, although quality of life work with nondisabled populations has focused on teens, seniors, and numerous disability and disease-related populations of various ages (see Renwick, Brown, & Nagler, 1996). Quality of life work with children who have intellectual disabilities is only beginning to develop (I. Brown, 1999b; R. Brown, 1999), and the quality of life in infancy and early childhood has yet to be directly considered. The importance of quality in the final part of life has been addressed in the sparse seniors' quality of life literature (e.g., R. Brown, 2000a; Raphael, 1996). Webb (1992) addressed quality within the very last stage of life, including dying and death. Further work needs to be carried out in these areas, and the work in the area of hospice care should not be ignored in relation to the field of intellectual disability. Lifespan, as a characteristic of family quality of life, informs us that quality needs to be considered and valued at all seasons of life.

Holistic Nature

Holism implies that all aspects of life and all the factors that influence quality of life are linked and influence one another. Holism within the family unit implies that the lives of all family members are linked and influence one another. In the same way that well-being in leisure and recreation has an influence on productive well-being, such as employment, so within a family the well-being of one member is likely to influence another (Velde, 1997). The emotional well-being of the individual with an intellectual disability is likely to affect the emotional well-being of other family members. Holism within families also implies that the factors that affect individual quality of life for family members are linked and influence one another, and that these factors also influence family quality of life (R. Brown, 1996, 2000b). Thus there is interaction among areas of well-being within the individual (personal holism), and there is interaction among family members (family holism).

Reliance On Perception And Values

Family quality of life, like individual quality of life, relies on perception and values. Family quality of life may be considered from the perception of individual family members or families as a whole, from the perception of some person or agency outside the family, or by using some objective criteria. It seems essential that family quality of life reflects the perceptions of individual family members and families as a whole, even though these perceptions arise from values held by family members. This is a challenge for family quality of life study, for such values differ among families and among members within families. Also, there remain the methodological questions of how to capture such perceptions accurately, how to determine if they are stable over time, and how to apply them in ways that will help to improve family quality of life. If the perceptions of others are used, the same challenges apply. The values that guide other people or agencies need to be made explicit in order to interpret the meaning of their perceptions for improving the lives of the families they observe (see Schalock et al., in press).

If objective criteria are used in describing family quality of life, it is highly likely that the criteria will be based on values of the families or the researchers. Even so-called objective criteria have a foundation in values. For example, it might be assumed that quality of life is better for families that get along well together 80% of the time than for families that act in hostile ways toward each other 80% of the time. In spite of how well-meaning this assumption may be, it still emerges from the value that family harmony is better than family discord. This example raises the question—if objective criteria are used, what values should inform them? Here, again, the values that have proven important to family life over thousands of years of human history might serve as the best guides.

Finally, the issues of major family disharmony, and deprived and abusive backgrounds, raise the concern that a family may not be the best environment for a particular person with intellectual disability. Severe abuse and deprivation may necessarily lead to the removal of a child from a family. The question is then raised: What quality of life issues should predominate in decision making that is involved in providing the individual with the best life options available? (see Clarke & Clarke, 2000).

Variability

Family quality of life, like individual quality of life, is extremely variable (R. Brown et al., 1994). Not only do individual families hold different values and strive toward different goals, but also the degrees to which they are successful in reaching a satisfactory quality of life differ markedly. This variability is important for both policy and practice, because it implies that the best and fairest ways to distribute resources—often referred to as equity—are to do so in ways that are not equal. Thus equity does not mean equality. It implies the recognition of diversity of individual family needs. This does not exclude some general standards for improving family quality of life. It does, however, assert that individual family needs are central to improving family quality of life.

Reflection Of Family Self-Image

The self-image of a family and its members is its way of perceiving itself as a unique social unit. Self-image is based on the many and varied individual and combined characteristics of family members and has been shown to be important in quality of life studies (R. Brown et al., 1992). These characteristics are combined to form a self-image that describes a family in terms of who it is, with whom it associates, in what productive activities it engages, what is most important to it, and what it hopes to achieve in the future.

Self-image can have a strong effect on a family's perceptions of what it wants to achieve and when goals have been achieved. It can also have a strong effect on happiness or satisfaction. For example, some families perceive themselves to be contented with very little materially, while others perceive themselves never to be contented at all. But self-image is also strongly related to empowerment, or family control. If control becomes external to the family, as is often the case when professionals carry out procedures, then family life may be disrupted and even damaged. On the other hand, giving greater control to families can change their self-image in positive ways. Thus one important aspect of the family quality of life concept is that it stresses the key role of self-image in determining attainment and happiness, and it emphasizes the critical relationship between self-image and family empowerment.

Relationship With Societal Issues

Families live within societies, and the characteristics and activities of those societies influence family quality of life. Human rights and antidiscrimination legislation, which have been features of many developed and some developing countries, represent a major strength in enabling families to achieve better quality of life. Other, more specific, characteristics of social functioning include, for example, physical access; home design and adaptation; acceptance on transport systems, when visiting banks, when paying electricity bills, attending local functions, or being fairly treated within one's own neighborhood (R. Brown, 2000c; Ferguson, 1997). When such accommodations are made for people with disabilities, they typically benefit society as a whole as well. For example, when it is made easier for a mother with a child who has a disability to get on a bus, it is usually easier for all other people to get on the bus as well.

Family quality of life will no doubt have to confront other societal forces. At the present time, economic rationalism is among the most formidable of these forces (R. Brown, 2000a); that is, quality of life recognizes a wide range of values and argues that success cannot be measured only, or largely, in monetary or economic terms. Improving the quality of family life where there is at least one member with an intellectual disability requires funds to meet family needs, but meeting such needs does not always match governmental fiscal priorities. For family quality of life to succeed as a process, it will have to be shown that enabling families to function effectively and qualitatively requires conceptual changes in social policy and that such changes are, in the long run, beneficial to societies. In this endeavor, the area of family quality of life is not alone, as similar challenges are currently being faced in the wider disability field and with related populations, such as seniors or people who have skiing accidents resulting in damaged limbs.

How To Describe Family Quality Of Life

The quality of life literature suggests three things are particularly important when we begin to describe family quality of life.

Families' Perceptions Of Their Own Lives

In spite of the challenges introduced (see above), a family's own perceptions of its life are important to family quality of life, because ultimately this is what determines how satisfied family members are with life and their approach to life. The degree to which others, claiming objectivity, consider family life to be satisfactory can also be useful for comparative purposes, or for presenting a new perspective.

A dilemma is presented here, because, although there are positions that families take as a group, there are separate and individual views of each family member. It is common in clinical and research work to obtain views from the major parent or caregiver, but proxy perceptions are poor measures for the perceptions of individual family members. Furthermore, if the views constructed by each family member are important content for counseling and improvement of quality of life (R. Brown, 1992), then it will be essential, although time consuming, to attain the views of each member. This raises the question of how best to do this methodologically: To what degree is it critical to zero in on the key issues for each family member compared to recognizing the collective views of the family as a whole?

Domains Of Well-Being

Considerable effort has been expended to date exploring and describing various aspects of life considered essential to examine the overall picture of quality of life. These are often referred to as domains, and those thought to be core to human life are sometimes referred to as core domains. In the individual quality of life literature, domains have almost always been generated based on the principle that the same domains should be considered for people with intellectual disabilities as for all other people (e.g., Goode, 1994; Schalock, 1990, 1996, 1997).

Some but not all of the individual domains developed might be adapted for use with family quality of life. Examples of domains from the individual quality of life literature include emotional, material, social, productive, and physical well-being (Felce & Perry, 1997); discrimination and rights (Schalock, 1997); spiritual and community belonging (Renwick et al., 2000). One way of looking at individual quality of life domains is to categorize them into two types, those that refer to personal health and behavior, and those that describe aspects of the environment in which people live (e.g., human rights and discrimination which have profound effects on personal well-being).

There are both advantages and disadvantages to looking at quality of life through the lens of "domains," as opposed to looking at life as a whole. The main advantage is that it is easier for people to think of specific aspects of their lives one at a time than to think of everything all together, and it is easier for researchers and those interpreting research to consider the implications of separate aspects of life. This clearly relates to the systems approach currently discussed in family and professional partnerships (Dale, 1996). The main disadvantages are that, by choosing particular domains, we may overlook others; the various domains may have unequal importance; and individual aspects of life cannot be fully explored in isolation because our lives are interactive. Indeed, a degree of artificiality becomes evident when we attempt to classify principles or information. These disadvantages have been recognized within the quality of life literature, which has asserted the holistic nature of quality of life and has clearly noted that changes in one aspect of life very much affect other aspects of life. If domains are used in family quality of life, their limitations will have to be emphasized and efforts to compensate will have to be made.

The domains that have emerged from the individual quality of life literature represent clusters of behaviors and actions associated with individuals. They are not unique to individuals with intellectual disability, but apply to all individuals, including individual family members. This suggests that individual quality of life domains might be applied to individuals within families, and that some combination of individual quality of life domains of family members might constitute family quality of life. It is also possible that an understanding of the individual quality of life of each family member is essential to an understanding of family quality of life as a whole. On the other hand, focusing on individual quality of life of family members overlooks the important question of whether total family quality of life is different from the sum of its parts and the question of how the family functions as a unit. We may need to look for some underlying factors that provide links among the quality of life of various family members and a clearer way to understand family quality of life as a whole. This important task is initiated in subsequent chapters of this book.

Values Of Families

The values held by individual families have a strong influence on how they perceive the quality of their family life. Because values are somewhat unique to individual families, assessing a family's life as a whole or through its domains requires adjusting or weighting what is observed in relation to the values held by specific families. For example, if a family has few material possessions and does not value having more, its quality of life cannot be thought of as low on that account alone (R. Brown et al., 1992).

How To Use The Concept Of Family Quality Of Life

The term *family quality of life* has a number of uses and can be used constructively in a number of contexts. Building upon our work in individual quality of life, family quality of life:

- is an ultimate goal, a "golden vision" for our work (I. Brown, 1999a);
- is an overarching concept for organizing positive values pertaining to families in the field of intellectual disabilities (Schalock, 1996);
- is a sensitizing notion (Taylor, 1994);
- underscores the essential nature of considering quality in everything we do;
- has the "potential to allow a new perspective in intellectual disability and to be a positive influence on those who work in the field" (Schalock et al., in press);

- is a principle that guides public policy development, services, support, and interventions (Schalock, 1997);
- is the outcome of assessment and measurement techniques (Cummins, 1997);
- is a concept that recognizes the importance of flexibility and choice within the family and service structures.

Family quality of life is a particularly useful concept to use in assessing the needs of families and responding to their needs with the appropriate policies and services. Its use during assessment is a way to ensure both that the concept as a whole and its subconcepts are fully considered, and that the goals of family quality of life (improving quality of life for individual families) are addressed.

One of the key aspects of assessment, using a family quality of life framework, is to ensure that each family member is able to have a say in representing his or her perceptions of personal and family needs. This is essential because the reactions of individual family members to the presence of a family member with a disability often differ considerably. It is also essential because the person with a disability often takes a central position within the family to which others adapt and respond. Some of those adaptations are positive and others are negative. If the family is not just to survive, but also to flourish, the views of each family member need to be heard and taken into account.

During assessment, it is perhaps natural that the initial primary concern is typically centered on the individual with a disability. The question is, though, whether or not this is the best approach to individual and family well-being. Reports such as those of R. Brown (2000c) suggest there are other important issues that now need to be addressed, including the need to more proactively listen, note, and respond to individual primary caregivers and consumers, though this is clearly foreshadowed in Hannam's 1975 work. Brown found that most caregivers had a clear idea of how their needs should be met; in verbalizing these needs their problems were eased. In many instances, these needs were not purely disability related, yet they were crucial to effective family functioning.

The best ways to listen to primary caregivers and collect information on their needs should also be addressed. When assessing, we need to keep in mind Goode and Hogg's (1994) "tyranny of quality." The question here is how is it possible to gain adequate information to assist without intruding, confusing, and overburdening family members. It seems that much good evidence has emerged from qualitative studies, and this suggests at this stage that family-centered narrative and ethnographic research is likely to pay dividends (Peter, 1997; Velde, 1997). Families, and particularly mothers, are good at telling their stories; one method of assessment may be simply to encourage them to write, or record on audio tape, their family stories and describe their family needs. As a follow-up, more refined and directed assessment might take place, and skilled counselors can use the narratives and other assessment information within the family quality of life framework to help families find the best methods for obtaining and enhancing their life of quality (R. Brown, 1992). In this way, assessment and the activities that follow it, using a family quality of life framework, should be directed to the needs and choices of the family, but this requires highly skilled professional attention (R. Brown, 1997b).

In assessment, then, family quality of life takes its major thrust from quality of life for individuals with disabilities but stresses the importance of stability of all family members. It is argued this must be addressed if a nurturing family environment is to be established and developed. For this reason, intellectual disability must be concerned with effective family quality of life.

Methods Of Inquiry

Academic study typically involves inquiry—seeking to explore and understand an area in ever-expanding ways for the purpose of furthering the breadth and depth of our knowledge. When an area of study is in its infancy, as is the case with family quality of life, it is important to consider what approaches to inquiry might be best.

Various methods of inquiry have been reflected in the quality of life literature to date, and there has been considerable discussion and debate about the merits of each. Much of the debate has centered on the enormous challenges faced in developing adequate measures of individual quality of life (Cummins, 1997) and on the different uses and applications of the concept. But the emerging consensus appears to be that a method should be selected that is most appropriate for the quality of life question to be addressed (Schalock et al., in press). For this reason, both qualitative and quantitative methods are useful (R. Brown, 1997a). Standardized scales, subjective measures, observation, description, and other methods of inquiry are all useful ways to address aspects of quality of life (see, e.g., Goode, 1994). But there is also agreement that to understand quality of life in the fullest possible way, it is important that both objective and subjective (perceptions of individuals and families) methods be used, and that multiple and complementary methods of inquiry are likely to result in a richer perspective on quality of life than reliance on any one method alone. There appears to be every reason to adopt this same approach toward family quality of life.

A Final Word

This chapter has suggested a number of concepts and issues for the study of family quality of life by describing the foundation of family quality of life, its spheres of interest, beginning conceptual and theoretical structures, and methods of inquiry. The authors consider these to be a good place to begin the study of family quality of life, and especially as a foundation for thinking about the material presented in subsequent chapters of this book. The concepts and issues introduced here will no doubt be amended and numerous others will emerge as theoretical and empirical considerations shape the evolving concept quality of life over time. This is both inevitable and desirable. The challenge for the immediate future, however, is to venture forward with knowledge that is currently available to determine how best to initiate work in the area of family quality of life.

References

Bottroff, V., Brown, R. I., Bullitis, E., Duffield, V., Grantley, J., Kyrkou, M., & Thornley, J. (in press). Studies involving individuals with Down syndrome and their relevance to a quality of life model. In M. Cuskelly, A. Jobling, & S. Buckley (Eds.), *Down syndrome across the lifespan*. London: Whurr.

Brown, I. (1994). Promoting quality within service delivery systems [editorial]. *Journal on Developmental Disabilities, 3*(2), i–iv.

Brown, I. (1999a). Embracing quality of life in times of spending restraint. *Journal of Intellectual & Developmental Disabilities, 24*, 299–308.

Brown, I. (1999b). Setting the foundation for a quality of life model in exceptional education [editorial]. *Exceptionality Education Canada, 9*(1–2), 57–59.

Brown, I., & Renwick, R. (1997). Understanding what we mean by quality of life [editorial]. *Journal on Developmental Disabilities, 5*(2), i–vii.

Brown, I., Renwick, R., & Nagler, M. (1996). The centrality of quality of life in health promotion and rehabilitation. In R. Renwick, I. Brown, & M. Nagler (Eds.), *Quality of life in health promotion and rehabilitation: Conceptualizations, research, and applications* (pp. 3–13). Thousand Oaks, CA: Sage.

Brown, R. I. (1992). Some challenges to counselling in the field of disabilities In S. E. Robertson & R. I. Brown, *Rehabilitation counselling: Approaches in the field of disability* (pp. 274–296). London: Chapman & Hall.

Brown, R. I. (1996). People with developmental disabilities: Applying quality of life models to assessment and intervention. In R. Renwick, I. Brown, & M. Nagler (Eds.), *Quality of life in health promotion and rehabilitation: Conceptual approaches, issues, and applications* (pp. 253–267). Thousand Oaks, CA: Sage.

Brown, R. I. (1997a). Quality of life: The development of an idea. In R. I. Brown (Ed.), *Quality of life for people with disabilities: Models, research, and practice* (pp. 1–11). Cheltenham, UK: Stanley Thornes.

Brown, R. I. (1997b). Quality of life and professional education. In R. I. Brown (Ed.), *Quality of life for people with disabilities: Models, research, and practice* (pp. 310–326). Cheltenham, UK: Stanley Thornes.

Brown, R. I. (1999). Inclusion [editorial]. *Exceptionality Education Canada, 9*(1–2), 3–4.

Brown, R. I. (2000a). Learning from quality-of-life models. In M. P. Janicki & E. F. Ansellow (Eds.), *Community supports for aging adults with lifelong disabilities* (pp. 19–40). Baltimore: Paul H. Brookes.

Brown, R. I. (2000b). Quality of life: Challenges and confrontation. In K. D. Keith & R. L. Schalock (Eds.), *Cross-cultural perspectives on quality of life* (pp. 347–362). Washington, DC: American Association on Mental Retardation.

Brown, R. I. (2000c). *Evaluation of options coordination.* Report to the Minister for Disability services, Minister for the Aging. Adelaide: Government of South Australia.

Brown, R. I., Bayer, M. B., & Brown, P. M. (1992). *Empowerment and developmental handicaps: Choices and quality of life.* Toronto: Captus Press; London: Chapman & Hall.

Brown, R. I., Bayer, M. B., & MacFarlane, C. (1989). *Rehabilitation programmes: Performance and quality of life of adults with developmental handicaps.* Toronto: Lugus Productions.

Brown, R. I., Brown, P. M., & Bayer, M. B. (1994). A quality of life model: New challenges arising from a six-year study. In D. Goode (Ed.), *Quality of life for persons with disabilities: International perspectives and issues* (pp. 39–56). Cambridge, MA: Brookline.

Brown, R. I., & Shearer, J. (1999). Quality of life: Some implications for the process of inclusion. *Exceptionality Education Canada, 9,* 83–103.

Clarke, A. M., & Clarke, A. D. B. (2000). *Early experience in the life path.* London: Jessica Kingsley.

Cummins, R. A. (1997). Assessing quality of life. In R. I. Brown (Ed.), *Quality of life for people with disabilities* (pp. 116–150). Cheltenham UK: Stanley Thornes.

Cummins, R. A. (2000). A homeostatic model for subjective quality of life. *Proceedings of the Second International Conference of Quality of Life in Cities* (pp. 51–59). Singapore: National University of Singapore.

Dale, N. (1996). *Working with families of children with special needs: Partnership and practice.* London: Routledge.

Felce, D., & Perry, J. (1997). Quality of life: The scope of the term and its breadth of measurement. In R. I. Brown (Ed.), *Quality of life for people with disabilities* (pp. 56–71). Cheltenham, UK: Stanley Thornes.

Ferguson, R. V. (1997). Environmental design and quality of life. In R. I. Brown (Ed.), *Quality of life for people with disabilities* (pp. 251–269). Cheltenham, UK: Stanley Thornes.

Goode, D. (Ed.). (1994). *Quality of life for persons with disabilities: International perspectives and issues.* Cambridge, MA: Brookline.

Goode, D. A., & Hogg, J. (1994). Towards an understanding of holistic quality of life in people with profound intellectual and multiple disabilities. In D. Goode (Ed.), *Quality of life for persons with disabilities: International perspectives and issues* (pp. 197–207). Cambridge, MA: Brookline.

Hannam, C. (1975). *Parents and mentally handicapped children.* Harmondsworth, UK: Penguin Books.

Hatton, C. (1998). Whose quality of life is it anyway? Some problems with the emerging quality of life consensus. *Mental Retardation, 36,* 104–115.

James, O. (1997). *Britain on the couch: Treating a low serotinin society.* London: Century Random House.

Neufeldt, A. H., & McGinley, P. (1997). Human spirituality in relation to quality of life. In R. I. Brown (Ed.), *Quality of life for people with disabilities* (pp. 292–309). Cheltenham, UK: Stanley Thornes.

Peter, D. (1997). A focus on the individual, theory, and reality: Making the connection through the lives of individuals. In R. I. Brown (Ed.), *Quality of life for people with disabilities* (pp. 27–55). Cheltenham, UK: Stanley Thornes.

Raphael, D. (1996). Quality of life of older adults: Toward the optimization of the aging process. In R. Renwick, I. Brown, & M. Nagler (Eds.), *Quality of life in health promotion and rehabilitation: Conceptualizations, research, and applications* (pp. 290–306). Thousand Oaks, CA: Sage.

Renwick, R., & Brown, I. (1996). The Centre for Health Promotion conceptualization of quality of life: Being, belonging, and becoming. In R. Renwick, I. Brown, & M. Nagler (Eds.), *Quality of life in health promotion and rehabilitation: Conceptualizations, research, and applications* (pp. 75–86). Thousand Oaks, CA: Sage.

Renwick, R., Brown, I., & Nagler, M. (Eds.). (1996). *Quality of life in health promotion and rehabilitiation: Conceptualizations, research, and applications.* Thousand Oaks, CA: Sage.

Renwick, R., Brown, I., & Raphael, D. (2000). Person-centered quality of life: Contributions from Canada to an international understanding. In K. D. Keith & R. L. Schalock (Eds.), *Cross-cultural perspectives on quality of life* (pp. 5–21). Washington, DC: American Association on Mental Retardation.

Schalock, R. L. (Ed.). (1990). *Quality of life: Perspectives and issues.* Washington, DC: American Association on Mental Retardation.

Schalock, R. L. (1996). Reconsidering the conceptualization and measurement of quality of life. In R. L. Schalock (Ed.), *Quality of life: Vol. 1. Conceptualization and measurement* (pp. 123–139). Washington, DC: American Association on Mental Retardation.

Schalock, R. L. (1997). Can the concept of quality of life make a difference? In R. L. Schalock (Ed.), *Quality of life: Vol. 2. Application to persons with disabilities* (pp. 245–267). Washington, DC: American Association on Mental Retardation.

Schalock, R. L., Brown, I., Brown, R. I., Cummins, R. A., Felce, D., Matikka, L., Keith, K., & Parmenter, T. (2002). Conceptualization, measurement, and application of quality of life for persons with intellectual

disabilities: Results of an international panel of experts. *Mental Retardation,
40 (6), 457–470.*

Taylor, S. J. (1994). In support of research on quality of life, but against
QOL. In D. Goode, *Quality of life for persons with disabilities: International
perspectives and issues* (pp. 260–265). Cambridge, MA: Brookline.

Turnbull, A., & Turnbull, R. (2001). *Families, professionals, and exceptionality: Collaborating for empowerment* (4th ed.). Lawrence: University of
Kansas, Beach Center on Families and Disability.

Velde, B. (1997). Quality of life through personally meaningful activity.
In R. I. Brown (Ed.), *Quality of life for people with disabilities* (pp. 12–26).
Cheltenham, UK: Stanley Thornes.

Warren, B. (1997). Change and necessity: Creative activity, well-being,
and the quality of life for persons with a disability. In R. I. Brown (Ed.),
Quality of life for people with disabilities (pp. 270–291). Cheltenham, UK:
Stanley Thornes.

Webb, S. B. (1992). Disability counselling: Grieving the loss. In S. E.
Robertson & R. I. Brown, *Rehabilitation counselling: Approaches in the field
of disability* (pp. 202–219). London: Chapman & Hall.

Woodill, G., Renwick, R., Brown, I., & Raphael, D. (1994). Being,
belonging, becoming: An approach to the quality of life of persons with
developmental disabilities. In D. Goode (Ed.), *Quality of life for persons
with disabilities: International perspectives and issues* (pp. 57–74).
Cambridge, MA: Brookline.

Part 2

FAMILY QUALITY OF LIFE INQUIRY IN FIVE COUNTRIES

The five chapters in Part 2 provide an overview of sociopolitical trends, family quality of life research, and future directions in family quality of life inquiry. The five countries are the United States, the United Kingdom, Israel, Canada, and Australia.

Chapter 4

Enhancing Quality Of Life Of Families Of Children And Youth With Disabilities In The United States

Ann Turnbull, Rud Turnbull, Denise Poston, Gwen Beegle, Martha Blue-Banning, Corine Frankland, Lisa Mische Lawson, Louise Lord Nelson, Janet Marquis, Ji Yeon Park, Matt Stowe, and Jean Ann Summers

University of Kansas
Lawrence, Kansas

A Day In The Life Of The Poston Family

May 12, 2000. As I was preparing for the day ahead, I was celebrating the 2-week anniversary of our move to Lawrence from Leavenworth, Kansas. We moved here for many reasons: to be closer to work and my doctoral program, to be closer to friends, to have more and better supports for my 13-year-old son AJ, who has autism, and to leave behind some of the physical reminders of life prior to my recent divorce. I knew that we would still have challenges here. AJ would still have autism and all the joys and challenges it brings, I would still be a single mother with two boys ages 11 and 13, and I would still have the duty to make a good life for myself and my boys. But at least here I expected to have more supports.

In the 2 weeks since the move, I had interviewed case managers and selected one (in Kansas, a Medicaid recipient has a choice concerning case management agencies) and checked out the local mental health organization for counseling for my 11-year-old son, Jim. I had also called several family practice physicians, only to find out that none of the ones I called accepted my insurance coverage. No matter whom I saw, I was going to have to pay more than I paid in Leavenworth. In an effort to hire people who could assist AJ at home and in our community, I had put flyers up all over the

51

University of Kansas campus and telephoned student employment services, the school district, and friends.

In those same 2 weeks, AJ had an escalating number of outbursts and refused to leave the house except to go to school, an ice cream store, church, and one special friend's house where there is a Nintendo. All he wanted to do was stay home and play Nintendo. Jim was dying to make friends, and, although I reminded him that it had been only 2 weeks, it was his opinion in his all-or-nothing 11-year-old way of thinking that he would NEVER have friends again as long as he lived. The staff at both Jim's and AJ's schools had been wonderful about getting to know them, accepting them, and making accommodations that they would need to facilitate learning at school. AJ was spending more time with "typical" peers than he ever had in the past. He had even brought home a real textbook with real homework for the first time ever.

On that day when I was celebrating, AJ had another violent behavior outburst—his third in four days. It started the same way that about one-quarter of his outbursts start. He was being a little mischievous, hassling his brother and messing around with a stuffed animal. As he came outside to wait for the bus, he started throwing his book bag—a sure sign that things were escalating. I went through my normal routine of diversion and calming, but this time he did not respond.

This is the sort of behavior that I worry about. Fortunately, it doesn't happen very often, only two or three times a week. But I must be constantly on the alert, waiting for it all the time. I know that the tension that accompanies this constant vigilance takes a toll on me. It also takes its toll on Jim. During this particular incident, AJ's violent reaction to my intervention resulted in him pinning me to the ground by the bus stop, with his fist full of my hair. When I finally broke free and returned to my newly rented home, just up the street from the bus stop, I was able to call his teacher, who came right over to help calm him down. Someone also called the police. So here we were, 2 weeks in our new home, and we already had the police at our door.

That incident was a harbinger of things to come. AJ had three more of those violent outbursts later that day. The police were called three more times—once to take AJ to the local hospital, once to defuse the situation, and the last time to take him in handcuffs to the juvenile detention facility. Many of the details of what happened that day are blurry to me. I was in a fog, physically hurting from his blows and emotionally hurting from the pain of feeling like a failure as a parent.

I also felt that I had failed to protect AJ from himself and his disability. Furthermore, I had failed to protect Jim from the emotional turmoil that accompanies each tantrum; Jim had been screaming at AJ to "Stop it, AJ! Stop hurting Mom!" Luckily, a good friend took Jim away from home early in the afternoon and kept him overnight, thereby sparing him from witnessing most of the violence—the police, the battering, the destruction.

I felt that I should have been able to handle the situation. After all, I know AJ very well and I have closely analyzed what causes his outbursts and how to defuse them. But he is getting so big and strong that I was physically almost helpless. I could only dodge his blows—not all of them, just some. A friend from work came over and was also trying to restrain AJ, but could not. I could only sit and watch and listen as my son destroyed our home. I know that money isn't the most important thing in life, but, in my household every cent counts, and I don't have extra to replace broken doors or windows, or to patch holes in the walls. None of the violence or destruction would matter at all if he seriously hurt himself, or me, or anyone else. The head of the local provider agency came over and helped us explore some options for AJ. We knew he could not stay at home alone with me. We also knew that he probably couldn't stay at home with anyone else either—the destroyed physical environment seemed to be a catalyst for more outbursts.

So my friend, the agency director, and I started looking for a safe place for AJ to stay. Our local hospital and mental health center said they did not have the capacity to keep adolescents on an in-patient basis. The head of the local agency was able to get him into the nearby state hospital for people with developmental disabilities on an emergency basis, but to admit him that night would mean a 2-and-a-half-hour drive with a violent young man at an hour when we were all exhausted—except the violent young man! The juvenile intake coordinator at the police station looked for a "bed" closer to us. She was very helpful, for she knew "the system" and coached me to use the right words, those that would get the result we needed for AJ—a short-term, emergency, in-patient facility where staff could stabilize him, keep him safe, and give me time to recover physically and emotionally and to figure out what to do next.

To consider hospitalizing AJ, no matter how dire his and our need at the time, was a huge step for me. I felt that no one could care for AJ as I could—even though I felt that I wasn't doing such a great job at the moment. I was afraid he would not be understood, that he would be restrained indiscriminately, that he might be pumped full of medication with potentially serious side effects, and that all of this would cause him to have even more behavior outbursts. I didn't trust the mental and physical health care systems to know how to care for him.

It took the kind and gentle, but persistent, urging of my friends to help me finally understand that this was best not just for AJ, but also for Jim and me as well. It is so difficult to decide when to "sacrifice" one family member's well-being for the well-being of others. In our case, both Jim and I had been sacrificing so long for AJ. I guess now it was time for him to give a little so that we could put our lives back together.

* * *

AJ has been in the hospital a little over a week, and I am just starting to feel a little less guilty about having him there. I am using the time to rest, plan for AJ's return, do things with Jim, catch up on work, and prioritize everything that I feel I have to do to keep my life running smoothly.

This whole incident has me thinking. First of all, I want never to be in the position again where things get so bad that the only solution is out-of-home placement, even if that placement is short term. Second, I need to have supports in place for AJ and a variety of preferred activities so that I don't use the Nintendo as a babysitter. It takes so much time and effort to keep him engaged in positive activities that I can't do it alone. Either I have no time left for anything else, or I become resentful at having to spend all my time outside of work being support person, case manager, therapist, friendship facilitator, and mom.

I had already tried to find assistants for AJ. I had flyers up all over campus, sent an ad to the student employment office, and called friends of colleagues, but so far I have come up empty. There are only a few more places I have to call. We have access to well-funded home- and community-based services, yet I cannot find qualified— or even unqualified, for that matter—people to hire as AJ's assistants. Once these assistants are in place and there are a variety of activities for AJ, then I think things will not come to a crisis again.

We are having a Group Action Planning meeting tomorrow. Our group consists of friends and professionals who meet on a regular basis to set goals and figure out "next steps" to accomplish the goals. The group did an excellent job getting me through the move to Lawrence and helping AJ's transition to the new school. But we didn't take care of the one thing I needed, which was to keep him safe at home. So that is our task now: finding a way to support AJ at home so that we all—AJ, Jim, and I—have a good quality of life. We have a lot to do at the meeting.

Denise Poston

Overview

This chapter provides an overview on policy, services, and research related to the quality of life of families in the United States who have children and youth with disabilities. It begins with an overview of the current sociopolitical trends and the current service delivery system, as of the middle of the year 2000. It then describes the Beach Center's research program on enhancing family quality of life (also as of the middle of the year 2000) and concludes by suggesting future directions for research, policy, and services. Throughout, we integrate examples of the Poston family as a way of grounding our concepts in the reality of family life, since it is our intention and hope that families everywhere will benefit from family quality of life research. Because we wrote this chapter in the beginning of the year 2000, we add a postscript to comment briefly on developments since that time.

Current Sociopolitical Trends

Families of children and youth with disabilities are affected by both general sociopolitical trends and by disability-specific trends.

General Trends

Two general trends of the 1990s have implications for family quality of life: the effects of policies that have encouraged strong economic growth, and the effects of changing views on the role of governments.

Demographics And Economics: A Mixed Picture

The United States has recently experienced greater overall economic health than at any time since the middle 1950s: the unemployment rate is lower; interest rates are generally lower; the paper wealth of investors has increased remarkably; there is an increase in the number of first-time home buyers and people trading up to larger houses; yearly, more households become linked to the Internet; and fewer families remain on public support (in part because of the economy and in part because of the welfare-reform laws that discourage such support). One view of these trends is that they help improve families' quality of life: a rising tide has lifted all boats.

The healthy national economy has also affected the field of disability. Supported and competitive employment of individuals with disabilities is higher than at any time since World War II (Braddock, Hemp, Parish, & Rizzolo, 2000). In addition, the closure or down sizing of the state facilities for people with disabilities, the creation of more home and community residential placements, the down sizing (from 12 to 6 or fewer residents) of community residential facilities, and increases in family support are proceeding unabated, fueled largely by a community-living ideology and by an economy that makes the ideology affordable (Braddock et al., 2000).

At the same time, there are more families whose countries of origin are not English speaking, more non-Caucasian families that are regarded as poor or working poor, and more families affected by "welfare reform" than at any time in the past half century (U.S. Census Bureau, 1996). The national poverty rate is 28% for children with disabilities and 16% for children without disabilities (Fuijiura & Yamaki, 2000). Indeed, the cooccurrence of poverty, single-parent families, cultural/linguistic/ethnic diversity, and disability is undeniable and has yet to be reversed (Forum on Child and Family Statistics, 1998; Fuijiura & Yamaki, 1997, 2000; LaPlante, Carlson, Kaye, & Bradsher, 1996; Newacheck & Halfon, 1998; Sherman, 1994; U.S. Census Bureau, 1996).

Politics: Moderation And The New Federalism

In the 1990s the United States witnessed at least three very different views on the role of government (H. Turnbull & A. Turnbull, 2000). The first emphasized an increased role for the federal government. This view was exemplified by efforts of the Clinton administration to establish a policy of universal, federally sponsored, and federally subsidized health care, and the failure of these efforts appears to represent a failure of support for the view that the federal government has a place in sponsoring large national programs.

A second view on the role of government emphasized a marked decrease in political intervention. This highly conservative view was evident in the actions of the 1994 Congress (the so-called Gingrich Congress) that involved efforts to enact a new "Contract With America," under which the federal government would abandon or significantly reduce its role in education, health care, and habilitation and rehabilitation services. These efforts also failed, signifying an apparent lack of support for reducing the role of government to such a degree.

The third view was more "moderate." This view held that the federal government has a legitimate role to play, but that it must "devolve" or transfer a great deal more discretion to operate programs that meet local needs to the states.

It seems clear at this writing that the moderate perspective has prevailed. There is increasing devolution of government rights and duties from the federal to the state-local level. This "new federalism" holds that issues that for the past 50 years have been regarded as national are in fact better handled by state and local governments. Accordingly, few new federal rights are being created. Likewise, state and local governments have increased discretion in administrating federally financed programs. One part of the key federal antidiscrimination law (Americans With Disabilities Act, 1990) was successfully challenged as unconstitutional in terms of Congress' power to enforce the equal protection provision of the 14th Amendment to the Constitution (*University of Alabama v. Garrett*, 2001). Other federal laws are being struck down as an unconstitutional exercise of federal power (*Alexander v. Sandoval*, 2001). The Supreme Court leads the way in policy making—a fact that is deeply disturbing, for its members are not subject to the corrective political process; they have life-time tenure. The federal role in disability policy is shrinking.

Disability-Specific Trends

Four trends that primarily affect individuals with disabilities and their families are the consolidation of rights, an emphasis on outcomes, the new paradigm of disability, and the linkage of core concepts and quality of life outcomes.

Consolidation Of Rights

The 1970s was the "civil rights era," a time when new rights to education, habilitation, rehabilitation, and community access were first established and when the emphasis was on *access* (removing barriers) and *benefit* (assuring that an accessible society provides individualized benefits). But the 1980s and 1990s were an era of *consolidation,* a time when rights were reaffirmed or improved, thereby contributing to families' quality of life. In 2000 and 2001, the Supreme Court began to vitiate the scope of antidiscrimination laws (*Kimel v. Board of Regents,* 2000; *Alabama v. Garrett,* 2001).

During the past two decades, both Congress and state legislatures have consolidated the rights of individuals with disabilities and their families in a number of ways. In the mid-1980s, Congress amended the federal special-education statute, Individuals With Disabilities Education Act (IDEA), to provide services to infants and children and to assure smooth transitions from school to the world of adulthood (H. Turnbull & A. Turnbull, 2000). In 1997 Congress strengthened parents' rights to share in school decision making, students' access to the general curriculum, students' protection against school discipline, and students' rights to "state-of-the-art" technology, called positive behavioral supports (H. Turnbull & A. Turnbull, 2000). In *Board v. Rowley* (1982), in *Irving Independent School District v. Tatro* (1984), and again in *Cedar Rapids Community School District v. Garret F.* (1999), the U.S. Supreme Court interpreted IDEA to sustain students' claims to an appropriate education and related services.

In 1988 Congress enacted antidiscrimination laws related to fair housing (Fair Housing Act Amendments). In 1990 it followed suit by enacting the "disability civil rights act," Americans With Disabilities Act (ADA), prohibiting discrimination in state and local governmental activities, public- and private-sector employment, transportation and telecommunications, and privately operated public accommodations.

As we said above, however, the constitutionality of these laws is now in doubt because of the Supreme Court's decisions. The era of consolidation may have been the last breath of liberalism in the United States.

Emphasis On Outcomes

The 1990s was a decade when Congress continued to emphasize process rights but added an emphasis on outcome rights. For example, when Congress first enacted the Individuals With Disabilities Education Act in 1975 (originally called the Education of the Handicapped Act), it emphasized how schools should transact their business with students with disabilities; the legal maxim "fair procedures produce fair results" governed (H. Turnbull & A. Turnbull, 2000). With the enactment of the Americans With Disabilities Act in 1990 and the reauthorization of the Individuals With Disabilities Education Act in 1997, however, Congress made clear that there are four *outcome* goals: full participation, equal opportunity, independent living, and economic self-sufficiency. Now families' quality of life is improved or affected by how well government achieves those outcome goals, not simply by how they process their services to families.

The New Paradigm Of Disability

The old paradigm of disability characterizes disability as a deficit within the individual that results in functional impairments associated with daily activities (A. Turnbull, Turbiville, & Turnbull, 2000). Accordingly, it focuses on "fixing" the individual's functional impairments and "fixing" the individual's parents (usually just mother) so that the person will be able to participate in the general societal experiences and settings. Figure 4.1 depicts the old paradigm's target of intervention.

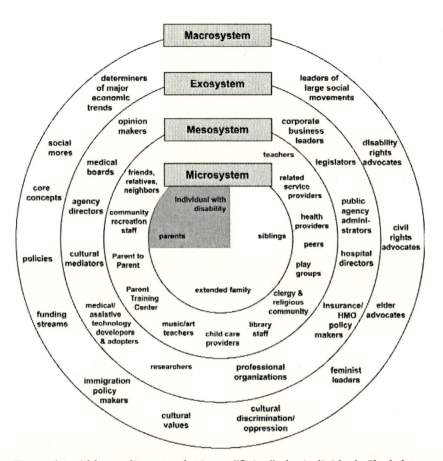

Figure 4.1 **Old paradigm: emphasis on "fixing" the individual. Shaded area represents target of "change efforts."**

The Americans With Disabilities Act (1990) and a new paradigm characterize disability as contextual and societal. A person has an impairment that is not a disability if sufficient supports and accommodations are available from and within the macrosystem, the exosystem, the mesosystem, and the microsystem, as illustrated in Figure 4.2. These environments either limit or liberate individuals with disabilities and their families. This paradigm then views disability as a social reaction to impairment. It emphasizes changes from "fixing" the individual and the family to "fixing" the social, policy, and physical environments, rather than "fixing" individuals (A. Turnbull, Blue-Banning, Turbiville, & Park, 1999). "Fixing" all such environments, it is believed, assures that adequate supports, services, accommodations, and relationships are available so that people with disabilities may accomplish the four outcomes goals.

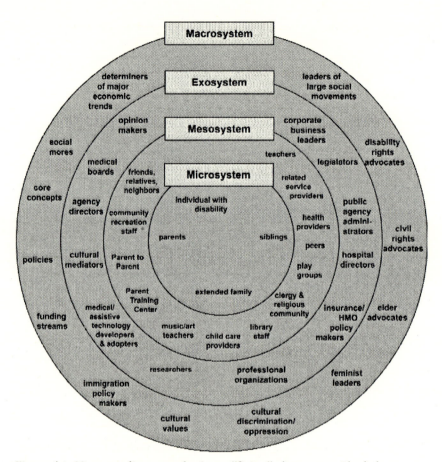

Figure 4.2 **New paradigm: emphasis on "fixing" the system. Shaded area represents target of "change efforts."**

Linkage Of Core Concepts And Quality Of Life Outcomes

The new paradigm recognizes that policy is a critical aspect of the environment in which people live. For this reason, it seeks to ground policy and practice explicitly in disability core concepts, and to link these core concepts to individual and family quality of life outcomes (H. Turnbull, Stowe, & Beegle, 2001). For example, the Individuals With Disabilities Education Act changed the policy and service-delivery environments (schools) by articulating the core concepts of disability policy and by authorizing services grounded in these concepts and targeted at outcomes. Furthermore, as illustrated by IDEA, the new paradigm also changes the family environment by strengthening families' rights with respect to their children's education. By changing the policy and service environments, advancing core concepts of policy, and assuring that policy and services target designated outcomes, the new paradigm addresses individual and family quality of life. We will discuss core concepts and family quality of life outcomes in the section that focuses on our current research agenda.

Current Service-Delivery Trends

The sociopolitical trends described above heavily influence current trends in service delivery.

General Trends

Partnerships

Traditionally, discrete laws and funding streams have sought to address narrowly targeted problems. Thus there are separate laws and appropriations for general education, special education, mental health, public health, social services, and others. These create a system of "verticality"—narrowly targeted problems and narrowly constructed policies, services, and funding streams. Table 4.1 illustrates this verticality in terms of the Poston family. The problem is that the Poston family does not fit into discrete vertical niches. This family, and indeed all families, typically have "horizontal" needs that are not sufficiently satisfied by verticality. Policies and services have dealt with only segments of families and children's lives; a wholistic approach has been elusive.

The general trend at the present time, however, is toward horizontality: cooperation, coordination, collaboration, integration, and transformation through such techniques as school-linked services, community-linked services, full-service schools, wrap-around services, and "bundling" (consolidation) of funding from different streams (Adelman & Taylor, 1997; Amato, 1996; Briar-Lawson, Lawson, Collier, & Joseph, 1997; Calfee, Wittwer, & Meredith, 1998; Coltoff, 1998; Comer, Haynes, Joyner, & Ben-Avie, 1996; Doktor & Poertner, 1996; Dryfoos, 1996, 1997, 1998; Dupper & Poertner, 1997; Franklin & Streeter, 1995; Lawson & Briar-Lawson, 1997; MacKenzie & Rogers, 1997; Raham, 1998; Sailor, in press; Skrtic & Sailor, 1996; U.S. Department of Education, 1999). We use the term *partnerships* to describe the gestalt, the general tenor, of horizontal organization.

The trend toward partnerships cuts across such diverse human-service fields as education, mental health, early childhood community development services, welfare reform demonstrations, and other poverty-related programs. Although some communities have achieved a degree of partnership, a truly service-integrated community, supporting families comprehensively, remains an unrealized ideal (Kagan, Goffin, Golub, & Pritchard, 1995; Schorr, 1997), especially for families of children with disabilities.

Table 4.1
Poston Family Needs In Three Service System Strands

Education	Human and Social Services	Health Care
• Updated and appropriate IEP for AJ incorporating behavior supports and goals • 12-month school year for AJ • Updated and appropriate IEP for Jim that focuses on supports that assist him without calling attention (from peers) to his need for support • Transportation to school for both boys that does not cause conflicts in daily schedule or childcare routines • Denise's continuing progress in her doctoral program	• New billing services for the HCBS waiver • Keeping track of upcoming changes in the HCBS system that affect the type and amount of services to which AJ is entitled • Coordination that allows AJ's participation with supports in a variety of community activities such as parks and recreation, equestrian therapy, scouting and the local youth sports "club" • Jim's participation in a variety of community activities such as swimming lessons, scouts, Big Brothers–Big Sisters, and music lessons • Supports for AJ so that all family members can actively participate in their church • Follow-up with juvenile justice regarding funding that may be available as a result of AJ's detention • Sexuality education for AJ • Regular respite care for Denise to have time with Jim, alone, and with friends • Finding and training AJ's personal assistants to provide supports at home and in the community	• Psychopharmacologist for AJ to prescribe appropriate medications that do not have side effects (drowsiness) that impact his ability to participate at school and in community activities • Counseling for Jim regarding his feelings about AJ and about his own diagnosis of ODD • Counseling for Denise • Keeping up to date on status of private medical insurance and Medicaid claims • Minimize drive time to obtain low-cost (free) medications (currently requires 45- minute one-way drive) • Family practice doctor to see the Poston family for first-line illness and injuries • Gynecologist for Denise • Dentist for the Poston family, one who is good with patients with disabilities or tactile sensitivities

Note. IEP = individualized education plan. ODD = oppositional defiant disorder.

Emphasis On Outcomes

An emphasis on outcomes is a sociopolitical trend and also a service delivery trend that has occurred simultaneously with the trend to service integration (Schorr, 1997).

This trend toward outcomes affects the disability service delivery system. For example, IDEA requires statewide or districtwide assessments of student outcomes. These assessments hold schools accountable for improving the outcomes for all students (Erickson, 1998; McLaughlin, 1998; H. Turnbull et al., 2001). Although students with disabilities have typically been excluded from state and national assessments, they are now included, and schools are held accountable for their outcomes (Vanderwood, McGrew, & Ysseldyke, 1998).

Disability-Specific Trends

The most significant trend for families has been away from the old paradigm of emphasizing parent involvement as a way to "fix" individuals with a disability to the new paradigm of family-centered services as a vehicle for "fixing" multiple environments.

Parent Involvement

When IDEA was first enacted in 1975, it authorized shared educational decision making by entitling parents to be members of their child's individualized education program (IEP) team. Although the IEP process was intended to provide a context for equal decision making among parents and professionals, a professional-dominated approach is prevalent, and there is scant evidence that the IEP process has empowering outcomes for students, parents, or educators (Smith, 1990; National Council on Disability, 1995; H. Turnbull et al., 2001). Moreover, the parents involved in educational decision making have been primarily mothers who have had limited influences on the decisions that are made in IEP conferences, mediation, and due process hearings (Able-Boone, 1993; Campbell, Strickland, & La Forme, 1992; H. Turnbull et al., 2001). This professionally dominated approach is particularly problematic for families from culturally and linguistically diverse backgrounds (Harry, Kalyanpur, & Day, 1999; Kalyanpur & Harry, 1999). It appears to exacerbate differences between the bureaucratic special-education culture and families from culturally and linguistically diverse backgrounds that rely more on relationships than legal procedures.

From Parent Involvement To Family-Centered Services

Since the mid-1980s the trend has been to move from parent involvement to family-centered services. We quote from a 1987 passage (A. Turnbull & Summers):

The term parent involvement sums up the current (1987) perspective. It means we want parents involved with us. It means the service delivery system we helped create is at the center of the universe, and families are revolving around it. It brings to mind an analogy about the old Ptolemaic view of the universe with the earth at the center … Copernicus came along and made a startling reversal—he put the sun in the center of the universe rather than the Earth. His declaration caused profound shock. The earth was not the epitome of creation; it was a planet like all other planets. The successful challenge to the entire system of ancient authority required a complete change in philosophical conception of the universe. This is rightly termed the "Copernican Revolution." Let's pause to consider what would happen if we had a Copernican Revolution in the field of disability. Visualize the concept: The family is the center of the universe and the service delivery system is one of the many planets revolving around it. Now visualize the service delivery system at the center and the family in orbit around it. Do you see the difference? Do you recognize the revolutionary change in perspective? We would move from an emphasis on parent involvement (i.e., parents participating in the program) to family support (i.e., programs providing a range of support services to families). This is not a semantic exercise—such a revolution leads us to a new set of assumptions and a new vista of options for service. (pp. 295–296)

The family-centered model is characterized by family choice, a family-strengths perspective, and the family as the unit of support (Allen & Petr, 1996). First, the family-centered model encourages families to take the lead in stating their priorities and having professionals respond to those priorities (Dunst, Johnson, Trivette, & Hamby, 1991; McBride, Brotherson, Joanning, Whiddon, & Demmit, 1993; A. Turnbull et al., 2000). Second, the family-centered model abandoned a pathology orientation and adopted a strengths orientation (Bailey & McWilliam, 1993; Dunst, Trivette, & Deal, 1988; Saleeby, 1996). Third, the entire family is the unit of support, not just the child with a disability and the child's mother (A. Turnbull & H. Turnbull, 2001).

The trend toward family-centered services reflects the new paradigm, emphasizing the family as an environment within and to which supports and services need to be provided to mitigate the effects of disability.

Currently the family-centered model prevails in early intervention and early childhood services for young children with disabilities (McWilliam, Lang, Vandiviere, Angell, Collins, & Underdown, 1995; Murphy, Lee, Turnbull, & Turbiville, 1995; A. Turnbull et al., 2000; Wehman, 1999). Research indicates, however, that the family-centered philosophy is stronger than its actual implementation (Katz & Scarpati, 1995; McBride et al., 1993; Menke, 1991). Moreover, at the elementary-, middle-, and secondary-school levels, the bridge from the old to the new paradigm is not as strong as it is

during the early years. The emphasis is still much more on parent involvement in IEP conferences and parent attendance at school events than on a
family-centered model and on an equalization of the power relationship
between families and professionals (A. Turnbull & H. Turnbull, 2001).

Family Quality Of Life Research Program

In this section we show how our research on family quality of life is consistent with the new paradigm trends we have just described. To make that
point, we first describe how we carry out our research for, with, and on
behalf of families: participatory action research. Then we describe the analytical framework for our research. Finally we describe the research agenda
that emanates from our analytical framework.

Participatory Action Research

The new paradigm acknowledges that research is itself an environment
that affects individuals with disabilities and their families. A means for
improving the research environment is participatory action research (PAR).
Under PAR, the ultimate beneficiaries of research (individuals and families)
are involved in all stages of the research (Santelli, Singer, DiVenere,
Ginsberg, & Powers, 1998; A. Turnbull, Friesen, & Ramirez, 1998; H.
Turnbull & A. Turnbull, 1989). Figure 4.3 illustrates six levels at which families and researchers can interact; three levels place researchers in the dominant role (old paradigm) and three represent researcher-parent partnerships
(new paradigm). At the Beach Center, we work at Levels 4 through 6. Our
work has particularly been influenced by the perspectives of families from
culturally and linguistically diverse backgrounds that have not typically been
part of the research process (Markey, Santelli, & Turnbull, 1998).

Overview Of Analytical Framework

Participatory action research is one way we have improved our research
environment to advance families' quality of life. Another way is assuring that
all research has a common basis. We call that basis our analytical framework.
Its role is to organize our research into a coherent and comprehensive whole.
In the old-paradigm research environment in social services, investigators
worked in relative isolation from each other, even when they were working
in the same research center. The result was that the benefits to the ultimate
beneficiaries of the research (in our case, families of individuals with disabilities) usually were not commensurate with the researchers' efforts or the dollars invested. To achieve outcomes that more positively affect families'
quality of life, we changed our own research environment by adopting an
analytical framework to assure that all of our research projects connect to
each other. The new paradigm demanded nothing less. Our analytical
framework has four major components (see Figure 4.4): core concepts and
overarching principles of disability policy, public policy, services, and family
quality of life outcomes.

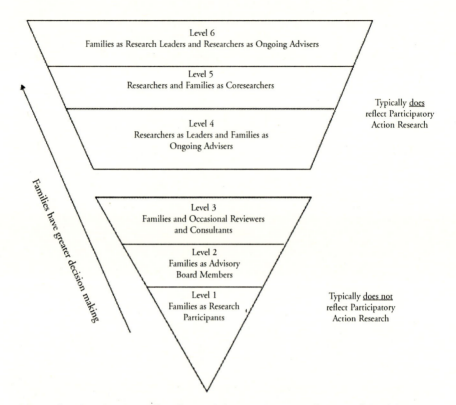

Figure 4.3 **Continuum of family participation in research. From "Participatory action research," by A. P. Turnbull, B. J. Friesen, and C. Ramirez, 1988.** *Journal of the Association for Persons with Severe Handicaps, 23,* **pp. 178–188. Copyright 1998 by The Association for Persons With Severe Handicaps. Reprinted with permission.**

The first component consists of research to identify the core concepts of disability policy. A concept is an abstract or generic idea generalized from particular instances; a concept is core if it is a central and often foundational part of disability policy, and if it reflects fundamental values—values that advance the quality of life for citizens with disabilities and their families and that are widely recognized as necessary for life, liberty, and the pursuit of happiness (Brakel, Parry, & Weiner, 1985; Levy & Rubenstein, 1996; Minow, 1990; Silverstein, 2000; H. Turnbull & A. Turnbull, 2000; H. Turnbull, Stowe, & Beegle, 2001).

The core concepts merge into principles that affect all families. A principle by definition is a comprehensive and fundamental law or doctrine; accordingly, core concepts of disability policy form into a taxonomy of principles affecting all families. Thus whatever principles govern and advance the

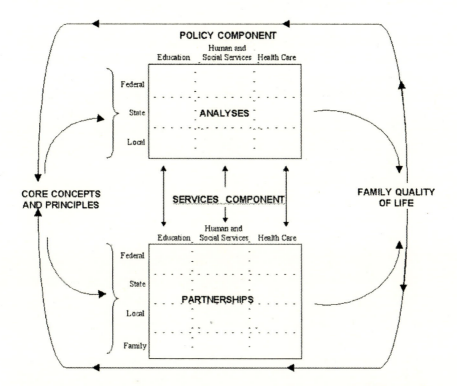

Figure 4.4 **New paradigm analytical framework for enhancing family quality of life.**

quality of life of all families should also do the same for families affected by disability. (Figure 4.2 places core concepts and generic principles at the macrosystem level, because they pervade not only that system but the other three systems as well.)

The second component of our analytical framework consists of research on public policy. Our assumptions here—assumptions that are central to our research agenda—are that core concepts and generic principles affect public policy; that core concepts and generic principles should be infused into policy at federal, state, and local levels (vertical implementation); and that they also should be infused across three service delivery strands: education, human and social services, and health care (horizontal implementation).

The third component of the analytical framework consists of research on service delivery systems. Because of the apparent benefits of partnerships among individuals with disabilities, families, and services providers (Adelman & Taylor, 1997; Burns & Goldman, 1999; Calfee et al., 1998; Dryfoos, 1997, 1998; Sailor, in press; Stroul, 1996), we are especially interested in the factors that facilitate or impede partnerships. We are also interested in how policy reforms, consistent with the core concepts and generic principles, can produce better outcomes through better service-delivery structures. In particular, we believe that partnerships that address interpersonal and structural components at the family-service provider, intra-agency, and interagency levels can empower families and professionals alike.

The fourth component of our analytical framework consists of research into family quality of life. We define a quality family life as occurring when the family's needs are met, family members enjoy their life together as a family, and family members have the opportunity to pursue and achieve outcomes that are important to their happiness and fulfillment.

There appears to be general agreement that a positive family quality of life should be an outcome of policies and services (Bailey et al., 1998; Accreditation Council, 1995; A. Turnbull et al., 1999; H. Turnbull & Brunk, 1997). Research in conceptualizing and measuring the quality of life of individuals with disabilities has far exceeded comparable work focusing on the family quality of life (Brown, Brown, & Bayer, 1994; Brown, 1997; Cummins, 1997; Felce & Perry, 1997; Gardner & Nudler, 1999; Renwick, Brown, & Nagler, 1996; Schalock, 1996, 1997, 2000). Researchers are just beginning to conceptualize and develop a taxonomy and a corresponding measurement system for family quality of life domains and indicators and thus for policy and program outcomes.

Our theory of change related to family quality of life outcome is as follows:

1. Core concepts of disability policy and overarching generic principles should shape policy (statutes, regulations, and court cases) at the federal, state, and local levels, and across the three strands of education, social services, and health care.

2. Policy shapes service delivery structures and processes at the federal, state, and local governmental level and across the three strands of education, human and social services, and health care.

3. Enhanced family quality of life results when policies and services are infused with the core concepts and principles, provide for horizontal implementation, and are delivered through partnerships.

4. Family quality of life domains or indicators should influence and be integral to core concepts and principles, so that, in turn, the core concepts' and generic principles' impact on policies and services will advance family quality of life.

5. Accordingly, there should be an unbroken loop in the relationship among core concepts and generic principles, policies, services, and family quality of life outcomes.

Our new research paradigm, then, relates to the outcomes of the new paradigm. Fundamentally we seek to "fix" multiple environments (see Figure 4.2) through new-paradigm research, rather than to "fix" the child or family, as was characteristic of old-paradigm research. We emphasize how research can result in a transformed ecology within which families, including children and youth with disabilities, can flourish as they interact with professionals within a responsive policy and service-delivery context (Garlow, Turnbull, & Schnase, 1991; Jones, Garlow, Turnbull, & Barber, 1996; A. Turnbull et al., 1999; H. Turnbull, Garlow, & Barber, 1991).

The Analytical Framework As A Basis For Research Activities

Our analytical framework (Figure 4.4) is the basis for our research on understanding and then enhancing family quality of life. Inherent in our research are efforts to develop measurement tools and to use them to carry out a research agenda that consists of policy analysis, explanatory research, and program evaluation or quality enhancement.

Development Of Measurement Tools

Overview. Perhaps the main reason that family quality of life research is in its infancy is that very little work has occurred in conceptualizing it and advancing a corresponding measurement system. Table 4.2 shows three studies we are carrying out, in which we have developed scales, indices, and matrices that we will use in our research.

- *Scales* have a validated factorial structure with domains and respective indicators. They will be used for explanatory research involving structural equation modeling.
- *Indices* are developed from the factorial structure of scales. They are shorter than scales and will be used for policy analyses or enhancement and program evaluation or enhancement.
- *Matrices* have been developed to assess the extent to which the core concepts of disability policy and domains of family quality of life are incorporated into federal and state statutes.

Table 4.2 gives a synopsis of our three research studies on developing measurement tools. It identifies the purpose, key research questions, research design, and current findings that have been or are being developed. To put our work into context, we briefly highlight the findings from each of these studies and then relate them to the Poston family.

To identify and define the core concepts of disability policy, we (a) analyzed the Constitution of the United States, Bill of Rights, and 58 cases from the U.S. Supreme Court or other precedent-setting decisions of other courts interpreting these documents; (b) analyzed nearly 45 Acts of Congress or pending bills; (c) carried out a literature review; and (d) conducted focus groups and individual interviews with policy leaders, senior-level program

Table 4.2
Overview Of Studies To Develop Measurement Tools

Study Focus	Purposes	Key Research Question	Research Design	Current Findings
Core Concepts	• To identify and define the core concepts of disability policy affecting families that have children with disabilities • To develop measurement tools related to the core concepts	• What are the core concepts—definitions, appropriate synonyms, and bases in key statutes, judicial cases, and practice?	• Focus groups and individual interviews consistent with rigorous qualitative procedures • Conduct test-retest reliability on the family and service provider indices • Conduct inter-rater reliability on the matrix for policy analysis	• Data confirm 18 core concepts, reveal 250+ factors influencing policy, and demonstrate inter-relationships of concepts, factors, and family quality of life outcomes
Partnerships	• To confirm or modify a conceptual model of partnerships between and among families and professionals • To identify domains and indicators associated with the components of partnerships • To configure the domains and indicators into scales and indices	• What are the domains and indicators of exemplary partnerships at the family-service provider, intra-agency, and interagency levels?	• Identified preliminary domains through literature review and PAR committee • Conducted 34 focus groups with parents, individuals with disabilities, service providers, and administrators (N = 169) • Conducted individual in-depth interviews with siblings and 20 parents with limited English proficiency • Constructed, pilot tested, and revised preliminary scale of family-service provider partnerships • In process of conducting large-scale field test partnerships • Will use confirmatory factor analysis to analyze responses	• The focus group data suggest six domains (with 10 indicators per domain) at the family-service level: communication, trust, respect, commitment, equality, and skills • The focus group data suggests a shift in our original conceptualization of inter-personal partnerships; Interpersonal domains appear to be homogeneous at family-service provider, intra-agency, and interagency levels
Family Quality of Life	• To identify domains and indicators of family quality of life • To configure the domains and indicators into a scale, indices, and matrix	• What are the domains and indicators of family quality of life for children with disabilities?	• Same as partnerships except for the following: – A minimum of 750 families will be involved in the field test – All family members will be asked to complete a scale rather than only the primary care provider	• Focus group data suggest a conceptualization of family quality of life with 10 domains, divided into two groups: those that primarily focus on the family as a unit and those that focus on individual members' impact on the family • The domains for the family as a unit are family interaction, daily life, parenting, and financial well-being • The domains for individual family members are emotional well-being, health, physical environment, productivity, social well-being, and advocacy

Note. PAR = participatory action research.

administrators, and family advocacy organization leaders at the federal and state-regional levels (H. Turnbull et al., 2001). Table 4.3 identifies and briefly defines the 18 core concepts; Table 4.4 indicates how six core concepts relate to family quality of life (as exemplified by the Poston family) and how the core concepts can conflict with each other when applied.

Table 4.3
Core Concepts Of Disability Policy

Disability Policy Core Concepts Principles	Definition and Constitutional
Antidiscrimination	Statutes, generally known as "civil rights acts," make it illegal to discriminate against a person with a disability solely by reason of the person's disability.
Autonomy	A person with a disability or the person's family has a right to consent, refuse to consent, withdraw consent, or otherwise control or have choice over what happens to him or her. Sometimes the concept of autonomy is expressed as "independence," "self-determination," or "full participation."
Empowerment/ Participatory Decision Making	These are the means by which a person or family or a duly appointed surrogate secures what he or she wants from a service provider system; the means is through participation with the system in consenting (see "autonomy") or otherwise participating in the decision-making processes by which the services that will be received are planned, developed, implemented, and evaluated.
Privacy & Confidentiality	Privacy refers to protection against unwarranted governmental interference in decision making that affects private interests. Confidentiality refers to infor-mation concerning one' self or family; it includes the person's or family's access to the information, rights of correction and expungement, and control over access to it by others.
Liberty	A person has the right to be free from unwarranted physical or other confinement by a government. Related is a claim to be treated with respect and dignity.
Protection Against Harm	A person has the right to be free from harm while in state custody or in the care of such private individu-als as family members or other caregivers.

(table continues)

(table 4.3 continued)

Disability Policy Core Concepts Principles	Definition and Constitutional
Individualized & Appropriate Services	These services are specially tailored to meet the needs and preferences of individuals with disabilities and their families.
Capacity-Based Services	The evaluation of the unique strengths and needs of a person with a disability or the person's family is the basis for capacity-based services. It includes a person- or family-directed evaluation of their resources, priorities, and concerns and their identification of the services necessary to enhance their various capacities. The term reflects the "strengths" perspective and rejects the "pathology" perspective.
Classification	Classification includes the processes (ways) and the standards (criteria) by which a person with a disability or the person's family qualifies (becomes eligible) to benefit from certain laws (antidiscrimination or other rights or entitlements). Sometimes eligibility is based on the severity of a person's disability or the family's extent of need.
Productivity & Contribution	Productivity refers to engagement in income-producing work and contribution refers to unpaid work that benefits a household or community. A synonym for productivity is economic self-sufficiency.
Integration	A person with a disability has the right not to be segregated, solely on the basis of disability, from people who do not have disabilities and not to be barred from participation in services that serve people who do not have disabilities. The prohibition against segregation includes a mandate for integration into generic services (as appropriate) and into the most typical environments (as appropriate).
Family Integrity & Unity	Policy presumes in favor of preserving and strengthening of the family as the core unit of society. That policy is reflected in services that maintain the family intact, assure responses to all family members, and respond to the family based on its cultural, ethnic, linguistic, or other socioeconomic traits and choices. Related are the concepts of family centeredness and cultural responsiveness.

(table continues)

(table 4.3 continued)

Disability Policy Core Concepts Principles	Definition and Constitutional
Family-Centeredness to Services to Whole Family	These services respond to the needs of the entire family of a person with a disability. They (a) support families to raise their children with disabilities in the family home, (b) strengthen the role of the family as the primary caregiver, (c) maintain the family's intactness and unity, and (d) reunite families with their children who have been placed out of the family home.
Service Coordination & Collaboration	Activities assist individuals with disabilities or their families to access and then to benefit from services from more than one provider system (interagency) or within a single provider system (intra-agency).
Cultural Responsiveness	These services respond to the beliefs, values, interpersonal styles, attitudes, cultural, ethnic, linguistic, or other socioeconomic traits of the person or family and therefore have the greatest likelihood of ensuring maximum participation of and benefit to the person or family.
Accountability	Accountability includes various methods of achieving the specified outcomes of services, especially procedural safeguards (legal accountability via procedural due process) and program-improvement measures.
Prevention	Prevention services seek primary, secondary, and tertiary prevention of disability.
Capacity	A service delivery system should have the capacity to implement any one or more core concepts, as appropriate for that system.

We have identified the following 18 core concepts of disability policy: (a) antidiscrimination, (b) autonomy, (c) empowerment, (d) privacy and confidentiality, (e) liberty (physical), (f) protection from harm, (g) individualized and appropriate services, (h) capacity-based services, (i) classification, (j) productivity, (k) integration, (l) family integrity, (m) family centeredness, (n) coordination and collaboration, (o) cultural responsiveness, (p) accountability, (q) prevention, and (r) professional capacity. Together these core concepts form the necessary components of policy that we assume, theoretically, to advance the quality of life of individuals with disabilities and their families.

Table 4.4
Illustrative Core Concepts As They
Relate To The Poston's Family Quality Of Life

Service Coordination and Collaboration

Without service coordination, AJ might not benefit from the many services and supports that are available (productivity domain), and Denise would be very stressed trying to do it herself or feel guilty that she could not do it herself (emotional well-being domain). The specific tasks involved are to (a) find, hire, and train assistants for AJ, (b) put together a schedule of activities and goals at home and in the community that are coordinated with AJ's educational activities and goals, and (c) manage, supervise, and coordinate and be accountable to AJ, Denise, and the other support team members.

Protection From Harm

Family-Centeredness

Integration

Family Integrity

During AJ's aggressive outbursts, he has the potential to harm himself and other family members, especially Denise (physical environment domain). Here there is a tension between the core concepts. By temporarily admitting him to the hospital, the Poston family chose to partially limit AJ's integration into the family (family interaction domain) and community as well as suspend family integrity so that (a) all family members can be safe, (b) the Poston family can be strengthened through supports and services, and (c) AJ can get a thorough psychopharmological evaluation.

Empowerment

The Poston family has chosen to convene a GAP (Group Action Planning team, which is a form of person-centered planning) to bring together friends and professionals from different service systems on an informal basis (advocacy domain and social well-being domain). The GAP serves to (a) bring information and options to the group, (b) provide input and support for Denise as she participates in the decision-making processes of the service systems, and (c) assist with service coordination.

These 18 core concepts of disability policy reflect nine principles. The first three principles—life, liberty, and equality—mirror the doctrines of our federal (written) Constitution, are the fundamental law of the land, and reflect our cultural, political, philosophical, and legal traditions. These are the *Constitutional principles*. Three other principles—dignity, family as foundation, and community—reflect widely held societal ethics, values, beliefs, and ideals. These are the *ethical principles*. The last three principles—capacity, individualization, and accountability—incorporate the qualities (capacity), foci (the individual beneficiaries), and procedures (legal and other accountability safeguards) that must be included in any policy to support its successful implementation. These are the *administrative principles*.

In addition, we have identified from our respondents' comments approximately 200 factors that facilitate, impede, and in other ways affect the development and meaning of core concepts and the translation of the core concepts into practice (e.g., administrative changes, shortfall in budget). These influencing factors affect policy development implementation, service delivery, and systems change across all sectors of the human service system.

To help policy makers, program administrators, and policy advocates apply our research on core concepts, we are developing three tools to measure core concepts: a matrix and two indices. *The Disability Policy Core Concepts Matrix for Policy Analysis* performs two levels of analysis: (a) the extent to which it is *appropriate* for a federal or state statute to reflect specific disability policy core concepts, and (b) the extent to which the statute reflects *coherence* with disability policy core concepts.

Because statutes have different purposes, it is not *appropriate* for every disability policy core concept to be incorporated into every statute. For example, it is arguably more *appropriate* for IDEA to reflect the concept of productivity than it is for the Developmental Disabilities Assistance and Bill of Rights Act (1995) to do so. This is so because IDEA has the explicit affirmative purpose of providing an appropriate education so the student will secure employment after leaving school. By contrast, the Developmental Disabilities Act creates statewide, systems-change opportunities, only some of which are related to productivity. Thus a first task for policy analysis is to establish a reliable rating of *appropriateness*.

An analysis is also needed of the extent to which statutes are *coherent* with respect to core concepts. Coherence addresses the consistency with which statutes incorporate the disability core concepts throughout all of their parts. For example, the administrative provisions of the law can align closely or weakly with the law's basic provisions, thus strengthening or weakening its implementation of core concepts. Thus coherence recognizes both the incorporation of the core concepts and internal consistency of adherence to the core concepts.

The two indices—*Disability Policy Core Concepts Index for Families* and *Disability Policy Core Concepts Index for Service Providers*—enable families and services providers, respectively, to assess the extent to which they believe it is important to incorporate the *appropriate* core concepts into service delivery and the extent to which they are satisfied that the *appropriate* core concepts are being *coherently* incorporated.

Measurement Tools for Partnerships. We began the process of developing partnership measurement tools by thoroughly reviewing partnership-related literature. Our review led us to conceptualize partnerships in the way that is shown at the top of Figure 4.5. This original conceptualization depicts partnerships at three commonly accepted levels—family members or service provider, intra-agency, and interagency. It also categorizes partnerships into interpersonal or structural components. Finally it suggests that cooperation, coordination, collaboration, and integration exist on a continuum from minimal to maximal partnerships, and it reflects our assumptions that service integration represents the most intensive level of partnership at the interagency level and that transdisciplinary teams are the most intensive partnerships at the intra-agency level.

Through our focus groups and individual interviews with family members and professionals, we identified six partnership domains and indicators associated with each domain. Table 4.5 reflects our analysis of the data from the focus groups and interviews. It identifies each domain and the associated indicators; it also exemplifies (via the Poston family) how these domains and indicators can impede or facilitate family quality of life. Figure 4.6 shows the process we followed to develop the partnership scale.

Our data suggested that our original partnership conceptualization (Figure 4.5) was inaccurate in terms of interpersonal partnerships at each of the three levels. Originally we hypothesized that the interpersonal partnerships would be different at each level and would therefore require different measurement tools. In our focus groups and interviews, however, family members and professional participants alike spoke about communication, trust, respect, commitment, equality, and skills or competence in very similar ways, whether they were talking about coworkers on the team, colleagues on an interagency planning group, or parent-professional relationships. We concluded that the characteristics of interpersonal partnerships may be universal across all levels of partnership—hence, our revision of the partnership model as shown in the bottom of Figure 4.5.

We are designing two parallel scales. The *Interpersonal Partnership Scale: Family-Professional* will be completed by families and will focus on family-to-professional partnerships. The *Interpersonal Partnership Scale: Professional-Professional* will focus on professional-to-professional partnerships and will be applicable to both intra-agency and interagency relationships. We also are developing a series of indices that will be helpful to families, agencies, and professionals to assess their satisfaction with the partnerships in their organizations and community and to identify areas for program enhancement.

We are field testing each scale in eight states, including a range of urban, suburban, and rural settings. We are asking each of 300 families to identify the primary care provider (or a coprimary care provider if this role is shared) who has the major interaction with professionals in services that the child with the disability receives. The *Interpersonal Partnership Scale: Family-Professional* asks respondents to rate the importance of items to them. To determine the factional validity of this scale, we are conducting a confirmatory factor analysis. The primary purpose of this confirmatory factor analysis is to help us determine if the indicators that we conceptualized as "fitting" in each domain are actually appropriately related to that concept. In addition, we hope to be able to make comparisons about the degree of importance parents place on these domains of interpersonal partnership at different child ages and on different types of services (health, education, or social services). We also hope to be able to determine whether families from different socioeconomic backgrounds, ethnic groups, and geographical locations differ in the relative emphasis they give to these domains of partnership.

Table 4.5

Domains And Indicators Of Interpersonal Partnerships

Domains and Indicators	Examples of Positive and Negative Partnerships
Communication • Resource sharing • Honesty • Clarity • Listen • Information coordination • Positive communication • Openness • Frequency	"AJ's new teacher and I have a longstanding relationship that started before AJ started at school there. I know he will really tell me like it is…it may take a while for him to find the best way to say something, but he is always honest with me about what he thinks is best for AJ." "There is nothing worse than people not returning phone calls. When I was trying to choose a case manager for AJ, people I called from several agencies never returned my calls. I don't want to have to fight for such a simple thing as returning calls."
Trust • Reliability • Safety • Discretion	"Before we moved, AJ had a behavior consultant whom both he and I could count on. She would come over to the house if AJ were having an episode. She always followed through on what she said she was going to do—training staff, developing instructional materials, or just calling to check on us." "When AJ was having some trouble in the self-contained class, the special-education director recommended a "distraction-free work area." This sounded like a good idea to me, . . . but when I finally went to see it, what I saw was the time-out booth they had built for him several years ago—a padded 6-foot-square box that he spent most of his day in. After that, I knew I had to question everything this person said to me."

(table continues)

(table 4.5 continued)

Domains and Indicators	Examples of Positive and Negative Partnerships
Respect • Child valuing • Courtesy • Non-intrusion • Nonjudgmental • Nondiscrimination	When AJ was having a series of violent tantrums and we had to call the police, I was so afraid that, once we got involved in the law enforcement system, both AJ and I would be lost in the bureaucracy of a system that deals with people who are not generally very nice people. I expected to feel like we didn't belong there. But they made me feel very at ease, treated me with respect—I had expected to be treated like a criminal, but I was treated as a mom who was going through a rough time with her son. Both the police officer and the juvenile intake coordinator were very nice, seemed caring, and understood that it was a difficult time for both of us. I'm calling officer Matt's supervisor and to let him know how good officer Matt was with AJ. This whole experience has really eased my sense of dread concerning the police." "At AJ's school in our old community, it was clear to both AJ and me that his teacher did not like him. She saw him only as a bundle of behavior problems. All her notes to me were negative, what bad behavior he had, what work he didn't complete; she never saw him as having potential. She didn't share at all in the vision I had for him. That, more than anything else, contributed to my feeling that I could never make positive things happen for him as long as she was there."
Commitment • Commit • Access • More than job • More than a case • Encourage • Consistent • Flexible • Sensitive	"When we were getting ready to move to the new community, we were talking about how best to prepare AJ for the transition. We all agreed that he should come visit the new school before he started, get to know some of the teachers and students, and get to know his way around. I thought that task would fall to me. But the behavior consultant, who really wanted AJ to succeed, volunteered to arrange her schedule to be with him for a whole day. She even drove him over there in her car. Since the move, we have kept in touch. She is one of AJ's 'cheerleaders'." "When I was interviewing case managers after the move, one let me know that she would not be available for any evening meetings at all. It made me feel like she really didn't care about the families she was working with."

(table continues)

(table 4.5 continued)

Domains and Indicators	Examples of Positive and Negative Partnerships
Equality • Clout • Validation • Reciprocity • Harmony • Empowerment • Options • Advocate • Place to the table • Equal	"I've always felt like an equal member of AJ's IEP team, but when Jim was evaluated for special education, the staff, especially the school psychologist, counselor, and resource room teacher, really made me feel part of the team. They made me feel good about how I was doing as a parent. They also respected my opinion concerning behavioral interventions that they set up for Jim. They didn't look to me as having all the answers, but we all felt that if we worked together, we could figure something out." "There was one time that I really felt like the doctors almost went out of their way to make me feel stupid. Thankfully, it wasn't here. It was in Germany, when AJ was 2 and he went in the hospital for a brain stem auditory response test. I spoke good enough German, so I knew the problem was not a language barrier. They acted like I didn't need to know any of the results because I was just a mother—only educated and trained doctors knew what all those charts meant. I really had to push to get the least little bit of information. We ended up having the test done again in the American military hospital."
Skills • Action • Special needs met • Learn • Expectations • Holistic	"AJ's new teacher is really good in many ways. First of all is his experience with AJ and lots of other kids. He plans and prepares for AJ's success by developing a visual schedule that AJ needs, by talking to the kids on the bus about AJ, and by working with each of his different teachers to help them understand how to best work with AJ. I feel that if he didn't do this, AJ would not be successful in school, and I would worry constantly about how school is going." "Sometimes I get so tired of hearing people say, 'I don't know' and not offering to help find out. One of AJ's case managers told me one time, 'Well, I don't know anything about that; when you find out could you let me know?' Well, I'm happy to share information, but it would have been nice if she would have said something like, 'We all need to know about that—let me find out about it, and I'll let my colleagues and you know as soon as I do.' But I felt that I had one more thing that I had to go do now. I didn't have the time or the energy at that point, so it never got done."

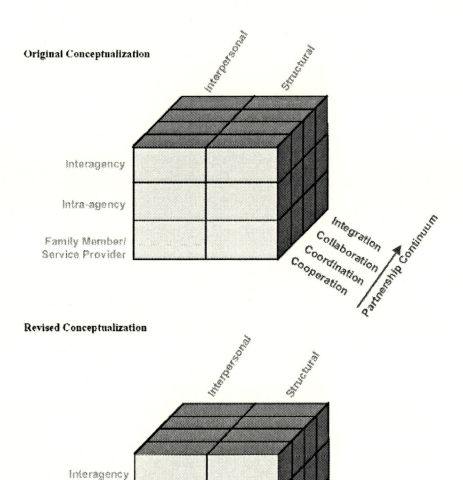

Figure 4.5 **Original and Revised Partnership Models**

Measurement Tools for Family Quality of Life Outcomes. We are following the same process to develop family quality of life tools as we are using in the partnership study (see Table 4.2 and Figure 4.6). The *Family Quality of Life Scale for Families* has comprised 10 domains—4 domains that are a function of the family unit as a whole and 6 that primarily function at the level of the impact of individual members on the family unit as a whole. The domains at the level of family unit were family interaction, daily life, parenting, and financial well-being. The domains at the individual level were emotional well-being, health, productivity, social well-being, physical environment, and advocacy. Table 4.6 identifies and briefly defines the original 10 domains, identifies the major indicators associated with each domain, and illustrates them via the Poston family.

Table 4.6
Family Quality Of Life Domains, Indicators, And Poston Family Examples

Domains and Indicators	Denise's Perspectives
Family Interaction • Relationships • Communication • Roles • Interactional environment	"We have dyads in our family, but limited interaction among the three of us. AJ and Jim's relationship consists of ignoring or teasing and fighting. I would love to be able to do something as a family without the constant bickering back and forth."
Daily Family Life • Household chores • Providing care • Daily routine	"I'm stressed a little about the afternoon after-school pick-up routine. The boys' schools both get out at the same time, and they are in different locations. I have to pick Jim up and then race home to make sure I am there when AJ's bus drops him off. If I'm not there, he might not get off the bus, or he would get upset because I'm not there. I need to be able to be in two places at once."
Parenting • Teaching/guiding • Supervising • Discipline	"I try to stay consistent with expectations for the boys, but it's difficult. Jim sees that the standard is different of him than for AJ. We have chores, allowance, bedtimes, and family rules. I think it helps set the tone for how I expect them to behave. It's difficult, being a single parent, to always be consistent—they sure can wear me down!"

(table continues)

(table 4.6 continued)

Domains and Indicators	Denise's Perspectives
Financial • Basic necessities • Health care, education, & transportation costs • Extras • Sources of income • Money management/ financial assistance	"I wanted the kids to go to a specific school in town, so I had to find a house to rent in that area. It just happened to be a newer area and much more expensive than other areas in town. I found a place, but it is smaller than I wanted—I had only so much to budget for rent and had to sacrifice space for location."
Emotional Well-Being • Positive thinking • Identity • Personal harmony • Adaptability • Control • Stress management	"With AJ in the state hospital now (temporarily), how am I to define my role as mother? Although it was difficult to care for him sometimes, at least my role was clear—there was daily caring and shepherding that took place. Now I'm still confused about how to 'be'. How do I be a woman, separate from my role as Mom?"
Health • Physical • Mental • Access to health care • Strategies to promote health	"Thank goodness we are all fairly healthy physically. I don't know how I could handle everything that goes on if I were sick or had a chronic illness. For us, finding doctors is an important thing, but not critical. Our mental health is another matter. We are doing okay, but I feel that mental health services are critical to keeping me able to go on. So now, I'm 'shopping' for a counselor. No one I knew had anyone they could recommend, so I'm calling different counselors, asking first if they accept our insurance, and then trying to figure out over the phone if he or she would be a good counselor for me. I've seen two different people. Although they were good, I still feel like I need to keep looking."
Productivity • School • Work life • Leisure • Personal development • Accomplishment	"School is a challenge for Jim—he's a smart kid, but unless he has a teacher who is flexible and has a sense of humor, he can get into trouble real easily. How he does in school has a direct relationship on his self-esteem. So we work hard to do what we can to help him succeed."

(table continues)

(table 4.6 continued)

Domains and Indicators	Denise's Perspectives
Social Well-Being • Relationships • Social belonging • Social support	"The biggest impact of our move on Jim was losing his friends. We are still close enough that he can see them every once in a while—but it takes a lot of effort to make that happen. He only has one friend in the new town so far. But I'm hoping he can make some friends in the neighborhood, at scouts, in church, and at school. For Jim, friendships are very important. He is really a social animal."
Physical Environment (safety, space, & comfort) • Home • School • Work • Neighborhood & community environment	"Our new home is much smaller than the one from which we just moved. This could be good news—once I get everything put away, it will be much easier to keep clean. I miss the space though. This house is bright and comfortable. I like it here and so do the kids. We were lucky to find a place in the right neighborhood (for schools), with a fenced yard for the dog, that is pretty much affordable. Now I just need to keep AJ from putting holes in the walls—during his last tantrum he broke three doors. So now I'm searching for a handyman to keep the things repaired without going through the landlord."
Advocacy • Skills • School • Health • Human service • Government benefits	"Everything having to do with 'the system' is always so difficult. I cringe when I think I'm going to have to ask someone for something out of the ordinary. I probably should do more work with the system to improve things for AJ, but I seem to have no energy to do this—what I do I do out of absolute necessity or guilt. I wish advocacy didn't depend so much on me."

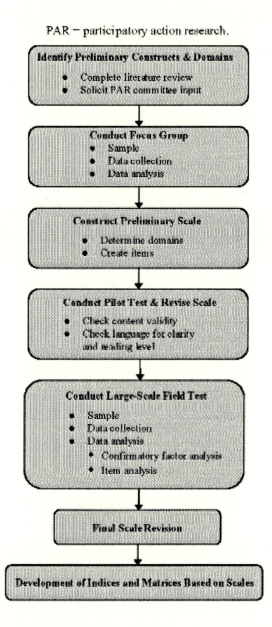

Figure 4.6 Steps in constructing family partnership and family quality of life scales, indices, and matrices.

We have field tested the scale with approximately 1,200 families of children with disabilities. In conducting the confirmatory factor analyses, we analyzed separately for family roles (e.g., mothers, fathers, individuals with a disability, and siblings). As a result of this field test, we reduced the number of family quality of life domains from 10 to 5 (Park et al., 2003): family interaction, parenting, support for the family member with a disability, family resources, and health and safety. In addition, we revised our family quality of life survey so that we included 41 different items, and we simplified the language that describes those items so that families can complete the survey more easily. In an additional analysis, we are exploring the impact of socioeconomic status, geographic location (urban, rural, suburban), lifespan stage, and possibly race or ethnicity. We also are examining different ways of aggregating the individual family member scores to attain an overall family score.

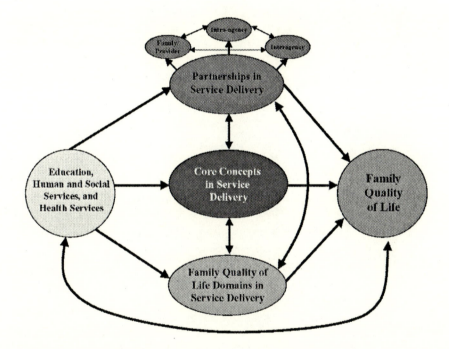

Figure 4.7 **Structural model for explanatory research.**

Once we develop the *Family Quality of Life Scale for Families,* we will convert it to a *Family Quality of Life Index for Families* and a *Family Quality of Life Index for Professionals.* Families and professionals will use these indices to report their perceptions of importance and satisfaction with how family quality of life domains are incorporated into service delivery.

The final measurement tool related to family quality of life is a *Family Quality of Life Domain Matrix for Policy Analysis*. This matrix will be used to assess federal and state statutes in terms of the *appropriateness* of incorporating family quality of life domains in the statutes and the *coherence* with which family quality of life domains are incorporated into the statutes. We will construct and use this matrix in a way that is similar to the way we construct and use the *Disability Policy Core Concepts Matrix for Policy Analysis*.

Overview Of Programmatic Research Agenda

With the analytical framework guiding us and with these measurement tools enabling us, we are carrying out a research agenda on three levels: policy analysis, explanatory research, and program evaluation and quality enhancement.

Policy Analysis. As we explained earlier, we are developing tools for analyzing policy and practice. With the two matrices, we are analyzing federal and state statutes to determine the degree to which they incorporate one or more of the disability policy core concepts (see Table 4.3) and family quality of life domains (see Table 4.6) (H. Turnbull, Beegle, & Stowe, 2001; H. Turnbull & Stowe, 2001).

Based on that policy analysis, we are developing a Disability Policy Grade Card. This card, developed for each statute that we analyze, describes the extent to which the statute (i.e., formal policy) advances the disability policy core concepts and family quality of life domains. More important, the grade card serves as a basis for policy enhancement through the legislative route (e.g., amendments to existing statutes and enactment of new laws) and/or the executive agency route (e.g., amendments to existing regulations, promulgation of new regulations, and adoption of guidelines governing the content of competitive contracts, grants, and cooperative agreements). In providing technical assistance to federal and state policy leaders, we give priority to statutes that are deemed to be highly *appropriate* for incorporation of disability core concepts and family quality of life domains but have low *coherence*.

Explanatory Research. Using the measurement tools, we can examine statistically the relationships among the core concepts of disability policy, service provision offered through partnership arrangements, and family quality of life outcomes. Based on the analytical framework, our hypothesized structural model (see Figure 4.7) suggests that a family's perceived quality of life is positively related to the services the family receives, and that the processes through which the services are delivered (incorporation of core concepts through authorized policies and empowering partnerships at the family-service provider, intra-agency, and interagency levels) will mediate the relationship between the services and the family quality of life outcomes. We are testing this structural model separately for each of the three service strands of education, human and social services, and health. We are also testing it in programs that are explicitly aimed at integrating services across strands.

In addition to investigating the mediating factors of this structural model, the relationship among the various factors can also be investigated in light of the family's structure (e.g., single-parent status), cultural and linguistic diversity characteristics, and socioeconomic level. As we stated earlier, these are the variables that have been found to place families of children with disabilities at highest risk (Fuijiura & Yamaki, 1997, 2000; LaPlante et al., 1996; Newacheck & Halfon, 1998).

Program Evaluation and Quality Enhancement. For policy analysis and explanatory research to benefit families (including children and youth with disabilities), we will be in a position to conduct thorough program evaluation and quality enhancement processes within strand-specific programs and in programs that reflect service integration. The Council on Quality and Leadership in Supports for People With Disabilities has taken a leadership role in combining principles of total quality management, reengineering, and disability state-of-art concepts (Gardner & Nudler, 1999). The Council focuses on personal outcomes for adults with developmental disabilities. We hope to extend the Council's work by focusing on outcomes for families of children and youth with disabilities, especially those families with single-parent status and lower socioeconomic status.

Research on an enhancement process should focus on increasing the incorporation of disability core concepts and family quality of life domains into services, infusing an empowering process into the family-service provider, intra-agency, and interagency partnerships, and ultimately increasing family quality of life outcomes. An appropriate methodology is a multiple- case-study design that allows for the analysis of individual cases as subunits as well as cross-case analyses designed to identify patterns (Yin, 1994). Case study methodology is a valuable means for exploring the impact and process related to quality enhancement (Campbell, 1994; Gardner & Nudler, 1999).

Implications Of Our Research

In this section, we will discuss implications of our research for improving the sociopolitical context, enhancing interpersonal and organizational partnerships, and shaping a future research agenda related to enhancing family quality of life.

For Improving The Sociopolitical Context

It is axiomatic within the new paradigm that policy is an environment that affects individuals with disabilities and their families. It is also axiomatic that those who have knowledge too often are irrelevant to those who have power. On the one hand, there are the generators and transmitters of knowledge (collectively, researchers); on the other, there are politicians and legislators, bureaucrats, and advocates (collectively, policy makers). This suggests two challenges: first, to connect the researchers and policy makers to each other and to answer the "so what?" question (now that we know something, *so, what* do we do with that knowledge?), and, second, to assure that research is both disseminated and used. Beyond mere dissemination and utilization, there is also the challenge of solidifying good policy and practice and then assuring that what is solidified does not become fossilized. To these ends, several strategies are apposite (H. Turnbull & A. Turnbull, 1996):

- create model statutes, regulations, and practice protocols;
- create teaching and technical assistance modules that contain the model statutes, regulations, and practice protocols and that are easily adaptable to multiple formats (e.g., print, voice, e-mail, and Internet);
- secure the use of the models and modules by state and local governmental policy leaders and their national and state associations (e.g., National Governors Association, National Conference of State Legislatures, National Association of State Directors of Special Education);
- secure the use of the models and modules by institutions of higher education as they carry out preservice and in-service (continuing) education of professionals and consumers;
- secure the use of the models and modules by advocacy organizations;
- persuade "insiders" to adopt the models, for it is always the case that a few members of a legislature, of an executive cabinet, or of a staff are the "play makers" in making or carrying out good policy.

For Improving The Service Delivery System

We have identified and measured the aspects of interpersonal relationships among the partners working with a family—those aspects that foster positive partnerships among members of the team and among professionals and family members. Assuming that our measures are validated, we will move both forward and backward in our analytical framework. That is, we will address several questions:

- What are the potential antecedents of positive partnerships? What are the administrative decisions, organizational procedures, and policies that nurture positive interpersonal partnerships among families, intra-agency and interagency team members? Our current work is focusing on identifying structures that we may consider "candidates" for having impacts on positive partnerships.
- Do these targeted structures and policies indeed have an impact on interpersonal partnerships, as we are measuring it? This will require a series of research studies, ranging perhaps from intervention

research to identification and measurement of exemplary programs across the country.

- Do positive partnerships also have a positive impact on family quality of life?

In general, our vision for the most direct application of this work is to provide policy makers, administrators, professionals and families with the ability to make *targeted* decisions and policy changes. We expect to develop self-assessment tools that will enable agencies and communities to identify strengths and challenges in the quality of their partnerships at all levels, use the tools to diagnose or identify those structural aspects of their organizations that require modification to improve partnerships, and measure the effectiveness of any innovations or changes made in their partnerships.

For A Future Research Agenda

One challenge in family quality of life research is to discover how to aggregate data to address the family as the unit of analysis. Typically research uses only mothers or, in far fewer cases, fathers as the unit of analysis when purporting to measure family perspectives. When we analyze our field-test data, we will investigate various ways to calculate a "family score" or a "family profile" from the scales that are filled out by several family members. Simple addition will not be the best representation of the family score, because the nature and degree of different family members' impact on the overall family is not the same. Different cultures have alternative interpretations of appropriate roles and influence of various family members (Lynch & Hanson, 1998); thus the aggregation of family scores must be highly culturally sensitive. Our challenge is to evaluate the potential benefits and drawbacks of analyzing scores separately for each individual family member compared to analyzing scores that aggregate family data.

Regardless of whether scores are individually reported or are aggregated, our participatory action research partners have consistently warned us that they fear that our scale might be misused by agencies to judge families as pathological or used as the basis of withholding services and supports from families. Thus we are committed to ensuring that this scale and others will not be used to harm families in any way. Instead, we will stress that our family quality of life tools can be used to measure the extent to which services meet the expectations of families; this is consistent with a new paradigm of "fixing" multiple environments. The old paradigm only assesses families and then uses scores to determine how they might be "fixed."

Future research can also create a database that accumulates and aggregates the scale results from diverse families. Policy makers can use this database to gain information about the impact of policies on the quality of life of families of children with disabilities according to various family characteristics (e.g., socioeconomic status, ethnicity, geography, or the severity and type of the family member's disability). Furthermore, this large database will enable researchers to establish patterns of family responses that are impossible to establish with smaller, localized samples. Jim Gardner at the Council on Quality and Leadership in Supports for People With Developmental Disabilities has created a model of such a database related to quality of life outcomes for individuals with developmental disabilities.[1]

In the future, researchers will be able to use the *Family Quality of Life Scale for Families* to measure families' satisfaction with their quality of life. This scale can be used in several ways:

- as a *planning tool* to establish individually tailored service or supports plans for families by determining the family quality of life indicators that are important to them and the extent of their satisfaction on those indicators;
- as a *strengths assessment* by identifying a family's individual, collective, and environmental assets, which will establish the direction and means of supports and services;
- as a *longitudinal evaluation* of service delivery and policy reform, since the ultimate outcome of changes in service delivery and policy would be enhanced family quality of life.

Before the *Family Quality of Life Scale for Families* is used as a planning tool, we need to explicate the issues that families may want to consider related to each of the domains. We envision having a supplemental checklist for each domain. The checklist will enable families to engage in individual and family reflection about priorities, possibilities, and the nature of the services and supports that would be most helpful to them. The development of these domain-specific checklists is one of our major research agendas.

A Year Later: A Future Day In The Life Of The Poston Family

AJ has learned to wake on his own with help from an alarm clock. Our GAP group recommended the clock as a way to help AJ be more independent and make things run more smoothly in the mornings. One of his personal assistants started coming at 6:30 A.M. to help him learn to get up with the alarm. Now I don't have to cajole him out of bed in the morning.

Both boys are doing well in school. Jim has a lot of homework, but we don't argue about it as much anymore. I think the counseling has

1.   See the website of Council on Quality and Leadership in Supports for People With Developmental Disabilities, National Center on Outcomes Resources: http://www .thecouncil.org

really helped him learn to communicate his feelings and take more responsibility for his own actions. We finally got Jim matched with a "Big Brother." Having a male role model in his life has been good for him. He has so many friends at school, scouts, and church that I can hardly keep up with his schedule. It has made my role as taxi mom harder, but he is so happy.

AJ is also blossoming at school. He goes to five different classes. The school staff has done an excellent job of modifying the curriculum so that he is learning the same subject matter as the other kids, but geared to his level and learning style. He is participating in a lot of after- school extracurricular activities with the support of his teacher and personal assistants. His teacher was instrumental in training the people whom AJ's case manager recruited. They all work together now, applying the same behavioral supports. The new medication helps take the edge off his impulsiveness. We haven't seen any side effects either, which is what I was so worried about. We have also been concentrating on how to deescalate the aggression once it starts.

I feel that life is really moving along smoothly. I finally completed my studies and received my doctorate. It sure feels good to have reached that goal in my life. AJ's service coordinator has taken a huge role in coordinating and monitoring the various services and supports for AJ. I am still very much involved, but now I'm able to focus more time on Jim and myself. I feel much less stressed, so I am a much more pleasant person to be around. With the supports that AJ has, we have actually been able to do things as a family now. We went to a movie last night and plan to go to the church picnic this Sunday. One of AJ's personal assistants joins in whatever we are doing; I guess our family has grown a little! That's okay, because they are all nice people and fit in really well with the three of us.

The new HCBS Medicaid funding policy took effect a few months ago. The proposed policy could have been disastrous for us because of the way the funds were to be allocated. But a group from Lawrence—people with disabilities, family members, and service providers—got together with people from other communities and mounted a campaign at the state level that forced a change in the proposed policy. We had to cut back a little on the amount we receive, but not as much as it would have been if we had not been advocates. The whole experience was good for me. I met some new people and feel like I really helped make a difference, not just for our family, but also for many other families.

The Lawrence group that worked on the HCBS funding issue has gotten back together and focused on a new project. We are trying to start a one-stop family support coalition. If we had had something like this when our family first moved to Lawrence, our transition would have been so much easier. We are talking to families throughout the community about what they think would be beneficial to their families. It seems that most people want neighborhood-based, family-centered and family-directed "centers" that are independent of the existing provider systems but know about all the available services and supports in our community. We hope to make that happen within the next 6 months.

Denise Poston

Epilogue

One must never underestimate the power of an idea whose time has come, the power of inertia, and the complexities of the policy environment. Family quality of life enhancement will inevitably be met by resistance to change. For that reason, researchers must embrace the complexities of all environments, understanding them and participating in them as participatory researchers. As the Chorus in Shakespeare's *Henry V* foretold in advance of Henry engaging in the Battle of Agincourt, combatants must "assume the port of Mars." Here lies an apt analogy: It is not enough to be a researcher, one must also be a warrior in diligent pursuit of making a difference. Knowledge is power only if the knowledgeable act powerfully.

Finally, because what we think we know changes as we conduct research, the challenge is to solidify policy and service delivery based on what we think we know now and then to critically assess innovations, lest they—and our research and knowledge—become fossilized. Winning the Battle of Agincourt was only the first of Henry's challenges; winning the peace thereafter was his second, and hence his marriage to Catherine of Aragon—truly an international metaphor for an international book such as this on family quality of life research.

Postscript: February 2002

Under the heading "General Trends," there have been a few changes. The text under "Demographics and Economics" should be changed to reflect the fact that a national recession is in progress, having begun in the fall of 2000.

The recession drastically increased the number of un- and underemployed individuals, and it is likely that among those who are now in those categories are many with disabilities. Likewise, the recession seriously impaired state governments' abilities to fund human and social service programs.

Also, the "9/11" incidents—the terrorists' destruction of the two World Trade Center buildings, the partial destruction of the Pentagon, and the failed attempt to further destroy symbols of American dominion—have skewed the federal and state governments' budgets to such a degree that the country's fiscal priorities no longer accommodate human services except in response to the "9/11" priorities.

Under the heading "Politics: Moderation and the New Federalism," it should be noted that the Supreme Court continues to eviscerate federal disability policy; Congress is being guided by a powerful right wing–ultraconservative leadership in the House of Representatives; and the omens for disability issues are dark.

Under the heading "Disability Trends," the consolidation of rights is still a priority, especially considering the attack on Individuals With Disabilities Education Act that has been launched by conservatives who seem to know little about disability (see Finn, Rotherham, & Hokanson, 2001).

Finally, for a complete review (as of fall 2001) of the Beach Center's work on core concepts and disability policy, see the series of articles published in *Journal of Disability Policy Studies 12*(3) (H. Turnbull, Beegle, & Stowe, 2001; H. Turnbull & Stowe, 2001).

References

Able-Boone, H. (1993). Family participation in the IFSP process: Family or professional driven? *Infant-Toddler Intervention, 3*(1), 63–71.

Adelman, H. S., & Taylor, L. (1997). Addressing barriers to learning: Beyond school-linked services and full-service schools. *American Journal of Orthopsychiatry, 67*(3), 408–419.

Alexander v. Sandoval, No. 99-1908, *slip op.* (U.S. April 24, 2001).

Allen, R. I., & Petr, C. G. (1996). Toward developing standards and measurements for family-centered practice in family support programs. In G. H. S. Singer, L. E. Powers, & A. L. Olson (Eds.), *Redefining family support: Innovations in public-private partnerships* (pp. 57–86). Baltimore: Paul H. Brookes.

Amato, C. (1996). Freedom elementary school and its community: An approach to school-linked service integration. *Remedial & Special Education, 17*(5), 303–309.

Americans With Disabilities Act of 1990. 42 U.S.C. § 12101 *et seq.*

Bailey, D. B., & McWilliam, P. J. (1993). The search for quality indicators. In P. J. McWilliam & D. B. Bailey (Eds.), *Working together with children and families* (pp. 3–20). Baltimore: Paul H. Brookes.

Bailey, D. B., McWilliam, R. A., Darkes, L. A., Hebbeler, K., Simeonsson, R. J., Spiker, D., & Wagner, M. (1998). Family outcomes in early intervention: A framework for program evaluation and efficacy research. *Exceptional Children, 64*, 313–328.

Board of Education v. Rowley, 458 U.S. 176 (1982).

Braddock, D., Hemp, R., Parish, S., & Rizzolo, M. C. (2000). *The state of the states in developmental disabilities: 2000 study summary.* Chicago: University of Illinois at Chicago, Department of Disability and Human Development.

Brakel, S. J., Parry, J., & Weiner, B. A. (1985). *The mentally disabled and the law.* Chicago: American Bar Association.

Briar-Lawson, K., Lawson, H. A., Collier, C., & Joseph, A. (1997). School-linked comprehensive services: Promising beginnings, lessons learned, and future challenges. *Social Work in Education, 19*(3), 136–145.

Brown, R. I. (Ed.). (1997). *Quality of life for people with disabilities: Models, research, and practice.* Cheltenham, UK: Stanley Thornes.

Brown, R. I., Brown, P. M., & Bayer, M. B. (1994). A quality of life model: New challenges arising from a six year study. In D. A. Goode (Ed.), *Quality of life for persons with disabilities: International perspectives and issues* (pp. 39–56). Cambridge, MA: Brookline.

Burns, B. J., & Goldman, S. K. (Eds.). (1999). *Systems of care: Promising practices in children's mental health.* Washington, DC: American Institutes for Research, Center for Effective Collaboration and Practice.

Calfee, C., Wittwer, F., & Meredith, M. (1998). Why build a full-service school? In C. Calfee, F. Wittwer, & M. Meredith (Eds.), *Building a full-service school* (pp. 6–24). San Francisco: Jossey-Bass.

Campbell, D. T. (1994). Foreword. In R. K. Yin, *Case study research: Design and methods* (2nd ed., pp. ix–xii). Thousand Oaks, CA: Sage.

Campbell, P. H., Strickland, B., & La Forme, C. (1992). Enhancing parent participation in the individualized family service plan. *Topics in Early Childhood Special Education, 11*(4), 112–124.

Cedar Rapids Community School District v. Garret F., 526 U.S. 66 (1999).

Coltoff, P. (1998). *Community schools: Education reform and partnership with our nation's social service agencies.* Washington, DC: Child Welfare League of America.

Comer, J. P., Haynes, N. M., Joyner, E. T., & Ben-Avie, M. (Ed.). (1996). *Rallying the whole village.* New York: Teachers College Press.

Cummins, R. A. (1997). Assessing quality of life. In R. I. Brown (Ed.), *Quality of life for people with disabilities: Model, research, and practice* (pp. 116–150). Cheltenham, UK: Stanley Thornes.

Doktor, J. E., & Poertner, J. (1996). Kentucky's family resource centers. *Remedial and Special Education, 17*(5), 293–302.

Dryfoos, J. G. (1996). Full-service schools. *Educational Leadership, 53*(7), 18–23.

Dryfoos, J. G. (1997). Adolescents at risk: Shaping programs to fit the need. *Journal of Negro Education, 65*(1), 5–18.

Dryfoos, J. G. (1998). *Safe passage: Making it through adolescence in a risky society.* New York: Oxford University Press.

Dunst, C. J., Johnson, D., Trivette, C. M., & Hamby, D. (1991). Family-oriented early intervention policies and practices: Family-centered or not? *Exceptional Children, 58*(2), 115–126.

Dunst, C. J., Trivette, C., & Deal, A. (1988). *Enabling & empowering families: Principles and guidelines for practice.* Cambridge, MA: Brookline.

Dupper, D. R., & Poertner, J. (1997). Public schools and the revitalization of impoverished communities: School-linked, family resource centers. *Social Work, 42*(5), 415–422.

Erickson, R. (1998). *Accountability, standards, and assessment.* Washington, DC: Federal Resource Center, Academy for Educational Development.

Felce, D., & Perry, J. (1997). Quality of life: The scope of the term and its breadth of measurement. In R. I. Brown (Ed.), *Quality of life for people with disabilities: Models, research, and practice* (2nd ed., pp. 56–71). Cheltenham, UK: Stanley Thornes.

Finn, C., Rotherham, A. J., & Hokanson, C. R. (2001). *Rethinking special education for a new century.* Washington, DC: Thomas B. Fordham Foundation and Progressive Policy Institute.

Forum on Child and Family Statistics. (1998). *America's children: Key national indicators of well-being.* [On-line]. Available: http://www.child-stats.gov/ac1998/highlite.htm

Franklin, C., & Streeter, C. L. (1995). School reform: Linking public schools with human services. *Social Work, 40*(6), 773–782.

Fuijiura, G. T., & Yamaki, K. (1997). Analysis of ethnic variations in developmental disability prevalence and household economic status. *Mental Retardation, 35*(4), 286–294.

Fuijiura, G. T., & Yamaki, K. (2000). Trends in demography of childhood poverty and disability. *Exceptional Children, 66*(2), 187–200.

Gardner, J. F., & Nudler, S. (Eds.). (1999). *Quality performance in human services: Leadership, values, and vision.* Baltimore: Paul H. Brookes.

Garlow, J. E., Turnbull, H. R., & Schnase, D. (1991). Model disability and family support act of 1991. *Kansas Law Review, 39*(3), 783–816.

Harry, B., Kalyanpur, M., & Day, M. (1999). *Building cultural reciprocity with families.* Baltimore: Paul H. Brookes.

Individuals With Disabilities Education Act of 1990, 20 U.S.C. § 1400 *et seq.*

Irving Independent School District v. Tatro, 468 U.S. 883 (1984).

Jones, T. M., Garlow, J. A., Turnbull, H. R., & Barber, P. A. (1996). Family empowerment in a family support program. In G. H. S. Singer, L. E. Powers, & A. L. Olson (Eds.), *Redefining family support innovations: Innovations in public-private partnerships* (pp. 87–114). Baltimore: Paul H. Brookes.

Kagan, S. L., Goffin, S. G., Golub, S. A., & Pritchard, E, (1995). *Toward systemic reform: Service integration for young children and their families.* Falls Church, VA: National Center for Service Integration.

Kalyanpur, M., & Harry, B. (1999). *Culture in special education.* Baltimore: Paul H. Brookes.

Katz, L., & Scarpati, S. (1995). A cultural interpretation of early intervention teams and the IFSP: Parent and professional perceptions of roles and responsibilities. *Infant-Toddler Intervention, 5*(2), 177–192.

Kimel v. Board of Regents, 528 U.S. 62 (2000).

LaPlante, M. P., Carlson, D., Kaye, H. S., & Bradsher, J. E. (1996). *Families with disabilities in the United States* (Disability Statistics Report No. 8). Washington, DC: U.S. Department of Education, National Institute on Disability and Rehabilitation Research.

Lawson, H., & Briar-Lawson, K. (1997). *Connecting the dots: Progress toward the integration of school reform, school-linked services, parent involvement, and community schools.* Unpublished manuscript, Miami University, The Danforth Foundation and the Institute for Educational Renewal, Oxford, OH.

Levy, R. M., & Rubenstein, L. S. (1996). *The rights of people with mental disabilities: The authoritative ACLU guide to the rights of people with mental illness and mental retardation* (rev. ed.). Carbondale: Southern Illinois University Press.

Lynch, E. W., & Hanson, M. (Eds.). (1998). *Developing cross-cultural competence: A guide for working with young children and their families* (2nd ed.). Baltimore: Paul H. Brookes.

MacKenzie, D., & Rogers, V. (1997). The full service school: A management and organizational structure for 21st-century schools. *Community Education Journal, 25*(3–4), 9–11.

Markey, U., Santelli, B., & Turnbull, A. P. (1998). Participatory action research involving families from underserved communities and researchers: Respecting cultural and linguistic diversity. In B. A. Ford (Ed.), *Compendium: Writings on effective practice for culturally and linguistically diverse exceptional learners.* Reston, VA: Council for Exceptional Children, Division for Culturally and Linguistically and Diverse Exceptional Learners.

McBride, S. L., Brotherson, M. J., Joanning, H., Whiddon, D., & Demmit, A. (1993). Implementation of family-centered services: Perceptions of families and professionals. *Journal of Early Intervention, 17*, 414–430.

McLaughlin, M. L. (1998). *Special education in an era of school reform: An overview.* Washington, DC: Federal Resource Center, Academy for Educational Development.

McWilliam, R. A., Lang, L., Vandiviere, P., Angell, R., Collins, L., & Underdown, G. (1995). Satisfaction and struggles: Family perceptions of early intervention services. *Journal of Early Intervention, 19*(1), 43–60.

Menke, K. (1991). The development of individualized family service plans in three early intervention programs: A data-based construction. *Dissertation Abstracts International, 52* (06), 2077A. (UMI No. 9134817)

Minow, M. (1990). *Making all the difference: Inclusion, exclusion, and American law.* Ithaca, NY: Cornell University Press.

Murphy, C. L., Lee, I. M., Turnbull, A. P., & Turbiville, V. (1995). The family-centered program rating scale: An instrument for program evaluation and change. *Journal of Early Intervention, 19*(1), 24–42.

National Council on Disability. (1995). *Improving the implementation of the Individuals With Disabilities Education Act: Making schools work for all of America's children.* Washington, DC: Author.

Newacheck, P. W., & Halfon, N. (1998). Prevalence and impact of disabling chronic conditions in childhood. *American Journal of Public Health, 88*, 610–617.

Osher, T. W. (1998). Outcomes and accountability from a family perspective. *Journal of Behavioral Health Services & Research, 25*(2), 230–232.

Park, J., Hoffman, L., Marquis, J., Turnbull, A. P., Poston, D., Mannan, H., Wang, M., & Nelson, L. L. (2003). Toward assessing family outcomes of service delivery: Validation of a family quality of life survey. *Journal of Intellectual Disability Research, 47*(4–5), 367–384.

Raham, H. (1998). Full-service schools. *School & Business Affairs, 64*(6), 24–28.

Renwick, R., Brown, I., & Nagler, M. (Eds.). (1996). *Quality of life in health promotion and rehabilitation: Conceptual approaches, issues, and applications.* Thousand Oaks, CA: Sage.

Sailor, W. (in press). Devolution, school/community/family partnerships, and inclusive education. In W. S. Sailor (Ed.), *Inclusive education and school/community partnership.* New York: Teachers College Press.

Saleeby, D. (1996). The strengths perspective in social work practice: Extensions and cautions. *Social Work, 41*(3), 296–306.

Santelli, B., Singer, G. H. S., DiVenere, N., Ginsberg, C., & Powers, L. (1998). Participatory action research: Reflections on critical incidents in a PAR project. *Journal of the Association for Persons With Severe Handicaps, 23*(3), 211–222.

Schalock, R. L. (1996). Quality of life and quality assurance. In R. Renwick, I. Brown, & M. Nagler (Eds.), *Quality of life in health promotion and rehabilitation: Conceptual approaches, issues, and applications* (pp. 104–118). Thousand Oaks, CA: Sage.

Schalock, R. L. (1997). Can the concept of quality of life make a difference? In R. L. Schalock (Ed.), *Quality of life: Vol. 2. Application to persons with disabilities* (pp. 245–267). Washington, DC: American Association on Mental Retardation.

Schalock, R. L. (2000). Three decades of quality of life: Mental retardation in the 21st century. In M. L. Wehmeyer & J. R. Patton (Eds.), *Mental retardation in the year 2000.* Austin, TX: Pro-Ed.

Schorr, L. B. (1997). *Common purpose.* New York: Anchor Books, Doubleday.

Sherman, A. (1994). *Wasting America's future: The Children's Defense Fund report on the costs of child poverty.* Boston: Beacon Press.

Silverstein, R. (2000). *An overview of the federal disability policy framework and general questions for analyzing the extent to which disability-specific and generic programs and policies reflect the federal disability policy framework.* Unpublished monograph, George Washington University, Washington, DC.

Skrtic, T. M., & Sailor, W. (1996). School-linked services integration. *Remedial & Special Education, 17*(5), 271–283.

Smith, S. W. (1990, September). Individualized education programs (IEPs) in special education: From intent to acquiescence. *Exceptional Children, 57,* 6–14.

Stroul, B. A. (1996). *Children's mental health: Creating systems of care in a changing society.* Baltimore: Paul H. Brookes.

Turnbull, A. P., Blue-Banning, M., Turbiville, V., & Park, J. (1999). From parent education to partnership education: A call for a transformed focus. *Topics in Early Childhood Special Education, 19*(3), 164–171.

Turnbull, A. P., Friesen, B. J., & Ramirez, C. (1998). Participatory action research as a model for conducting family research. *Journal of the Association for Persons With Severe Handicaps, 23*(3), 178–188.

Turnbull, A. P., & Summers, J. A. (1987). From parent involvement to family support: Evolution to revolution. In S. M. Puescel, C. Tingey, J. W. Rynders, A. C. Crocker, & D. M. Crutcher (Eds.), *New perspectives on Down syndrome* (pp. 289–306). Baltimore: Paul H. Brookes.

Turnbull, A. P., Turbiville, V., & Turnbull, H. R. (2000). Evolution of family-professional partnership models: Collective empowerment as the model for the early 21st century. In J. P. Shonkoff & S. L. Meisels (Eds.), *The handbook of early childhood intervention* (2nd ed.). New York: Cambridge University Press.

Turnbull, A. P., & Turnbull, H. R. (2001). *Families, professionals, and exceptionality: Collaborating for empowerment* (4th ed.). Upper Saddle River, NJ: Merrill/Prentice Hall.

Turnbull, H. R., Beegle, G., & Stowe, M. J. (2001). The core concepts of disability policy affecting families who have children with disabilities. *Journal of Disability Policy Studies, 12*(3), 133–143.

Turnbull, H. R., & Brunk, G. L. (1997). Quality of life and public policy. In R. L. Schalock (Ed.), *Quality of life: Vol. 2. Application for persons with disabilities* (pp. 201–210). Washington, DC: American Association on Mental Retardation.

Turnbull, H. R., Garlow, J., & Barber, P. (1991). A policy analysis of family support for families with members with disabilities. *University of Kansas Law Review, 39,* 739–782.

Turnbull, H. R., & Stowe, M. J. (2001). Five models for thinking about disability: Implications for policy. *Journal of Disability Policy Studies, 12*(3), 198–205.

Turnbull, H. R., Stowe, M., & Beegle, G. (2001). *Portraying the core concepts of disability policy: A taxonomy framework for disability policy.* Unpublished monograph, Beach Center on Families and Disability, Lawrence, KS.

Turnbull, H. R., & Turnbull, A. P. (1989). *Report on consensus conference on principles of family research.* Lawrence, KS: Beach Center on Families and Disability.

Turnbull, H. R., & Turnbull, A. P. (1996). The synchrony of stakeholders: Lessons from the disabilities rights movement. In S. L. Kagan & N. E. Cohen (Eds.), *Reinventing early care and education: A vision for a quality system* (pp. 290–305). San Francisco: Jossey-Bass.

Turnbull, H. R., & Turnbull, A. P. (2000). *Free appropriate public education: The law and children with disabilities* (6th ed.). Denver: Love.

University of Alabama v. Garrett, 531 U.S. 356 (2001).

U.S. Census Bureau. (1996). Almost half of the nation's chronic poor are children. *Census and You, 31*(9), 1.

U.S. Department of Education. (1999). *To assure the free appropriate education of all children with disabilities.* Annual Report to Congress on the Implementation of the Individuals With Disabilities Education Act, U.S.C., §§ 1400–1485 (Supp. 1996). Washington, DC: Author.

Vanderwood, M., McGrew, K. S., & Ysseldyke, J. E. (1998). Why we can't say much about students with disabilities during education reform. *Exceptional Children, 64*(3), 359–370.

Wehman, T. (1999). A functional model of self-determination: Factors contributing to increased parent involvement and participation. *Focus on Autism & Other Developmental Disabilities, 13*(2), 80–86.

Yin, R. K. (1994). *Case study research: Design and methods* (2nd ed.). Thousand Oaks, CA: Sage.

Chapter 5

Family Quality Of Life In Wales

Stuart Todd, Pauline Young, Julia Shearn, and Stephanie Jones
University of Wales College of Medicine
Cardiff, Wales, United Kingdom

Daring To Be Ordinary: A Welsh Mother's Narrative

Whilst this is my story as a parent of a child with an intellectual disability, with its own personal twists and turns, it is by no means unique. I believe it can be duplicated with only a few variations all over Wales and the U.K.

A few years ago, in 1995, I was invited to speak as a parent of a son with intellectual disabilities at a multiagency conference. I called my presentation "Not Waving, but Drowning." This title was taken from a poem by Stevie Smith, a poem about a girl out at sea. She is signaling to the shore that she is in trouble, but everyone on the beach thinks she's just waving at them. So they wave back! It is, of course, metaphorical, but it encapsulates what happens to families with people with disabilities. People see you coping. Everything seems fine. You even believe yourself that this is true. But underneath you are floundering, and as a family you either won't acknowledge this, or else you don't want to ask for help as you strive for an appearance of whatever passes for "normality." The subject of my presentation was [parenting through the] transitioning from childhood to adulthood. For me, the experience just left me feeling as lost as after that initial disclosure that you have a disabled child, only here there are fewer props to help. I learned that making adjustments was going to be a lifetime phenomenon.

Anyway, I began my presentation with the following tale: "Once upon a time, there were two teenagers. One, a girl, began fighting her teenage battles with her parents early. She wanted her own domestic space, and she wanted to invite her friends in to play loud music. She was given a key to the door, and she was allowed, occasionally, to stay out late. In time, she had friends who were becoming boyfriends. Through both heated and reasoned exchanges, her parents learned the lesson from the poet C. Day Lewis that 'the beginning of love lies in the letting go.'

"The other teenager was a boy. Older than his sister, he nevertheless was unable to articulate his demands. Because he was intellectually disabled, his parents sheltered him from many situations they instinctively felt were threatening, keeping him a child as long as possible. In doing so, they were encouraged by an education system that provided him with a safe harbor in a school well away from his own community where he was segregated from ordinary children and where his only friends were children like himself. The years went by, and the end of his school days drew near. One day, there was a letter in the post addressed to their son inviting him to open a bank account and offering good terms to students intending to attend college. On the same day, he had a letter from his Member of Parliament asking for his support in the next election. A few days later, he was offered 10 free tickets if he would agree to celebrate his birthday at a well-known city night-club. His parents realized, with a good measure of shock, that this time there had been no process of letting go. Instead, it felt rather as if they were being asked to throw a new-born infant into the sea."

I concluded this opening with the comment that this was not a fairy tale. I knew these teenagers very well. I was and am their mother. These events taught me that parents' lives are changing and evolving all the time. We got Matthew off to a decent school, and then we thought we could relax. Family life did have a semblance of order, of manageable routine. Then, suddenly, it seemed there was the boy/young man, fully grown. School will end, and all the things that happen to a normal child—friendships, college prospectuses—these are not appropriate. We had a newborn baby all over again, and it felt as though we were throwing him into a kind of abyss. And all these prompts of "normality" in junk mail form! All that did was confirm that our child wasn't like most others. We still had to ask ourselves, "What happens now? Where does he go?" Life was turned upside down again and in a very dramatic and drastic way.

I then suggested in my talk that something radical clearly needed to be done, and that the single, guiding principle informing that change should be that all children and young people with intellectual disabilities be offered the same opportunities to develop their skills and interests as every other child and teenager. Furthermore, for this principle to be effective in practice, these opportunities must be socially recognized and valued.

And then there is my own personal future too. It seems just as hazy as Matthew's. My life is still bound up very much in what happens to Matthew. While he was at school, there was a predictable pattern to our lives and, with constant juggling with paid help, we could just about cope as working parents, although the school holidays were a nightmare. Now that predictability has gone. In terms of a career, do I have the same opportunities as all my female colleagues? The answer is no! Matthew's "hidden" needs, such as not sleeping and our inability to take holidays, clearly impacted on my career and John's, my partner. I am an academic as well as a parent, and just try to get a paper written when you've had little sleep for a week! Yes, I know we all go through this when kids are babies, but it doesn't last for 20 years.

I didn't talk about our problems in college. The academic world has only just got used to the fact that staff have kids at all, let alone "weird" kids with very special demands. Of course people all know, but you hide it anyway, all those signs of needing additional time. I didn't want to be seen falling down on the job or attributing difficulties to my "unfortunate" family circumstances. And that promotion, that career move, would be withheld, because they would say, "You wouldn't be up to it!" It is hard and, I would suggest, harder for me than for some of my colleagues. But what can legislation do to help those of us with similar problems?

Pauline Young

Introducing The Issues

Pauline's suspicion that her experiences might be applicable to many mothers of disabled children in the United Kingdom would be confirmed by a cursory glance of the research literature on parents' experiences. There is no doubt that parents in other countries would also relate easily to her experiences. However, it is more Pauline's observations that being a parent of a person with intellectual disabilities involves making a series of adjustments over the life course that we take as one of our chief concerns here. Becoming a parent of a child with disabilities is not an event that is confined to those early years following disclosure, but is a continual process of facing novel and difficult problems that require fresh perspectives. Parents' experiences are not static but may vary in time and in response to a range of age-status turning points.

We focus mainly on the experiences of the transitional years, from a novel perspective of mothers commenting on their lives in the middle years and its struggles, challenges, opportunities, and constraints. Riches (1996) has argued that the transitional years are among the most critical for families to deal with. Substantial research literature suggests that these years are difficult (Baxter, Cummins, & Polak, 1995; Grant & McGrath, 1990; W. Mitchell, 1999; Suelzle & Keenan, 1981; Thorin, Yovanoff, & Irvin, 1996; Wikler, 1986; Wikler, Wasow, & Hatfield, 1981). This research has highlighted several key issues: heightened levels of parental anxiety; the indeterminate nature of the transition from child to adult services; and dealing with what has been termed "chronic sorrow," the emotions prompted by the felt disjuncture between the developmental status of the adolescent and nondisabled peers. These themes are all evident in Pauline's opening autobiographical commentary. Missing from many accounts of the transitional years, but emerging in Pauline's, is some concern over parents' views of their own lives and their own expectations. For sure, the transitional years are double edged, and the child's transition to adulthood may be a transition that serves as an impetus for ushering in the midlife years of parents, a stage in the typical parental career associated with its own distinct but potentially troublesome meanings (Carr, 1997; Gergen, 1990).

Midlife is a complex transition encompassing a wide spectrum of experiences, including contradiction, change, opportunity, and loss (Levinson, 1996). A characteristic and anticipated feature of the middle years of parenting is the expansion in the lives of mothers in particular, as family responsibilities are restructured. They have, therefore, been viewed as years that provide greater opportunity for women to attend, without guilt, to their personal lives (Sheehy, 1991). Women find themselves in a situation of moving the direction of their lives from family to personally meaningful, but previously suspended, commitments (V. Mitchell & Helson, 1990). For both mothers and their adolescent children, the transitional years have been described as the "enlargement of boundaries" (Bassoff, 1987). Both may experience greater freedom to move beyond the family as the main source of social relationships and come to establish new definitions of the self (Ackerman, 1990).

Yet research typically views the transitional years in unidimensional terms from which the expectations and changes in the lives of parents themselves are obscured. When parents are asked to give their views in research studies, it is often to talk about the lives of their sons or daughters. In many ways, their own lives are hidden and private. In this chapter, we seek to incorporate the moving perspective of life and capture something of the way in which the world and life looks to a group of mothers at a distinct phase in their maternal careers. We deal with the identities and biographies of women at midlife who earlier in their lives had become the mothers of children with intellectual disabilities. It seeks to link their personal histories with the opportunities and constraints of the present, and the possibilities of the future.

Much of our understanding of family life is bounded by a view that being a parent of a person with intellectual disabilities is a discrete role and one untouched by wider social, biographical, and historical role influences. Yet what it means to be the mother of a person with intellectual disability will be a complex interaction between self, time, culture, and history (Hareven, 1982). The perspectives of individuals are shaped by their cumulative life history, specific historical conditions, and wider cultural contexts. How individuals appraise their lives, and the expectations they invest in and derive meaning from, will be very much influenced by their location within historical and social time. Such an understanding formed a critical basis for our research so as to provide a deeper understanding of the lives and experiences of individuals (Elder, 1994). Thus this chapter can be conceived of as examining mothers' own views of the "goodness of fit" of their lives in personal, social, and historical ways.

The midlife years of parenting provide an interesting area for study (Todd & Jones, 1999) as parents have lived through and experienced some dramatic changes. Their experiences will be radically different from those of parents who have preceded them. To begin with, many of the reforms that have altered the landscape of intellectual disability services in the United Kingdom were introduced when the children of these parents were born. For example, at the time of this study, the All-Wales Strategy (Welsh Office, 1983), a strategy of considerable ideological and practical reform (Felce et al., 1998), was itself 15 years old. This cohort of parents, then, can be characterized as parents of the reform years; it is interesting to observe what impact such changes have had upon their experiences and aspirations. Further, this cohort of mothers will have been encultured in the changing attitudes toward, and practices in, the relationships among women, time, and society that provide a broad social and historical context within which lives are lived and interpreted.

We recognize that no single study and no single chapter can do full justice to the richness, complexities, and contradictions of those links. Here we are less ambitious and deal with the nature and breadth of relationships outside of the domestic and family sphere and with issues of identity and self-fulfillment, important elements of a quality of life approach. Our aim is to examine some of the ways individuals receive support that reinforces their sense of self, their sense of location within the world, and the opportunities that exist for self-realization. Perhaps our concern is with parents' appraisal of their life projects and the extent to which they find ways of sustaining valued and coherent narratives (Giddens, 1991). Our approach very much follows that outlined by Woodill, Renwick, Brown, and Raphael (1994) which asserts that "Quality of life is the degree to which the person enjoys the important possibilities of his or her life. [This] can be simplified to: How good is your life for you?" (p. 67).

Welsh And United Kingdom Policy

In contemporary Western societies, debates about the most appropriate forms of care for people with intellectual disabilities have taken on new resonances and directions in the final two or three decades of the past century. These decades were characterized by the emergence of wide-ranging critiques of the nature and function of institutional care highlighting its oppressive social control functions. The pressure for reform has grown over this period, and it is now widely accepted in policy that people with intellectual disabilities have a right to be included in the ordinary rhythms and routines of the community. Institutional forms of service provision have been displaced, and the community has become the new locus for the provision of care. These trends were witnessed within Wales, a constituent country of the United Kingdom of some 3 million people. The All-Wales Strategy (AWS) (Welsh Office, 1983), which formalized these trends into policy, has been recognized as a radical and value-led effort to secure for people with intellectual disabilities and their families as full a life as was possible within their own communities. The strengths and weaknesses of the AWS have been described in some detail elsewhere (Felce et al., 1998). Here we simply offer a broad outline of its intent alongside other relevant United Kingdom policies, insofar as they relate to families.

The AWS was described as containing "bold and imaginative proposals for a radical new service in Wales" (Audit Commission, 1987, p. 8). Behind it were three guiding principles, which, it was emphasized, applied to all people with intellectual disabilities however severe their disability. It stated that people were to have a right to normal patterns of life within the community, to be treated as individuals, and to receive additional help from the communities in which they lived and from professional services. It acknowledged and sought to rectify the historical legacy of inadequate and poor standards of services for individuals and their families. It called for progressive reform and offered privileged political patronage and the provision of significant extra resources for its realization (Felce et al., 1998). A key mechanism through which these aims might be translated into practice was the various activities involving a partnership of parents and people with intellectual disabilities, such as involvement in planning at a national and local level, and participation in individual planning (IP) meetings. Although the AWS valued and sought to stimulate further the resources of communities, this aspect of policy was only vaguely defined. Thus at the core of the AWS was the development of a network of professional, individual planning, housing, respite, and domiciliary support services and a diverse range of day services within most areas of Wales. Rather than being an example of policy directed at enhancing care by the community, the AWS must be properly regarded as a policy directed toward the reform of services and the maintenance of people within their own homes. As Felce et al. (1998) have argued:

> its proposals remained firmly rooted in the reform of deficient services, reform which would be likely to decrease segregation and promote community participation for those served, but would leave the nature of the community relatively unaffected. The AWS, therefore, represented a move from institutional treatment to community treatment. (p. 280)

Although the intentions and aims of the AWS for service reform were clearly laid out for people with intellectual disabilities, there was little mention of the specific and individual needs of carers and how these might be met. Rather, it simply recognized the "hardships" families faced and the need for short-term service intervention to "provide breaks which would not otherwise be possible" (Welsh Office, 1983, p. 5). As we argue below, such aims do lend themselves to full understanding of the day-to-day experiences of families and how services might impact upon them. The AWS did not outline in detail the objectives of service development as it related to family life, although several other policy statements were introduced in the 1980s and 1990s that set these out more explicitly. These more explicit statements identified the family home as the ideal site for the delivery of care and reinforced the idea that effort should be directed to enhancing the family's capacity to care. These became more central, and more focused efforts at recognizing and responding to the needs of carers developed (Heaton, 1999). The latest development occurred in 1996, when carers became the exclusive object of policy with the implementation of the Carers (Recognition and Services) Act 1995 (Department of Health, 1995). Thus while early reform-oriented policies referred to families only in passing, the intention of policy became increasingly evident in the 1980s: to supplement but not supplant the care giving by family, friends, and neighbors.

The formal, postwar health and welfare system has been increasingly built around the family, and women in particular, and has been prompted by both ideological and fiscal pressures (Parker, 1990; Twigg & Atkin, 1994). There is general agreement that the welfare state was in a state of "fiscal crisis" and that, as in other European countries, this could be resolved only through supporting families and other informal carers to act as service providers (Twigg & Atkin). The new economy of welfarism in the United Kingdom and elsewhere has been underpinned by the social relations of gender. Informal care became the orthodoxy and relied to a large extent upon women providing unpaid services for dependent close kin. The reality of family care, inasmuch as it involves people with intellectual disabilities, is overwhelmingly provided by mothers (Parker & Lawton, 1994). Thus, although family or community may be the ideological pivots of reform, in reality it is able to be realized largely because women provide the resources. Service workers and professionals were to have the task of supplementing and sustaining these resources. This view of responsibility for care giving was recognized formally in the Griffiths Report (1988):

Publicly provided services constitute only a small part of the total care provided to people in need. Families . . . provide the majority of care in response to needs which they are uniquely well placed to identify and respond to. This will continue to be the primary means by which people are enabled to lead normal lives in community settings. The proposals take as their starting point that this is as it should be, and that the first task of publicly provided services is to support and where possible strengthen these networks of carers, consulting them about their needs and those of the people they are caring for, and tailoring the provision of extra services (if required) accordingly. (p. 5)

Within United Kingdom policy, therefore, the family has been conceptualized as the mainstay of provision, while the task of the services around them is to protect and develop this resource. In so doing, carers have been increasingly viewed as the users of services themselves (Heaton, 1999). This suggests the need for a more careful understanding of the day-to-day realities of families' lives and of how services might impinge upon them. This was to be achieved by offering carers independent assessment of their own needs in addition to assessment of the needs of their relatives. This notion lay at the heart of the Carers Act (Department of Health, 1995) which, as Heaton (1999) argued, brings carers into a new relationship with professionals:

So positioned, informal carers' relationships with, on the one hand, patients, and on the other, formal service providers, exemplify contemporary disciplinary practices using relays: the informal carer is the supervisor of the person they care for, who in turn is supervised by the statutory health and social care services. (p. 773)

In summary, the implementation of policy has generally followed this pattern: Family members are viewed as the primary providers of care whose activities are supervised, supported, and scrutinized by the development of a network of professional agencies, processes, and bodies.

The Growth And Patterns Of Support Services In Wales

I am now looking back not just over the last 5 years, but over 20. My son, who has Down syndrome and is also severely autistic, is now 24 years old. In Wales, we have benefited from the All-Wales Strategy for Mental Handicap, and numerous government policies in the health, social care, and education fields. The All-Wales Strategy raised expectations, and some pieces of government legislation, such as the Carers' Act, do give qualified powers to families to campaign for the best quality service and the highest standards of care. The All-Wales Strategy has now come to an end, and, as new policies come into effect, it is perhaps timely to take stock of its effects.

I didn't know about the Strategy for years. We first heard about it when Matthew was at school in Barry, and the head told us about something called respite care and that it could be obtained at a local hostel. It took a long time to persuade us to let Matthew go—but we did. He loved the new arrangement, and it suddenly felt as if we'd won the lottery. For the first of the overnight stays, John sat by the phone all night. Soon it became a routine, however, and every 10 weeks or so we had a night to ourselves. We were just becoming acclimatized to this when I heard that there were plans to shut the hostel. I went to a parental protest meeting, and found myself with a group of very angry parents facing a young professional who was adamant that residential respite wasn't what parents needed. I was so incensed that I found a public voice I hadn't used since my CND days. I stood on a chair and became very articulate, denouncing the guy and his theoretical suppositions about "social role valorization" and receiving a massive ovation from the crowd—though I have to say I was shaking and very upset!

From there I was invited to join the Parents Federation (of which I knew nothing) and that was the beginning. Again, in parenthesis, I think all parents come to protest as a personal outburst against some part of the system that impacts severely on their lives. Then we go through a sort of "pain barrier" and fight others' causes, first alongside, and then apart from, our own. I had high hopes for the Strategy, though I very soon realized that the majority of the money was targeted at the minority of the population, that is, at those who were moving from the long stay institutions.

Nonetheless, there were great, and much needed, service innovations—and carers HAD to be part of the planning, delivery, and monitoring process. This represented a shift in culture in a way that seems amazing when I look back. Our views were important, but, in addition, they had to be seen to be the voices behind policy and planning. It was scary and a bit heady for those of us in the front line. But we were encouraged to raise our heads, to plan for a future that looked a whole lot better than the dreadful privations of the past. If there is a legacy that I would hang on to from the All-Wales Strategy, it is that it raised expectations. I think we can continue to capitalize on that.

What about services? In my case, these were few for years. A lot of stuff was put in place for adults, but not much for kids. The big and burning issue was always respite care—as it still is today. When I ask myself, "What HAS changed over these years for those of us with children and young people with intellectual disabilities?" I would have to report sadly, "Not very much!"

Pauline Young

The landscape of service provision for people with intellectual disabilities and their families underwent radical transformation in the last 20 years of the last century. Indeed, the data in this section suggest much has changed for families. There is increased support available in a variety of forms for families. In addition, they find themselves drawn into a palpable network of service professionals. Yet, despite such service provision, it is also imperative that we return subsequently to Pauline's summary comment on the felt lack of change and attempt to resolve her stated contradiction, that the more things change the more they seem to be the same.

In 1983 the institutional model was the cornerstone of residential provision in Wales, although its infrastructure was in a state of decline. Of the 3,100 people with intellectual disabilities living in some form of residential service, the majority (66%) were living in large-scale institutional care. Of the remainder, very few lived in what could be considered ordinary staffed housing in the community. The launch of the All-Wales Strategy (AWS) signaled an end to this situation, and the pursuit of ordinary housing stock was the favored objective for people currently living in atypical services and for people who were currently living with their families but who needed to leave home. By the end of the 1980s, 1,200 places had been created in ordinary housing, each setting accommodating on average three people. The reform of residential service provision was, therefore, considerable and had led to small-scale community housing becoming the established model for provision. However, the development of ordinary housing in Wales had little impact upon the

majority of families. Most of the people living in these new service settings had moved there from institutions (Evans, Todd, & Beyer, 1994).

Although the overwhelming majority of families were untouched by the
scale of residential reforms, support services to families did develop. Policy
has gradually come to be more explicit about the importance of the family
as a locus of care, and services have developed that set as a goal-building
capacity for families to provide care for longer periods of time. In Wales, this
typically took the form of short-term residential (respite) care, domiciliary
care, and the presence of a professional network. The development of domiciliary services was welcomed by families as an important means of enabling
parents and people with intellectual disabilities to spend more time apart
and for each to engage in independent activities for a few hours each week
(Evans, Felce, de Paiva, & Todd, 1992). Such a service was novel within
Wales at the launch of the AWS, but was soon found throughout the prin-
cipality over its course. It was an area of significant service expansion (Evans
et al., 1994; Perry, Felce, Byer, & Todd, 1998). In 1983 there were 47 families who received domiciliary support in Wales. By 1988 it was estimated
that there were 1,858 families receiving such support, and this number rose
to 1,914 families by 1995 (Perry et al.). Later, the growth of domiciliary support became more or less suspended so that between 1988 and 1995, there
was only a 4% increase in domiciliary provision. Unlike domiciliary support,
the development of short-term care continued after 1990. By 1995, 2,278
families in Wales used short-term care, almost twice as many families as in
1988 (Perry et al.). The development of short-term care in Wales was notable
also for a radical change in the way this service was provided. Prior to, and
also in the early years of, the AWS, the bulk of short-term care was provided
in atypical settings. In 1988 over 50% of short-term care still took place in
such settings. By 1995 this had dropped to only 18%. Then, short-term care
was more likely to be provided in ordinary staffed housing or was family-
based, 51% and 31% respectively. The development of short-term care in
ordinary housing represented a significant move toward more typical settings
with a hope that some of the ill-considered and damaging depersonalization
and experiences noted by Oswin (1984) would be avoided.

The AWS can, therefore, be seen as making a positive response to the
existing inadequacy of both the quantity and quality of short-term care
(Bayley, 1973; Oswin, 1984) and services providing a break of a few hours in
the evening or at weekends also became an established aspect of family support. Such developments led to a situation where there was a dramatic reduction in the proportion of families that had no access to, or made no use of,
one or other of these services (Todd, Shearn, Beyer, & Felce, 1993).
Furthermore, over the course of the AWS, there was significant growth in the
level of professional fieldwork staff, such as social workers, community nurses,

and family physicians in contact with families and in the number of families reporting being involved in IP meetings (Evans et al., 1994). Individual planning meetings involved a regular discussion between family members and service professionals concerning the views on the appropriateness and felt gaps in service provision to the person with intellectual disabilities.

There were, however, some areas of concern that detracted from the gains provided by practical support services. First, approximately one in five adults with intellectual disabilities living in the parental home had no access to any form of daycare in 1990, a proportion that had increased slightly since 1986 (Todd et al., 1993). Second, there had been a move toward greater part-time day occupation (Evans et al., 1994). Twelve percent of adults living at home had only part-time levels of day occupation in 1990, compared to 9% in 1986. Looked at another way, between 1986 and 1990, there had been a decrease in the proportions of adults living in the family home who had full-time forms of day occupation, from 74% to 68%. Daycare provides a frequent, regular, and substantial form of respite for caregivers. Thus, although families had greater access to domiciliary and short-term care, a substantial and increasing number of parents had adult offspring with intellectual disabilities with no daytime provision for all or part of the week. This was a particularly significant problem for families whose sons and daughters were leaving their full-time education and facing the prospect that daycare would become more irregular.

A third area of concern was that the scale of IPs never reached a level where the majority of families reported being involved or being offered a planning meeting with professionals. Early research on the recent implementation of the Carers Act (Department of Health, 1995), offers little indication that support might be offered to families in a more coordinated fashion. Williams and Robinson (2000) reported that only 22% of carers reported having received a carer's need assessment and that the majority of those were "in crisis." In addition, they reported poor outcomes in terms of the services discussed, with only 18 of the 42 services discussed being provided after approximately 1 year. Furthermore, they noted that these assessments were limited in scope and did not take into account important aspects of carers' lives, such as their own employment needs or the future accommodation needs of their relatives. They observed that whilst family members were prepared to vocalize strongly the needs of their relatives with disabilities, they were much more hesitant to ask for services for themselves. This appears to be in complete contrast to their tenacious character in "fighting" or "battling" for services for their sons and daughters.

[They] were not forthcoming about their own needs. They were not used to thinking in those terms, and, as parents, they often still felt totally bound up in their son's or daughter's lives even after they had reached adulthood. (Williams & Robinson, 2000, p. 17)

At the same time, there was little evidence to suggest an increase of support available through the resources of families' local communities. Indeed, data suggested shrinkage rather than growth in this respect and reflects the death or infirmity of relatives, the movement of siblings, and the reduced capacities of individual supporters (Grant, 1993; Todd et al., 1993). There is evidence here too that the accessibility of informal support is influenced by cultural and social norms and that these change with age. Thus, as children age, parents become more reluctant to ask for help from neighbors and friends, because they feel unable to reciprocate the support received.

In summary, Welsh services, as they have touched the lives of families over the past two decades, reflect policy by focusing on providing support to families to maintain people with intellectual disabilities within the family home. The support provided has certainly increased, but it does not seem to be available to all families. Furthermore, the AWS led increasingly to families becoming enmeshed within a professional and service network, albeit not always in a coordinated or comprehensive fashion. In the remainder of this chapter we examine the impact that changes have had upon families and upon mothers in particular.

Research

It is not our intention here to comment upon family quality of life in a rounded fashion, as other authors have in this text. To do so would be to go beyond the original intentions of the research. The research sought to describe the experiences of a group of women who become mothers of children with intellectual disabilities. The data drawn upon below were derived from three separate but related studies conducted by members of the Welsh Centre for Learning Disabilities between 1994 and 1999. In all, 89 parents were interviewed, often on several occasions. Their ages ranged from 28 to 75, and those of their offspring with intellectual disabilities ranged in age from 5 to 44. Our decision to study separate groups of parents was based upon a belief that, although care giving represents both an activity and identity, the nature of both is likely to alter over time. Thus, 18 mothers of young children with intellectual disabilities and their employment aspirations were the focus for one study conducted in 1995 (Shearn, 1997). A second study concerned the lives and support needs of 33 parents of adults with intellectual disabilities conducted in 1994 (Todd & Shearn, 1996b, 1997). The data that are drawn upon more extensively were from a third study of 38 parents during the middle years of parenting conducted over 1998 and 1999 (Todd & Jones, 1999). These were parents of young people with intellectual disabilities aged 13 to 18. All the people with intellectual disabilities were living in the parental home.

Professional Encounters And Identity Threats

I remember visiting our local primary school with my 4-year-old daughter and suggesting, half in jest, that we might think of sending Matthew to his local school in company with his sister. There was a sudden flash of anxiety on the head's face, just in case I might be serious! I also recall the teacher at the local special school (for those with "mild" intellectual disabilities) sending me a note home telling me that my son had been "diabolical" all day and that she'd found it hard to cope with him! I remember my anger that a specialist teacher couldn't cope for the 6.5 hours of the school day, when I was expected to cope for the other 17 hours, and 24 hours at weekends and school holidays.

Then, by chance, at a meeting at the Wales National Sports Centre in Cardiff, I heard a headmaster speak about his special school in the Vale of Glamorgan. He spoke with such pride about the achievement of his pupils. After a year-long battle, which threatened to involve the secretary of state for Wales (the most senior elected minister in Wales at that time), we managed to get our son transferred from his current school to that special school, where he then spent 12 happy years. He received an individualized education program, and all staff were specialist trained, very experienced, and understood his (and our) needs. We felt that there was a proper relationship between school and home. We were encouraged by their approach and attitude. Yet I felt something that has persisted over the years — that there is a social cost to specialized and segregated provision for both the children and their families. The school was not local. For Matthew, this meant he had little out-of-school contact with children in our community or with those children who attended his school. It was isolating and certainly didn't help in the transition process.

New government guidelines suggest multiagency planning to secure individually tailored programs for "special children," but they speak only of "commitment" not "process." At present, families are shuffled among agencies wrangling over who should fund what therapies and practical support. Joined-up thinking should also mean joined-up funding, so that families are not sent from agency to agency asking for help and advice in an attempt to delay the moment when someone will actually put a support program in place! If all or even some of these measures were in place, then transition—the smooth movement from school to life in the outside world—would have been at least partly addressed.

As it was, we were sent, unprepared and rudderless, it seemed, into a world where there were very few options for our son. "Residential college?" suggested our social worker. "What for?" we asked. The answer was clear: It would keep Matthew within the education system for another couple of years, meaning that the fees and costs would come out of the education budget, thus delaying the day when Social Services would have to find funding for some sort of day activity. We visited the college. Matthew would be living in residence 4 nights a week, and would be coming home at weekends. The hostel was pleasant, but he couldn't take his toy cars. It was not "age-appropriate." I mentioned the small and ancient teddy bear that accompanies me on trips abroad, and the vast array of soft toys that my 21-year-old daughter takes back and forth to university. We won that battle and Matthew duly went to "college."

We discovered that the social program was good. The carers helped Matthew to learn new skills, such as making his bed and laying out his clothes. The formal education, though, was as bad as the social program was good. "He can't count," wailed the teacher in her first report home. I hi-tailed it to college, and was told that Matthew did not know what to do with a pencil and paper except to scribble and then tear it up. "Have you tried taking him out into the car park and asking him to count the different colored cars?" I asked. She did, and, small wonder, my son could count. This experience sent me off to educational resource centres to buy practical equipment so that Matthew's teacher had a teaching program that related to his abilities and needs.

We lurched through those two years and grew ever more anxious about the future. Matthew left college, and, though there were murmurings about service provision, nothing happened for several months. The transition process was a farce and nothing useful really happened. College was a kind of afterthought and was really a leave of marking time. The gap between the college term ending and the day-service provision beginning was a very difficult time for us. We had to get in a good deal of help in order to continue working, and arrangements were not satisfactory. It was costly, Matthew was bored and fed up—and showed it. The friends he'd made at college disappeared, as had the friends he'd made in school. He, and we, felt very isolated. Finally we were offered an individualized program of activities for 4 days a week, and life for all of us began to improve. Although we are pleased with Matthew's service, I know it is currently under threat. We live in fear of a scaling down of day services which, it will be argued, will be no one's "fault" but simply the result of the current climate of "economic stringency."

As for professionals, our experience has been mixed, I suppose. Our medical service is dire in that, although they will always see Matthew quickly if we ask, they have no training to deal with him. They always provide their service through us, even when we are seeking advice because we don't know what is wrong. There always appears to be palpable relief when we leave with him. Fortunately, he is rarely ill. Medical professionals like to "cure" people, I suppose, and they can't cure Down syndrome and autism. A memory that sticks with me is the first midwife I met after Matthew's birth who told me, "Forget him and have another. Put him away." When she visited, she wouldn't even look at him. Shortly afterwards, we had a very good health visitor, not a specialist, but she made Matthew her study and she was wonderful to us. She got us portage, which was very helpful, as it involves parents helping their disabled children in such a positive way. Social workers have generally been good, but I tend to be given the ones who are more clued up because I'm trouble, I think, so this probably isn't the case for everyone. I ask for policies and procedures—in all, I ask a lot of questions!

I am lucky, but I have NEVER let a professional patronize me and get away with it. A good relationship between parents and professionals has to be based on openness and trust. If someone doesn't know the answer to a question I would prefer to be told that directly. If I have to wait for a service, I would always prefer to be told that, rather than sit expectantly for months while nothing happens. For our part, we shouldn't expect professionals to know everything or to respond to us immediately. But decent communication processes, and an honest, caring approach would make the process so much easier for parents. Sometimes, I think professionals forget that parents are anything other than caseload numbers and, because they often have a heavy workload, they neglect to make the small gestures that mean so much to carers who are at the end of their tether.

Most of my experiences have been good, as I have said, but I have a wealth of horror stories from other people. These include being given no notice for a meeting, being given no choice of when meetings occur, having to wait for hours with no apologies or reasons, or meetings postponed or cancelled at the last minute (mostly, by health professionals). Stories include sudden changes of personnel, with people leaving and no one knowing anything, and having a "temp" in place who doesn't know anything about the family. Some parents complain of cancelled reviews when they have had to go to great lengths to secure time off or to make childminding arrangements.

It all comes down to three C's: communication, courtesy, and consideration! Parents also need to be open and explicit about their needs. Dealing with it from the other side, I know that sometimes parents are not very direct in telling you what they really want! Parents need to be empowered to criticize so that they don't feel they have to put up with a second-rate service, or that their children will be penalized if they make a fuss. But parents also need to be prepared to listen to new ideas, new opportunities, and perhaps a different take on a service, since we do find it difficult to accept and deal with change!

Pauline Young

Drawing families increasingly closer into a network of professionals and agencies has become the hallmark of recent policy, as described above. Yet, as Pauline's reflections and data presented in this section suggest, the value of professional intervention is generally welcomed even if it is not straightforward. Good professional relationships by no means always occur, but, when they do, they are seen to be highly supportive. If there was a sense of continuity in this world of changing service personnel and provision, it was in the nature of parents' engagement with it. For many, as with Pauline, these encounters are cast as "struggles" (Chamberlayne & King, 1997) that are often "endless" (Williams & Robinson, 2000) and where, all too easily, families can feel scrutinized and evaluated. Not unsurprisingly, then, parents approach the transitional years with a degree of pessimism and resistance, and they believed they would only receive appropriate help after a period of struggle:

I'd love to see him have a job. I don't want him going to a Centre. I can't see him in a place like that. But given our experiences, I don't think anything will happen without a fight. I'm expecting a fight for his rights. Unless things change, I should imagine that'll be what it'll be like.

Pauline Young

As others have suggested, dissatisfaction with professional encounters can have long-lasting effects and help shape the ways individuals anticipate future ones (Annandale & Hunt, 1998). For many, negative relationships with service professionals had been a long-standing feature of their parental careers. Often the roots of these lay in their initial encounters during the period of disclosure. Parents were extremely keen to have us listen to these early accounts, and the frequency and intensity of their telling signifies that they had not come to cast "closure" over those events. One parent, for example, used the word "raw" to describe her feelings of those encounters some 16 years later. Coyle (1999) has argued that many accounts of dissatisfaction with professionals involve more than emotions; they also reflect a sense that one's personal identity is under threat. Certainly it seemed parents felt that from the beginning that their competence and moral worth was being placed under scrutiny, and this had been acutely felt over many years. Their own valued sense of self as "ordinary mothers," a commonly used expression in our interviews, was undermined in their dealings with professionals. Many mothers stressed that their commitment to be parents was not special, but simply "what any mother would do":

> My mates remind me that I'm doing a good job. They say they don't know how I cope, but they don't realize it's what we'd all do. I hate being praised 'cos I think I'd do what any mum would do in my situation. I keep going for her, fighting for her. I fought to get her into a mainstream school. I fought with doctors. My friends say really positive things about me, but I just say, "I'm just a mum and you'd do the same." Being a good mum is paramount in my life, number one. God knows it is tough! I suppose it's about being there and not giving up. Supporting them as much as you can.

There was little doubt that this was the way many mothers characterized their role as parents, but that in many different ways it was undermined by their contact with service agencies from the beginning, as the following comment illustrates:

> It was obvious to me at birth. It was obvious, you know, that she was handicapped. I noticed her hands were not normal. She was a poor color. She didn't look like my other babies. She was kept with me but it was obvious she wasn't right. Within 24 hours, and on my instigation, they told me. But I found out they had known, but they didn't want me to reject her. How could I do that to a child of mine?

The felt lack of sensitivity from service personnel was repeatedly stressed. They were viewed as abrupt and lacking in consideration for the mother. In another case, one mother reported how devalued she had felt after one such encounter:

> They sat us down, about twenty people in this room. They were all geneticists and pediatricians and social workers, obviously interested in the case, and they said, "Well, there is no future for Geraint." In fact, the neurologist asked, "Has Geraint ever had a cold? No? Well, the kindest thing from my point of view when he does is to let nature take its course and not treat him." I couldn't believe that a doctor was telling me this, you know. He was my son. He was 13 months old. Although he was a horrid baby, you know, I loved him just the same, and in fact the social worker said to us afterwards, "You know, if you want to move on and get on with your lives, and leave Geraint here, we've got some sort of country place that certain children go to." I couldn't possibly do that. I felt totally inadequate, really, and I was made to feel that by these health professionals. It was absolutely horrendous. I was just shell-shocked.

Many parents also felt that it was all too easy for them to be viewed as needlessly worried, or, as one mother commented "a neurotic mother." In general, their faith in professional expertise was seriously tested in those early years, and many come to fight and resist professional domination:

> I was 36, and I was refused amniocentesis. I was told it wasn't needed. But I felt it was. The doctor refused. I wanted it. I knew there was something not right. I mean I'd had 2 children, and I felt it wasn't right. I was told I was being neurotic. But that's the story of our lives. The number of times I've been told I'm being a neurotic, fussy mother and been proved right! Once, for example he was sent for a hearing test and the doctor looked at him and said, "Is he normal or subnormal?" "That's it, c'mon!" I said and picked him up. "Oh, oh, wait, where are you going?" I said he's a normal Down syndrome child. "Well, we'll put grommets in." I said, "But, excuse me, you haven't given him any tests yet!" "Ah, but these children . . ." So I said, "I'm sorry, I don't think he needs grommets." So I went back to my doctor and said I wanted to see a specialist. She wrote down that I was confused, a fussy mother. Can you imagine? But I persisted. So he had three tests, and there was nothing wrong with his hearing. I don't think it should be like that.

Another parent described her ongoing relationships with professionals as ones that cast doubt upon her parental competencies:

> I think social services can be a bit judgmental. Like I was really pleased when I saw your fags [cigarettes] fall out of your briefcase.

I hid all the ashtrays and that before you came. I didn't think I could smoke in front of you. My friend said, "Never smoke in front a social worker, what with Sharon's bad heart 'n all." I remember a social worker saying to me once that I should be baking cakes with her. Then that was it, gone and never seen again. I don't bake so why should I bake with Sharon? Just because she's doing it at school? It's not the kind of help I need. I don't need people telling me what to do with her 'n all. She was a real pain. What did she know about me or Sharon? They think you don't know what you're doing and it's their job to tell you. To be perfectly honest, it's like all the interviews I've had with them. They say, "Oh you're not pre-pared to let her do this." And I said, "I'm prepared to let her do anything that's going to make her independent." I don't know where they get the idea that you don't want her to do this and you don't want her to do that.

Despite being intended as a way to relieve parenting difficulties, profes-sional relationships were viewed by some as adding to them. They felt their status as "good mothers" was one they had to achieve and be granted, rather than to have it afforded without question. However, over time, these moth-ers had acquired new competencies to deal with professionals. They became more willing to "tough it out" as advocates of their sons' and daughters' needs. For these mothers, this was a core dimension of "good motherhood":

I didn't know much about learning disability before I had Steph. Well, I think Steph has made my life stronger; it's shaped it for the better. Oh sure, my life has changed. Almost everything that's hap-pened to me is in some way related to Steph having special needs. But in a lot of ways it's been for my good. I've searched high and low for information. It doesn't come looking for you. I've had to fight for her, whereas before I'd just saunter through life taking it easy. It wasn't in my personality to be a fighter, but no one else could do it for her.

However, although these mothers felt they had struggled to be treated as ordinary mothers this had come at a particular cost that, for many, became apparent only during the middle years of parenting. During the transitional years of their children, there were decisions to be made about placements in adult services. It seemed that a mother's role in such meetings was to advo-cate for her child, rather than for herself. Thus parents were careful not to let their own interests and needs spill over into the discussions. Mothers' wider interests, as we describe below, are considerable but are not treated as a legit-imate subject for discussion. Mothers themselves felt that they ought not cross this threshold since this might be construed as "selfish":

How do you think that would've looked? "Thanks for sorting out Joe. Now let's deal with me! What are you going to do for me?" I'd be a right selfish cow wouldn't I? You know, well it would be like, "We've got this package for Joe and this one for you. Now choose which one you want!" I'd cop for that, wouldn't I, if I chose the one for me. You're not going to get into that situation with them. Anyway I can fight my own battles. Joe can't.

Mothers' views of their own lives and how any proposed changes in service provision might impact upon them personally are not directly brought into discussions with professionals. If many of the encounters parents had with professionals seemed to be around conflicting notions of the "good mother," there was some agreement that "the good mother" placed her child's needs before her own. Responding to a question about how much her desires and aspirations for her own life influenced her conduct in transitional meetings, one mother replied:

> You learn you can't have everything you want from [professionals]. You take what's best from what's on offer. Best for her really. I couldn't do something just because it was more convenient for me, because I wanted it. I go in there for her. You've got to be able to live with yourself afterwards, haven't you? It's got to be the right thing for her. I think I've got a right to a life myself, and it kind of niggles away at you sometimes. But it's "Let's roll up the sleeves and work for her."

One mother was clear that the role "good mother" was one she was expected to perform and that it was less acceptable for mothers of children with intellectual disabilities to have a public life beyond the family home. Furthermore, it appeared that mothers sensed that the idealized standard of the "good mother" was more stringently applied to them than to other mothers:

> All mothers are sometimes made to feel guilty if they go out. But if you're the mother of a handicapped child, they think you should be at home. They really think you should be there with them all the time.

The data in this section suggest that there are certain risks for mothers in being drawn into a network of professionals and agencies. These interactions form an important feature of parents' lives once their children are recognized as children with intellectual disabilities. Despite the value attached to expanding the number and range of professionals, the outcomes for families are not automatically beneficial, and the quality of the relationships needs to be critically examined rather than assumed to be helpful. This view is generally in line with research findings that attest to the significance of positive, affirmative, and empathic relationships with service professionals (Grant, McGrath, & Ramcharan, 1994). It appears, though, that relationships with professionals can sometimes be "identity-threatening" and, in this case, it is the maternal identity that is exposed and at stake in professional encounters.

Running Faster Just To Stand Still: The Changing But Hidden Contexts Of Midlife

It is certainly true that when a family embraces a child with a disability, that family hits the ground running. In many cases, we run ever faster in order to remain on the same spot!

What other major differences has having a child, then an adult, with a disability made to my life. In some ways, this is not easy to answer. When I was very young, my parents divorced. In my small home town, this was still fairly rare, and my school friends would ask, "What's it like to have divorced parents?" To this, I would always respond, "I don't know, because I don't know what it's like to have my parents living together!" This is also the answer to the present question: Matthew has always been there, we love him dearly, and we cannot imagine life without him. There are, however, some obvious factors that have changed. We have not been very mobile as a family. When Matthew was small, he could and would escape, Houdini-like, from all houses and gardens, and run off at high speed, careless of traffic or any other danger. Our house was locked up like a fortress every night, but he would still often work out how to find and use keys and other ways of escaping. Many times, the local police would bring him home in a police car with the flashing light and siren to entertain him (if not our neighbors!) and offer him just the kind of reward that encouraged his running. So family holidays were nonexistent—there was nowhere safe to take him—and friends, though well-meaning, didn't always appreciate our problems. Public places were generally unsafe, since, without warning, he would take off at the speed of light. I wouldn't tie him to me once he grew beyond the toddler stage, since that would have drawn unwarranted attention and such restraint seemed cruel. The result was that we didn't go very far as a family group. We went only to parks and play areas where walls and fences were high and gates were few. We grew used to taking turns to visit people or to go away. We had no extended family living nearby, and baby-sitters were not very happy to supervise a very active child who didn't sleep but could escape the premises if not carefully watched. Not sleeping was another issue. At 24, he still wanders the house at night, and we sleep lightly and take it in turns to ensure that he is brought back to bed, and doesn't do things like turning on taps with the plug left in the basin.

After his birth, I'd seriously believed and considered that I should give up work and concentrate on Matthew. A psychologist, one of the first professionals we saw other than the GP, assessed Matthew at the hospital. Then he assessed me, though I hadn't asked him to. He told my husband, John, that I needed to get back to work! He told me subsequently that he felt that my own health, physical and psychological, would be badly compromised if I didn't resume my career. This was probably the best bit of advice I ever had. I went back to work, though I never had support from services. A nurse I knew offered to help. I could trust her with Matthew and she cared for him for 18 months. As Matthew got older and his routines started to change, we thought it would be best for someone else to care for him at home. I have remained friends with both these women, which I believe says something about the ways in which women relate to and understand each other. We share something!

I think there are many issues for the parents of a disabled child in finding and maintaining work. I do clearly feel some guilt about being a working mum. I've never felt the need to apologize for doing so, but I missed both my kids' first steps—silly to regret it, but I do! Fortunately, Matthew is not sick, and he doesn't have long-term health-care needs. Many of my parent friends, on the other hand, have endless hospital trips, and there is no proper provision for flexible working in such cases. Some organizations do offer caring leave. One of my employers offered me 5 days per annum caring leave when I joined them, but there is a long way to go before this is widely available. I am aware that many women sacrifice good career opportunities in order to campaign for better quality of lives for their disabled children, and I think how frustrating this must be. My work in an academic environment has time off that coincides nicely with school holidays, so that has worked fairly well, except that other academics manage to complete research projects in the holidays and I could never do this. There was virtually no service for Matthew in any of the holiday periods.

I have asked my husband what he would have liked to have done with his life without the constraints of a child with a disability. He ventured that he might have been more active in pursuing his career (he is also a university academic), but that moving around the country when you need the intervention of specialized services—which vary in quality and quantity from area to area—is not an easy option. He did speculate light-heartedly that, had Matthew been perfectly able, he would probably be worrying about a whole series of other things, such as why his son was wasting a good education and not looking for a good job to pay off his university debt! He then seriously commented that, for us as a family, there was an additional problem. Ours is a family that lives very much for the things of the mind. We love books, conversation, the arts, and music. To have a son who cannot share in any of this has increased our sorrow, and, in some way, has compounded our guilt. We tried, when Matthew was younger, to engage in more practical pursuits, such as sporting events and outdoor activities, but these do not come so naturally to us, and we have often wondered if Matthew would have been better off in different family circumstances.

As for me, I would have loved to have traveled more. I have been fortunate in that I have taught in the United States for short periods, and engaged in study tours of Canada and Egypt, but these trips are always undertaken knowing that I leave my son with his father and that we cannot be together exploring and enjoying the experiences such opportunities bring. We did once venture to the United States as a family with Matthew to visit a brother and sister-in-law who live there, but that experience—never to be repeated—rates a whole chapter to itself!

And what about our daughter? To begin with, I would have liked more children, so there might have been a brother or sister to share her childhood. She has said that she feels like an only child, but with none of the privileges that go with that role. She has often had to take second place for attention, she has often naturally fallen into the role of carer even at a very young age as a result of the expectations of others, and she has a deep awareness of the effects on family life of a sibling with an intellectual disability. When my daughter became a teenager, in particular, she joined the two of us as an additional carer, despite our best efforts to preserve as "normal" a life for her as possible. Now that she is an adult, my husband and I do have more breaks together. We went for a wonderful week to California 2 years ago, the first holiday we had taken together for many years, leaving Kate "in charge." There have been, however, some benefits for her. Kate is mature beyond her years, confidently espouses the cause of the underdog, and wherever she goes she challenges what she deems to be a lack of awareness of disability rights issues and solidly champions equal opportunities and antidiscriminatory practice! Until she professed an interest in working in the media after her university studies, we had grave anxieties that she might turn into a social worker—a good, but highly exploited and underrated profession subject to a rapid burn-out rate!

Pauline Young

Pauline's autobiographical lens begins to open out and capture a more panoramic, and perhaps more personal, perspective of her life, a view researchers and services seem to recognize in only a blurred fashion, if at all. As the data above suggest, mothers themselves find it awkward to express personally salient interests. In this silent space, we seem to forget that behind many of the tasks and interactions of being a mother might also lie a wife, a friend, and a colleague. We examine in this section some of the struggles mothers engage in as they strive to have a life outside of the family home. This includes the worlds of socializing and employment, worlds that figure as important in the transitional concerns of young people with learning disabilities but not, it seems, for their mothers. Pauline commented that the advice given to her to maintain her career was "probably the best bit of advice I ever had." All too few mothers are given such advice, however, and consequently feel, as Pauline initially did, that they ought not to resume their careers for some years, if ever. There is little doubt from our data that mothers of people with intellectual disabilities experience employment difficulties (Shearn & Todd, 2000; Todd & Shearn, 1996b). Most women expect a career to be part of their lives, and employment is seen as a salient expression of their self-identities (Martin & Roberts, 1984). Increasingly mothers combine family and domestic work with paid employment, and the return to full-time work becomes more likely as their children age (Kiernan & Wicks, 1990). It appears that these trends do not apply to mothers of children with intellectual disabilities, as their employment rates are significantly lower than for mothers in general (Baldwin & Glendinning, 1983; Shearn, 1998). Of 78 mothers of school-aged children with intellectual disabilities surveyed in one county in Wales, only 31% worked in any form of employment, and less than a fifth of them (that is 6% of the sample) were in full-time employment. This compares to an employment rate of 67% for all mothers of similarly aged children, two fifths of whom worked full time. Furthermore, 67% of the nonworking mothers reported that they wanted work in the future. Work was seen as a highly valuable activity, as is neatly captured as "survival of the self" in the comments of one mother:

My mum heard of a little part-time job going, just photocopying. I can remember going to work. Oh! The sun was shining. I had the car and I had the radio on. And it was lovely. The kids were in school. It was nice on my own, in my own car, playing Gloria Gaynor, "I Will Survive." I was going to earn money. I was actually going into work and mixing with people. It was a new experience for me. It was just wonderful.

The introduction of the middle years of parenting threatened mothers' employment status and aspirations. A number of key changes were taking place in mothers' lives in the transitional years. To begin with, and as Pauline also stated, the departure of other children from the family home was, in the short term at least, experienced as a loss of support. Jill, for example, found that she had to give up her part-time job when her other children left home:

I did have a part-time job. It was a sorry thing that I had to give it up, but I was torn. I was actually office manager so it wasn't the sort of job that you could, you know, let people down. It was very flexible for me, they were marvelous about school holidays and bringing work home, you know, [and] it was very much a give and take job. But it was really thanks to my children being home because they were older teenagers so I could pop into the office for an hour and they would watch Sarah. Once they'd gone, I was really stuck. I just felt I wasn't being fair to Sarah at all. I would be busy, perhaps doing the paperwork, and I was constantly [saying], "Hang on Sarah, wait a minute, wait a minute."

At the same time, their teenagers with intellectual disabilities were undergoing important changes in service provision. They were leaving the world of school with its predictable schedule and entering one that was much less predictable and could, as we described earlier, be of much shorter duration. Not surprisingly, many mothers felt that the adolescent years were so full of uncertainty that the prospect of their maintaining employment was now in jeopardy, despite the importance they placed on it. This prospect is not viewed simply in terms of a loss of activity, but as a threat to their very identities:

I don't know whether I'll be able to continue like this. I'm not very hopeful. When Geraint leaves school, there might not be any services available to him. It's always been in the back of my mind as well that when he reaches 19, I'm going to have to give up work. [But work is] what keeps me going you know, it gives me some sort of reason for existing, I suppose. I can be me, as opposed to being Geraint's mum or Dave's wife, and when I'm at work, I'm Jane, a person in her own right, with my own identity.

The transitional years with its shifting and less precise resources ushers in a perspective that, in general, life is beginning to lose a sense of ordinariness. Life no longer seems to feel the same. Although mothers had always faced restrictions, their context of those was beginning to alter and many felt a growing sense of being left behind as their lives become less normative. As one mother noted: "Everyone stays at home when their children are young, don't they?"

This change is brought about not only by the diminishing opportunities for work but also by the difficulty socializing with friends. These mothers' friends had careers that were unfolding in a very different fashion. As the following comment teasingly suggests, the attitude of "nothing too unusual is happening" is disrupted in the middle years:

> We used to get together with our mates on a Saturday afternoon in the pub down the road. They didn't mind having kids in there and so we could all go there and have a laugh without having to find people to look after them. They just played in the garden. So Saturday used to be a great deal, and you bundle all your problems with the school and the doctors away and just relax. We don't anymore, though.

Mothers in the middle years begin to sense that their lives are no longer "like other mothers." Having other children at home allowed them to find flexible ways of coping with the demands of care giving. They could, for example, go out in a way that fitted with the pattern of life of their peers:

> We had our nights out, my husband and I. If we wanted to go to the pub, one of the kids would stay in and I'd say, "Right, we're walking round the pub." There was nothing in my life that was different to anyone else's then.

Mothers in the middle years of parenting anticipate that family demands will increase, because services might not be as generously available for their growing children and there would be fewer resources to call upon the family itself. At the same time, they feel their lives are beginning to move away from those of their peers, as Rachel was beginning to experience:

> I get out with my friends about once every 2 months. We go out in a gang. But I'm beginning to notice how different my life is from theirs. If I want to go out, it's got to be really organized. They can do what they want. I don't see them during the day because they're out working. They just get on and do what they want, but my life's really different. When Sonia was younger I had a lot of friends. We used to go out together, and our husbands used to baby-sit. We were all tired and busy. My life wasn't any different from theirs. Not really. It just

creeps up on you gradually that your life is really different. I know it sounds a bit trivial, but when our kids were 10 or 11, well, my friends were beginning to leave their kids on their own for the odd hour or so. You don't think about those things until they happen. Even now, if I run out of milk, I have to say, "Come on, you're coming with me." She causes a fuss and says she wants to stay, but I can't let her do that. She's never been left on her own. Well, I've done it about twice, just to pop round and get some milk from the shop. But it's horrible, my heart is thumping, it's nerve racking. What if a social worker called when I was out? I'd die, I'd be mortified. They'd think I did it all the time. It might be a hassle, so she comes with me. I don't think I could trust her. Even when she's in the house with me she's done some silly things, like turn the gas taps on by mistake. So she's at risk for injuring herself. You just learn not to trust her. It could turn into something major and you'd never forgive yourself. So now there's a huge difference between myself and my friends. They're mostly working and go out whenever they fancy it.

All in all, families felt they were unable to find the right resources to meet their wider social needs, needs that had changed according to their expectations of what typical social lives for people their age should be. Now there was simply both insufficient and inappropriate time (Todd & Shearn, 1996b). We have described the weakness of formal family support services in considerable detail elsewhere (Felce et al., 1998; Todd & Shearn, 1996a) and have argued that their temporal organization does not dove-tail with the temporal rhythms and flow of parents' social or working lives and aspirations. Flexibility, that key ingredient Pauline identifies, seems so lacking. As currently fashioned, support does not permit the maximization of engagement in a life outside of the home, and indeed does not seem to be based upon meeting such needs. Rather, support seems to be based upon an assumption that motherhood involves overbearing and tiring demands, and is designed to offer mothers opportunities to rest, relax, and recharge their batteries. However, and for the most part, mothers are not looking only to relax but also to invest time in a range of personally salient activities and commitments. Such concerns are not part of any transitional planning meetings. There seems to be little support for promoting a more encompassing and active view of mothers' lives.

So far, therefore, the data suggest that mothers' sense of self is threatened in different ways. Professional encounters seem to silence personal aspirations and focus, and not always positively, on "being mother." During the middle years, their sense of self is further threatened by a growing inability to act out personally salient activities. We now turn to the way mothers incorporate these events into their life stories, and how this reveals the meanings they give to being the mother of a person with learning disabilities.

Weaving Together The Strands Of Stories Of Living

This may not seem relevant, but it is! My mum was a single mother who was born into a very poor agricultural laboring family. Though she was very bright and was offered a scholarship to go to a local grammar school, enormous financial constraints meant that she stayed at the village school till she was 14 when she left to go into domestic service. She married very young at 17 (to get out of service, I think), and had me at 19. She became a single mother when I was 14, and we went to live with my grandparents. Mum was a shop assistant, and very determined that my life should not echo hers in any respect. I was encouraged to stay on at school after 16—the only child to have done this in the family—and Mum had to fight very vocal objections from family members to this!

I was actually all set for a musical career. In those days, I was a very competent pianist. I won prizes at festivals and got a scholarship to the London Royal Academy of Music as a performer. But I had a major problem: public performance actually made me ill! I used to get appalling migraines, and I was truly the most nervous concert pianist you could possibly imagine. In the summer of my A levels, I suddenly realized that I was embarking on a career path that was potentially disastrous, despite massive encouragement from a whole range of very intimidating people! Anyway, much to my mother's disappointment, I took a year out and did all sorts of things to earn a living because there was no way Mum could keep me. I finally went to university to study music, intending to teach it, but, again, got sidelined when I met a young and very radical university professor of English. He persuaded me to go for a subject change. So I eventually graduated with a degree in English and stayed on for a year-long education diploma and went to teach at a grammar school.

I was very happy for 2 years. I had absolutely no thoughts of marrying before or when I was in college. Although I liked kids and enjoyed teaching very much, I was not even vaguely tempted to consider having any of my own! I started to apply for a variety of jobs around the world, in Vancouver, Sweden, and Southern Italy. I was offered jobs in Sweden and Sorrento and, while I was considering options, a friend from college days phoned me and told me about a job vacancy back in Wales, at a college of education, for a lecturer in English. The competition would be fairly fierce, but how about it? So I went with very little hope of getting it. There were two posts going, and 14 of us were interviewed over 2 full days. By coincidence, my friend got one post, and I was offered the other.

So, abroad was on hold! I intended to stay only a couple of years, although I thoroughly enjoyed teaching students, visiting schools, and watching people teach—a great learning curve. The chap who had told me about the job had been on the periphery of my college circle, but to cut a long story short and to echo the ending of Jane Eyre (with a little less romance!), "Reader, I married him!" We were actually married in the summer of 1971. I was 29, and suddenly the option of a family loomed into a sort of perspective, if only because family kept on asking when we were going to produce. My mother, in particular, kept on about my age and impending decrepitude.

I had three miscarriages before I was pregnant with Matthew, and, by this time, the thought of another miscarriage was horrendous. My patient gynecologist, a very nice woman who became more of a friend than a doctor over the years, took me into hospital where I spent 3 months on bedrest.

While I was there, they carried out a number of tests and discovered that I had a translocated chromosomal pattern that could result in an abnormality of some kind. I had six amniocentesis tests and none of them worked for a variety of reasons. I tell you all of this to show an aspect of my nature, a kind of strength through adversity. I was 5 and a half months pregnant, and I was asked if I wanted to proceed with the pregnancy. I was adamant that I should. I felt that this child was meant to be born. After all the problems and all the tests, he was hanging on in there. The thought at that stage of a late termination was just impossible to contemplate. So he was born, and, as they say, the rest is history.

I have to say that in the days immediately after his birth, I felt as if I'd been handed a life sentence, and I was extremely depressed. I was set apart from other expectant or new mothers in the labor ward. I had left from that ward, but after Matthew's birth I found all my belongings had been moved into a single, high walled, high windowed room in what was once an old isolation ward. Looking back now, this seems so tellingly symbolic, a ritual rites de passage of being separated before being returned to the world. Seemingly, I was not allowed to be, and was being told I could not be, like those other women I had been with only hours before.

I can't describe with any real justice the depth of my depression. But it all ended the minute I picked Matthew up for the first time. I fell in love with him, and that was it. I was going to give up my teaching career and dedicate my life to working with Matthew. As a parent of a child with a disability, you start with a blank page of understanding. Researching, asking questions, and learning about child developmental techniques was how I imagined my life would be. While I was in this "missionary zeal" stage, we went to see a clinical psychologist. He gave us some useful information on Matthew, then sent me out of the room to get coffees while he told John to "get Pauline back into her career. Don't let her stay at home and turn herself into some kind of monstrous martyr."

After much soul searching, that is exactly what I did. When I was pregnant, we'd had such dreams of what having children would be like, and I was really looking forward to being a mother. The minute you have a disabled child, though, you are a mother apart.

And I felt such dreadful guilt. It was clearly "my" problem. I'd saddled a partner with this burden, although I would have to say that John embraced the situation absolutely from day one, ringing up friends and relatives and being very open and positive. I didn't ever imagine I would have a disabled child and I didn't want to, if I'm honest. Nobody wants that to happen. I felt such a conflicting mixture of anger and guilt.

I still get angry sometimes at the things that we have been unable to do as a family. My salvation is my work. The psychologist was absolutely right. I would have been an absolute monster if I had dedicated my life to Matthew, and been even less easy to live with than I am now! I never assumed, given the way I am and the way I was brought up, that I'd ever be tied in this way.

When I look back, what I wanted was to see the world, to remain independent, and to have a career that would finance travel to the more remote parts of the globe. Earlier in my life, I had taken a year out and I did so many things. I worked on a farm potato picking, in a tomato packing factory, and in a printing firm. I learned how to ice cakes on a regular 5 A.M. shift in a bakery, and to pull pints at a variety of pubs. I knew that I could turn my hand to lots of things, and so I assumed that I would always be able to earn enough to fund an independent lifestyle. John and I had similar plans to travel and go adventuring when we were first married. The compromise has been that he stays at home and I get to travel a little. He is more home oriented than I am, but I still feel guilty, and it is a whole lot less fun when you can't travel as a whole family. I am fortunate in that I am curious about people generally, find them interesting, and find it easy to make acquaintances of them. I do like to meet challenge.

Pauline Young

This section of the chapter deals with a form of challenge, the role of biography in shaping and contextualizing mothers' experiences of the present. Our analysis examines the nature of the link between the inner and outer worlds of carers (Chamberlayne & King, 1997). This approach has a rich potential for exploring how carers' lives are "lived out" and the personal meanings through which carers' appraisals of their situations depend. It is here that life is given a certain quality, one hewn from historical and personal circumstances. Certainly, mothers varied in the ways they defined their lives despite facing similar challenges. They differed in the way becoming and being a mother of a person with intellectual disabilities was incorporated into, and impacted upon, their biographies and the narratives of their lives. We present two such responses and offer them only as idealized categorizations. No one mother's story fit one or other category perfectly but they are highly suggestive for social care practices.

Valued Consistency

One group of mothers recognized that considerable change was taking place in their lives in terms of family structure and relationships with others. Yet it was evident that, within this fluid world, they also expressed satisfaction with the continuing salience of "mother" in their lives. It was felt to offer the most authentic expression of their identity. Being and continuing to be a mother presented an important link between their past and present lives, and even across generations. Put simply, the durability of their maternal identity felt right! This aspect of their self-identities was an important reflection of themselves when they were growing up:

I got engaged at 18 and married when I was 20. I left school halfway through my A-levels. "I'll get engaged instead," I thought. That's how it was. It's difficult to explain to people, but then you were looking for a husband. I don't think career came into it. I was bright. I got a scholarship to a private school, I got 8 O-levels. I could've done A-levels [but] things were just different. The head came and asked us about university and I was thinking, "Hold on a bit. I want to get married." I'd already met this fella. She asked me, "Where are you going?" I said, "I'm not."

Life was different then I suppose. You didn't think in terms of career. I was the first person in my family to get O levels. But finding a husband was a romantic thing, it was what you do in life. If you weren't married in your 20s, that was it, you were on the shelf. Things have really changed in 30 years. I've been married 27 years. Sometimes I love him and sometimes I hate him, but at the end of the day, no, I wouldn't like to have my time over again. I've had a fortunate life. I'd found Mr. Right.

Then I had kids. That's what I really wanted. I love kids. If I could've, I'd have six kids. We had the two, as Paul didn't want too many kids. So two was enough. But I wanted more, it's in me. I love them. I hate it when people say, "He's lucky to have you." He's not. I'm lucky to have him. They can't face [this] concept at all. How can you be lucky to have someone like Joe? I did go back to work for a year but I stopped working. Having more kids seemed right.

These mothers sensed, though, that their lives were more akin to the lives of women of previous generations, and there was some unease that others might devalue their role and judge them as "failing in a modern world." Thus there is a dual risk for these mothers in their interactions with others in their social or service-based networks. They could be seen as "failing mothers" in professional contexts and "failed individuals" in the wider world. Thus, for this group of mothers, they not only asked for resources or support but also wished to have the salience of their roles as mothers valued and respected:

I suppose I was unlucky to be born when I was. If I had been born when my grandmother was, I'd be perfectly content. My grandmother was born in 1900. After she had children, her house was her domain. When the children left home, she was nearly 60. She did nothing then. You didn't go on holiday in those days. I don't like this idea about achieving. As women, carers aren't valued by anyone except the people they care for. Society as a whole doesn't value us. Single mothers [go] back into work [because] looking after your children isn't a good thing to do. Looking after your children doesn't count as a career.

It's a commitment and I work hard at it. Why can't what I do be valued? It's a career to me. It's a valuable thing to do. It's not a chore. But woman are like . . . it's one of those things, isn't it? . . . that women just . . . just . . . I think women must be born with an in-built guilt complex, you know.

I've never wanted a career in terms of work. I was never career steered. It was get married and never have a career. Years later, people say, "How can you not have a career?" But I'm quite happy being a mum. It suits me.

Women's roles have changed dramatically. My daughter would love to stay at home and look after her kids. That sounds how it should be to me. But that's going against the flow now. Maybe it all just goes toward making my role as a woman look small.

These mothers considered that they were managing successfully in a role that they felt natural and comfortable with. However, as well as risking the label of being an "underachiever" or "out-of-time" in the modern world, there was also a concern that the scale of their investment in the maternal identity may cause them difficulties in later years. This was evident with Rhian, whose daughter approached the outer margins of her life expectancy:

I do try and be positive about the future. When I went to college, I was preparing for life without her. Maybe I should've gone to college earlier. At least she used to go to bed early and I could've done the course work without much interruption. Now I'm just as busy try-ing to keep her occupied as I used to be, only more so because she's awake for longer now. I think I've got a lack of confidence about me. I can talk and talk about Shelia but when it comes to myself, I just feel brain-dead. So I'm pretty frightened of going to work really. Then, if Shelia were ill, well I just couldn't commit myself to being at work regularly. I'd have to leave there and then. It's not that I want to go to work for the work, but sometimes I'd just like the company.

Maybe I'll work in the community in the future. I can't think about the future. I just try and keep to here and now. Think about her quality of life now. That's all I want. I don't really think beyond that. Not for myself. Well, I suppose I do unconsciously. I do have some kind of plan. I'm doing BSL [British sign language], so that might help me work in the community [later]. But I'm thinking too much about it.

For this group of mothers, the future and the attitudes of others threat-ened to disrupt their lives more than the past or present. They might, there-fore, be viewed as determining their roles as a mother of a person with intellectual disabilities as a form of "biographical reinforcement" (Carricaburu & Pierret, 1995). Their current lives appeared consistent with life stories and were thus endowed with much positive meaning. To be sure, all mothers in the study reported the positive features of being mothers of children with intellectual disabilities. What made this group different was that becoming and being a mother had always had a central place in their sense of self and in organizing and planning their lives. Their biographies were very much constructed around this role. Being a mother had been, and continued to be, a salient "preferred identity" (Charmaz, 1987). It was one very much at risk in professional encounters as described earlier. The difficulties for this group of women were not so much related to having a child with intellectual disabilities as in dealing with the attitudes of others who imagined that such a role could not be fulfilling and fulfilled by "ordinary mothers."

Disrupted Narratives

For another group of mothers, the identity of mother was, and continued to be, important. However, many felt that it was beginning to dominate and offer too narrow a reflection of their identities. "Mother" was just one of several roles they valued. Yet they were frustrated in their attempts to express these other important profiles and annoyed at the inability of others to see these without inferring they were "indifferent mothers." For them, the events and properties of midlife offered *biographical disruption* (Bury, 1983). They were not the person they once thought they were and they questioned the appropriateness of living "like any other mother." Contained in the narratives of this group of mothers were references to what might best be described as "critical incidents." These are incidents that "are the most likely to occur at particular times in the individual's life. They are a useful area to study, because they reveal, like a flashbulb, the major choice and change times in people's lives" (Measor, 1985, p. 61). In Jayne's account below, there is no incident as such, only the emergence of vague and unsettling questions of uncertainty over her identity. It is a form of "reality shock" whereby old patterns of activity and interpretation begin to provide an inadequate basis for carrying on in a routine way, that is, with the previously unreflexive nature of day-to-day life itself. Often accounts like Jayne's were sprinkled with existential concerns such as, "Who am I?" or "I don't feel myself."

It's kind of like being in cold-storage, you know. Day-in, day-out you're just getting on with it. Keeping the routine together kind of thing. Making sure everyone's happy, everything's in its place. Then it's "Bong," and I'm thinking, "Where have the years gone?" And I'm thinking, you know, it sounds daft but I'm thinking, "Where am I? Who am I?" He laughs when I say it to him. And he'll give me a cuddle and say, "You're Jayne!" He doesn't . . . well it's not easy to understand. I don't really feel myself. It's just in those odd moments of the day. It's what happens when you think!

In these mothers' accounts of their lives, the present seemed to involve a fear over the impending loss of self and heightened feelings of differentiation from other mothers. They were becoming different, and this was located in what was felt to be a unidimensional existence. They were being seen as "mothers" only, and this hid a range of other salient interests and roles, real or desired. This feature of care giving was outlined by Todd and Shearn (1996a) and was supported by this mother:

> I'm sort of like being pushed into the background. Because everything's the kids, the kids, the kids. Nothing for me like, you know what I mean? They demand your attention all the time. Sometimes you forget who you are. Well that's why I'd love to go to work because I'd have an identity. I'd know who I was! I'd be me!

For many mothers, the ability to go out when one pleases is the taken-for-granted hallmark of the midlife years of most parents. An inability to follow through with long-held aspirations left some mothers reviewing their lives in a negative fashion, as did Lucy, for example. For Lucy the midlife years were viewed as a milestone, encouraging reflection and self-appraisal and pessimism about her self in the future.

Well, I don't say I had great ambitions, but the thing is, having got so far, there've been many times when I think, "What have I done?" Especially when you turn milestones and you think, "Oh gosh, all I've done is this," and the other end of the stick is thinking that you've got to do this for the rest of your life. I used to say to [my husband] Stephen, "What do I do? All I am is somebody's mum."

Importantly, this group of mothers had not surrendered important components of their lives when they first become mothers of children with intellectually disabilities. Previous conceptions of self continued to exist, if silently, in the way mothers struggled with the resources at hand to lead as ordinary a life as possible. Aspirations for self did not vanish at the point of "disclosure." Rather, it may not be for some years after that mothers begin the process of assembling a story of what it has all come to mean. It is, perhaps, in their midlife years and as a response to some of the typical events of midlife that some mothers begin to really understand what it has meant to be mothers of disabled children. The inability, or reluctance, of services to adopt a more rounded view of mothers' lives from the beginning is paid for by mothers painfully losing something of themselves. Measor's (1985) notion of "critical incidents" being like a "flashbulb" is well illustrated in Jill's account below, with the repeated use of the phrase "all of a sudden." Behind Jill's felt distress was a sense that her strategy of "being like anyone else" was becoming an immensely awkward and demanding one. It no longer held.

I don't do anything really. People know that after, well, once Sarah comes in at four o'clock, I'm finished . . . I can't . . . anything that crops up of an evening time, I can't do, I can't. Well, I just can't do it. I mean, going back to what you were saying about family situation, it was, I think it was my sister's 30th wedding anniversary a couple of months back. It was all arranged. My brother-in-law had organized a night out. There's a boat down at the bay there. You know, he'd hired that out as a surprise and everyone was hush-hush, and it was all exciting. Everything was organized and I was taking Sarah because, you know, as I say, I didn't have a sitter. And all of a sudden, I just rang my other sister at seven o'clock in floods of tears and I said, "I'm not coming." She said, "Don't be stupid. What do you mean, you're not coming?" And I said, "I can't," and all of a sudden I just couldn't handle it. I said, "I can't. To get Sarah sorted out, to get myself sorted out and then to come home." I'd planned everything, I was going to get a black cab to come home and put Sarah to bed, and I just . . . it was all too much for me. All of a sudden I felt, "This is just too much to do." It was too difficult to get out and she said, "Oh! We'll come and collect you, don't worry. We'll look after Sarah." It was just . . . everything was on top of me, you know. All of a sudden I just thought to myself, "Oh look, don't try and be like the others because you can't be." I do try and I think sometimes you do try to be the same as everybody else. When something like this happens, it just hits home to you that you're not a family like others. So don't try and pretend you are, because you can't do it. My sister tried all ways. She came around all, "Oh come, it'll be great," and I said, "I just can't," and I was just really screwed up. I said, "I've just had enough of it, I've had enough of trying to keep up a brave face," and now and again it just takes over, you know. It's just too much trouble. It's too much.

As their children begin to age and some leave the family home altogether, and as their peers begin to acquire different lifestyles, this group of mothers viewed the middle years as a turning point in their lives or as a form of identity transformation (Strauss, 1992). That is, they began to feel they were not the people they once thought they were. During these years, and in contrast to the time when their other children had lived at home, many mothers anticipated or felt they would receive less support in their caring duties. The following comment is interesting for the way it suggests that a certain transformation in perspective might occur during these years, that is, the change from being a mother to a carer:

The kids would come in from school and first thing they'd make a cup of tea, watch *Neighbors,* and I'd say, "Keep your eye on Sarah a minute, will you?" and I would prepare tea. That's gone completely. Thinking of the teenage years, in my circumstances, I was not a carer until, say, the last 5 years.

Discussion And Implications

The first chapter of this book set out some of the complexities of, and challenges for, comprehending family quality of life. In a very modest fashion, our chapter underlines rather than resolves many of these challenges. It emphasizes, in particular, the need to look at family life in the round and with some understanding of its dynamic qualities. We recognize the value of defining the notion of family and how the quality of life of a family, or any other collective, rather than that of individuals can be understood as important. However, we do little to develop such understanding. Rather, we prefer to realize that it is typically mothers who are charged with the responsibility of managing and maintaining a day-to-day sense of family, regardless of, and sometimes at the expense of, their participation in other social groupings and activities. How mothers of children with intellectual disabilities define family, its quality, and their responsibility for both seems to be an important task for refining and developing family quality of life.

Furthermore, our approach is also partial in that it is largely qualitative. Such an approach does seem to maximize the potential of the concept of quality of life to reveal important but hidden concerns in peoples' lives, as others in this volume have argued. It encourages individuals to identify the salient and relevant content and plots of their lives, and how parts of them ought to be interpreted. It permits a new perspective on what living as a mother of a child with intellectual disabilities implies by urging that mother to reveal the rounded and living individual behind the maternal mask. It must be stressed that this can be a difficult and awkward task for mothers, given the felt prohibitions outlined above. There remains, however, the task of coupling quantitative and qualitative data together. This is not a simple exercise, since it is not so much the type of data that distinguishes one mother from another, but more their assumptions about the world from which data are obtained. Bringing research findings together is, therefore, a difficult exercise, but one that encourages and requires reflexivity and circumspection.

The data above deal with moving perspectives of the ways individuals update and integrate the past, present, and future, and the perspectives that emerge from the interaction among the individual, time, and society. Thus although mothers may share some concerns by virtue of their status as women and as mothers of children with intellectual disabilities, there is much that distinguishes them from each other, in particular as a result of their unique biographies. The link between individual and society has intrigued sociology for decades; there may be much to learn from endeavors in that field, because in this interaction a sense of quality is constructed. In the accounts provided by parents, quality of life cannot simply be read off from their status as parents of disabled people, from their age, or from the

range of services they receive. Rather, it requires a more detailed understanding of many components that might make for a quality of life. Further,
as generations pass, what counts as quality of life may change and a younger
cohort of mothers may have very different views of what life ought to be like.
Our views need regular updating and some degree of sensitivity to historical
as well as cultural differences. Groups of parents may be separated by place
and time.

We have approached some of these concerns through the concepts of
identity and biography and through narratives—devices mothers use to exert
some control in identifying the salient features of their lives for particular
audiences. We have done so in the belief that a notion of the quality of living is found in the way lives are lived out within certain temporal, cultural,
and historically determined spaces, and by particular individuals. Identity
refers to that understanding of oneself that is shaped in time, social interaction, and self-awareness. It refers not simply to the way one is known by others, but also to the way one wishes to be known by others. The motivations
and aspirations of the self can also provide the basis for a sense of well-being
(Simon, 1997; Thoits, 1992). In the way it involves a relationship between
self and others, it refers to the "goodness of fit" between individuals and the
world around them. This appears to be one instrumental way of thinking of
quality of life. Furthermore, and inasmuch as these relationships alter in
time and are projected into the future, individual biographies provide some
important insights into the implications of becoming and being the mother
of a child with intellectual disabilities. For many, but importantly not all, the
data suggest that being and becoming a mother of a child with intellectual
disabilities poses a number of identity and biographical puzzles for women.

There seems to be one key feature that differentiates their lives from
other mothers, and this feature is more than just having a child with intellectual disabilities. It is, as Redmond (1997) described, that they "acquire
professionals in their lives." At one level, the number of services and professionals to which parents have access is an important measure. However, the
data about services and professionals do not describe the quality and impact
of those potential resources. The data here suggest that, although parents
have found themselves at the middle of a greater professional network, this
situation may contain some risks. Mothers may all too easily view these relationships as restricting and based upon a form of pernicious supervision. The
threat revolves around the identity of mother, the quality of which can be
called into question. For some mothers in particular, having their roles and
contributions as mothers validated and valued is crucial to their sense of self.

This surely has implications for professional practice, and, in particular,
for basing interactions with parents around the issues of empathy and building upon rather than detracting from existing parental competencies, as

Nolan, Grant, and Keady (1997) have argued. More open-ended or equalized relationships between professionals and parents may have important outcomes, but they must also permit more of the person behind the parental mask to be revealed. Interestingly, mothers themselves were unsure whether such concerns were legitimate. Yet they had a powerful impact on the experience of what it means to be a mother of a child with intellectual disabilities. Beyond making these desires legitimate and unremarkable, the issue becomes one of thinking creatively about matching support to the type of lives individuals feel are personally important to them. For some of the mothers in this study, this is about reducing that palpable sense of differentness and disruption that marks out those middle years. Examples in this study include employment and social and recreational activities, areas that have been identified as important in an increasing number of studies of mothers of children with intellectual disabilities (Shearn, 1998).

We have argued elsewhere that such an approach presents difficult challenges for service development. It requires that we move beyond the limited and possibly misleading use of the term *respite* to think more proactively. We have used an understanding of identity at both theoretical and practical levels to identify and build upon those aspects of support that might maintain a salient or preferred identity (Felce et al., 1998; Todd & Shearn, 1996b). In short, it is about identifying those features of support that are interpreted as supportive (Lynam, 1990) and aligning them more closely to an active and dynamic model of family lives (Nolan et al., 1996, 1997).

The ways individuals make sense of their lives alters over time. Becoming the mother of a child with intellectual disabilities does not, in one instant, change the very foundations of a woman's life. Nor does it seem immediately to require a new definition of self. There is a resolve that the status of their children will not alter their sense of competence and identity, at least in terms of their personal identities as "ordinary mothers." One should not, therefore, be seduced by a notion that being the mother of a child with intellectual disabilities implies becoming a different type of person. The future need not yet be transformed and the past still seems a solid enough anchor for living in the present. There exists some commonality of experience with other mothers. There exists a level of coherence. It is not until the years pass that the contexts of mothers' lives change, so that previous views of oneself and one's life are called into question. For some, there are very positive answers to be found from their past lives. For others, there is a sense of fracture. These may be painful years. The issue here, from a quality of life perspective, is the extent to which there are opportunities for self-fulfillment, and clearly there appear to be few. Do mothers dare to be ordinary? It is in these years that such a question becomes increasingly daring and therefore under resourced.

We end this chapter with Pauline's concerns and desires for the future. It captures many of the concerns we have raised throughout this chapter. It is undoubtedly personal. It also contains those sticky and difficult emotions that we feel are shared by many parents and points toward the need for a more substantive study of the emotional contexts of parenting a child with intellectual disability. Emotions do not reflect the character of an individual, but rather the shortcomings of the world in which we live. Thus when it comes to the ambitions of family quality of life, it is that time when parents no longer wish to outlive their children that we might begin to think that the efforts and hopes of the past are beginning to bear fruit.

Pauline's Dream

What of the future? Almost every family I know that cares for an intellectually disabled relative lives very much from day to day. The future is a particularly scary place. Services change, key people leave their jobs and move on, policies come into place that look for "efficiency savings," and the vulnerable and less articulate are easy targets for money-saving politics. We can't afford to do more than raise our eyes from the common daily tasks, and look up occasionally into such an unknown and fearful place as the future.

But I do fantasize, of course. If I won the national lottery (unlikely, since I rarely remember to buy a ticket!), I would buy a beautiful piece of land and build homes for my son and others like him. There might be individual flats and houses, some staffed, some not, some shared, some not, where families could take their relatives to choose what kind of home they would like. Some would offer more or less independent living, others would have live-in staff, selected by the residents to care for their needs. There would be beautifully kept gardens and grounds, maybe a football pitch, a bowling green, a nine-hole golf course, a swimming pool and a decent medical centre. It goes without saying that I would of course hire the most imaginative architect to design and build these masterpieces of real estate!

My desire for the future is to find some space in my life without my son. This must sound dreadful to you, but I would like to look forward to being in charge of my life a little more and for John and I to have more quality time together. That's how it is for most parents after all, so why should it be different for me? To go away for the weekend, or on holiday, would be wonderful.

We both get very tired, especially when Matthew has a sequence when he won't go to bed until two in the morning. I think that we both feel we've come to the end of the line in terms of what we can provide for him. We feed him, clothe him, care for him, and give him his own space. But most of his activities are facilitated by others these days, and we would just like that little bit of extra time to ourselves.

The trouble is that I cannot see this happening. But I still keep it as a goal. There is no money to accommodate those people living with their families. Unless and until we get too old, or become ill, I cannot see Matthew ever leaving us. I can't dwell on this, or I would be racing to the doc for pills. So it is put a long way on the back burner of our thoughts.

I know what would be ideal for us all: Matthew in a good, caring, but not isolated, environment; us nearby for visits and trips away with him, but able to make choices about things that we [now] have no control over; visits away; long days out; and regular good nights' sleep. I think when you have a disabled child/adult you cannot afford to be too fanciful. The things that most people take for granted are not always open to you and so they become the goals toward which you turn your thoughts. You also have to believe that one day they will happen. Otherwise, you'd drive yourself insane, I think.

I don't think you can be fully yourself as the parent of a disabled son—who you are, what you want. You are always subsumed by the greater responsibility and role of caring. It is always there, lurking in the back of your mind even when you are physically away. "Is he okay? He is very vulnerable. What if they don't realize he gets badly sunburned? He shouldn't drink Coke. He has no road sense. He won't tell them he wants the toilet."

I think parents only want peace of mind. But how do we get it? Well, some form of appropriate care in a good setting for their offspring before they become too old to care is what all parents would say. That means slightly different things to each of us. We all worry about abusive carers, neglectful regimes, and cost-cutting exercises that will adversely affect our children. All of us will carry those worries into our graves, if there is not a consistent process developed within our society that offers continual high-quality care to our relatives. This brings me back to the desire of many of us carers that our daughters and sons with disabilities should die before us. Even thinking that thought makes me feel guilty! But I know from conversations with other mothers, most often when we are on our own, that this guilt-ridden hope is a common, if private, one. Although we would like to believe that in some future time and place we could confidently entrust our children to a caring community, current experience makes us believe otherwise.

Pauline Young

References

Ackerman, R. L. (1990). Career development and transitions of middle-aged women. *Psychology of Women Quarterly, 14,* 513–530.

Annandale, E., & Hunt, K. (1998). Accounts of disagreements with doctors. *Social Science & Medicine, 46,* 119–29.

Audit Commission. (1987). *Community care: Occasional Papers No. 4.* London: Her Majesty's Stationery Office.

Baldwin, S., & Glendinning, C. (1983). Employment, women, and their disabled children. In J. Finch & D. Groves (Eds.), *A labour of love* (pp. 77–96). London: Routledge & Kegan Paul.

Bassoff, E. (1987). Mothering adolescent children. *Journal of Counselling & Development, 65,* 471–474.

Baxter, C., Cummins, R., & Polak, S. (1995). A longitudinal study of parental stress and support: From diagnosis of disability to leaving school. *International Journal of Disability, Development, & Education, 42,* 125–36.

Bayley, M. (1973). *Mental handicap and community care.* London: Routledge & Kegan Paul.

Bury, M. (1983). Chronic illness as biographical disruption. *Sociology of Health & Illness, 4,* 167–182.

Carr, D. (1997). The fulfillment of career dreams at midlife. *Journal of Health & Social Behavior, 38,* 331–344.

Carricaburu, D., & Pierret, J. (1995). From biographical disruption to biographical reinforcement. *Sociology of Health & Illness, 17,* 65–88.

Chamberlayne, P., & King, A. (1997). The biographical challenge of caring. *Sociology of Health & Illness, 19,* 601–621.

Charmaz, K. (1987). Struggling for a self: Identity levels of the chronically ill. *Research in the Sociology of Health Care, 6,* 283–321.

Coyle, J. (1999). Exploring the meaning of dissatisfaction with health care. *Sociology of Health & Illness, 21,* 95–123.

Department of Health. (1995). *Carers (Recognition and Services) Act 1995.* London: Author.

Elder, G. (1994). Time, human agency, and social change: Perspectives on the life course. *Social Psychology Quarterly, 57,* 4–15.

Evans, G., Felce, D., de Paiva, S., & Todd, S. (1992). Observing the delivery of a domiciliary support service. *Disability & Society, 7,* 19–34.

Evans, G., Todd, S., & Beyer, S. (1994). Assessing the impact of the All-Wales Strategy. *Journal of Intellectual Disability Research, 38,* 109–133.

Felce, D., Grant, G., Todd, S., Ramcharan, P., Beyer, S., McGrath, M., Perry, J., Shearn, J., Kilsby, M., & Lowe, K. (1998). *Towards a full life.* London: Butterworth Heinnemann.

Gergen, M. (1990). Finished at 40: Women's development within patriarchy. *Social Psychology of Women, 14,* 471–493.

Giddens, A. (1991). *Modernity of self-identity: Self, society in the late modern age.* Cambridge, UK: Polity Press.

Grant, G. (1993). Support networks and transitions over two years among adults with a mental handicap. *Mental Handicap Research, 6,* 36–55.

Grant, G., & McGrath, M. (1990). Need for respite: Care services for caregivers of persons with mental retardation. *American Journal on Mental Retardation, 94,* 638–648.

Grant, G., McGrath, M., & Ramcharan, P. (1994). How family and informal supporters appraise service quality. *International Journal of Disability, 41,* 127–141.

Griffiths, Sir R. (1988). *Community care: Agenda for action.* London: Her Majesty's Stationery Office.

Hareven, T. K. (1982). *Family time and industrial time.* Cambridge, UK: Cambridge University Press.

Heaton, J. (1999). The gaze and visibility of the carer: A Foucauldian analysis of the discourse of informal care. *Sociology of Health & Illness, 21,* 759–777.

Kiernan, K., & Wicks, M. (1990). *Family change and future policy.* York, UK: Joseph Rowntree Foundation.

Levinson, D. J. (1996). *The seasons of a woman's life.* New York: Knopf.

Lynam, M. J. (1990). Examining social support in context. *Sociology of Health & Illness, 12,* 169–194.

Martin, J., & Roberts, C. (1984). *Women and employment: A lifetime perspective.* London: Department of Employment/O.P.C.S.

Measor, P. (1985). Critical incidents in the classroom: Identities, choices, and careers. In S. J. Ball & I. F. Goodson (Eds.), *Teachers' lives and careers* (pp. 61–77). Lewes, UK: Falmer Press.

Mitchell, V., & Helson, R. (1990). Women's prime of life: In the 50s? *Psychology of Women Quarterly, 14,* 451–470.

Mitchell, W. (1999). Leaving special school: The next step and future aspirations. *Disability & Society, 14,* 753–771.

Nolan, M., Grant, G., & Keady, J. (1996). The Carers' Act: Realising the potential. *British Journal of Community Health Nursing, 1,* 317–321.

Nolan, M., Grant, G., & Keady, J. (1997). *Understanding family care: A multidimensional model of caring and coping.* Buckingham, UK: Open University Press.

Oakley, A. (1980). *Women confined.* Oxford: Martin Robertson.

Oswin, M. (1984). *They keep going away.* London: King Edward's Hospital Fund for London.

Parker, G. (1990). *With due care and attention: A review of the literature on informal care.* London: Family Policy Studies Centre.

Parker, G., & Lawton, D. (1994). *Different types of care, different types of carers.* London: Her Majesty's Stationery Office.

Perry, J., Felce, D., Beyer, S., & Todd, S. (1998). Strategic change: Development of core services in Wales, 1983–1995. *Journal of Applied Research in Intellectual Disability, 11,* 15–33.

Riches, V. (1996). A review of transition from school to community. *Journal of Intellectual & Developmental Disabilities, 21,* 71–88.

Redmond, B. (1997). Family support services: The need to challenge old stereotypes. *Irish Social Worker, 15,* 4–7.

Shearn, J. (1997). *Only mothers: The experience and meaning of employment for mothers of children with learning disabilities.* Unpublished master's thesis, Cardiff University, Wales.

Shearn, J. (1998). Still at home: The participation in paid employment of mothers of children with learning disabilities. *British Journal of Learning Disabilities, 26,* 100–104.

Shearn, J., & Todd, S. (2000). Maternal employment and family responsibilities. *Journal of Applied Research in Intellectual Disabilities, 13,* 109–131.

Sheehy, G. (1991). *The silent passage.* New York: Random House.

Simon, R. W. (1997). The meanings individuals attach to role identities and their implications for mental health. *Journal of Health & Social Behavior, 38,* 256–274.

Strauss, A. (1992). Turning points in identity. In C. Clark & H. Robboy (Eds.), *Social interaction* (pp. 135–158). New York: St Martin's.

Suelzle, M., & Keenan, V. (1981). Changes in family support over the life cycle of mentally retarded persons. *American Journal of Mental Deficiency, 86,* 267–361.

Thoits, P. A. (1992). On merging identity theory and stress research, *Social Psychology Quarterly, 54,* 101–112.

Thorin, E., Yovanoff, P., & Irvin, L. (1996). Dilemmas faced by families during their young adults' transition to adulthood. *Mental Retardation, 34,* 117–120.

Todd, S., & Jones, S. (1999). *Mothers at midlife.* Cardiff, Wales: WCLDARU.

Todd, S., Shearn, J., Beyer, S., & Felce, D. (1993). Careers in caring: The changing situations of parents caring for an offspring with learning difficulties, *Irish Journal of Psychology, 14,* 130–153.

Todd, S., & Shearn, J. (1996a). Time and the person: The impact of support services on the lives of parents of adults with learning disabilities. *Journal of Applied Research in Intellectual Disabilities, 9,* 40–60.

Todd, S., & Shearn, J. (1996b). Struggles with time: The careers of parents of adult sons and daughters with learning disabilities. *Disability & Society, 11,* 379–402.

Todd, S., & Shearn, J. (1997). Family secrets: Parental management of disclosure. *Disability & Society 12,* 134–178.

Twigg, J., & Atkin, K. (1994). *Carers perceived.* Buckingham, UK: Open University Press.

Welsh Office. (1983). *The All-Wales Strategy for the Development of Services for Mentally Handicapped People.* Cardiff, Wales: Author.

Wikler, L. (1986). Periodic stress in families of children with mental retardation. *American Journal of Mental Deficiency, 90,* 703–706.

Wikler, L., Wasow, M., & Hatfield, E. (1981). Chronic sorrow revisited. *American Journal of Orthopsychiatry, 51,* 63–70.

Williams, V., & Robinson, C. (2000). *In their own right.* Bristol, UK: Norah Fry Research Centre.

Woodill, G., Renwick, R., Brown, I., & Raphael, D. (1994). Being, belonging, and becoming: An approach to quality of life for people with developmental disabilities. In D. Goode (Ed.), *Quality of life for people with disabilities: International perspectives and issues* (pp. 57–74). Cambridge, MA: Brookline.

Chapter 6

Family Quality Of Life In Israel

**Shimshon M. Neikrug, Jean Judes, Dana Roth,
and Batya Krauss**
Tel-Hai Academic College
Upper Galilee, Israel

The pessimist resembles a man who observes with fear and sadness that his wall calendar, from which he daily tears a sheet, grows thinner with each passing day. On the other hand, the person who attacks the problems of life actively is like a man who removes each successive leaf from his calendar and files it neatly and carefully away with its predecessors, after first having jotted down a few diary notes on the back. He can reflect with pride and joy on all the richness set down in these notes, on all the life he has already lived to the fullest. . . . He will think, "Instead of possibilities, I have realities, not only the reality of work done and of love loved, but of sufferings bravely suffered. These sufferings are even the things of which I am most proud, though these are things which cannot inspire envy." (Viktor Frankl, 1959/1986, p. 144)

Family life with a child with a developmental disability may not inspire envy. Indeed, there may never have been a woman who, in the long nights during her pregnancy, did not pray that *it* would not happen to her and her family. "It" is having a child of realities instead of a child of possibilities. "It" is having a life that includes the hardships and sufferings that accompany raising a child with a disability. The fears of an increasing percentage of these women become realities as medical science gives the gift of life to infants who until recently would not have survived. Their survival with disability and the growing numbers of families raising children with disabilities makes accurate knowledge regarding family quality of life important and valuable.

When we consider the way our society values beauty and productivity, it is easy to understand the bases of fear of having a child with disability. In our society stereotyped, negative images of people with disabilities are presented in many places, including the mass media, literature, folktales, and hostile jokes. These are abusive to the people who are the brunt of these images. These images of disability are pernicious and destructive to the well-being of people with disabilities and their families even when they are not based on objective reality. In addition, these images of future family life are, all too often, based on stereotypic, unrealistic information. Young parents have little access to accurate information that would help them meet life's challenges realistically.

In this chapter we seek to provide an improved understanding of families with developmental disabilities in Israel based on realities rather than stereotypes. We shall attempt to deal with several of the major cultural, political, and social issues that affect the lives of people with disabilities, their families, and caregivers in Israel. We shall also attempt to understand better the unique day-to-day challenges facing families with developmental disabilities by developing a picture of the service delivery systems and various organizational supports available to individuals and families. Family quality of life in families challenged by disability is to a large extent related to the quality of services that are intended to meet their needs. Finally, we intend to explore the issues that contribute to the quality of family life: supports and services as they play out in a particular sample of families that have children with disabilities in Israel.

Origins Of Health And Welfare Services In Israel

The State of Israel was established in 1948, at which time the central government took responsibility for developing health and welfare services for the population. The new state did not need to develop a service system from scratch, but rather was able to build on models that had their roots in two sources: Israeli health and welfare services developed from the Jewish charitable tradition on the one hand, and the social traditions that the pioneers who founded the new state brought with them from the countries of their origin on the other hand. Traditional Jewish concepts of welfare developed from a religious obligation from biblical and rabbinical law. These developed into a complex system of human services that operated in most of the countries of the Jewish Diaspora. Jewish health and social services developed because, in many of the countries of the Diaspora, organized services did not exist, or, if they did exist, as second class citizens Jews were not allowed to avail themselves of the public philanthropic services or of the services provided by other religious traditions.

Until the modern period, the care of people with disabilities or chronic disease took place in the home. The community offered financial help when needed, and surgeons and barbers (who applied leeches and let blood as well as cutting hair) attended the ill and disabled in the home. As early as the 11th century, Jewish communities throughout Europe began developing regular organizations, called societies (*chevra*), to better organize and specialize charitable activity. The societies offered a wide range of services, including providing tuition grants for indigent students, free loan societies, "bridal" societies to organize weddings for the poor, and burial societies. Among the most universal of these societies were the Bikur Cholim societies which organized home visiting and care for the chronically ill and disabled, provided for medical and nursing care, assisted in the purchase of medicine, and offered spiritual consolation.

In the modern period, as services became more professional and bureaucratic, the organized Jewish communities formalized their concern for the disabled. In the Jewish communities of the Diaspora, the trend to professionalism became superimposed on traditional values and practices. In most cases the traditional societies were replaced by specialized services for those who were blind, deaf, intellectually and physically disabled, and others.

As Jews immigrated to Israel throughout the 19th century, the religious charitable societies responsible for the establishment and management of health and welfare services accompanied them. Toward the end of the 19th century, world Jewry became concerned about the greatly distressed health conditions in the Holy Land. Through support and assistance from Jews in the Western countries, the first hospitals were established in the major cities.

During the early years of the 20th century, the wave of immigration coming primarily from Eastern Europe brought with it the socialist concepts being developed in their countries of origin. Socialized health clinics were developed throughout the country, freeing the new settlers from dependence on the system of religious- and charity-based services. These clinics were supported by the workers' movement and later developed into a highly modernized and professional health system.

When the State of Israel was established in 1948, human services became the responsibility of the new nation-state. Health and welfare services became the concern of national policy rather than a religious and humanitarian issue, but the central government did not replace the various services already in place. The fact that there was already a vibrant, although fragmented, welfare system in Israel eased the task of the new central government, but it created a situation that would continue to interfere with the development of comprehensive, planned service.

Three major forces worked in parallel to determine the nature of health and welfare in the country. First, there was a strong traditional voluntary sector that traced its origins back throughout Jewish history. Second, a movement toward socialism imported from Eastern Europe and Russia brought new values and concepts of social organization. Third, the concept of the "welfare state," which was then flowering throughout the Western world, had a strong impact on the newly developing governmental sector. This unique history has led to the development of a complex social welfare and health system. The health system includes services based on: (a) direct governmental action (government hospitals, ministerial policy, and tax-based funding); (b) public, nongovernmental, health-maintenance organizations (the continuation of the labor union sick funds and health clinics); and (c) services based on private philanthropy. All three sectors succeeded to survive and develop over the years. Together they provide special-needs children with health services, special education, psychological counseling and support, paramedical services, occupational therapy, pensions, institutional and community housing, assistance in making housing and public buildings accessible, and information services.

A significant improvement in the situation occurred in 1995 with the passage of the National Health Law. The new law strengthened, but did not replace, the outdated and ineffective sick fund structure. It guaranteed universal and compulsory health coverage and a basic "basket" of services for all Israeli citizens. The result is that, at the present time, families that use predominantly the services included in the "basket" receive a generally adequate level of health service. Indeed the quality and cost of service in Israel is on par with the European standard. Israel falls between Ireland and Norway with an expenditure of 7.6% of gross domestic product on health service.

Families with special health needs that are dependent on frequent use of numerous services, and services not included in the general basket, find themselves in a complex system of public services, services partially government funded, private services, fraternal services, union-affiliated services, and others. These all have different catchment areas, eligibility requirements, and fee structures. Families with disability often find themselves torn between the rules, regulations and demands of numerous service organizations that have little or no structures for interfacing and coordinating their services.

Current Sociopolitical Trends

The social and political environment for families challenged with disability and other special needs populations exists within the general sociopolitical trends that affect all families in Israel. Israel today is a complex society with a growing hi-tech, start-up, "yuppie" class alongside serious social problems. These problems include political insecurity, uncontrolled unemployment, and the rapid development of an underclass. The present situation has been particularly complicated for the families with special service needs. Families with problems stemming from disabilities are further challenged by these general problems.

In Israel, the sociopolitical environment is changing quite significantly. As in many other countries, the processes of privatization, budget cuts, and tightening eligibility requirements are well under way. The health system of hospitals, clinics, and other services organized by the labor movement was once a monopoly covering over 90% of the population. The National Health Law has brought competition to the health delivery system. Now at least three others (nongovernmental organizations or NGOs) compete with the labor union health system to enroll clients into their health insurance schemes. The result of these conditions is that, as government moves to limit its responsibility for offering services, services in the public nongovernmental sector are under pressure to become increasingly cost-effective and many special services are being cut back or eliminated completely.

The Finance Ministry is a powerful actor in the efforts toward budgetary cutbacks and privatization. Government promises of high benefit outlays by the National Insurance Institute create the impression of an increase in government spending for social services. However, most of the social service ministries will not spend significantly more than they have in the past and some of them (i.e., Ministry of Education) face significant budget cuts. The 1998 budget represented the third consecutive year of stagnation or erosion of Israel's social service budgets. The Education budget for 1998 was similar to that of 1997. The health system budget expanded by 4%, but this increase is in a deficit-burdened system that neglects vital needs, such as long-term nursing care (Swirski, San-Zangy, Connor, & Swirski, 1997).

While government is cutting back on its human service commitments to its citizens' well being, gains are being made in advancing the civil rights of people with disabilities. Efforts are being made to more fully integrate people with disabilities into all aspects of community life. The Special Education Law (1988), amended in 1991, has included child development services in the National Health Insurance Law. The age of eligibility for disabled child benefits from the National Insurance Institute has been lowered from 3 years to newborn. The Equal Rights for Persons With Disability Law (1998) was a breakthrough. This law addresses issues of equal employment and access to public transportation, but it has yet to be implemented. A commission was to have investigated the lack of implementation but has not managed to resolve the issue. There is considerable optimism that this legislation will be implemented soon, and that it will set the basis for equal opportunity in social life as well as in law.

At the same time as government is cutting back on human services, the voluntary sector is hard pressed to pick up the slack. At this time, it would be good if not-for-profit organizations could expand in response to these cutbacks. However, private philanthropy from abroad is under siege by hundreds of small Israeli NGOs of various sorts for financial help to compensate for the erosion of their funding base. This undermines the centralized organization of Jewish charities, and places the NGOs in competition with each other. The organized Jewish communal philanthropy from abroad is under considerable pressure to rechannel funds to needs of the Jewish communities at home. In addition, many Jewish communities abroad are confused about the quality of the relations between Israel and the Jewish communities in the Diaspora, and about the areas of tension that have developed between these traditional partners. This may further weaken the base of philanthropy from abroad. Israeli internal philanthropy is still in the early stages of organization and is still too weak to offer a solution.

In summary, families that have children with disabilities in the State of Israel receive many services, grants, and benefits. The problems are due to two situations: the lack of a coordinated service delivery system, and the breakdown of the values of the welfare state. Families of children with developmental disabilities are served by a complex, and not very well integrated, system that is in disarray, lacks a stable funding base, and has no clear organizing concept. The result is that families are served by a number of organizations of different and often-competing auspices, which offer service of different quality and at different cost levels to the family. Often there are major service gaps. Information on the availability of service and eligibility of the client is unavailable or even intentionally withheld. With the welfare state in Israel undergoing retrenchment, which includes serious cutbacks in universal access to human services, there is greater inequality than ever before. Rural areas, minorities, and the poor receive significantly less service. In these times of emphasis on the global economy, ever smaller segments of the population control an increasingly large portion of the wealth. The existence of a rapidly growing for-profit sector offers the wealthy an alternative to the universal sectors described above and siphons off a potential force for social change by distancing the wealthy from the problems of the less fortunate.

In Israel, as well as in many other developed countries, we begin to see what may be termed a postmodern stance of mistrust toward government and its potential for providing quality services to the population. This stance potentially extends to the political process and to the main institutions of the society—the military, social welfare and social justice. What is emerging is that citizens are no longer able to believe in the ability of the political process to bring peace, the military to provide security, and the state to provide adequately and fairly for the needs the poor, the disabled, and the minorities. At this point, there develops a social ecology wherein all families worry about their ability to provide their children the quality of life to which they strive. Alternatively, when families challenged by disability and other groups under pressure are able to create quality family lives, they become a source of hope for the society as a whole and proof of the hardiness and sustainability of our families and our communities.

Special-Needs Children In Israel

As indicated above, services to children with developmental disabilities and other special-needs children are provided under various auspices. These include the National Insurance Institute (the Israeli social security system), the Ministry of Health, the Ministry of Labor and Social Affairs, and the Ministry of Education. In addition, services are provided by the local government, health insurance programs (health funds), as well as private, voluntary associations, religious and philanthropic organizations, and a growing for-profit industry. Perhaps because of the fragmentation of the service system, until very recently there were no central statistics regarding the population of special-needs children, their needs, or the degree to which the existing services meet those needs.

Since 1981, children 3 to 18 years of age with serious disability are eligible for an allowance from the National Insurance Institute. The law that allowed for this was amended in 1991 to include children from birth to age three. Now that all children with disabilities are receiving public funds, the first accurate and reliable set of information regarding the prevalence of children with developmental disabilities and other accurate statistics are becoming available.

The criteria for the child disability allowance are quite severe and only 14,000 of the 160,000 children in Israel with disabilities qualified for an allowance from the National Insurance Institute in 1999. At age 18, youth are no longer children by legal definition and become covered by the General Disability Allowance, also administered by the National Insurance Institute. The data describing the population of people with developmental disabilities who have reached age 18 years is quite interesting. Of all individuals receiving the General Disability Allowance, only 15.9% have developmental disabilities. For 93.3% of these individuals, the allowance is the only source of income. Their physical condition is considerably worse than the condition of the rest of the General Disability group. Fifty percent of the individuals with developmental disabilities had 75% or higher medical disability, as compared to only 34% of the entire General Disability population. Interestingly, although the percentage of people with problems of internal medicine is relatively low among the developmental disabilities group, the percentage of hospitalizations in the developmental disability group is significantly higher than other disabilities (Wasserstein, 1998).

There is even less known about people with disability who are over the age of 18 years than about children with disability. There are 38,600 veterans of the Israel Defense Forces with disabilities of 10% to 40% severity, and some 11,100 people with work-related disabilities of 20% to 40% severity. The largest group of people with disability for which there are statistics are the 113,300 aged 18 to 65 with a medical disability greater than 40% severity and who receive various types of benefits from the National Insurance Institute.

These statistics do not include less severely disabled people, nor those who are employed and earn more than the disability benefit. These people are not eligible for additional benefits and do not appear in the statistics.

People with disabilities over the age of 65 receive old age pensions and receive no supplementary benefit, and thus are not counted in the statistics.

Recently the first comprehensive study of services to families and children with disabilities was carried out by the JDC–Brookdale Institute and the National Insurance Institute (Naon, Morginstin, Schimmel, & Rivlis, 2000). This study focused attention on the population of noninstitutionalized children with "special needs" in Israel, using a multidisciplinary medical, professional, and paraprofessional panel to evaluate and estimate the actual percentage of children who require special services. Because it is a source of valuable information, a number of its findings are described below. The data presented are based on three sources: (a) a subset of a national survey of all children in Israel; (b) face-to-face interviews with the families of the children sampled; and (c) a panel of professionals who reviewed the cases to determine the degree to which the needs of the children were being met.

The national survey and face-to-face interviews showed that 12.8% of children in Israel who lived in the community could be defined as special-needs children, with 40% of those having multiple disability (as compared to the 5% of children in Israel who qualify for a General Disability Allowance). The concept of special-needs children includes: (a) 4.3% of all children in Israel who have chronic diseases or other problems that do not impair functioning or require constant care, (b) 0.8% who have problems that interfere with function on a temporary basis, and (c) 7.7% who have long-term disabilities and require ongoing medical care. The types of services received by special-needs children, and the percentage of children who currently receive each type, are shown in Table 6.1.

The data in Table 6.1 show that most special-needs children are receiving at least one special service. However, less than 40% receive specialized medical care, and only about one third receive paramedical care. The findings indicate a severe and significant degree of underservice for children with special needs (only 2% receive more than one service). The lack of service is notable in all areas but most blatant in the area of information to the family and psychosocial services. The findings for the subpopulation of children who receive Disability Allowance show that these children are comparatively better served. Of these children, 66% receive specialized medical care, 63% receive paramedical therapies, 27% receive psychosocial treatment, 62% receive special education, 57% get supportive services, and 20% receive information and guidance.

Table 6.1
Percentage Of Identified Special-Needs Children
Who Receive Various Special Services

Medical Services	**39**
Treatment by specialist	35
Various medical treatment	5
Homeopathic service	2
Paramedical Treatment	**34**
Physiotherapy	10
Occupational therapy	15
Speech therapy	11
Sports/art activities	16
Nonconventional treatment	1
Psychosocial Services	**19**
Treatment by psychologist	15
Treatment by social worker	6
Educational Services	**51**
Private teacher	26
"Big Brother"	8
Special education	27
Supportive Services	**26**
Individual nurse care	0
Individual nonprofessional	17
Transportation	23
Information and Advice	**12**
Receiving at least one special service	83
Receiving more than one service	2
Receiving Social Insurance payments	8

In general, the service that these children receive falls far short of the amount of service that the children should receive based on professional criteria. Comparing the recommendations of the professionals in the panel to the figures above provides another way for us to see how severe the underservice is for the families of children with disabilities. The panel found that 75% of the children should be receiving paramedical therapies (compared to 33% in 2000), 83% should be receiving psychotherapy (compared to 18% in 2000), and 69% of the families should be receiving information and counseling (compared to 0.9% in 2000).

The reports by a panel of professionals, commonly called the Naon Report, are another source of information. Table 6.2 shows the Naon Report percentage of children by age group who were reviewed by the multidisciplinary panel and found not to be receiving the services that they require on the basis of a purely medical evaluation. One striking finding here is the considerable degree of underservice for school-age children. Psychosocial services for the child and advice (counseling) services for parents are particularly problematic in all age groups.

Table 6.2
Percentage Of Special-Needs Children Not Receiving Required Services For Three Age Groups

	Age 0–5	Age 6–11	Age 12+
Medical Services	28	51	58
Paramedical Services	30	52	58
Psychosocial Services	78	77	77
Educational Services	77	58	64
Supportive Services	48	24	44
Information and Advice	86	82	92

A further breakdown shows that the gap between received and required services is greatest for children with developmental disabilities and those with physical disabilities. Those with chronic illness are somewhat better served compared to those with what is referred to as disability of the senses, such as being blind or deaf (Naon et al., 2000).

The Naon Report also looked at the degree and extent of the inequality with which these children received special services (Naon et al., 2000). Among the most important factors associated with inequality are age of the child, minority status, and area of residence. Children birth to age 5 receive relatively fewer services, and children ages 6 to 11 receive the most services in all areas except psychosocial service. Children 12 years and older again receive fewer services in all areas except psychosocial service. This is due to the fact that services offered by the educational system do not continue when children leave school, even when they are needed.

People with disabilities suffer from lack of adequate service as adults as well as during the younger years. There is a growing awareness of the need for more employment opportunities for adults with developmental disabilities. This includes sheltered workshops and the development of additional solutions outside the sheltered framework. Currently there are only about 11,000 people with disabilities employed in sheltered employment services, while a similar number await placement. Of the 11,000 people employed, only a very few are in supported employment positions on the open market. Most of the people in sheltered employment earn a very low wage and the work is repetitive and low-level.

Level of services is also related to size of towns and cities—the smaller the town, the less service is received. People living in low socioeconomic towns and villages typically receive less than one half the amount of service as the population as a whole. In addition, people living in minority villages receive only about one third the amount of service as the national figures (Naon et al., 2000). The findings of the Naon Report also indicated that a considerable degree of the inequality in service between various sectors is due to income. The poor suffer more. The study found that 92% of the children from families at high socioeconomic levels received at least one special service to meet their needs, compared to only 67% of the children from families at very low socioeconomic levels. Shockingly, 42% of the children from families at high socioeconomic levels received paramedical therapy compared to only 6% of the children from families at very low socioeconomic levels. In the area of education, similar inequality was found. Of children from families at high socioeconomic levels, 39% received private lessons to meet their needs, compared to only 8% of the children from families at very low socioeconomic levels.

Rural families, when compared to urban families, experienced problems with transportation to the main centers, lack of availability of quality services for the general population, and low income. In urban areas, 93% of all special-needs children received at least one special service, whereas only 67% of such children in the outlying towns received one special service. Supportive learning services (in mainstream education) were provided to 59% of all urban special-needs children, but only to 33% of such children in rural areas. In the main cities, 42% of these children received at least one of the paramedical services (e.g., physiotherapy, speech pathology), but only 20% of special-needs children in rural areas received such services. In rural areas with a very low socioeconomic profile, the proportion of children with disabilities is particularly large: 11% as compared to 7.7% of the total population of children in Israel.

Arab families also suffer unequally. A number of factors combined to result in a severe underservice for Arab families. The rural Arab population is more financially distressed than the rural Jewish population and is politically weaker. There is a shortage of Arab students in the medical and paramedic fields. There is a major shortage of trained professionals who speak Arabic. While 43% of Jewish children with special needs receive service from medical specialists, this is true for only 21% of Arab children. The same inequality is to be found in the other service areas. Among the more glaring examples are psychosocial service is 21% for Jewish children with special needs as compared to 8% in the Arab sector, paramedical treatment is 39% compared to 9%, and sessions with a private teacher is 30% for the Jewish sector compared to 7% in the Arab sector. There is a growing awareness of these inequalities and several Israeli NGOs have tried to intervene, but the gap between the rural Arab population and the predominantly urban Jewish population is considerable. Beit Issie Shapiro, the institutional partner in our study, has instituted two major initiatives to develop services in the Arab sector, but, without a major commitment of government to improve the quality of service to the poor, the minorities, and the rural areas, this is proving challenging.

Family Quality Of Life In Israel

The Family Quality of Life study in Israel has consisted of looking at the subjective reports of parents of children with developmental disabilities in order to understand the degree to which the families have found satisfactory solutions to the problems facing the family as a whole. The goal is to explore and measure family quality of life in families that have children with developmental disabilities and to identify factors that contribute to the improvement of quality of life of children with disabilities who live with their families.

This project has adopted the premise that family quality of life is the primary environmental influence on quality of life for children. We attempt to understand the concept of family quality of life by investigating the various dimensions that have been identified as being related to quality of life in the literature. This is seen as a first step to understanding how quality of life can be improved in the families of the children we serve. We attempt to study the subjective reports of parents of children with developmental disabilities to determine the degree to which the family has found satisfactory solutions to the problems facing the family as a whole. The emphasis is placed here on family attributes, which can collectively be referred to as quality of life of the family as a whole. It is our position that a family that has found such satisfactory solutions not only lives in a way that brings benefits for the family as a whole, but also is improving the quality of life of children with disabilities. Thus the quality of life of children with disabilities and the quality of life of their family members are interwoven, both influencing and depending upon one another.

The initial thrust for an Israeli study resulted from the interest on the part of Beit Issie Shapiro, our partner agency. The organization is interested in developing measurement methods of family quality that are able to detect any changes in the life of the family as a result of the treatment of the child with disability. During the course of treatment of the child with disability, there is a tendency to view the outcomes of the treatment process on the child-as-individual. The family-oriented service philosophy requires an information system that is sensitive to the outcomes of treatment in the entire family system. The practical application of the study will be the understanding of how the treatment of the child affects the family as a whole and how improving the lives of children with disabilities requires the improvement of all-over family quality of life.

It is easy for the service system to underemphasize the importance of family in the lives of the children being served. It is also easy to ignore the effect of service for the child with disabilities on the family as a whole. Children with disabilities often leave home early in the morning and return from their schools and therapy programs late in the evening with little time or energy left for meaningful interaction with their families. They are often seen by service providers as living in a closed system that includes the child, teachers and therapists, but that is distant from the family. How professional interventions affect family life is often ignored or relegated to a position of minor importance.

The main direction of the present study is to gather information on the levels of family quality of life in relation to the various domains of family life in families with disability. The focus of this work is on factors that contribute to family quality of life. Further research should relate to questions such as: Is there a relationship between the therapeutic gains of the child in the agency and the quality of life in the family? Is there a relationship between gains in quality of life for the family and personal, social, and behavioral effects on the child with disability?

Instrument

In our exploration of family quality of life, we used the Family Quality of Life Survey (Schalock et al., in press). This instrument was developed out of the efforts of the three-country initiative in research of family quality of life: Israel, Canada, and Australia. The Survey was developed through the collective expertise of the international research team, and from their considerable discussions over time. The instrument addresses nine key domains of family life: (a) physical health, (b) financial well-being, (c) family relationships, (d) support from other people, (e) support from disability-related services, (f) careers and preparing for careers, (g) spiritual and religious concerns, (h) leisure, and (i) community and civic involvement. It is the theoretical premise that these domains contribute significantly to family quality of life when considered in terms of: (a) how things in the domain are viewed at this point in time; (b) optimism or pessimism: the likelihood that things will improve (in at least some of the domains) or get worse in the future; (c) the availability of opportunities for all family members; (d) access of family members to the available opportunities (skills, barriers, and enablers); (e) initiative for taking action to improve and provide hope for the future; and (f) satisfaction with things as they are.

A Hebrew language version of the instrument was developed for the Israeli study. A pretest of the instrument was carried out to determine the quality of the translation and the appropriateness of the instrument in the Israeli context. The translation was presented to a panel of respondents similar to the parents to be included in the study, and, after amendments were made, a Hebrew language version was finalized.

Sample

The Family Quality of Life Survey instrument was used in comprehensive interviews with a group of families with children with multiple disabilities that agreed to participate in the project. The sample is composed of parents of children with multiple disabilities who are leaders in the Israeli Forum for Families With Children Who Have Multiple Diagnoses. The purpose of the Forum is to draw attention to the special conditions and needs of children who have multiple diagnoses and to bring about social and political change. The organization also serves as a self-help body that offers information and considerable mutual emotional support to its members.

The leadership of the Forum was chosen to be included in the study. The leadership of the organization includes a cross-section of ages, socioeconomic status, countries of origin, education, as well as children of a range of ages from age 5 to late teens. The members share a commitment to social activism and social change for the benefit of their children. Not only were they central in the organization and establishment of the Forum, but also they are active in other disability-related organizations. They are well known in the community, and many sit on committees on the national and local government levels.

Two of the authors (Neikrug & Krauss) met with 20 members of the Forum individually in their homes and participated in meetings of the organization. The interviews were conducted using the Family Quality of Life Survey as an outline only. The sessions were informal and lasted an average of 2 hours each. We approached the sessions in an exploratory manner giving the respondents considerable freedom to direct the sessions. The information was organized into the nine key domains of family life of the research instrument. The parents we spoke with were willing to discuss their problems, but they were quick to point out that, in addition to the problems, there is much quality in their lives that never gets recognized. They wanted the experts and professionals who serve them and their children to know their strengths as well as their problems.

Because the sample is composed of leaders of the Forum who are activists and advocates, we do not imply that their quality of life is in any way representative of other families. Our interest was to learn about the way these parents view their families. We are concerned more with the similarities that they share than the variability we find among them. The data were analyzed qualitatively to identify trends and patterns. In the following sections we will relate the major areas of similarity among the families. We will attempt to describe their shared problems of family life, as well as the ways that they strive for solutions. We will include statements of the families as they describe the ways they strive for quality in their lives.

Israeli Families With A Disabled Child: Findings

In this section, we report on the findings of our interviews with the 20 families. We present the findings around three themes: family stress, service delivery, and informal community and family support. Throughout, the "voices" of the parents themselves are used to illustrate our findings.

The Voice Of The Families

Razi is my own special child. He was my first-born child. Now he is 8 years old with blond hair and a killing smile. Razi also has enough problems to fill several textbooks. Since Razi was born I had two more beautiful sons who have no more problems than they should for their ages and BINGO we are a family. Nothing happens to anyone of us that doesn't happen to us all. Whether it is Re'emi cutting another tooth, my husband working until midnight and coming home to find me a basket case, or the operation for Razi's legs that we are trying not to think about—all these happen to us as a family. When I want to check how things are going in my life, first I check out my family's quality of life.

When Razi was born 8 years ago, there was no sense of tragedy. He was born by Cesarean section in the 28th week of my pregnancy because I was in a state of advanced toxemia and there was concern for my life. My husband is a scientist, and I was a young social worker then. We had great faith in the medical system with all the advanced equipment and the highly trained staff. We were sure that they would keep our baby alive and all would be right.

All the delays in development that we noticed in the first months of Razi's life were due, we were assured, to Razi's being born prematurely. When we finally received the diagnosis of cerebral palsy, we were well on our way to being adjusted to the idea that we had a "special-needs" child. We were managing and we believed that, when we would need help, it would be there for us. Indeed, our first experience with the service system went very well. At age 18 months we placed Razi in the therapeutic daycare program for babies at Beit Issie Shapiro. Even though I was not totally uncritical of the services that Razi received, we felt that we were understood and supported and that we were getting the care for Razi that he needed. At the time, we didn't know how rare those feelings would be in our continued contacts with the service delivery system.

Rather early on it became clear to us that the other children in Razi"s classes would be his friends for many years to come, just as we would be in contact with their parents. We began to encourage conversations with other parents. We found that many of the hurts that we felt were not idiosyncratic responses to our personal situation, but part and parcel of the experience of raising a child with severe disabilities. Mostly, we all had similar problems securing the public services that are necessary for the quality of life of children with disability. Not the least of the complaints we heard was the fact that public agencies saw the few laws and administrative guidelines that protect the rights of our children as being "suggestions" only. The service system was not morally or practically bound to honor those rules or make them known to the families. Second, any expression of displeasure or complaint was disregarded and interpreted as a projection of anger that originated in the ambivalent feeling that parents have toward the child and the disability.

By the time Razi was 3 years old, my husband Ari and I were meeting regularly with other parents, socially and informally, and we were sharing information and experiences. We were clear that our responsibility as parents requires that we provide for our children every opportunity that will allow them to improve their functioning and reach greater independence. This meant that we were going to have to learn how to deal effectively with bureaucrats who see their role as protecting the public purse from parents with insatiable demands and that we could not do this successfully in isolation from other parents.

During the past 5 years, we have grown into a formal organization. We have a name: Israeli Forum for Families With Children Who Have Multiple Disabilities. This year the Ministry of the Interior listed us as a not-for-profit organization. I became the general director of the association and Ari is on the board of directors. It is a family affair. The Forum has all the early signs of success. I already have the home telephone numbers of the social issues journalists of the various newspapers, and they expect to get newsworthy material from me. I am in regular contact with dozens of members of Knesset [Israel's parliament], and I am a familiar figure in the halls of the Knesset building and in the various committee meetings. We have 250 active members and our newsletter is passed out at most of the special schools in Israel.

We are challenged by the very severe problems (only we know how hard "multiple disabilities" can be), and yet we are able to find quality in our lives. We think that this says much for all families with problems. When I think of my life and my family, I hear the voices of all the families of children with severe disability. For, although we are different, we are so much the same. Our lives are so heavily dominated by the same hospitals, doctors, therapists, form filling, chauffeuring, and waiting and crying, that the differences among us are less than the similarities. We organized the Forum so that the voice of the families could speak to the professionals, to the decision makers, to the politicians, to those who have access to their ears, and to those who want to hear us because they care.

A current example of how our public activity in the Forum relates to our family quality of life is our efforts in getting better schooling for Razi. He now is in a private school for children with cerebral palsy. It seems to me that the better situation would be for Razi to learn in a special class integrated into the same school system as his brother. He would be included in the aspects that he can be part of, and separate in those parts that should be geared to his special educational needs. But we cannot bring this situation about no matter how much money we might have and how much energy we might have invested to make this happen. By working through the Forum and bringing the weight of the Forum to bear on the issue, though, we can improve Razi's chances for a better education and improve the chances for a better education for all children with disabilities.

In preparation for this paper, I met with the leadership of the Forum individually in their homes and interviewed them according to the Family Quality of Life Survey used in the Israeli study presented above. The members viewed this context as an opportunity to raise our voice and be heard. Because of the fact that I, too, am a mother of a very special child and a leader in the Forum (or in spite of these facts), the families that I interviewed accepted me into their homes and shared very difficult and intimate material openly with me. There was a strong willingness to participate in this study and to understand its importance. I speak for us all when I say that there is so much quality in our lives that never gets recognized and that should be known especially to the experts and professionals who help us but who often only see our problems. It was understood that we would be able to inform the study with our perceptions of life with a child diagnosed as having multiple disabilities.

Our members viewed this as an opportunity to raise our voices and be heard. This is an opportunity for us to be the authors of the information about our lives and not simply the subjects of studies. This is an opportunity for us to have our voice heard.

Batya Krauss

Family Stress

Many of our initial observations correspond to the findings in previous studies. These show that the existence of a child with a disability challenges the family's ability to function well to meet its needs and adapt to the ever-changing pressures of the environment. It should not be surprising that we found that living with a child challenged by disability is a source of strain on the family system. The literature documents numerous stressful and problematic aspects of care giving (Anthony-Bergstone, Zarit, & Gatz, 1988; Biegel, Sales, & Schulz, 1991; Seltzer & Krauss, 1994; Turnbull, Brotherson, & Summers, 1986). Studies that compare parents of disabled children with parents not challenged by a child with disability show that parents of disabled children score significantly higher on stress (Beckman, 1991).

The existence of a child with a developmental disability taxes all the family's resources. Our study gives strong support to the reality of the difficulties of families with a child with disabilities. What is surprising is that we found that these families are able to meet the challenge and raise their families optimistically and successfully. They even find the time and energy to participate in their communities and take part in social action.

The single most frequent problem raised in our interviews with parents is related to the high cost of securing special services. The cost is expressed in terms of resources, finances, and emotions, energy, and time. Family resources are stretched to the limits. The family is hard pressed to offer the care and give attention to all family members equally, due to the drain of resources that the special needs of a special child require. To the family committed to meeting the needs of all its members fairly, the challenges of the future can seem insurmountable.

As in other research, financial problems and emotional strains are characteristic of most of the families we interviewed (Wallander, Pitt, & Mellins, 1990). Almost all the families, at all the socioeconomic levels, raised the problem of finances. This is explained by the extremely high cost of services and equipment that is not supported by government allowances. Private school fees, therapeutic horseback riding, swimming, supplementary physical therapy, other therapies, special equipment, home adaptations, and other expenses are part of the long list of additional and "optional" services that parents want to offer their special-needs children. They do this along with trying to meet the needs of their other children in a fair way. Finances were identified as the greatest barrier to service delivery. Often the desired service was not available or was not included in the "basket of services" offered by the government, and private family insurance is very rare in Israel. Much of the family income goes to providing special services at the expense of extracurricular programs for the other children, vacations for the family, and the other "extras" that are important to family life.

Time strains and tiredness were the next most commonly mentioned problems. There are not enough resources in these families (time or energy) to give their children what they believe they require while managing the needs of all the family members. This was true of the more affluent families as well as the less affluent. The needs are greater than the resources.

You ask about finances. Well, we are a lucky family. Both my husband and I are well-paid professionals. By Israeli standards we can be considered well to do. Because of our child's disability, we receive the maximum allowance from the government: $536.85 a month. We did a budget that includes therapies, school fees, transportation, diapers, and babysitters and it came to $1,050. This does not include practical nursing, medicine, and the one-time expenses such as a computer (and software), wheelchair, special bed, etc., or lost time from work. We somehow manage to give all these services to our child . . . What do less fortunate families do? Are they always compromising? Do they always feel guilty?

The Problems Of Services

Children with multiple disabilities and their families have many of the same fundamental problems as other families with disabilities. However, as our respondents pointed out, children with multiple disabilities clearly have more unmet needs and are more dependent on the service system. The ability to make use of existing services is, to a great extent, dependent upon the family's motivation for the service and its ability to accept the way services are offered. Motivation to seek and use services may stem less from the characteristics and needs of the child and more from the family's perceived need for services and the optimism that the benefits from services will outweigh the difficulties inherent in receiving them (see also Dunst, Trivette, Hamby, & Pollack, 1990; Margalit, Raviv, & Ankonina, 1992; Rimmerman & Portowicz, 1987). There is an implicit economy in which the family weighs the expected advantage of the service against the effort, time, family stress, and other costs of participation in the service.

Research has shown that many families in need of help are not connected to professional services (Smith, Fullmer, & Tobin, 1994; Wood, 1993). On the other hand, social workers and other helping professionals often find that families are resistant to their outreach efforts (McCallion & Tobin, 1995; Sutton, Sterns, Schwartz, & Roberts, 1992). These findings are not paradoxical. The single most virulent criticism of, and dissatisfaction with, the service delivery system expressed in our interviews with parents was related to the hurts involved in securing needed services.

> To get my son's leg braces paid for, we had to prove that our son could walk. This seems reasonable, but our son has cerebral palsy and can't walk. He needs braces for improving his posture. They tell me the rule dates from the time of the big polio epidemic of the 1940s when all children who could be helped to walk with braces where given them. The criteria were never changed to include children like our son with cerebral palsy who may never walk but still will benefit from the braces. To get the braces we need from the system, I put chocolate a few steps in front of him so as to encourage him and said, "Now, Honey, try and walk for the nice man." He took two bumbling steps and fell on the chocolate. This was so demeaning! Getting the braces was important, but it was not necessary for it to be so cruel.

There are several issues that recurred in our interviews with the families regarding the difficulties involved in interfacing with the service system. These difficulties include: getting information, proving eligibility, coordinating, wasting time, managing the system, repeatedly giving the same information, as well as the negative physiological meanings inherent in the process. As indicated above, the service system in Israel is composed of a complex set of public, private, philanthropic agencies as well as others that don't fit neatly into these categories. The complex rules, regulations, and eligibility requirements are not rational, and this often results in service lacuna or overlapping of services. Not only is this complicated for families, but also the time and emotional energy spent in engaging with numerous agencies that have little communication among them, attending staffings, and developing relationships with professionals from different systems, taxes the already overburdened families.

In spite of these burdens, the families maintain contact with the service system and request more service, not less. The families in our study expressed strong feelings about being relegated to a back position in the decision process regarding important decisions about their children. In the 1990s there has been a shift in the role of families in the service agency. The literature shows that, when family-centered and service-oriented approaches are adopted, a considerable degree of family satisfaction has resulted. Many professionals in Israel feel that services are moving away from agency-centered approaches in assessment and intervention and moving toward a family-centered approach. The families are still very critical. There are still significant differences between parent and staff views of the actual and desired level of implementation of family-centered services.

As parents become more knowledgeable about service systems and better understand the nature of their children's problems, they feel more able to identify what services their children need. Most parents we interviewed felt that their children were not receiving necessary therapies, medical care, or special education. This feeling was a source of both anxiety and anger.

Families identified problems of accessibility among the many barriers to services. Many families said that inadequate coordination and accessibility of services was a major cause of unmet needs. Coordination of services and lack of information and guidance regarding the service delivery system may be particularly important for families of children with multiple disabilities.

Other families related to the arbitrary nature of the rules and regulations of the system. One family complained that they were told not to buy a wheelchair for their child, as it would interfere with his motivation to walk. The family chose the wheelchair to increase the child's independence. Not only did they not get support from the therapists in this, but also they were told that they were being bad parents. Another parent spoke about the tyranny of the rules and regulations:

> This is my dilemma. My child is mentally retarded and deaf. She can go to a special school under the auspices of the Ministry of Education. She is, however, also a cerebral palsy child, and cerebral palsy children must go to a school for the physically disabled where she won't learn even the basic skills of living that they teach in the school for the mentally retarded. So I can choose to give her an education at the price of her having malformed legs. This is crazy!

Considering the depth of the feelings that questions about the relationship between families and agencies brought up, it seems wise for agencies to consider developing a family-centered approach to policy and practice. There must be recognition that the family is the constant in the child's life, while the service systems and support personnel within those systems are typically only a temporary element. The family-centered approach to policy and practice is based on a philosophy of organizing assistance collaboratively, in accordance with an individual family's wishes rather than on the basis of overall policy. Individualizing family services and practice, focusing upon the family as the unit of attention, and structuring service delivery so as to ensure accessibility and minimal disruption of family life, would be major steps forward in improving the relationship between families and agencies (Higgins, 1997).

Informal Family And Community Support

One general set of questions presented to the respondents concerned the support system within the family and the support provided by the community of friends and relatives. We found that the predominant family system among our families was a clearly defined nuclear family composed of a child or children and one or two natural parents (parents in one family were divorced, and those in a second were separated). We also found an actively engaged, extended family that was in close (even daily) contact, shared in the division of labor, and is referred to—often together with the nuclear family—when the respondents gave information about their "family." The parents felt that the extended family (their siblings and their parents) was somewhat more involved than they would have been if not for the disability. Sisters and mothers (especially on the maternal side) were most often cited in connection with direct childcare and instrumental tasks such as shopping and transportation. In part, this may be due to the relative lack of mobility of the Israeli family with parents, siblings, and other family members living in the same cities and often in the same neighborhoods.

Almost paradoxically, the families indicated a clear preference for the nuclear family being responsible for meeting its own needs, with as little additional help from extended family as possible. We found a hierarchy of preference in which the family: expects and demands help from formal services; strives to meet other needs by nuclear family resources (especially when there are older children without disability); accepts help from neighbors, especially for typical neighboring activities (babysitting, shopping, etc.); turns to good friends for emotional support; and sees the family of origin as being there for every type of need (including financial aid, acting in *loco parentis*, etc.), but should be turned to sparingly and "saved for a rainy day."

Within the nuclear family, the findings were related to the place of the family in the family life cycle. In the younger families, the fathers took over many direct-care, housekeeping, and kitchen tasks, although most mothers still accepted more responsibility in these areas. As the families age, paid help became more financially possible and the other children took more responsibility in family activities, thereby giving the mother more respite time. Sharing of family tasks was common (and somewhat more egalitarian) in families where both parents were employed outside the home. The majority of mothers interviewed were working outside the home in career jobs. Several mothers explained that working not only brought in necessary funds, badly needed to pay for special services, but also gave the mother much needed respite from the problems of the home.

> There are still millions of things we'd like to do for our son that we can't, but much of what we can do is because of help we get from family, friends and just good people. For example, my parents live close by and do hundreds of things for us. One neighbor has four teen-aged and young adult girls who give all my kids love, attention, babysitting, and even make them little presents from time to time. The instructor at the nearby pool gives 2 hours each day to kids with disabilities—free of charge. We do okay financially. We're not a welfare family by any means, but we would be able to do a lot less if we didn't get help. As I see it, the people who help us benefit as much as we do.

In general, we found that helping is also related to residential location. The urban families were making more use of formal services than rural families who relied more on informal services. In contrast, among all our respondents, only the rural family living in a kibbutz received adequate formal and informal support. The kibbutz is organized in a way that families can readily access services. However, the kibbutz movement in Israel is experiencing difficult financial and philosophical strains and is also privatizing and cutting back on services. Still, it seems that the kibbutz is far more able to adjust to the special needs of its members than the more typical rural or urban living situations.

We found an interesting and inverse relationship between the family's insecurity and low sense of efficacy of their parenting, and the use of informal supports. The parents with most need for informal support were often least able to access the informal support system. It is as though receiving help is another sign of their incompetence as a family. The more secure parents found it easier to ask for the information and assistance necessary for them to make good decisions and solve potential problems. In addition, family adaptation in the less able families was further challenged by the behavior problems that are often associated with disabilities. Both children with mental retardation and those with chronic illness exhibit significantly more behavior problems compared to children without disability (Gortmaker, Walker, Weitzman, & Sobol, 1990). It has been found that behavior problems in children with disabilities are predictive of poor family adjustment (Wallander et al., 1990). In our study, where most families were strong and functioning well, there were few feelings of being threatened or embarrassed by the problems of their children. Yet our families felt that there is a considerable proportion of families that are embarrassed to the point that they are not willing to seek informal help that would lead to better family adjustment.

In Israel the governmental and nongovernmental sectors are offering a greater variety of services today than ever in the past. These informal, local, community supports are often critical for successful family functioning. The ability of the family to overcome the difficulties and access these supports is often a major predictor of successful family functioning.

The Strength Of Families

Providing care to a family member is, for many families, a rewarding experience and a source of loving pride. The literature shows that caring for a child with special problems over time is beneficial to the quality of family organization. For example, Seltzer, Greenberg, Krauss, Gordon, and Judge (1997) noted that siblings of adults with mental retardation were significantly more likely than siblings of adults with mental illness to perceive that the brother or sister had a pervasive influence on their life decisions and to evaluate their sibling experience as mostly positive. In addition, siblings of adults with mental retardation had a closer relationship with the brother or sister with the disability than siblings of adults with serious mental illness.

The good news that permeates our study is that, despite the stress, there is a strong sense of family in Israel, and it usually manages to function in the face of severe stress. The son, daughter, brother, or sister with the disability is, in the families we interviewed, a part of a dynamic system that includes that child in a loving, protective, family nest. In the face of significant stressors related to the disability as well as the stressors affecting all families in Israel, these families function remarkably well. If we had expected to find a group overwhelmed by the problems of raising a family under the conditions described above, we could not have been more surprised. In fact, we found the members able to be powerful, resourceful people, actively engaged and seeking help from others to plan strategies and tactics. We found people able to think creatively and reflectively about their situations and the situations of others, and to act purposefully.

The families tend to adapt to, and compensate for, the problems presented by the special children without significant negative impact on functioning of the whole family unit. The findings of several studies elsewhere suggest that this is true in other families as well (Gallimore, Weisner, Bernheimer, Guthrie, & Nihira, 1993; Kazak & Marvin, 1984; Saddler, Hillman, & Benjamins, 1993).

Our interviews indicated a tremendous capacity for care, love, and resilience in the families. In general, the parents felt that they were able to develop the necessary social competence and problem-solving skills necessary to manage the challenges that caring for a child with disability has placed before them. These families indicated a considerable ability to adapt to the increased demands of caring for the special needs of the child with disability, finding the resources to meet these special demands, and, at the same time, meeting the usual demands placed on the modern family and all its members.

Successful adaptation to disability does not mean that the families have the ability to access all the necessary supports and services. The families were clearly struggling to cope with their children's unmet needs, and to reduce disability-related problems for the child and family. However, for most of these families the inability to solve all their problems was not an indication of family incompetence. Rather it is seen as societal failure. There is a strong resistance to accepting negative messages about oneself and family. The families do not see themselves as being dysfunctional. They maintain a sense of family identity and a sense of their ability to act and to exert some control over their environment. They seem to have developed a critical understanding of disability-phobia in society and have developed a natural awareness of the structures of oppression. They see such organizations as the Forum as a context for creating strategies for overcoming them. We asked one father, after he described his typical "36-hour" day, to explain how he had the time and energy to be active in the Forum and work for social change. He answered that it is his anger at service agencies and his activism that keeps him going.

Discussion: Thinking About Family Quality Of Life

Our present study has adopted the premise that the quality of family life is the primary environmental influence on developing quality of life for children. We have come to understand that quality of life in its broad sense is what all families want, though they may mean very different things by this term. In this study we have taken the position that quality of life relates to specific domains of living (e.g., income, health, opportunity, relationships, services, values), which, in turn, reflect and describe the degree and nature of a particular family's "good life."

Dynamic Patterns Of Family Life

The image that is developing for us is that the holistic view of family quality life is composed of specific domains of living that come together and approximate a recognizable pattern. The pattern that each family develops is a reflection of its values. For several of the families we interviewed, the "recognizable pattern" had to do with social activism and advocacy and the other dimensions of life clustered around that theme. Another family may find that its involvement with its faith community gives shape to the wholeness of its life. For a third family, "getting by" or "doing well" may be the basic pattern that gives structure to its life. Within the basic pattern, the other dimensions find their place. How each dimension fits into the developing pattern is, at times, unclear. Families are often aware of the apparent incongruity of the different aspects of their families' lives. As one father told us in droll humor, "If asked what is more important to me, work or family, I'd say, 'Family, of course! Why else would I work 16 hours a day?' "

Measuring family quality of life is a complex undertaking. The various dimensions that comprise the whole of quality life are of different sizes (or importance), and they increase and decrease in size along with life's vicissitudes. Some dimensions are readily seen as inherent parts of the family pattern. Other parts don't easily fit into the family style. What is more, the entire pattern is in dynamic rotation, turning as different aspects become more or less central in the life of the family over time. One dimension may be responsible for much of the family quality of life and then, in a moment, the whole pattern rotates. At that point, one dimension may lose its meaningfulness while another takes its place.

In life, the dimensions are in a dynamic condition of change. Dimensions such as health, social support, or finances can change abruptly as the family's fortunes change. A family with normally high satisfaction with its quality of life can perceive things very differently if interviewed during the hospitalization of the main family provider. On the other hand, the change process can be so slow in evolving that the family members are unaware how much they have changed. Our goal is to find the family patterns that are presumed to be of a more long-term character and should provide relatively constant quality of life scores over time, in spite of life's fluctuations.

Resilience

We have found, contrary to what may be expected, that our families are surprisingly resilient. They have a great capacity to do well while facing extremely difficult life situations. Our evidence leads us to support prior research and theory in human development that has clearly established the innate capacity of families for resilience. Resilience is the result of having such traits as self-esteem, self-efficacy, autonomy, and optimism, and it also encourages the development of these qualities. Families are surprisingly able to develop social competence, problem-solving skills, autonomy, and a sense of purpose in the face of considerable adversity. They reflect a strong critical consciousness of the role of oppression in our society and how it affects quality of life. This understanding can be the basis for cooperation toward positive social change.

As we attempt to understand how family quality of life can be improved, we also realize the importance of the social service agencies. How professional interventions with the person with a disability can improve (or decrease) family quality of life is often ignored or relegated to a position of minor importance. Service agencies can do much to support family resilience. Agencies can encourage the development of social support and social action networks based on models similar to the model of the Forum mentioned in this chapter. True cooperation between family and agency may not only improve direct service, but also be a powerful force for social change. Agencies can also learn more about the knowledge and the skills families have developed through the necessity of managing family life in the face of disability. Families have important expertise, and that expertise can and should be brought into the service organization.

Social service agencies communicate expectations by the way they are structured and organized. Policies that support resilience respect the way humans behave. Policies that are inclusive of multiple perspectives—especially those that include perspectives of silenced groups—advance a critical consciousness that supports resilience. Services can build from perceptions of family strengths and can create ongoing opportunities for self-reflection, critical inquiry, problem solving, and dialogue.

It is our hope that this study will underscore the importance of family quality of life for professionals in the agencies that support families with children with disability. We have seen that even highly resilient families can experience significant detriments to their quality of life when service agencies do not operate on the basis of a family-centered approach to policy and practice. We have presented a view of families that struggle to raise a child challenged by disability, to meet the needs of other children in the family, and to fulfill the family responsibilities placed upon it in our society. This is a tribute to the inherent strength of the family. However, to achieve a positive quality of life, families struggling with disability need "empowering environments." To create these empowering environments, agencies that provide services to individuals with disabilities have to change the way they serve their clients and, in the process, to help clients maximize their quality of life.

We still have a distance to go to reach a more definitive conceptualization and measurement of family quality of life. We wish to extend our study to a more representative sample of families with disability. We must gather information on Israeli families without disability and compare them to families with disability. As we continue, we hope that our study will throw increasing light on the nature of the concept of family quality of life.

Quality Of Life 20 Years Down The Road:
An Advocate's Perspective

Several years ago we began to understand that Razi not only had cerebral palsy, but that he was different in another way. My husband, Ari, and I had to adjust to the terms *autistic* and *multiple diagnosis.* We also had to adjust to the fact that the problems that we faced in obtaining adequate services for a "normal" cerebral palsy child were nothing compared to the problems in dealing with the service system around the "multiple diagnosis."

Children with autism and cerebral palsy are caught in a labyrinth of rules, regulations, and confused responsibility. Ministry of Health, Ministry of Welfare, the HMOs all are somehow involved. The Ministry of Education is theoretically responsible, but lacks even the minimal resources. Even within the Ministry of Education, there seems to be very little communication between the "special" educational system with the associated entitlements for therapies and the "normal" education system where inclusion may be possible.

The problems that we are facing increasingly have less to do with dealing with the bureaucracy to receive entitlements. More and more, they are about the fact that adequate alternatives for children with multiple disabilities simply do not exist. It became clear to us that if Razi is to have any chance at all for a "normal" life in the future, new alternatives will have to be developed. This requires not only political pressure, but also systemic societal change. We could not even consider doing this alone. Ari and I are not alone. Other parents were dealing with the same problems as we are. What will be necessary in the future will be to change the agenda from managing the system to creating social change.

In general, things are getting better in Israel. Two years ago the adults with disabilities staged a major sit-in strike in front of the Ministry of the Treasury. For weeks, people in wheelchairs were shown in all the media as they braved the Jerusalem winter to bring the most absurd of the administrative regulation to public awareness. We brought our children and sat in protest with them. Since then there have been many signs of change. The Knesset has passed the new equal rights law for people with disabilities and an overseeing agency has been appointed. We see more and more people with disabilities on television talk shows. There are public service broadcasts on television showing the effects of the hurtful and illegal barriers to the mobility of people with disabilities. There is still much to be done, but, at least for the present, we feel that we have access to the public ear in a way that was not available before.

We are trying to stay in the public eye. In any case, families like ours are in the public eye. My family has long accepted the fact that people will stare at us. It doesn't matter if we want it or not. People can't help staring. Does this mean that we should hide from the public, or should we work toward change? It is normal to stare at people who are different, but there are different types of staring. Now I say, "Come! Look! Learn! Do!" There are thousands of potential advocates out there—we just have to get them.

I am telling all this as the preface to discussing our family quality of life as we see it today and as it seems that it will be years from now, in the future. The quality of our family life is tied to the quality of life of the many hundreds of other families in our situation, and it will have to continue to be this way in the future. Perhaps it is tied to the quality of life of all people in Israel who are challenged by differentness of all kinds.

Our responsibility to our family has become integrally involved with our responsibility to our society. In the future, it will be even less possible to achieve what we need as a family by our own efforts. We must bring more and more parents, grandparents, friends, and people with understanding hearts into the process. We must attract more key people to advocate for the necessary social changes, and we must be in the public agenda.

Along with the positive signs that augur for a better future, major worries loom ahead for my family. As great as the difficulties of arranging adequate education for Razi has been, the worries of what will be after the age of 20 are far greater.

In many ways, Israel is leaving its socialist past behind, and postmodern, global, changes are occurring in many areas—but not in the area of services for people with special needs. The Israeli government, through its agents, "knows" what is best for the child and for all Israeli children. Social policy has little concern for individual differences. Today the government's answer for people with severe disability is to place them in institutions. There is actual hostility to group homes or other means by which people like Razi could live in normal neighborhoods with neighbors and a community.

Finances strongly influence policy. An institution receives $4,000 per month to care for a severely disabled person. Living outside of an institution, the same person receives about $700, the same as a legally disabled person who is able to meet his own problems of community living. Israel, today, may be the only modern society that is building new institutions for people with severe disability and is proud of it! True, these are small institutions of 16 to 30 beds, but they are nevertheless institutions in all ways. This may be an outgrowth of the Israeli romance with group living, as in the kibbutz movement and the army, but in our own lives we strive for privacy and freedom of choice. The major goal for the future is to guarantee that people with disabilities should be able to claim to live as others do as a right.

I expect that my family will become a vanguard in bringing about the necessary social change. Both Ari and I come from strong religious families where we learned values of social justice and social responsibility. We would have been active in social issues even if we did not have a child with disabilities, but probably without the same degree of passion. Social action has been a positive contribution to our family quality of life until now and will be so in the future. Social action is not an additional problem that draws energy and resources away from the family. Social action has changed us from being victims of a cruel fate, to actors, leaders, navigators of our lives. We would not have chosen this to happen, and I cry more than I wish to, but it did happen.

Our family cannot deny that Razi's special needs have led us all to our involvement with the social problems of disability. If one of our children were a very successful athlete, we would be gearing our life to his schedule of competitions and travel around the world. Our family life is contingent upon the needs, desires, and interests of the members of the family. The quality of our family life is dependent on how well we succeed in living our family life. This is the kind of family that we are. Being involved with Razi and making it possible for him to lead a normal life is a source of pride for us. In many ways, it is both a drain on all our resources, as well as a source of strength and family growth.

As Razi's brothers grow, they will have to make some kind of adjustment to the facts of Razi's different-ness. It is our job to lead them to loving acceptance, just as it is our job to lead them in the direction of moral responsibility in general. We will have to do this through an awareness and respect for their special-ness and a loving support for their own separate life interests and goals. In the end they will make their own lives and the directions that they take will cause us, as a family, to readjust to them. How well we do this will either add or detract from the quality of our family life.

It is our hope that the quality of our family life will not be dictated to us by the conditions in which we find ourselves. We create the quality of our family life in the way we interpret the things that happen and in the ways that we act in the face of these realities. We can either reenforce our self-image and our self-respect, or we can act in ways that lead us to shame and loss of self-respect. For us, quality of family life is being a family of quality people. The struggle for quality of family life is only in part an issue of dealing with disability. To a much greater extent, it is the result of being courageously committed to making the world a better place. This is the challenge that we take upon us as a family.

A high quality of family life is necessary if we, as parents, are going to be able to raise all our children to be emotionally healthy, secure, and optimistic adults who will eventually take on the challenge of being parents themselves. What contributes to our positive quality of family life is the implementation of our values into our everyday life. The more we are successful in doing this, the more quality we experience. One of the main things that I have learned in meeting the parents of other children is that families vary widely in their values, and that families differ greatly one from the other. What makes us happy and proud and gives quality to our life is different from those things that are important to others. What is good and right for our family may differ greatly from the next family. The service system would do well to understand this and take into account what we want and need as a family when they make decisions about our children. It is our task to learn how to communicate with them so that they see us and hear us and understand how we can be colleagues in creating ability.

Batya Krauss

Conclusion

We wish to conclude with the voice of one family:

We are the parents. We are responsible for our families. We do a heck of a good job meeting our responsibilities. We are parents of all our children. Although you often only consider the needs of one of our children, we are the family for all of us. We are the best families our children will ever have. We are the ones who administer your professional help between one session and another. We will be here long after our allotted sessions with you are over.

We have problems. Some of us are divorced. (Do they still say "broken homes"?) Some of us would probably be better off divorced. But families with special-needs children don't have the monopoly on marital problems.

We never seem to have nearly enough money to give our children what they need, but again we are not alone in that either.

Our other children are not always helpful or even considerate. Sometimes they are jealous. Sometimes their families embarrass them. Are your children any different?

We have anger and even rage. Who knows what our neighbors say about us behind closed doors? But this is the truth and it fills the air when we meet.

We are a family! We have taken on an outrageously difficult job of child rearing, and we have not let our side down!

We have lots of pride. Listen to our pride.

References

Anthony-Bergstone, C., Zarit, S. H., & Gatz, M. (1988). Symptoms of psychological distress among caregivers of dementia patients. *Psychology & Aging, 3,* 245–248.

Beckman, P. J. (1991). Comparison of mothers' and fathers' perceptions of the effect of young children with and without disabilities. *American Journal on Mental Retardation, 95,* 585–595.

Biegel, D. E., Sales, E., & Schulz, R. (1991). *Family caregiving in chronic illness.* Thousand Oaks, CA: Sage.

Dunst, C. J., Trivette, C. M., Hamby, D., & Pollack, B. (1990). Family systems correlates of the behavior of young children with handicaps. *Journal of Early Intervention, 14,* 204–218.

Frankl, V. (1959/1985). *Man's search for meaning.* New York: Washington Square Press.

Gallimore, R., Weisner, T. S., Bernheimer, L. P., Guthrie, D., & Nihira, K. (1993). Family responses to young children with developmental delays: Accommodation activity in ecological and cultural context. *American Journal on Mental Retardation, 98,* 185–206.

Gortmaker, S. L., Walker, D. K., Weitzman, M., & Sobol, A. M. (1990). Chronic conditions, socioeconomic risks, and behavioral problems in children and adolescents. *Pediatrics, 85,* 267–276.

Higgins, C. (Ed.). (1997). Family-centered service delivery. *Families and Disability Newsletter, 8,* 2.

Kazak, A. E., & Marvin, R. S. (1984). Differences, difficulties and adaptation: Stress and social networks in families with a handicapped child. *Family Relations, 33,* 67–77.

Margalit, M., Raviv, A., & Ankonina, D. B. (1992). Coping and coherence among parents with disabled children. *Journal of Clinical Child Psychology, 21,* 202–209.

McCallion, P., & Tobin, S. (1995). Social workers' perceptions of older parents caring at home for sons and daughters. *Mental Retardation, 33,* 153–162.

Naon, D., Morginstin, B., Schimmel, M., & Rivlis, G. (2000). *Children with special needs: An assessment of needs and coverage by services.* Jerusalem: JDC–Brookdale Institute, National Insurance Institute.

Rimmerman, A., & Portowicz, D. J. (1987). Analysis of resources and stress among parents of developmentally disabled children. *International Journal of Rehabilitation Research, 10,* 439–445.

Saddler, A. L., Hillman, S. B., & Benjamins, D. (1993). The influence of disabling condition visibility on family functioning. *Journal of Pediatric Psychology, 18,* 425–439.

Schalock, R. L., Brown, I., Brown, R., Cummins, R. A., Felce, D., Mattikka, L., Keith, K., & Parmenter, T. (2002). Conceptualization, measurement, and application of quality of life for persons with intellectual disability: results of an international panel of experts. *Mental Retardation, 40* (6), 457-470.

Seltzer, M. M., Greenberg, J. S., Krauss, M. W., Gordon, R. M., & Judge, K. (1997). Siblings of adults with mental retardation or mental illness: Effects on lifestyle and psychological well-being. *Family Relations, 46,* 395–405.

Seltzer, M. M., & Krauss, M. W. (1994). Aging parents with co-resident adult children: The impact of lifelong caregiving. In M. M. Seltzer, M. W. Krauss, & M. P. Janicki (Eds.), *Life course perspectives on adulthood and old age* (pp. 3–18). Washington, DC: American Association on Mental Retardation.

Smith, G. C., Fullmer, E. M., & Tobin, S. S. (1994). Living outside the system: An exploration of older families who do not use day programs. In M. M. Seltzer, M. W. Krauss, & M. P. Janicki (Eds.), *Life course perspectives on adulthood and old age* (pp. 17–38). Washington, DC: American Association on Mental Retardation.

Sutton, E., Sterns, H. L., Schwartz, L., & Roberts, R. (1992). The training of specialists in developmental disabilities and aging. *Generations, 16,* 71–74.

State of Israel. (1988). Special Education Law, 5748.

State of Israel. (1999). National Health Law, 5759.

Swirski, S., San-Zangy, M., Connor, E., & Swirski, M. (1997). *Looking at the budget of the State of Israel.* Tel Aviv: Adva Center.

Turnbull, A. P., Brotherson, M. J., & Summers, J. A. (1986). Family lifecycle: Theoretical and empirical implications and future directions for families with mentally retarded members. In J. J. Gallagher & P. M. Vietze (Eds.), *Families of handicapped persons: Research, programs, and policy issues.* Baltimore: Paul H. Brookes.

Wallander, J. L., Pitt, L. C., & Mellins, C. A. (1990). Child functional independence and maternal psychosocial stress as risk factors. *Journal of Consulting & Clinical Psychology 58,* 818–824.

Wasserstein, C. (1998). *Recipients of general disability allowance 1996–1997.* Jerusalem: National Insurance Institute.

Wood, J. B. (1993). Planning for the transfer of care: Social and psychological issues. In K. A. Roberto (Ed.), *The elderly caregiver: Caring for adults with developmental disabilities.* Thousand Oaks, CA: Sage.

Chapter 7

Family Quality Of Life In Canada

**Ivan Brown, Barry Isaacs, Barbara McCormack,
Nehama Baum, and Rebecca Renwick**
University of Toronto
Toronto, Ontario, Canada

Barbara's Family Story

Quality of life is an elusive goal—a state of mind, health and well-being that can rarely be sustained for long periods of time in our family. I might tell you in the morning that we experience a deep and profound quality of life, only to see my daughter choking and gasping for breath, and for her life, hours later with me, panic-stricken, by her side. At those times, and quite a few others, I think we have none.

The past 11 years, since my daughter was born, have been a roller coaster of such challenges and emotions. I have learned the hard way to take life in very small bites and measure our happiness moment by moment. This is how I survive and remain positive, enthusiastic and energetic. The alternative is too grim to contemplate.

My daughter's birth, 11 years ago, marked a turning point in my life. If it were only about becoming a mother, it might have been comparatively easy. But instead, Sarah's birth apparently unleashed a torrent of appalling bad luck, and we have limped from crisis to crisis ever since. Fortunately, the bad luck has been accompanied by a growing sense of gratitude, appreciation, and wonder for everything that life has to offer. Keeping these feelings in balance is how I stay sane.

My first 24 hours with Sarah were, perhaps, the most perfect of my life. I had moved to Canada alone in 1985 after several years in South Africa. My family, both parents, one sister, and three nieces, were still in England where I was brought up. In Canada I met a wonderful man and was now happily married with a challenging executive-level job, a new house, and a longed-for baby. I sometimes

185

wonder now if it were just a dream. Sarah had her first obvious seizure when she was 24 hours old. Over the next several days, her seizures spiralled out of control as doctors ran increasingly complex tests to discover the reason. The news unfolded. Half her brain is missing, she will never walk, she will never talk, she is blind, and so on. By the time they told me she had a single kidney, I barely heard. As I gazed at her wracked little body, it was impossible to believe that she, or I, would ever experience any quality of life again.

Five days later, Sarah's father had emergency open heart surgery for which he was given less than even odds of survival. For weeks his life was in the balance before he rallied. Now I was almost a widow, too. Finally at 4 weeks, I was let go from my job—paid off after 14 years because the new president thought I had too much on my plate. It had been a steep fall from my perfect day. Shock and grim determination sustained me through those early days. I hardly knew what had hit me. But I did manage to form an inseparable bond with my new daughter. Sitting in the hospital with Sarah in my arms, I promised her that I would do everything in my power to make her life as good as it could be.

Many things have happened since, mostly not very kind. We had moved to Nova Scotia to reduce the pressure of big city living, only to find few services, a poor climate for Sarah's health, and no work opportunities for me. Then my husband left us, 8 years ago, and we moved back to Toronto. The challenges continued, obtaining services, finding a school, managing Sarah's care, being Mum and Dad to Sarah while painting my own walls and fixing the plumbing. But I was also building a new career in the world of disability by managing the Canadian subsidiary of a U.S. product supplier. Sarah was the poster child for our multisensory environments and was seen and talked about on TV, radio and in print. For a child who had never said a word or taken a step, this was quite an achievement.

By early 1999, things seemed to be calming down. I had won some battles for services for Sarah and now volunteered on government committees and hospital boards to make services better for all children with disabilities. Sarah was settled in an integrated school setting, and, though her health was still alarming (she stopped breathing from time to time), she had dozens of little friends who filled her day. She was, and is, as predicted when she was born. Sarah can neither walk nor talk; she cannot see, feed herself, or do most things other children can. She weighs nearly 60 pounds. She requires 24-hour-care, and, although I have some help, I am "it" much of the time.

Since her birth, I have treated Sarah as normally as possible. Dressed in "cool" clothes, she makes a fashion statement that aids acceptance by her peers. In fact, she is quite the jet-setting child with several trips to England, California, Florida, Virginia, and Barbados—to name a few destinations—on her own frequent flier card. I am concerned that we will travel less as she grows more. We go to the shops, movies with good soundtracks, swimming, and on trips. Oftentimes, Sarah will sail through episodes so poignantly that I am in tears at what she cannot see or enjoy, or at the kindness of strangers. Sometimes she is equally ignorant of my fury when someone talks about her inappropriately in her presence or stares unacceptably long. She loves music and delights in noises, from the clattering of dishes to sneezes and sirens. I have resisted G-tube feeding so that she may enjoy the taste of food. She samples everything from pureed curry to chocolate—the latter being preferable. We enjoy our scented garden each summer, our walks and outings, and most of all, our nightly snuggles together on the sofa.

But although on the surface things have been moving along, I have wondered at times how long I could keep up the pace. I was weary of fighting battles, of having a complex-care child, of the loneliness of being a single parent in a big city with no family. Perhaps I was just physically and mentally tired. But instead of things becoming easier, the challenge suddenly intensified. Last September, I was diagnosed with cancer and had major surgery that rendered me weak and helpless. My mother died in October followed, by the death of Sarah's little friend, aged 9, who shared the same rare diagnosis, Aicardi syndrome. Sarah became ill yet again, and in December my sister's daughter died of leukemia the day before her 22nd birthday. I lost my hair and energy through 6 months of chemotherapy and treatment. Once more it was a challenge just to stay afloat, to have hope.

It sometimes takes the jolt of a serious diagnosis to put the world back into perspective. And this most certainly did. My earlier "problems" quickly assumed a very different perspective, to the point of triviality. And just as they diminished, so my appreciation for life increased. From my gratitude to Canada with its supportive and caring social structure, to the outpouring of help and support from many different sources, to the appreciation of the tiny things in life—after 10 years of trying, Sarah has finally learned to give me a kiss—it has been an extraordinary journey to discover what quality of life is all about.

Last weekend Sarah was asked to be the flower girl at the wedding of the first nurse who ever cared for her, when she was 5 months old. As it was a Scottish wedding, Sarah was dressed in a red tartan silk crinoline dress, her wheelchair decorated, her hair coiffed and ribboned. The bagpiper sounded his first note, and, as the bridal procession began, Sarah burst into the most magnificent smile, thrilled by the sound and sense of occasion. Equally dressed up, I pushed her chair down the aisle, proud of my beautiful daughter, of all we have come through together, and of such caring friends who include us in their lives. On that day we enjoyed the most exquisite quality of life. We will deal with tomorrow, tomorrow.

Barbara McCormack

Introduction

Barbara's story of her daughter Sarah, a story that will be continued throughout this chapter by a series of brief comments, vividly illustrates the impossibility of describing quality of life for families that have a son or daughter with intellectual and developmental disabilities. The sheer number and intensity of the barriers, challenges, and joys faced by the various members of such families—and the fact that they often change from day to day—suggests an immense complexity that we cannot hope to capture fully. Whenever we presume to study family quality of life, then, it is imperative that we begin by recognizing our limitations in being able to do full justice to the topic, and especially to the individuals with disabilities and their family members.

Instead, our aim in such study is to describe and measure family quality of life in a more general way—delving into the richness of personal experience at times in an imperfect way—and to identify some of the factors that promote and act as barriers to family quality of life that families hold in common. The core value behind studying family quality of life is that all families are entitled to lives of quality, and that families that have a son or daughter with an intellectual disability are especially so entitled. This value supports the main purpose of studying family quality of life outlined in chapter 1 of this volume, namely, to work toward maintaining and improving conditions that lead to "the good life" for families.

This chapter sets the stage for studying family quality of life in families that have sons or daughters with intellectual disabilities in Canada. It outlines the entitlements, the sociopolitical trends and the services available to such families, it reports on some initial findings from interviews with 28 families, and it suggests some implications of these findings both for families living in Canada and for our future work in family quality of life.

Current Entitlements, Sociopolitical Trends, And Services In Canada

What Are Entitlements?

Entitlements are benefits established by governments in response to the needs of a class of individuals, into which a particular individual fits after appropriate evaluation and classification. Entitlements may take the form of formal or informal policy or regulated practice, or they may be contained within laws or even in the constitution of a country. Entitlements are essential to all citizens of all countries, because they set out the boundaries within which we are free to live and carry out our life activities and they identify the types of supports we can expect along the way, as well as the types of barriers we are likely to encounter.

A clear set of entitlements is beneficial to citizens of countries in two main ways. First, entitlements help countries to function in orderly, prescribed ways that governments direct. It is often considered that it is most helpful to countries—though not always to individual citizens or to individual families, since the set of entitlements may not support their particular interests—if the range of entitlements is clearly described. Countries that do not clearly describe entitlements for their citizens either must rely on cultural customs to direct what people are entitled to, or risk the chaotic behavior and action that typically results from citizens being unsure of what they should do, how far they should go, and what they can expect to receive. Second, entitlements are beneficial because they are usually associated with protecting the rights of the various marginalized groups of people who live in all countries, including individuals with intellectual disabilities and their families, and with ensuring that the supports they require to live within their own country are in place. The degree to which entitlements work to enhance the lives of marginalized people is one of the principal thrusts that drives work in quality of life, and the degree to which entitlements work to enhance the lives of families is one of the principal thrusts that drives current work in family quality of life.

Canada's Constitutional And Legal Entitlements

Canadian Constitution

The Canadian Constitution clearly sets out the general entitlement of people with intellectual disabilities in two important ways (Rioux & Frazee,

1999). First, it declares that all citizens are equal under the law. In practical terms this means that all the laws of Canada must provide equal protection and equal benefit to each one of us, no matter who we are and whether or not we have a disability. Second, the Constitution specifies that special laws or programs can be set up if their purpose is to help disadvantaged citizens. A number of factors related to possible disadvantage are specifically mentioned, one of which is mental or physical disability.

Section 15 of the Constitution Act of Canada (1982) provides (among other things):

1. Every individual is equal before and under the law and has the right to equal protection and equal benefit of the law without discrimination and in particular without discrimination based on race, national, or ethnic origin, color, religion, sex, age, mental or physical disability.

2. Subsection 1 does not preclude any law, program or activity that has as its object the amelioration or conditions of disadvantaged individuals or groups including those that are disadvantaged because of race, national or ethnic origin, color, religion, sex, age, mental or physical disability.

In addition to constitutional entitlement of people with intellectual disabilities, Canada has put in place a number of laws that also describe the human rights entitlements of all citizens as well as all people who live and work in the country or who are simply visiting (Rioux & Frazee, 1999). The most important of these laws are (a) the Canadian Charter of Rights and Freedoms (1982), (b) the Canadian Human Rights Act (1985), and (c) Human Rights Codes in every Canadian province and territory.

Canadian Charter Of Rights And Freedoms

The Charter (Constitution Act, 1982) came into force in 1982 and is the "supreme law" of the country. Its particular importance for people with disabilities is that it specifically guarantees that people with mental or physical disabilities shall have the "equal protection and equal benefit of the law." At the time, Canada was the only nation in the world to extend this guarantee (Rioux & Frazee, 1999). Since the Charter is the supreme law, it applies to all levels of government in the country. Thus all federal, provincial and territorial, and municipal laws must comply with the Charter of Rights and Freedoms—including laws about education, health care, immigration, transportation, taxation, and many others—by guaranteeing equal protection and equal benefit to people with disabilities.

The Canadian Human Rights Act

This Act was adopted by the Parliament of Canada in 1985. It prohibits employers and service providers from discriminating on the basis of any one, or combination, of several personal characteristics: physical and mental disability, race, color, country or place of origin, religion, age, sex, marital status, same-sex partnership status, family status, sexual orientation, and pardoned criminal history (in some cases). The Canadian Human Rights Act applies to all federal government offices and employees, including those private companies that are federally regulated, but does not specifically apply to private business, organizations, or individuals. However, it does function as a strong ongoing example of entitlement—especially through the Canadian Human Rights Commission which promotes and enforces this law—and many businesses and organizations have adopted some or all of its principles.

Example: The Ontario Human Rights Code

Every province and territory in Canada has enacted human rights codes. For example, in Ontario, the province where the current study took place, the Ontario Human Rights Code is in effect and is enforced by the Ontario Human Rights Commission. Like the Canadian Human Rights Code, this Code protects people with "handicap," broadly defined to include people with physical, mental, and intellectual disabilities, as well as most other characteristics listed in the Canadian Human Rights Code, from discrimination. It extends these protections, however, by having a much broader application. It protects every person who lives in, works in, or visits Ontario in four broad areas (Rioux & Frazee, 1999): (a) employment, except that covered by the Canadian Human Rights Act; (b) service provision, including that by government, community agencies, hospitals, schools, and recreation services, as well as private service providers such as insurance companies or banks; (c) housing, including rental units, homes for sale, and long-term care housing; and (d) organizations and association, including unions, clubs, special societies, and others.

Enforcing Constitutional And Legal Entitlements

Constitutional and legal entitlements represent a formal set of rules. In Canada, as in other countries, they are written in rather broad, nonspecific language. One of the responsibilities of the Canadian justice system is to interpret how these entitlements are to be applied in any particular situation. Such interpretations are made in provincial courts, federal courts, and in the Supreme Court of Canada.

The first case that was decided in the Supreme Court of Canada that cited the Canadian Charter of Rights and Freedoms looked at whether or not discrimination had to be intentional. The Court ruled that discrimination can result whether or not discrimination was intended. For example, if a building were erected in such a way that people are required to use steps to enter it, this could be discrimination against those who cannot physically negotiate steps—even if the builders had no intention of keeping out people who cannot use steps. This case was important because it set out one of the basic rules for interpreting discrimination cases: that it is the *effect* of something, not the *original intent*, that the law applies to (Rioux & Frazee, 1999).

Entitlements In Five Areas Of Law

Entitlements apply to numerous areas of law. Five areas of law that are of particular importance to people with intellectual disabilities and families who have sons or daughters with intellectual disabilities in Canada are (a) consent and substitute decision making for personal care, including personal care provided by health and social services, (b) income, (c) living arrangements, (d) education, and (e) health (Peppin & Baker, 1999). These entitlements are similar in all provinces of Canada, although there are some differences arising from the fact that they are primarily a result of provincial legislation. Entitlements in Ontario, with reference to federal entitlements where appropriate, are used below as an example of Canadian entitlements since the study took place in Ontario.

Consent And Substitute Decision Making For Personal Care

Two Ontario laws, the Health Care Consent Act and the Substitute Decision Act, set out the guidelines and procedures for giving consent. They deal with capacity to make a treatment decision, disclosure of information as part of the informed decision-making process, and the specific rules for both substitute decision making and when emergency decisions can be made by professionals without waiting for consent. Both Acts apply equally to people with and without disabilities.

Income

In Ontario, adults with intellectual disabilities who are not capable of earning their own living are entitled to a disability pension through the Ontario Disability Support Program (ODSP). Although the amount of the pension varies according to housing costs, the current maximum is $930 per month. For those capable of some work, the Ontario Works Act provides a considerably lower pension and the criteria for eligibility are considerably more stringent. Both plans allow for the pensions to be "topped up" by some employment earnings. Other income programs available to the general population—such as welfare, Canada Pension Plan disability benefits, and workers' compensation—are equally available to people with intellectual disabilities. People with intellectual disabilities who are 65 or older are entitled, like all others their age, to receive both the federal Old Age Security pension, the Guaranteed Income Supplement—currently at a maximum level for about $920 a month, as well as other benefits for seniors. Financial entitlements that are available through tax credits include: a disability income tax credit, Ontario tax credit (for which a small portion of rent paid may be claimed), GST (federal goods and service taxes of 7% on most goods and services), and PST (Ontario provincial sales tax of 8%) partial rebates, and a medical expense income tax credit.

Living Arrangements

The Ontario Tenant Protection Act sets out entitlements for people who rent in Ontario. Perhaps the most important of these entitlements is controls on rent increases for people who continue to live in the same rental units. Another source of living arrangement support is the 240,000 social housing units that offer geared-to-income rents in Ontario. Although these are not specifically for people with disabilities, individuals with intellectual disabilities and low-income families where a member has an intellectual disability almost always meet the eligibility criteria.

There are still about 1,000 people living in institutions for people with intellectual disabilities in Ontario. There is no entitlement to continue living within institutions, as all are scheduled to be closed within the next several years. However, all who are currently in institutions are entitled under current government policy to supported community living, usually in semi-independent supported living situations. There is no legal entitlement for adults with intellectual disabilities in Ontario to receive supported housing, but the practice has been over several decades that people who do receive such services through community agencies continue to receive it.

Education

Ontario amended its Education Act in 1980 to make public schools responsible for the education of *all* children from age 5 (or from age 4 if the school board offers a junior kindergarten program) to the age of 16, the years when school attendance is compulsory. This amendment required school boards to provide education for children with any disability in the most integrated way possible. In addition, public secondary schools were made responsible for the education of all such children and young adults with intellectual and all other disabilities between the ages of 17 and 21, should they choose to continue attending school. In addition, through special application, school boards can receive funding to continue education for young adults with disabilities beyond the age of 21 if alternative programs are not available in their areas. In addition, some community colleges enroll a limited number of adults with disabilities in their various programs, offering a certificate for satisfactory participation. Children and young adults with special learning needs are not guaranteed to be placed within regular-stream classrooms, but the amended Act assumes that they will be unless it can be shown that their educational needs are better met in another setting.

At the same time, entitlement to educational and developmental services for young children was guaranteed by Ontario's Day Nurseries Act. This Act established a comprehensive system of early childhood education across Ontario that was required to offer special services designed to meet the needs of young children with disabilities between the ages of 2 and 5.

Health

Health laws in Canada entitle all citizens, including all people with disabilities, to health care. Because Canada's 10 provinces have separate responsibility for health-care practice, the regulations that govern this practice are slightly different within each province. In Ontario, health care is paid for by public funds through the Ontario government. Although not every medical procedure is covered by the plan—especially those that are consider more "optional"—visits to physicians' offices, hospital stays, and almost all procedures ordered by physicians are covered. In addition, people who receive ODSP (a substantial percentage of people with intellectual disabilities) or welfare receive their medications free of charge. People who are 65 years of age or older, including people with intellectual disabilities, pay a yearly fee of just over $100 for any medications they might use throughout the year.

Social Services Available For Individuals With Intellectual Disabilities And Their Families

The trend in Ontario for the past number of years has been for people with intellectual disabilities to use, wherever possible, the services that are available to the general population. This trend has resulted in large numbers of people with intellectual disabilities, like people with other disabilities, becoming involved in generic social, health, education, and many other services. Still, some special services are required for people with intellectual disabilities and their families because or their special needs.

Numerous programs are in place in Ontario to provide these services, and these are funded through several ministries of the Ontario government. The Ministry of Community and Social Services, in particular, funds a wide variety of programs for adults with intellectual disabilities and for families of children with developmental delays.

There is no special entitlement to any of these services. A great many are currently carried out by community agencies that receive most of their funding from MCSS (and sometimes another ministry, such as Education or Health). Individuals, families, or advocates simply apply for services at these community agencies, and, if there is an opening and if the eligibility criteria are met, the services are initiated. People often have to wait for services, however, because agencies do not have sufficient resources to accept all applicants. At the present time, there are also some initiatives by Ontario government agencies to grant funding to individuals or families who may then purchase the services they need at a community agency of the individual's or family's choice. Some other initiatives allow individuals or families to spend money granted to them, provided that the family or another designated party assumes responsibility for spending the money only for the purposes for which it was given. In practice, then, although no one is specifically entitled to any social services at all, all individuals with intellectual disabilities and their families are entitled to any service available if there is a match between the need of the individual and the mandate and resources of the service, or if they assume responsibility for spending money granted. However, some degree of advocacy is usually required to gain access to both funding and services, which are limited, and, because of this, funding and services are available to individuals and families in ways that do not always match their needs.

A number of programs are especially helpful to families that have children with intellectual disabilities (Brown, 1999). Among the most helpful are

- Special financial assistance to families with children who have severe disabilities;
- Special Needs/Special Services at Home, providing funding for supports to children and adults who live in family homes;
- infant development programs, supporting and training parents of infants up to the age of 2;
- Parent Relief, providing for temporary, alternative care to relieve parents;
- Family Support Program, providing advice, assistance, and case management to families that have children with intellectual disabilities;
- Family Home Program, which provides funding and support to families willing to share their homes with children or adults with intellectual disabilities.

Numerous other programs are less directly helpful to family members, but do support the family indirectly by offering services to the family member with an intellectual disability. These services include: community job and volunteer placement and support, sheltered workshops, life skill development programs, behavior management programs, supported independent living, group living programs, and the adult protective services program.

Service Challenges for Families

Dealing with the array of available services is a considerable challenge that is often both daunting and stressful for family members. Currently in Ontario, individuals and families can usually receive some needed services, but there are three main barriers. First, because of the considerable number of families and individuals in need of some services, it is not always possible to access the needed services without waiting. Second, because each child with developmental delays or adult with intellectual disabilities has unique needs, the services available do not always address those needs in the ways that family members would like. Frustration expressed over the years with services that are too "program-centered" has resulted in some move toward more individualized or "person-centred" approaches (Galambos, 1999). Now, many of the programs that involve families are able to be tailored to the specific needs of families fairly well. A third barrier to services for family members is that a great many simply do not receive as much service as they would like. Caring for a son or daughter with an intellectual disability takes a great deal of time, and a great deal of physical and emotional energy. Most parents—even those who already receive services—would enjoy receiving more support than they currently do (Renwick, Brown, & Raphael, 1998).

Current Policy Influences On Services

Services for people with intellectual disabilities and their families have traditionally been quite good in Ontario, compared with services in other jurisdictions. Still, they have not responded to all the needs expressed, and there has been an ongoing advocacy movement throughout the last half of the 20th century from families and service providers for continued improvements to services. Beginning in 1995, the Ontario government altered its policy priorities, and these have influenced the degree to which services are available to families that have sons or daughters with intellectual disabilities. No new money has been made available for services provided by community agencies, but, because new children are being born and life expectancy is increasing, the available funds have to serve more people. On the other hand, there have been some new initiatives that provide relatively small amounts of money to individuals with intellectual disabilities and their families, and occasionally to a community agency for a specific program. Recent policy documents from the Ontario government have been explicit on three points:

- It is essential to the overall well-being of Ontario that public spending on social programs, including programs to people with intellectual disabilities, be contained.
- The current level of public spending on programs for people with intellectual disabilities should be used for as many people as possible and for those most in need.
- Support for people with intellectual disabilities must come from a "partnership" of families, communities, and government.

An additional aspect of recent policy is the assumption that community agencies themselves, groups of families, and others will generate new ways of addressing needs with essentially the same amount of overall funding as was previously allocated. Although this has led to a few innovative projects, it has not yet resulted in any substantial restructuring of services or the emergence of new credible ways to make services and supports available to those who need them. On the other hand, it has not resulted in many programs being eliminated, even if general stagnation and lack of expansion have characterized service agencies since 1995. Some expansion of services has occurred for families, however, where families take the main responsibility for the support of their son or daughter and the service provides some support to the family.

Economic Changes That Are Likely To Affect Government Policy

Current government policy that influences services to individuals with intellectual disabilities and their families arose from an *apparent* need in 1995 to protect the viability of Ontario as an economic growth area by containing Ontario governmental spending. Immediate dangers that were cited included high provincial income taxes and government deficit spending. By early 2000, however, these apparent dangers had been neutralized. Ontario's income tax rate had been lowered substantially, and the Ontario government budget was registering a surplus. With the principal arguments for not spending on programs for people with intellectual disabilities gone, it seems probable that there will be renewed activity from parent groups, community agency groups, and other groups to advocate for more funding for better services. In addition, the Ontario government itself has recently begun to develop disability-related policy that is more relevant to the current economic reality.

The Shape Of New And Expanded Services

The form that new and expanded services will take, should they occur in the future, is not yet clear. It seems unlikely that the service-centered system, consisting of government-funded community agencies carrying out programs according to their mandates, will be readopted. What seems more likely is that the variety of innovative individualized and person-centered (or family-centered) programs that have begun to emerge over the past few years will be expanded and that the program-centered services will be gradually phased out. If this should be the case, it will provide more options for individuals and families, but, at the same time, it may require them to take considerably more responsibility for acquiring and maintaining the services and supports they do receive.

Because both acquiring and maintaining services requires skill, time, energy, and other resources, this will represent an additional burden upon families unless creative ways to support them are also adopted. There is an additional danger for those families that do not have a family member who has the skill, time, energy, or other resources required to acquire and maintain services. These families are in grave danger of being neglected or forgotten unless serious measures are taken to ensure that they are included.

Research With Families

The Need For The Current Research

The voice of families that have a member with an intellectual disability was the driving force behind the initial development of most services in Ontario. In earlier decades of this century, groups of parents set up the first schools in homes, church basements, and community centers, and developed the first vocational workshops wherever they could (Porter et al., 1999). These same parents banded together and advocated for—and received—government-funded special schools and places where their sons and daughters could spend their days in productive ways. At the same time, other parents successfully advocated for—and received—government funding for a variety of community-based programs that offered residential services and life skills development.

The structure of the more than 320 community agencies throughout Ontario that support people with intellectual disabilities and their families is evidence of the involvement of families. All are directed by volunteer boards of directors, which typically include family members. Although the day-to-day business of these agencies is carried out by professional staff, it is still traditional for board members to take an active interest in their agencies' affairs, and sometimes to be actively involved in a personal way.

Still, the voice of families has diminished within the service system over the past few decades as the voices of professionals and of the Ontario government, that provides most of the funding for the agencies, have increased. A predictable consequence of this was that many services began to operate primarily from the perspective of their ongoing mandates, not from the perspective of the changing needs of families. One indication that the needs of families are not the driving force within services was the emergence several years ago in Ontario of a strong parent advocacy group, the Family Alliance, that established a goal of advocating for government funds to provide services and supports to families that families actually wanted and needed. Such advocacy continues today among members of this and other groups.

Community agencies have responded to family advocacy by changing their approach to some degree. The term *support* has all but replaced the term *service,* in an effort to appear more person-centered (Brown, 1999). Services have adopted goals of meeting individual and emerging needs. Government policy has followed, rather than led, this change through publication of policy documents (e.g., Ontario Ministry of Community and Social Services, 1997), although such policy documents do represent a formal attempt to strengthen the notion that the services that are funded and carried out are those most needed and wanted by individuals with intellectual disabilities and their families.

Thus the voice of families can be heard faintly, but there is no formal way of ensuring that it will continue to be heard. The current research team recognized a need for ensuring that the voice of family not only is heard by both government and the service system, but also is an integral part of its planning and service implementation.

Conceptualization Of Family Quality Of Life

Quality of life was considered by the research team to be a useful construct through which families could express their voices. The principal reason for thinking in this way was that the basic thrust of work in the quality of life area has been to emphasize the importance of quality in the lives of people with intellectual disabilities, and to strive toward personal and environmental improvements that will lead to improved life quality (Brown & Renwick, 1997). Although almost all the work carried out to date in quality of life and intellectual disability has involved adults at the individual level, it seemed reasonable to the researchers that the same key ideas that are being solidified in the study of individual quality of life might be usefully applied to family quality of life.

Those ideas have been developed and expressed in writing by some of the researchers and were further developed through a set of discussions among researchers in three countries, Australia, Canada, and Israel. The ideas were further refined through discussions with researchers from Wales and the United States.

These key ideas support the general purpose for engaging in work in the area of family quality of life, namely, to work to maintain and enhance the lives of families that have a member with an intellectual disability. Quality of life is seen as an overarching concept, one that represents an area of study and subsumes numerous other concepts. This concept is considered to be useful as an overall goal for work in family quality of life, as a useful policy and service principle, as a way to describe outcomes, and as a process for improving people's lives. Quality of life can be assessed and measured using a variety of methodologies, and these should describe a blend of characteristics that are held and valued by all families everywhere and characteristics that are held and valued by the family being assessed or measured.

The research team adopted the conceptualization of family quality of life developed by the three-country team described in Israel chapter. That conceptualization included examining six dimensions in each of nine key areas of family life. Four of the six dimensions were examined in the present study: attainment, opportunities for improvement, initiative of family members to make choices, and satisfaction. The nine key areas of family life are health, financial well-being, family relationships, support from other people, support from services, careers and preparing for careers, spiritual and cultural life, leisure, and community and civic involvement.

Methodology

Recognizing the complexity of family quality of life, the research team set out an overall plan to look initially at some key areas of family life, and to follow these by indepth interviews with some of the families (for a full explanation of the methodology, see chap. 2). To begin to put this plan into action, the research team from Canada interviewed the main caregiver or caregivers of 28 families that have a son or daughter with an intellectual disability in Toronto, Canada's largest city with a population about 2.5 million. According to population estimates (Brown, 1999), Toronto houses 60,000 to 75,000 families that have a son or daughter with an intellectual disability. The families were selected from two community agencies, Surrey Place Centre and the Muki Baum Association. Each of the two participating agencies provides a unique and broad set of services to individuals and families that have member with intellectual disabilities, and the two are situated in different parts of the city.

Profile Of Participating Families

Family Makeup

The 28 families surveyed ranged in size from 2 to 8 members, with a mean family size of 5.21 members. Some family members did not live within the family home full time, however, and the mean family size for those who did live full time within the family home was 3.86 members. Of the 28 families, 23 had both mother and father present, 4 had only mother present, and 1 had only father present. The mothers ranged in age from 37 to 74 with a mean age of 53.56 (SD = 9.20), and the fathers ranged in age from 42 to 73 with a mean age of 54.65 (SD = 7.36). Fifteen families had a daughter with a disability and 13 had a son with a disability. The children with disabilities ranged in age from 10 to 36 with a mean age of 21.93 (SD = 8.26).

All 28 families had children other than the son or daughter with an intellectual disability. Twenty-one had other female children and 14 had other male children. The number of children per family ranged from 2 to 5, with a mean of 2.74 children per family. Twelve of the 28 families were partly made up of other relatives, and 3 of the families each had a family member who was a long-term nanny/caregiver.

Types Of Disabilities In The Families

The families had children with a wide array of disabilities. These included attention deficit disorder (ADD), arachnoid cyst, autism, Down syndrome, tuberous sclerosis, seizure disorder, epilepsy, and Landau Kleffner syndrome. Some children had multiple disabilities such as ADD with seizure disorder, autism, or psychiatric disorders. All were considered to have resulted in developmental delay in childhood and intellectual disability in adulthood.

Responsibility Within Families

The parents who were interviewed were asked about the degree of responsibility they personally have in the day-to-day affairs of their families. Seven sets of parents have much more responsibility than they would like, 10 have more responsibility than they would like, and 11 have about the amount they would like. No parents wanted more responsibility than they currently have.

These same parents were also asked about the degree of responsibility they personally have related to their son or daughter with a disability. Here, the parents in 7 families had much more responsibility than they wanted, 11 had more responsibility than they wanted, and 10 had about the right amount of responsibility for them. Again, no parents claimed they would like to take on more responsibility than they currently do with regard to their son or daughter with a disability.

Eighteen of the 28 sets of parents chose the same category (the remaining 10 were all within one response category) for the two responsibility questions, suggesting that the degree of responsibility they feel is strongly related to the degree of responsibility they feel for the disability. To explore this further, the parents were asked who is most involved in the life of the children with the disability. The responses suggested parents, sometimes with the help of their children, accept most responsibility: mother (7 families), mother and father (6 families), parents and siblings (9 families), parents and other people (5 families), and other people (1 family).

Profile Of Nine Major Areas Of Family Life

Health Of Families

When families were asked about the health of the family as a whole, 14 responded that it was "good," 9 responded "very good," and 1 responded "excellent." Four families described their health as "fair" and none selected "poor." Seventeen of the 28 families responded "yes" when asked if there had been any major health concerns, other than disability, that impacted the family during the past year. The major health concerns that they identified included: high blood pressure, heart problems (some involved open heart surgery or triple bypass surgery), pneumonia, chronic bronchitis, emotional stress, bipolar disorder (manic depression), dementia (including Alzheimer's disease), seizures, a retinal tear, enlarged lymph nodes, heart burns, chronic back and shoulder pain, frailty due to old age, spinal cord and hip problems, prostate cancer, pituitary problems, and diabetes. In addition, 3 of the families had experienced deaths of at least one family member during the past year.

All families engaged in some activities, such as eating well and exercising, to improve their health. Some health needs were not met by services, however, because they were not available at all, because they were available but were in locations that were too far from where the families lived, and sometimes because of long waits for health services.

> We may not recognize the physical and emotional impact of living with disability—coping every day, we forget that life was, or could be, any different. I often compare my life with Sarah to the young family with a newborn baby—the sleepless nights, the desperation of interpreting and calming cries and screams, the incredible emotion and energy we bestow on the relationship, the worry and the concern. But although the new family may experience this stressful life for a few months, we live this way all the time. Almost inevitably, as the years roll by, there is a physical price to pay. In our case, my diagnosis of cancer may have been that price.

> The health of the family is critical to quality of life, but few of us manage to strike the right balance of taking good care of ourselves while we take care of our child's extensive needs—there is just not the time, energy, or resources. Difficult though it may be, we do need to recognize the long-term risk and be kind to ourselves whenever possible.

> Barbara McCormack

Financial Well-Being Of Families

When families were asked about their total income, 12 responded that they were either "well off" or "managing well with some extra" money; 11 families stated that they were "doing okay," and 5 described their overall financial situation as "just getting by." None of these families described themselves as "struggling." The total income reported by the families reflected a fairly wide range: 8 of the families had combined family income of more than $90,000, 13 families had family income of between $45,000 and $90,000, and 5 families had less than $45,000. Two families declined to comment.

On average, the 28 families spent $581.43 a month on care, support, or equipment for the family member with an intellectual disability. Twenty-two of the families said that all of their basic needs were met by the money they had available, but 13 families, including 8 families that said all their basic needs were being met, described themselves as not having any money left over at the end of the month.

Nine of the 28 families have plans to try to increase the income of members who contribute financially to the household. These plans include working more, hoping work will improve (e.g., through promotion, getting more business), and having additional family members enter the workforce after they finish their education. In 22 of the 28 families, family members were engaging in activities that should enable them to earn more money in the future—taking courses or programs that would improve their skills and portfolios.

> Disability is expensive. From the outlay for home renovations to the price of vehicle modifications, from the price of specialized equipment to the cost of lifelong care, from the cost of diapers and medications to the fees for therapeutic services, this is a world with a high price tag. We are fortunate to live in a socially aware country where help is available to defray some of the costs. Nevertheless, it is a constant challenge to pay for this unanticipated lifestyle. Yesterday our nursing agency, without notice, increased their nursing rates from $25 to $34 an hour—a $700 per month impact on our lives. I'm still trying to fathom which hours to cut, or how to raise the extra money. The challenge continues.
>
> Barbara McCormack

Family Relationships

Families were asked about 10 aspects of family relationships (see Table 7.1). Most of the families reported carrying out these activities "a lot" or "quite a bit" although helping each other do things, going places together, doing things as a family, and helping solve family problems were a little less highly rated. Few families reported "not much" to the categories and no family reported "not much" to all of the categories. A great many families mentioned that sharing meals together was an activity that contributed significantly to maintaining good ongoing family relationships.

Table 7.1
Number Of Families Reporting Family Relationship Activities

Activities	Degree of Involvement			
	A lot	Quite a bit	Same	Not much
Help each other do things	9	13	5	1
Go places together	11	6	10	1
Enjoy each other's company	11	15	2	0
Support each other in times of trouble	19	7	1	1
Help solve family problems	14	6	8	0
Trust each other	23	4	1	0
Work together toward family goals	16	7	4	1
Have a sense of belonging together	20	7	1	0
Generally have similar values	15	12	1	0
Do things as a family	12	9	5	2

How I wish our family had stayed together and given Sarah the family life, two parents, and extended family that she deserves. Sadly, the stress of our lives tore my husband and me apart, not an uncommon story in the world of severe disability. Had we understood, been forewarned, or guided through, the many pressures we faced, perhaps we could have made it work. Today, my husband and his large family are rarely in our lives, and my family lives an impractical 3,000 miles away. Instead, Sarah has her own slightly different "family" consisting of me, our good friends and her many nurses and caregivers—each one a valuable contributor to our daily lives.

Barbara McCormack

Support From Other People

Most families described family life circumstances that involved considerably more physical and emotional demands than would be typical of families that do not have children with disabilities. An important aspect of family quality of life, therefore, is the amount of support that such families get from other people.

When asked to describe overall support from relatives, friends, and neighors, no clear trend emerged from the families' responses. The number of families that indicated that support from other people was excellent or very good was similar to the number that indicated that such support was only fair or poor. A closer look at the sources and types of supports from others, however, provides a clearer picture. Families were asked about the degree to which they receive both help doing practical things and emotional support (e.g., listening, trust, empathy) from two sources: (a) relatives and (b) friends and neighbors. Their responses (see Table 7.2) provide striking evidence that most families receive very little practical assistance from others, and that only a few more families receive emotional support.

Table 7.2
Number Of Families Reporting Degrees Of Practical And Emotional Support

Support Source	Degree of Support				
	A great deal	Quite a bit	Some	A little	None
Practical help					
Relatives	0	1	4	4	19
Friends and neighbors	0	3	3	2	20
Emotional support					
Relatives	4	5	6	4	9
Friends and neighbors	3	8	7	3	7

One factor that appears to play a role in support from relatives and friends, in particular, is how physically close they live to the families. It is difficult, and often impossible, for those who live far away to provide practical assistance, and distance requires more effort to provide emotional support. One father said, "We have no relatives living in Toronto" and a mother commented, "All our relatives live in Europe, and we can't travel there because of Joe."

Families' overall ratings of support from others and their more specific ratings in Table 7.2 seem, at first glance, to be somewhat contradictory. This apparent contradiction may be explained, at least in part, by families' efforts to seek support. About half the families are actively seeking more support from others, and the other half are not. Those not seeking support are, for the most part, the same families that are happy with their level of support from others. The inference is that they are not seeking more support because, although some families do not get much support from others, they do not particularly want it. Some comments from family members lent support to this inference. For example, one mother said, "We don't ask for help from relatives or friends because we try to do as much as possible independently." Another said, "We don't ask for help because we don't see it as necessary." Some families claimed that other people have their own responsibilities, and they do not want to impose too much: "There is a friend supporting [me] now, but I can't expect more than she is providing."

The overall effect of the degree of support on parents' social lives was also recorded. Seven sets of parents described their social lives as "about what I would like"; 12 said their social lives were "somewhat less than I would like"; 9 responded "much less than I would like." It seems from this that a great many parents probably see the presence of disability in their families as interfering with their wishes for social life.

> My friends are the mainstay of my life. Some have been there for me for more than 20 years, and other more recent friends are involved with disability or have a disabled child themselves. These wonderful people provide me with a wealth of emotional support, caring, friendship, and a social life, of sorts. Practical support is more diffi-cult—it feels like an imposition to ask them to take responsibility for a child with a life-threatening condition, and most are nervous of handling Sarah. As a result, almost all of Sarah's direct care is with paid, professional help.

> For my part, I try to be a good friend, a willing ear, and sometimes a mentor for my friends, but I feel constrained from offering much prac-tical help; I'm mostly overwhelmed just managing my own life. I think my friends understand that I do what I can, and that I think of them even more. We have yet to make much progress with the neighbors

and their children, despite living in the same midcity Toronto house for 5 years. With no siblings to "break the ice" and little time to spare, these relationships hover with unrealized potential.

Barbara McCormack

Support From Disability-Related Services

All of the families interviewed received at least some services, as they were identified as users of services of the two participating community agencies. When asked about availability of disability-related services in areas where they lived, the typical response was that there are some services available. The main types of services used are shown in Table 7.3.

The families' needs are not all being met by the services in their communities, mainly because families sometimes prefer to meet the needs within their own homes and because they have not yet sought out the services.

Table 7.3
Number Of Families Reporting Use Of Seven Types Of Services

Type of Service	Number of Families
Special benefits or funding	22
Special education	20
Supported employment	19
Supported living	18
Day programs or activities	20
Case management	21
Specialized medical services	22

Families of children with complex care needs are highly dependent on the services available from the Ontario government and community agencies. In fact, we could not manage very long without them. As a result, and together with many other vocal parents, I have become involved with advocacy groups and committees working for improved services and changes in government policy wherever our children are concerned. Little did I know when I became involved that I would end up being a prime recipient of many beneficial changes that have recently occurred in our service structure. Apparently, a single mother with a life-threatening condition of a child with a life-threatening condition makes for a powerful story!

Unfortunately, the services available in Canada differ, sometimes dramatically, from province to province and, with few exceptions, can be difficult to fathom, navigate and negotiate, especially for recent arrivals to our country. Inevitably, it is those families who can advocate for themselves and "work the system" that receive the most services. Others may not realize their entitlement and get left by the wayside. We need to develop a safety net that "catches" all those who need services, and offer lifelong case management to support families through the many transitions in their lives.

Barbara McCormack

Spiritual And Cultural Beliefs

When asked how important spiritual or cultural beliefs were, 23 families responded that such beliefs were "extremely" or "quite" important; 3 families said "somewhat" important; 2 said "only a little" important. Additionally, when asked to what degree spiritual or cultural beliefs guided the way they think and act, 21 families indicated "very strongly" or "quite a bit"; 4 indicated "somewhat"; only 3 said "a little." Clearly, spiritual or cultural beliefs are important to most families. Somewhat surprisingly, though, such beliefs appeared not always to emerge from the broader social environment in which the families live. Five families said their social environments encourage spiritual and cultural beliefs "very much"; 7 said "quite a bit"; 6 said "some"; 8 said "a little"; 2 said "not at all."

When asked more specifically about opportunities to develop spiritual and cultural beliefs, 19 families indicated that there were "a lot" or "quite a few" opportunities available to them, and 9 families indicated "some" opportunities, "a few" or "hardly any." When asked to what degree their family actively seeks out opportunities to develop spiritual or cultural beliefs, 17 indicated "a great deal," "quite a bit," or "some"; 7 indicated "a little"; 4 said "hardly at all." It appears that the majority of families have opportunities available to them to develop their spiritual and cultural beliefs and actively seek out these opportunities to strengthen their beliefs. According to family members, most of these opportunities come from "activities and courses available at [places of worship]" or "religious community centres."

To help better understand how spiritual and cultural beliefs function as supports to family members regarding disability, families were asked three questions about the degree to which their spiritual and cultural beliefs related to disability within their families: (a) To what degree does your spiritual/cultural community accept intellectual disabilities? (b) To what degree does your spiritual/cultural community help you physically and emotionally to deal with intellectual disability? (c) To what degree do your spiritual/cultural beliefs help you personally to accept and cope with intellectual disability? The responses of the participating families are reported in Table 7.4.

It is somewhat discouraging that fewer than half of the families reported "very much" or "quite a bit" to any of the questions. The lack of help of spiritual or cultural communities in helping parents deal with disability is particularly noteworthy. This preliminary data suggests that spiritual or cultural communities and beliefs may not provide strong support to many families for relating to disability, even though their beliefs are important to them (none of the families indicated dissatisfaction with their spiritual or cultural beliefs). Perhaps the reason for this is that beliefs are important to family members for other purposes.

Table 7.4
Number Of Families Reporting Degrees Of
Spiritual And Cultural Support

Support Source	Degree of Support				
	Very much	Quite a bit	Some	A little	None
Spiritual or cultural community					
Accepts disability[a]	7	6	10	0	4
Helps deal with disability[a]	4	4	1	3	15
Beliefs help accept disability[b]	4	6	6	6	4

[a]1 missing response, [b]2 missing responses.

When I look at the dynamic between myself and Sarah, it seems obvious that we were made for each other. I feel privileged to be her mother. Whether this is part of a vast eternal plan, God's will, destiny, fate or sheer coincidence, I cannot be certain. What I do know, however, is that Sarah has added incredible value, meaning, depth, and richness to the lives of many people, and, most especially, to me.

Our friends, by and large, are not strongly connected to specific religious communities, although many schools, group homes, and day programs do have a religious affiliation. Nevertheless, my circle of parents all believe that their children who have disabilities have a vital and significant role in the world today, and that their lives make the world a more loving, peaceful and understanding place.

Barbara McCormack

Careers And Preparing For Careers

Having a son or daughter with an intellectual disability affected the education and careers of some of the parents interviewed. In 7 families, one or both parents had given up some education to care for their child with a disability. Five families reported the mother giving up her career, at least temporarily, to care for her child. Overall, parents in just 18 of the 28 families reported that they had been able to prepare for, and have, the careers they wanted.

On the other hand, 18 families expected that there would be no obstacles for their family members being able to work or go to school in the near future. As well, 5 families described their families' careers and preparations for careers as "excellent"; 9 selected "very good"; and an additional 9 selected "good." Four families chose "fair" and none selected "poor." One family declined to comment. Of the 28 families, 19 reported that they have family members working "quite a bit" or "a great deal" toward furthering their careers and education, while only 1 reported that this was occurring "hardly at all." Overall, 21 of the 28 families were "satisfied" or "very satisfied" with their families' careers and preparations for those careers.

> Working in the field of disability, I continually come across people whose careers have been irrevocably changed by the "touch" of disability in their lives. Many who work with disability bring firsthand experience to their new careers. Among my friends, several of the mothers have given up working outside the home, and many fathers have seen their careers stagnate, lost time at work or, in extremes cases, lost jobs. Some are tied to work they detest simply because of the insurance benefits package. The unpredictable nature of our children's health and lives does not often fit with a typical, progressive work profile, which often creates torn loyalties and conflicts both at home and at work. It would have been impossible for me to continue my high-tech career and manage Sarah, so I am fortunate to work for a company which values my understanding of disability while tolerating the constraints it imposes on my working life.
>
> Barbara McCormack

Leisure And Enjoyment Of Life

For many families, the things they do in their leisure time to enjoy themselves add substantially to their perceived quality of life. When asked to what degree their family does things together for fun and enjoyment of life, 5 families responded "a great deal"; 9 families responded "quite a bit"; 9 families responded "some"; 4 families responded "a little"; 1 family responded "hardly at all." Families reported a wide variety of leisure activities, including sports, camping, biking, swimming, bowling, going to movies and theatre, attending concerts, shopping, walking, hiking, swimming, travel and vacationing, watching television, doing arts and crafts, socializing and visiting, working out, going out to dinner and parties, and reading.

Most families reported that there were "a great many," "quite a few," or "some" things they could do in their neighborhoods for fun and enjoyment. Six families reported only a "few" or "hardly any" opportunities for fun. However, all reported barriers that keep their families from enjoying these opportunities. These barriers are summarized in seven categories: barriers associated with the disability itself (16 families), lack of time (6 families), lack of money (4 families), lack of respite (2 families), the health of a family member (1 family), lack of energy (1 family), and the negative views of others (1 family). By far, the most common barrier to family leisure and enjoyment is limitations associated with the disability. For example, one mother said, "When he is there, we can only do things if he feels like it," and another claimed that "because of our daughter's disability, we can't do many things as a family." Despite these barriers, however, all 28 families, when asked to describe their overall fun and enjoyment of life, said "very good," "good," or "fair."

> I usually say, "What social life?" when I am asked about it, because it has certainly changed since Sarah and I have become a family. The greatest loss is spontaneity; there is no such thing as "yes, let's go" to an unexpected invitation. Today, every hour away from Sarah has to be meticulously planned in advance, and every outing has a starting and ending time. Another major barrier to a social life is the incredible cost of care services. My minimum outlay per hour is $16, but most often Sarah needs qualified nursing help at $25 to $34 an hour. That makes the standard "movie and burger outing" a serious financial investment. I do get some respite hours, but I try not to use them frivolously. It's easier, and cheaper, to invite people over for a meal.

> Sarah comes along on quite a few outings, especially in summer, and usually just fits in on with whatever's happening. At a Moody Blues concert, she tried to rival the sound system as she sang along, and we had to beat a hasty, red-faced, retreat. She stayed silent at the Christmas Carol concert until they began to sing "Silent Night," and she decided to make the night a noisy one!

> Barbara McCormack

Community And Civic Involvement

Parents of participating families were asked about the extent to which they participated in community and civic activities. This included participation in social, cultural, religious, or political affairs within their home communities. Thirteen of the families described their community and civic involvement as "a great deal" or "quite a bit"; 7 families said they had "some" involvement; 8 families perceived their involvement as only "a little" or "hardly at all."

When asked specifically what they did, parents in 24 of the 28 families identified at least one community and civic activity in which they were involved. It is interesting to note, however, that no family identified more than three community and civic activities in total for all its members. The activities reported included volunteering, attending religious services and groups, fund raising, donating money, and supporting cultural activities. In addition, 16 families voice their opinions publicly, 9 write letters, and 4 contact their elected officials. Of the 4 families not involved in community activities, 3 indicated that they felt it was not possible in their area to contribute to how things are by being involved in community activities. These 3 families were all either dissatisfied or neither satisfied nor dissatisfied with their families' contributions. Of the 24 families involved with their communities, only 3 were dissatisfied with their contributions.

> My work with advocacy groups, the board of directors of Canada's largest rehabilitation/chronic care facility for children, and a recreation center for people with disabilities, has served to place me in the middle of a large number of activities and initiatives. As a result, my network of friends, contacts, and acquaintances has expanded enormously. I find providing input is empowering—it feels that I have some control in a life that runs seriously amok. Even if no one takes any notice, at least I have tried to give a different perspective. Second, participating feels as if I'm giving something back to the society from which we have received so many benefits. If I cannot use my time and experience to do this, then why should I expect anyone else to make a difference for me? Third, and to be totally shameless, my involvement has ended up helping us in ways I never anticipated or even thought of several years ago. Sometimes things seem to happen for a reason.
>
> Barbara McCormack

Four Measures Of Family Quality Of Life

Four general measures of family quality of life were developed for each of the nine areas of life. These four measures corresponded to four concepts: attainment, opportunities, initiative to access opportunities, and satisfaction.

Attainment

Attainment refers to getting, having, or accomplishing something that the family wants. For example, attainment in health refers to being healthy, attainment in spiritual and cultural beliefs refers to having developed and using such beliefs, and attainment in leisure refers to enjoying leisure activities. Attainment was measured in each of the nine areas by scoring the response to a single question asked. For example, the question for health was: "Thinking of your family as a whole, how would you describe your family's health?" Response options were excellent (score of 5), very good (score of 4), good (score of 3), fair (score of 2), and poor (score of 1). A similar single question was asked to assess attainment in the other eight areas of life. The mean attainment scores for the 28 families for the nine areas of life are shown in Figure 7.1.

The attainment ratings in Figure 7.1 show that these families perceive their achievement to be best in the areas of family relationships, spiritual or cultural beliefs, and careers or preparing for careers. Attainment is rated lowest in the supports areas and in community involvement.

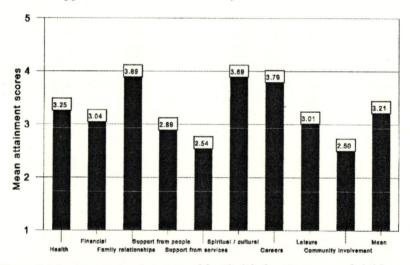

Figure 7.1 **Attainment in nine areas of family life for 28 parents of children with intellectual disabilities.**

5 = excellent; 4 = very good; 3 = good; 2 = fair; 1 = poor.

Opportunities Available To Families

Families live within physical and social environments that have varying types and numbers of opportunities. The term *opportunities* refers to options that are available within a family's environment and that are relevant to the family's needs. *Opportunities* was measured using a single item for each of the nine areas of life. For example, for the domain of leisure and enjoyment of life, parents were asked: "Are there opportunities in the area where you live for your family to have fun and enjoy life?" Response options were as follows: a great many, quite a few, some, a few, and hardly any. The mean opportunities scores for the 28 families are shown in Figure 7.2 for each of the nine areas of life.

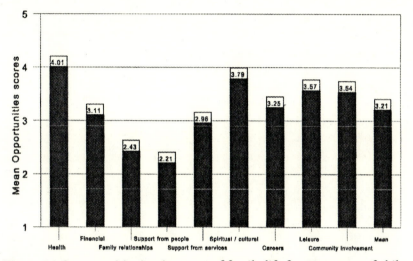

Figure 7.2 **Opportunities in nine areas of family life for 28 parents of children with intellectual disabilities.**
5 = a great many; 4 = quite a few; 3 = some; 2 = a few; 1 = hardly any.

Relevant options are viewed by the families to be available to them most in the areas of health, spiritual or cultural beliefs, leisure, and community involvement. Opportunities for support from other people was perceived to be particularly poor. The lower ratings for family relationships may result from the question referring to opportunities from outside the family to help maintain or improve relationships. It is possible that a different response would have emerged had the question referred to opportunities the families created themselves within their own families to help maintain or improve family relationships.

Family Initiative To Access Opportunities

Opportunities may be available and relevant to a family's needs, but families also need to take advantage of them, if they are to help improve a family's quality of life. Families may not take advantage of opportunities for many reasons, such as physical barriers, lack of time, insufficient skills, or simply because they do not wish to. Thus family initiative to access opportunities is a measure that is closely tied to the measure of opportunities. Having opportunities available from which to act is a pre-condition for measuring family initiative to access opportunities, but having opportunities alone does not promote family quality of life if families do not act to access them.

Family initiative to access opportunities was measured by scoring responses to a single question asked in each of the nine areas of life. For example, for the domain of support for disability-related services, families were asked, "To what degree do members of your family advocate for, or monitor, disability-related services?" The mean family initiative to access opportunities scores for each of the nine areas of life are shown in Figure 7.3.

Initiative was perceived by families to be highest for careers or preparing for careers, health, and family relationships. Families rated themselves as showing the least effort in the areas of seeking support from other people and becoming involved in community and civic affairs.

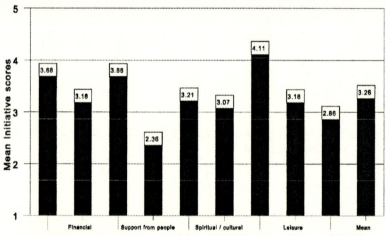

Figure 7.3 **Initiative in nine areas of family life for 28 parents of children with intellectual disabilities.**
5 = highest degree of initiative exercised by family;
1 = lowest degree of initiative exercised by family.

Family Satisfaction With Life

Overall satisfaction with family life was the final question asked in each of the nine areas of life of the survey. An example of this question for the domain of community and civic involvement is, "All things considered, how satisfied are you with your family's contribution to community and civic affairs?" The mean satisfaction scores for each of the nine areas of life are shown in Figure 7.4.

The 28 families expressed the highest level of satisfaction in the areas of family relationships, spiritual or cultural beliefs, and careers or preparing for careers. The lowest levels of satisfaction were shown for the two support areas: support from other people and support from services.

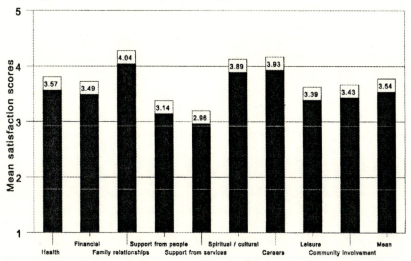

Figure 7.4 **Satisfaction in nine areas of family life for 28 parents of children with intellectual disabilities.**

5 = highest degree of satisfaction exercised by family;
1 = lowest degree of satisfaction exercised by family.

Relationship Among The Four Measures

It was expected that the four measures of family quality of life would be related to one another to some degree. A preliminary examination of relationship was carried out by computing correlation coefficients for each pair of measures in each of the nine areas of life examined. Significant coefficients were found ($r = .35-.77$, $p < .05$) for attainment and satisfaction scores for all areas except spiritual or cultural beliefs, indicating that those who have attained well are well satisfied and those who have not attained are dissatisfied. Initiative was similarly related to attainment in four of the nine areas of life, financial, spiritual or cultural, and leisure, and careers or preparing for careers ($r = .36-.68$, $p < .05$), which suggests an interesting hypothesis: attainment may result, at least in part, from initiative to access opportunities. It was expected that initiative to access opportunities would be related to the availability of opportunities, but, surprisingly, this was the case for only one of the nine areas of life, spiritual or cultural beliefs ($r = .55$, $p < .01$). This suggests another interesting hypothesis: Those who take initiative to access available opportunities may be as inclined or more inclined to do so when opportunities are not as available as when they are.

The four measures of family quality of life all correlated significantly for only one of the nine areas of life, careers and preparing for careers ($r = .47–.77$, $p < .01$ for all six pairs). Exploring the factors that account for the strong relationship among opportunities, initiative, attainment, and satisfaction in this aspect of life will be an interesting area of future study. It will be equally interesting to explore the more precise ways the measures are interrelated in the various areas of life.

Key Issues Emerging From The Research Findings

A number of issues can be identified from the information gathered from the 28 families that participated in this survey:

- In spite of descriptions of life circumstances that would be considered by most people to be difficult, the overall life satisfaction of these families was fairly high. This is in keeping with the tendency within all populations to be fairly optimistic about their life satisfaction (Cummins, 1995), and may reflect a human ability to find satisfaction from the particular circumstances of our lives.

- Families do not receive a great deal of support from other people. They do not have as much support as they would like, they see few opportunities to get more, and, perhaps as a consequence, they don't try very hard to find more support from others. Families show relatively low satisfaction in this area of life. A few women mentioned that their extended family refused to see that help was needed. In other cases, parents did not want to burden other people with their child's difficult behavior.

- Families also have difficulty receiving disability-related supports to satisfy all their needs. Most families felt that there were several unmet service needs. Reasons included a long wait for services, services did not help enough, and the services were not available in their area. One woman commented that poor treatment by health-care staff discouraged service use by her family. The scores in this areas show that disability-related services are somewhat insufficient, and that families have relatively low satisfaction. This suggests that support from services is an area of life that detracts somewhat from overall family quality of life.

- Family relationships, spiritual and cultural beliefs, and careers appear to be quite good contributors to family quality of life.

- Families with sons or daughters with intellectual disabilities are not highly involved in community and civic activities, but, on the whole, are not particularly displeased with this state of affairs.

- Families varied considerably in the amount of money available to them. For a number of families, money was not a problem at all, but for others it was. Families, especially those for whom money was already somewhat of a problem, worried about the stability of their financial situation in the future.
- Many families felt that they do not spent a lot of leisure time together and had a moderate dissatisfaction with this.
- The quality of family life is strongly affected by the health of even one member with a serious health problem.

Implications Of Research

Implications For Improving Entitlements And Services

Individuals with disabilities are well protected in Canada under various legal entitlements. This protection is, for the most part, at the individual level, however, rather than at the family level. The question that emerges within the family quality of life context is this: If families want to, or are encouraged to, take on the primary responsibility for their sons and daughters with intellectual disabilities—even through their adult lives—what protections and entitlements do such families need?

Implications For Entitlement Policy

Three suggestions emerge from the conversations with the participating parents and relate directly to the development of entitlement policy. These involve entitlement by families to:

- Reasonable services that meet the individual needs of the family member with a disability. Some people need more services than others, and these change over time. These needs must be individually assessed and addressed in an ongoing way.
- Reasonable services that reflect the unique makeup and strengths/needs of each family. Each family has its own set of abilities and support needs that emerge from the unique structure of each family. Because these differ widely, such differences must be monitored in an ongoing way and services need to match the specific family needs.
- Case management and advocacy services. Few families are able to do this on their own, and require help from professionals who know the service and political systems and can access them.

Implications For Family Members' Protection Policy

Families with a member who has an intellectual disability may also require special legal and/or policy protection to ensure that their own rights are not compromised because of the occurrence of disability in their families.

Examples of such protections include freedom from discrimination at work because of time and energy required to deal with disability in the family, equal access (which may require special privileges) to public places and leisure opportunities, and access to specialized health and medical care (which may also require special privileges).

Implications For General Population Support Policy And Practice

A striking finding of the conversations with the 28 families is how little support they get from outside the family. This finding is consistent with an earlier study where 35 randomly selected sets of parents were interviewed about their lives (Renwick et al., 1998). It suggests that both policy and practice methods need to be developed that:

- assist community and civic organizations and processes to understand the need to support families better;
- assist faith and cultural communities to understand the need to support families better;
- assist relatives, friends, and neighbors to understand the need to support families better;
- assist parents to understand the need to seek support outside the family.

Implications For Disability-Related Policy

Within the research findings, there is an implied need to continue to strengthen disability-related policy that is based on a social and human rights model (Bach, 1999). What seems much more explicit is the lack of policy directly related to the needs of families, and the need to develop such policy. In Ontario, this will probably have to be done at the level of the government of Ontario to be effective, and will require considerable focused advocacy by individual family members, family organizations, service organizations, and others. There may some willingness within government ministries to begin to develop such policy, although there will no doubt be a natural tension between providing equal access to supports for all families and guarding against such supports costing more than the government wishes to fund.

Implications For Improving the Sociopolitical Context

Study of family quality of life focuses attention directly on addressing the question: How good is life for family members? This has simply not been a strong focus of attention in the past, either within the general population or within the disability field. Perhaps partly as a result, the general population and the political system have remained largely unaware of and unconcerned with the needs of family members. If the larger sociopolitical context is to be influenced in ways that favor recognizing and responding to the needs of families better, study of family quality of life will have to make an impact on developing entitlements to families, on developing government policy related to families, and on the way services are funded and delivered.

Implications For The Future Research Agenda

There appears to be a clear need to develop a broad and systematic research agenda to address family quality of life. In developing such an agenda, three decision areas are important to consider. The first decision area is the types of broad questions we should ask that will guide the content of the research agenda. Three broad questions are

- To what degree can, or should, we attempt to capture the complexity of family quality of life?
- What role, if any, do measures of family quality of life play in promoting the quality of families' lives?
- If we do use measures of family quality of life, what are the best ways to include the real life experiences of families?

A second decision area in setting a research agenda involves what is best to include. Again, it seems instructive to borrow from the work on individual quality of life that has been done in the field of intellectual disabilities. A best practice application that has developed here is to maintain and enhance those aspects of life that already add quality to life, and to work to improve those aspects of life that detract from quality in life (Renwick, Brown, & Raphael, 1994). Adopting this to family quality of life, it seems reasonable to undertake research first to identify the various factors that currently contribute to and detract from family quality of life, and second to explore how such factors can be maintained and enhanced or improved. The research here also suggests that we need to develop and measure the effectiveness of strategies to help families close the gaps between their real-life experiences and the levels of family quality of life that they feel is desirable.

Finally, a third decision area in setting a research agenda in family quality of life involves what methods are best to use. Previous research in this area, a qualitative study by Renwick et al. (1998) and the current study, suggest quite strongly that any attempts to understand the phenomenon of family quality of life need to include the telling of the stories of parents and other family members. At the same time, there may be some objective quantitative measures that may be both relevant and helpful. Because we do not know the best methods either to describe or measure family quality of life at the present time, however, it appears best to recommend a comprehensive approach where information from various sources and use of various methods can be compared and assessed for its credibility. This will involve a very careful examination of methodological issues and will be a strong challenge for family quality of life researchers.

A Parent's Voice: Barbara's Closing Thoughts

In the months that have passed since I wrote our opening story, the wheel of life has continued to turn, and with it my deepest attention to the subject of quality of life. We were recently told that if Sarah does not have two major surgeries for her dislocated hips and scoliosis, she will likely end up "twisted like a pretzel"—completely rotated at her waist to face the back. Untreated, this will result in increasingly painful episodes from the dislocation for her, and we will not be able to have her sit upright. She might spend years lying on a stretcher-type wheelchair, wiped out with muscle relaxants, her internal organs affected by their restricted space. However, both surgeries (a year apart) are highly complicated, long, initially painful, and fraught with risk. She might die during the procedures or recovery phases from a list of potential hazards that run off the page. Moreover, there is not much time to decide, as the deterioration is rapid. We could start surgery now, except that now she is a happy, laughing little girl not yet suffering too many ill effects from these problems. Now she is a young girl who might live another 15 to 20 years, though possibly far less.

If this were not a real-life story, it could be a question in an ethics textbook. Should Sarah have surgery? What is more important to her quality of life—the longer, more difficult life, or the risk of death for later gain? Even her two orthopaedic surgeons could not agree.

Being forced to play God with my child's life has been an unnerving experience. I have had to consider deeply her quality of life and what adds value to her little world. I have had to choose for her and her alone, despite my own agonized fears that I may lose her, and the possible ramifications on every facet of my own life. Yet even this dreadful dilemma has not detracted from the quality of life we share today. It has simply made our time together more precious.

Thus, although we can attempt to define and quantify the areas of life that affect quality, we must consider the personal context of the family—what we each want and expect from our lives, what we believe life to be, and how far we have come along the path of disability. Most often, disability has a shocking impact on family life, from the initial stunning impact of diagnosis to the waves of aftershock that radiate out and affect every single aspect of life. Years on, our lives barely resemble what they started out to be, and we have become quite different people with significantly altered values. Is there a way to measure quality of life more accurately, taking this journey into account?

To survive and thrive in this new world, families of children with disabilities have to find new parameters to assess quality of life. It is not the quality we had or expected to have, and it is not always immediately apparent. From that world-stopping moment of diagnosis, we have to invest major time and energy redefining the notion of quality in our individual situations. Acceptance is key. Those of us who are able to embrace disability, and incorporate it into the core aspects of our daily lives, often find greater purpose and satisfaction than those who struggle against their fate, angry and resentful at the intrusion of disability. Can quality of life indicators capture our attitude to, and acceptance of, disability?

We find our quality of life in small, unexpected places and draw intense joy from the tiny miracles, such as the movement of a hand, a smile, a first word, or a single step. Gradually, we experience life on an altogether different plane from the one we remember, and, with it, our expectations change. We learn to live in the moment, to cherish the good things that happen, and acknowledge that bad times may be around the corner. We develop a remarkable resilience to deal with life's challenges and seek out the good in whatever is thrown our way. Can we assess our resilience on a scale of 1 to 10? Can we plot a graph of our changing attitudes and expectations? Is there a measure for the intensity of our feelings? How much does this affect our overall quality of life?

There are still so many questions, but this valuable research has set the stage for further investigation, insight, and understanding of the many nuances that affect quality of life in families of children with disabilities. For my part, despite the hardships, I consider my life with Sarah to be one of exceptional quality where we travel a rich, wonderful, and extraordinary journey together.

Barbara McCormack

Authors' Note

The authors gratefully acknowledge the important contributions of Joanna Pacia, Asthma Dost Mohamed, Tara Levkoe, Alan Fung, and Kevin Shi to the writing of this chapter.

References

Bach, M. (1999). Current views on developmental disabilities. In I. Brown & M. Percy (Eds.), Developmental disabilities in Ontario (pp. 33–42). Toronto: Front Porch.

Brown, I. (1999). What do we mean by developmental disabilities in Ontario? In I. Brown & M. Percy (Eds.), Developmental disabilities in Ontario (pp. 17–31). Toronto: Front Porch.

Brown, I., & Renwick, R. (1997). Understanding what we mean by quality of life [editorial]. Journal on Developmental Disabilities, 5(2), i–vii.

Canadian Human Rights Act, R.S., 1985, c. H-6 July 1996. Human Rights Code, RSO 1990. Retrieved May 27, 2003, from:
http://lois.justice.gc.ca/en/H-6/

Constitution Act, 1982, Part I—Canadian Charter of Rights and Freedoms, § 15(1). Retrieved May 27, 2003, from:
http://laws.justice.gc.ca/en/charter/

Cummins, R. A. (1995). On the trail of the gold standard for life satisfaction. Social Indicators Research, 95, 179–200.

Galambos, D. (1999). Individual approaches to support. In I. Brown & M. Percy (Eds.), Developmental disabilities in Ontario (pp. 43–58). Toronto: Front Porch.

Ontario Human Rights Code. (1990). Human Rights Code. Retrieved May 27, 2003, from:
http://www.e-laws.gov.on.ca:81/ISYSquery/IRLC94B.tmp/11/doc

Ontario Ministry of Community and Social Services. (1997). Making services work for people: A new framework for children and for people with developmental disabilities. Toronto: Author.

Peppin, P., & Baker, D. (1999). Entitlements in four areas of law. In I. Brown & M. Percy (Eds.), Developmental disabilities in Ontario (pp. 67–82). Toronto: Front Porch.

Porter, J., Melville-Bennoch, J., Gouse-Sheese, J., Emerson, L., Grossman, A., Massé, D., & Reda, R. (1999). Developmental disabilities and Ontario's schools. In I. Brown & M. Percy (Eds.), Developmental disabilities in Ontario (pp. 109–117). Toronto: Front Porch.

Renwick, R., Brown, I., & Raphael, D. (1994). Linking a conceptual approach to service provision. Journal on Developmental Disabilities, 3(2), 32–44.

Renwick, R., Brown, I., & Raphael, D. (1998). The family quality of life project: Final report to the Ontario Ministry of Community and Social Services. Toronto: University of Toronto, Centre for Health Promotion, Quality of Life Research Unit.

Rioux, M. H., & Frazee, C. L. (1999). Rights and freedoms. In I. Brown & M. Percy (Eds.), Developmental disabilities in Ontario (pp. 59–66). Toronto: Front Porch.

Chapter 8

Family Quality Of Life In Australia

Roy Brown, Ruth Davey, Jo Shearer, and Margaret Kyrkou
Flinders University
Adelaide, South Australia, Australia

"Heroes" by Ian Corlett[1]
Dedicated to Rebecca, and all who understand.

BIRTH:
> *New life leaps out,*
> *But there are no wildflowers,*
> *No birds singing.*
> *For this new life is broken,*
> *Handicapped. A burden of shame,*
> *A disappointment forever. . .*

A Family Experience

Sarah is 27 years old and lives at home with her parents, Linda and James. Linda works in the disability sector and James is a lecturer at a South Australian university. Sarah has a younger sister, Samantha, aged 20 years, in her final year at university, and a younger brother, Joe, aged 16 years, who is nearing completion of his high-school education. Here Linda introduces her story:

Sarah's intellectual disability was first detected at the age of 3 years, when it was discovered that she had not reached developmental milestones considered the "norm" for her age. It seemed that Sarah would benefit from a longer than normal period at the kindergarten, before moving onto school. Unfortunately, the kindergarten staff perceived themselves unable to cope and insisted a parent be present most of the time. James' comment illustrates our feelings at the time and underscores the need for training in disability for all teachers, whether preschool, primary or secondary students. "Teachers at kindergartens and schools can't cope unless the parent attends most of the time as a free helper. I seemed to be visiting such places lots of the time, yet I know Linda did much more, and this has added to my

1. Excerpts (in italics) from the poem"Heroes" by Ian Corlett (c) 1999, used by permission of the author.

guilt burden. To find your child was the first such child to be accepted into that kindergarten or school demonstrates how poor the system still is. Of course we had to fight for this right." There is an ongoing demand on parents' time, above and beyond that which would be considered the norm in caring for children.

Health and medical care feature prominently in our lives, sometimes because of long-term major problems, sometimes because of short-term variations. Sarah suffers from a cardiac condition that has led to complications with chest infections, usually leading to pneumonia and hospitalization. Up until the age of 18 years, Sarah was admitted to the Children's Hospital. She was very upset on her last admission to hospital, after her 17th birthday, when she was told she would soon have to go into an adult hospital. It wasn't long before that dreaded admission to the general hospital occurred. Sarah has been admitted to hospital several times. In the pediatrics ward, Sarah was seen as a child with a disability. In the adult ward, Sarah is seen as "disability" first and person second.

Sarah did not know the nurses or medical staff and they did not seem to understand her needs. We were extremely worried about her being in the hospital and this put additional stress on our family. The staff at the Children's Hospital were used to carefully watching patients with disabilities, whose understanding and self-help skills were still at the level of a young child, whereas in an adult hospital the staff were not used to supervising patients to this same degree.

One night we visited Sarah, who had already been in hospital for 2 days. As we walked out to the toilet with her, a nurse said, "Oh, we didn't think she could walk on her own." On another occasion, we got out of the lifts [elevators] to see a white streak moving rapidly down the passage [Sarah] followed by a blue streak [the nurse]. Another night, I was holding Sarah while yet another doctor tried to insert a drip connection. Suddenly Sarah bent down very quickly and pulled out the newly inserted drip with her teeth. Sarah's behavior means that you feel that you must be forever vigilant and this feeling leads to tension, headaches, and worry about what she will do next. On the rare occasions she has been cared for by respite workers, the relief for her family is unbelievable.

Family relationships in general seem to suffer and assume different perspectives than those in families without a member with a disability. Sarah's behavior leads to upsets within the family. The impact of

Sarah's behavior and special health needs on her siblings has far-reaching effects. Internal challenges ordinarily faced by families are exacerbated by Sarah's behavior. Sarah listens to her radio late at night, the sound carrying through to the other bedrooms, and she has refused to wear headphones to lessen the noise. Sarah also tries to help around the house picking up clothes, and likes to make sure all the doors are closed. Samantha's comments illustrate the effect of Sarah's behavior: "I find it so easy to forget how annoying Sarah can be when I am not at home, but when I am at home she drives me insane . . . she refuses to leave my stuff alone. Every single day she insists on closing my bedroom door, I've tried everything. I've wedged it open, I've told her not to do it but she doesn't listen."

Part of the challenge lies in the uncertainty of the future. Family members' roles become distorted. Responsibility can be excessive. Siblings can sometimes become so anxious for the welfare of their parents that they become pseudo *in loco parentis*. James often talks about the parents' role and the load placed on Sarah's siblings. James says, "We have a very tough parenting role, far beyond the normal load and so easily glossed over by the community around you. Massive guilt follows (or was present from birth) and is expressed on many occasions against people or your children who do not understand what is wrong and probably blame themselves. Siblings can be so wonderful and almost becoming a friend. It is a depressing period as the family grows older and as you feel increasingly cornered by the family member with a disability as she and you age. This is contrary to most people's expectations of a peaceful and less wearing time as children grow and depart from the family. Retirement freedom is now not a possibility. Responsibility remains into the foreseeable future and on, to distant old age."

Responsibility is often displaced to siblings. James says, "As Sarah has approached adulthood, we have become more worried about her relationships, her understanding of relationships, and what the future holds for her. We are worried about her vulnerability and likely exploitation. It is now far less worrying for us if she goes out with her younger sister and her friends to a nightclub. However, this is not necessarily the way Samantha looks at this situation and perhaps we are being unfair to her in placing this responsibility upon her. Samantha and brother Joe are often embarrassed by some of the things that Sarah says and does that are age inappropriate. Samantha's friends look at Sarah strangely at times. Samantha is tired of watching out for Sarah, and would just like to relax and have a good time herself. Lots of young men approach Sarah, and either make some excuse to leave after talking to her for awhile or seek to take advantage of her and ask her to come outside."

Dual disability further exacerbates the problems initiated by intellectual disability. Sarah's life is further complicated by obsessive-compulsive behavior, a condition only recently verified by the psychiatrist. Obsessive-compulsive behavior increases the tension and frustration within the family unit. This behavior manifests itself in a thousand little routines: Items are placed within larger items, in a plastic bag or a biscuit tin, and then hidden somewhere else. She tidies up beautifully, but where are the keys to the car, the spare keys to the house, the tissue box when you sneeze? The whole family is affected by these routines. Sarah's psychiatric disorder has complicated her support needs. Dual disability is at last receiving some attention through a fledgling specialist service. After a year's trial there are now the beginnings of a protocol for discourse between the entity that funds intellectual disability and that which funds mental health. Services lack the necessary resources to handle the ever-increasing number of people surfacing with dual disabilities, and there is an extremely long waiting list for services.

The challenges inherent in these experiences focus on the need for training, education and support services in order to foster Sarah's development and alleviate the pressure on the whole family. Little is known about the long-term impact on siblings, and so we look to the future with some trepidation.

Introduction And Information Base

This chapter concerns issues related to the quality of life of families in Australia who have a child with intellectual disability. It takes its material from several sources, presenting various accounts of the experiences of families and children, largely from South Australia.

In total, 107 families provided information through a mixture of in-depth interviews and questionnaire responses that include parent and siblings commentary. Information has been drawn from an evaluation of disability services in South Australia (R. Brown, 2000b), a qualitative research study by one of the authors (Shearer, 2000), and other studies, including a three-nation study (with Australia) which is currently underway (I. Brown, R Brown, & Neikrug, 2000).

The material covers a wide age-range for people with intellectual disabilities, including adults and children. Males and females were included, although there was a bias toward female involvement in some of the studies, both in terms of the people with disabilities and the primary parent respondent (who in most cases was the mother).

The families do not represent a random sample. They are families who have a desire to provide information about their experiences. Many of the reporters are mothers who came from traditional families of European background where there is a mother and father. The content is largely narrative and phenomenological. The report on carers' perspectives (Peters, 1998), based on 100 family cases involving intellectual and allied disabilities, suggests that the qualitative commentary in this chapter is consistent with the major numerical trends in South Australia. The opening vignette has summarized the collective experiences of a family. Other aspects of this story, along with remarks from a variety of additional families, continue to be presented throughout the remainder of the chapter.

The people with intellectual disability are diverse, including those with Down syndrome, cerebral palsy, autism spectrum disorder, and dual disability (where issues of mental health as well as intellectual disability are involved). The parents profiled include postgraduate students in disability studies who have children with disabilities and as such are in favourable positions to provide information on the topic.

This account is not one of the norm or of incidence, but is an attempt to tell developmental stories illustrating families' concerns. Different generations face different issues, and different families tackle their situations in different ways. Each is an exploration with expectations, fears, resolutions, successes, and failures. We believe both hardships and hopes need to be described. The changing service system needs to address the benefits and the pains so that practitioners and policy makers can work with families collectively and adjust their responses to ever-changing family needs. Families in our narrative have grasped the challenge of living with disability; indeed, throughout our chapter there sparkles the human spirit. The chapter opening, featuring the poetic words of one of our parents, epitomises this theme.

There is also a need to recognize different scenarios, such as single-parent or blended families. There are additional issues surrounding families from Aboriginal backgrounds, where both disability and family are conceived in different terms, in that the primary caregiver can be a member of a large extended family (e.g., grandmother or auntie), who is regarded as part of the immediate family. Those families' needs are great (V. Brown, 2000).

There are also families from non-European backgrounds, particularly those from Asian descent, where issues of language, immigration, and culture interact with disability concerns, such as those relating to the fear and shame of having a child with a disability and the responses from large extended families (Helbers, 1997).

This chapter addresses the theme of quality of life and exemplifies the concepts involved in a family quality of life model. But the model is far from complete, so we identify other concepts and practices important to parents.

We look at the resources within Australia that are available for families who have children with a disability, and then we examine the implications of these resources for future development in the context of quality of life, thus raising challenges for professionals and service agencies. Throughout our discussion we aim to identify questions and suggest improvements.

A Look At Australian Services

Parmenter and colleagues (Parmenter, Cummins, Shaddock, & Stancliff, 1994) recognized, in their historical overview of disability services, that in Australia there had been an attempt to give people with disabilities and their families more control in the way they conduct their lives. The term *quality of life* is now embedded in the rhetoric of strategic planning documents, but many questions regarding the meaning, implications, and application of the model remain.

One government document states that quality of life "refers to the health, well-being and level of contentment of individuals, families and communities" (Department of Human Services, 1999, p. 39). Another refers to improving the quality of life for people with a disability by removing barriers that prevent them from accessing life's opportunities (Disability Services Queensland, 2000). Although it is necessary to acknowledge the increasing commitment to the importance of quality of life for people with a disability and their families, the meaning of the term *quality of life* in these documents can still be debated, particularly in relation to individuals and families. There is a danger that the term can be presented but its challenging implications not practiced (R. Brown 2000a).

The Australian Population And Federal System

Australia is populated by approximately 19 million people, the majority of whom (65%) live in capital cities and inhabit coastal regions. Almost three quarters of the Australian land mass is relatively uninhabited. The structure of the Australian government consists of a federal system (known as the Commonwealth Government), with six individual states and two territories having their own legislatures. In addition, there are divisions of local government within each of these states. Australian parliamentary structures are based upon the British Westminster system. The demographic picture and federation structure of the country is much like Canada.

Following the white settlement of Australia, policy and practice were largely influenced by British policies and practices. Strong Christian values guided the nature of relief in both government services and private charities. Institutions, nursing homes, asylums, and sheltered workshops based on charity and/or medical models of care and control were predominant. In the early 1900s the Commonwealth (federal) Government began to provide means-tested invalid (disability) pensions. Toward the 1950s, after the Second World War, the Commonwealth Government ratified the Social Services Act (1947). This act was to become the guiding legislation for disability over the next 30 years.

The civil rights movement of the 1960s and 70s influenced the way people viewed disability and highlighted discriminatory practices that existed at that time. The implementation of the Handicapped Person's Assistance Welfare Act (1974) broadened the provision of support to people with a disability. Subsequently, in 1983, the Commonwealth Government of Australia funded the Australian chapter of Disabled People's International. This development occurred in conjunction with the establishment of the Disability Advisory Council of Australia and a commissioned review of the Handicapped Person's Assistance Welfare Act (1974) undertaken by Senator Don Grimes, which was to become a landmark development in relation to disability services.

Critical Legislation

Four major developments in legislation have occurred since that time: (a) the establishment of the Disability Services Act (1986), (b) the Human Rights and Equal Opportunities Commission Act (1986), (c) the establishment of the Disability Discrimination Act (1992), and (d) the establishment of the Commonwealth/State Disability Agreement (CSDA) in 1992.

The lead in Australia has been taken from older, more populous Western countries and as such a similarity to these countries in terms of service developments and attitudes has emerged. From the point of view of disability, there has not been the same coordinated approach to advocacy nor the same detailed or primary involvement of people with disabilities and their families in the development of policy and service systems. Further, there has been less emphasis on human rights and discrimination. However, at a state level, disability services and equal opportunities acts are providing a stage for increasing advocacy, including both family and environmental issues.

Services In Australia

We describe below services available to people with a disability and their families across Australia in the year 2000, and then give more specific examples from the services of South Australia as an example of the state system.

As briefly mentioned, significant developments in both state and federal legislation and policy, regarding disability, have developed over the past 15 years since the Grimes report (1985). Essentially there were seven positive consumer outcomes of the Grimes report: (a) a place to live, (b) paid employ-ment, (c) competence and self-reliance, (d) community participation, (e) security, (f) choice, and (g) a positive image. This development reflects increasing empowerment and respect for people with a disability and a clear direction toward the encouragement of community participation. Yeatman, in 1996, noted that, "For the past ten years Australian Commonwealth, State and Territory governments have pursued approaches to people with disabili-ties which regards them as entitled to the same rights as other citizens" (p. 1).

In 1991 the initial 5-year Commonwealth/State Disability Agreement (CSDA) was established in an attempt to unify disability service provision across the nation and address the funding inequities that existed among states. A policy of fiscal balance was implemented based on a "per capita" ratio. Currently, the second CSDA agreement expires in 2002.

The federal government's legislative and funded services and provisions relevant to disability can be summarised as follows: Commonwealth legisla-tion, employment services, work-oriented rehabilitation services, financial assistance, advocacy, and research. State and territorial governments are responsible for the following: state legislation, accommodation services, recre-ation services, day options, respite, case management, early intervention serv-ices, education, community services, advocacy, transport, equipment, information and resource services, and research. Local governments provide community support services specifically for aged and younger people with dis-abilities and a range of generic local community services.

In general, a common philosophy of service provision exists across the states and territories of Australia. Essentially, each state is responsible for accommodation support, personal care, community services, respite care, social and day activity programs, information and resources (with a focus on community participation), and the development of individualized funding. In addition, the state governments are also responsible for health, education, and the justice systems, each of which interface with the disability sector.

The type of support services available to families varies, and the level at which one can access these services differs. Federal and state services aim to integrate and coordinate many of these services. Overall, each of the states and territories within Australia function similarly in relation to the services provided to people with a disability and their families, although variation does occur. This variation becomes noticeably significant when a family, or person, with a disability relocates to another state and seeks the same sup-ports. Sometimes services improve; sometimes they do not.

A State Example: Options Coordination

Within South Australia the regional boundaries of the major disability service providers and local governments have not always been aligned, caus-ing inequities among regions and across local government constituencies.

Inequities have also existed among disability groupings. Yet there is an attempt to put in place an equitable system of services through an organization called Options Coordination.

Options Coordination represents a model for case management and comprises five agencies for five different disability groupings: intellectual disability, adult physical and neurological disability, children with physical and neurological disability, sensory disability, and acquired brain injury. One of the aims of this initiative is to see whether it is possible to provide umbrella services for all disabilities. There are merits to this approach but also challenges, particularly with regard to how individual variability is accommodated in terms of needs across and within disabilities—a key concept in any quality of life model (R. Brown, 2000b).

Allied with Options Coordination are many government-funded incorporated organizations (e.g., respite agencies, therapy services, recreation agencies, tenancy support and community accommodation agencies, specific disability organizations, and advocacy agencies). The complex web of services often confuses families, hence the advent of Options Coordination.

As the name Options Coordination implies, choice and control are gradually devolved to the consumer, with some self-managed packages now in place. However, although this system relates to all disabilities, the development of self-managed packages is more evident among adults with physical and neurological difficulties than among people with intellectual disability.

Employment

Although employment for people with an intellectual disability is a Commonwealth responsibility, postschool day activity falls into the domain of state government. Projects allocate funding resources for people who are in transition from school to employment. Eligible consumers may choose from an array of accredited day options that focus toward employment. In addition, the Commonwealth Government provides funds to vocational rehabilitation agencies in each state. These agencies provide services for training, placement, and follow-up.

Inclusion In Education

For a number of years, and certainly as far back as the 1970s, there have been pilot schemes demonstrating how children with disabilities can be supported in regular classes (Davey & Morgan, 1977). In more recent years, programs of inclusion have developed to different degrees in different states, with the involvement of support officers (or teacher aides). This has now led to major revisions in some state curricula so that regular teaching can include children with various disabilities.

Satisfaction With The Service System

Across Australia, studies (Knox et al., 1995; R. Brown, 2000b; McKenzie, 1999; Shearer, 2000) indicate that reasons for dissatisfaction and inadequacy concerning disability services for families revolve around power and control, consultation and involvement, access to services, access to information, professionalism and knowledge of staff, the relationship between support staff and family, levels of funding (particularly for accommodation), equipment provision, appropriate supports for individual needs, and the degree of flexibility. These all relate to family quality of life, not just to the quality of life of the individual with a disability. More recently Cummins (2001) particularly highlights the significantly lower overall assessment of quality of life for families where disability is present and advocates that such families must be provided with increased levels of support to sustain community and family care. Cummins concludes that "families, most especially mothers, are paying a very high price for providing care" (p. 97). This point is brought out in the R. Brown report (2000b) where parents, especially single mothers, were recognized as facing extreme burdens of care particularly where multiple disabilities and behavior problems occurred.

How well do disability services work? A recent survey (R. Brown, 2000b) suggests there are a number of concerns and issues. The system appears to meet the needs of many individuals and families, but quite often the lack of funds, changing personnel (in some areas), high workloads with attendant stress, and insufficient appropriate community accommodation and relief support result in notable levels of complaint. Further, there remain challenges concerning the appropriate level of care and support for families with older members with intellectual disabilities and the issues of dual disability remain a challenge. Finally, and probably underestimated in most communities, there are the issues related to the financial and human support required to access relevant community services and operations in areas such as leisure, the arts, and spirituality. Unfortunately these areas of life are frequently not seen as rehabilitation resources, and yet they appear to be major resources that can contribute to a satisfactory level of quality of life for families.

Future Possibilities

One hopes Australia is now poised to focus on further enhancing quality of life for people with disabilities and their families. It is anticipated that there will be an increasing desire to understand what constitutes "quality of life" for the disability sector, both in theory and practice. However, the principles and application of quality of life not only need to be understood at policy levels but also need to be regularly practiced within front-line service delivery.

Quality Of Life And Families

Changes In The Field Of Intellectual Disability

At least two major changes in the field of intellectual disability over the past 25 years are crucial to an understanding of family needs and service delivery. First, children with intellectual disabilities are living much longer. Those with severe and profound levels of disabilities, as well as children with multiple disabilities, are surviving from birth in much greater numbers. Second, children with intellectual disabilities no longer enter institutions. The majority live at home with their parents and other family members. As a result of these changes, family has become the major service unit and each of its members is dramatically affected by the circumstances related to the disability of one of its members.

Studies On Family Quality Of Life

Although the quality of life of children with disability is now becoming recognized as an important research concern (see R. Brown & I. Brown, 1999), few studies have interviewed families with a quality of life theme in mind, and few children with disabilities have been consulted about their lives within those families. For example, a recent Australian text (Porter & McKenzie, 2000), although covering many critical issues germane to quality of life, has only one reference to this term. Some studies (e.g., Mitchell & Winslade 1997) discuss family research and quality of life models within the context of disability. Rasmussen (1993), McPhail (1996), and, within Australia, Knox et al. (1995), Peters (1998), and McKenzie (1999) have explored similar concerns and have interviewed family members. Also Shearer (2000) interviewed mothers and fathers and children with a disability. Cummins (2001) has reviewed subjective family quality of life from a more quantitative perspective. On the whole, issues specific to families with one or more children with disabilities have not yet been sufficiently explored within the constructs of quality of life (Goode, 1999). Careful analysis of family needs in the field of disabilities (*Demand for Disability Support Services in Australia,* 1997) presents quantitative data but does not discuss the underlying quality of life issues. This is a glaring shortcoming because, in providing services, it is important to address the personal issues of all the family members.

Focus On The Family

Persons with intellectual disabilities are central in the family context and a family's life tends to revolve around them. That also seems to be true of different types of disability, including, for example, acquired brain injury (Anstey, 2001). The centrality of the child is itself a concern, since a family functions in all its parts, not just around the child with a disability. By contrast, our research approach is family centered. Its results may or may not generalize to families as a whole, but they provide questions and suggestions relevant to practice and future research. Similarly, Turnbull, Poston, Park, and Lawson (2000) are currently developing a new model for exploring family dynamics in the context of disability and quality of life. Within this model the child (or adult) with a disability is no longer the focus of most of the researchers' attention, but each family member's needs are given appropriate weighting. Thus rather than a disability-centered family, an integrated and balanced family model can be encouraged.

In the present chapter we look at the positives, the negatives, and the challenges in disability-affected families, although we look at them from the point of view of families that believe they have, to a considerable degree, accommodated to disability. These families reveal not just challenges and frustrations that are at times severe, but rewards and frequently positive developments—in short, a reasonably balanced view of the issues. These portrayals are "models" from which ideas and potential solutions, including the variety of supports that are likely to be required, emerge.

WALK:

> *First steps; new horizons!*
>
> *She walked unaided, unassisted, out. Out beyond!*
> *Out*
> *the front door*
> *to answer the call*
> *of a world*
> *beyond*
> *the horizon. She toddled*
> *outside,*
> *(I wept at her side),*
> *A few steps*
> *then stop for a rest;*
> *To explore*
> *the new world*
> *rushing to greet her.*

Families And Children With Intellectual Disability

Quality of life studies enable us to look at children with disabilities in new ways. The following two responses relating to the child's bedtime at home clearly indicate differences in family experiences and values:

I think with Ellen she's an only child in a sense because she is the only one left. And I think, you know, we go off into that room together and she's by herself . . . it's pretty tough when she says her room's dark . . . And I think because we've got adult children we know how quick children grow up. I mean our kids were babies yesterday and now they're having babies of their own. So, it's fine to have her fall asleep in our bed.

From a baby I discouraged having her sleep with us. I wouldn't allow it, basically wouldn't allow it. I said to Lisa [mother], no I'm not . . . we've got our own relationship and we want to be able to sleep at nights and things like that. So she has always been encouraged to sleep in her bed . . . she likes her bed.

Clearly, quality of life is relevant not just to children who have a disability but also to the whole family. Although the theoretical components of quality of life are recognised (International Association for the Scientific Study of Intellectual Disabilities [IASSID], 2000), we still need to ask how well family experiences and these concepts converge and whether the principles emerging within the field of quality of life are consonant with family experiences.

Family Perceptions

We have alluded to the conceptual understanding and importance of perception. Quality of life is related to personal perceptions and, in this particular context, the dynamic interaction of those perceptions within the operative unit, the family, which are all encompassing. Accordingly, we favor Bronfenbrenner's model (1979) as particularly useful within a quality of life framework (IASSID, 2000; Mitchell & Winslade, 1997). Researchers may continue to debate whether the stated perceptions, which may be verbal or nonverbal, are objective or subjective phenomena. However, they are undoubtedly the outward reflections of the people concerned, the interwoven fibers of memories, feelings, fears, and dreams, and such perceptions are what cause people to interact, respond, develop, or deteriorate (see Andrews, 1974). For that reason, they merit our careful attention as central to an understanding of what causes people to do the things they do. They must now become central to any comprehensive understanding of the child with a disability in the context of the family.

In family quality of life, the perceptions of the mother, father, and each child become relevant. The recording of such detail is not regularly carried out by services. It is a time-consuming activity, and perhaps is seen by some as an infringement of privacy. But individual perceptions tell us much about the values and approaches employed by a family, and it is into this matrix of individual perceptions that services are delivered. The topic "quality of life" appears to appeal to families and represents a sensitising approach (Taylor, 1994) that enables people to respond. Of course, services should be ameliorative, but they also should be preventative in a broad family sense, helping to ensure that the family continues to be an effective functioning unit. A proactive approach relates to individual-member and family-wide self-image and empowerment.

We believe it is particularly important, wherever possible, to involve information directly from each family member because individual perceptions are both personal and varied. It is interesting to ponder, for example, why children with disabilities have not been in a position to provide first-hand accounts of their own perceptions of quality of life. Timmons and Brown (1997) indicate that children represent the least empowered members of society. This impotence is heightened among children with disabilities, making it unlikely that they will be consulted (Goode, 1999), especially when they have minimal or no language.

It has been a fairly well held belief that professionals and parents know best what is good for their children. It is now recognized, however, that parents may not always represent the perceptions of their children. Timmons and Brown (1997) quote examples where highly skilled and well-motivated parents are surprised when they hear of their children's wishes, choices, and needs.

One of the central issues for family quality of life research is that no one individual can entirely stand as proxy for another, notwithstanding the importance of information which is provided by an individual. A quality of life model requires direct statements from individuals, not necessarily as a valid reflection of objectivity but as a valid reflection of personal viewpoint. Shearer's (2000) study revealed that parents' accounts largely agreed with those of the child with a disability, but there were differences of time, place and name of activities, and individuals. For example, one child was asked, "Tell me about your school friends." The child replied, "About my school friends, we play." The interviewer then asked, "Who are they?" The child said the names of all her friends. When this child's father responded to the same question, he said: "[Chloe] says she has a lot of friends, and they all seem to say hello to her. I'm sure she's got a couple of close friends, but last year at school she was at everyone's birthday party, but at the beginning of this year I think there is only one popped up so far. So whether the other children feel they are too old for her or what, I don't know." More important, parents thought in more abstract terms and on different time span issues than their child. They were also aware of boundaries both of a physical and psychological nature that had not entered their child's perception. One mother was conscious of screening the experiences of her daughter and commented, "You can't stop what goes on at school, but you can make sure it's the nice little kids who come to play." These accounts clearly indicate different responses within the same family, thus highlighting different perspectives.

Social Inclusion And Exclusion

Research also reveals issues of inclusion and exclusion, with all that these processes bring in terms of family and child adaptation. Inclusion or exclusion is not just about the person with a disability, but about each family member and the lifestyle they pursue. Different members tackle situations in different ways, depending on circumstances and the value systems involved and on the experience of previous occasions.

> It proved extremely difficult to include Sarah in family gatherings because of her inability to cope with change and larger numbers of people. Sarah's difficulties have meant that we cannot socialize as a family group at occasions outside the family home. This repeated challenging behavior has led to some difficult decisions to avoid uncomfortable and embarrassing situations for both Sarah and ourselves.

Or again . . .

> We decided that one parent would attend a social function while the other stayed home with Sarah. Personal relationships under these circumstances are very fragile and lead to tension at other times also.

Also . . .

> We won a massive social burden in having a disabled family member, many people having too much difficulty coping with your problem and back off inviting you places. Being stared at is part of the game and hurts constantly. To have a young person who lies on tram floors or who is scared of buses and makes a scene getting on is awful.

What is the role of services here? To enable the family to function optimally is critical. Respite or relief may be required, but it is often required as need arises and it cannot always be forecast in advance. Also, services should recognize the importance of enabling a family to live a normal social life. Formerly, families tended to cope socially because their child was institutionalized. Now, with the child within the family home, new stresses, strains, and exclusions occur. Thus the degree of exclusion or inclusion has to be recognized within the quality of life model to accommodate the diversity of family needs.

The issues of social vulnerability are a constant concern for parents and represent issues of inclusion and the setting of boundaries. These issues are relevant to educational inclusion:

When Jackie was about 7 or 8 we suddenly got a phone call from the school. Jackie had her bag packed and was going to her Nanna's place. One of the kids saw her crossing the road. They (the teachers) didn't even know she'd left. The school panicked (thinking, how are we going to stop this? We can't have her just disappearing like that), and when we went to the school to discuss it, all sorts of issues started coming out. Jackie had not been cooperating, we found out that she was going under her desk and sitting there, refusing to come out, and sometimes she would just totally refuse to come in from the playground, and they didn't know what to do. I asked why they didn't tell us these things before. The big problem, as I saw it, was that they didn't know how to handle her. I explained to them that they should expect her to comply like the other kids. We discussed what we'd do. They went around the school and put red lines at certain points where all the ways going out of the school could probably be. Every day, for a couple of weeks, the support teacher would take Jackie to these points and teach her that the red line meant stop go no further. In the end I couldn't pick her up from school without her getting to the red line and saying, "Stop, no go Dad." I reassured her that with me it was okay. It was a rule and it worked, she never went out again past that red line. I suppose it's like any kid, they need a boundary but she needed a physical one. She needed to know where she could go to.

As this example shows, risk and behavior have to be balanced with the rights and benefits of inclusion. Society punishes those who take risks and falter, but learning and adaptation depend on sensible risk taking, which, by definition, can involve "things" going wrong. Increasingly professionals eschew risk because of potential legal implications (duty of care). In so doing they may frequently cause delays in the child's adaptation and learning. Services and societies need to deal with these issues: so do professionals (including lawyers) who work in the area of liability and insurance.

Choices

Families often find that it is difficult to attain choices when a child with an intellectual disability is involved. This difficulty influences all family members. Part of the issue is that the challenges are frequently about small procedures or items that have cumulative and potentially massive effects. Services tend to be interested in megaproblems, whereas families have to deal with nuance and millions of minor challenges and choices, and their "dealing with" can constitute major stress for families. It is not in the service systems' interest to allow family stress to build up because family situations are then likely to become more acute and chronic, with family breakdown or other costly losses more likely. Isolation and emotional stress tend to be coprevalent.

It is these concerns that services and management systems have to come to grips with. Initial funding of a small number of hours of support, used in a flexible way, either inside the home or outside on a regular basis, may diffuse potentially stressful situations and enable the family to maintain some harmony. An assurance of regular support is psychologically reassuring and offers both a stable base for planning and opportunities to consider real choices.

Emotion And Intimacy

In some families emotional issues can become critical, leading to a spiral effect that influences family interaction with its attendant stresses and damage to members' self-image. It is to such instances that the concept of holism applies, namely, that we cannot afford to overlook how one aspect of a person's life affects other aspects and their associated relationships, potentially causing stress to all of the family.

> A couple's sex life suffers due to the worry over having "another" such child, despite medical advice to the contrary (by this time you don't trust such advice anyway even with your own reading on the subject). A couple need each other to survive during such times. The child we had after Sarah has been a wonderful gift, though, and probably has returned some balance to our psyches. The decision to have another child was not taken lightly, but the pregnancy was a very testing time. Somehow Linda seemed to manage better than I.

This represents a different aspect of holism than is normally associated with a quality of life model, where the individual alone is concerned. Intimate relationships between partners may be changed or stressed due to worry or anxiety. This may affect personal and family decision making, having far-reaching effects throughout the family. Individuals may be strong enough to overcome the difficulties, but, even so, the effects may be felt over a long period of time.

Family Progress

The quality of life model raises other issues for the family. For example, whose responsibility is it to help individual members reduce the challenging effects of the child with a disability living in the home? Some of the difficulties would be unlikely to occur if the individual were institutionalized, but we are well aware of the effects of institutionalization. The challenge is to see how the negative aspects of family and community inclusion can be countered, for they are very real. As Linda (mother) notes, speaking about James (father):

And what of the effect upon James himself and his career? He felt that he could not leave me for long periods of time in the early years when Sarah was so often ill and needing to be hospitalized. He felt I could not cope with Sarah's special needs, together with the demands of Samantha and Joe, so he made a deliberate decision to not attend conferences and other work-related events outside of South Australia. This behavior then affected his work and chances for promotion. In later years, at times when he has felt particularly bitter, he regrets the effect that this has had on his university career as a lecturer, and reflects on what might have been.

Family quality of life is closely associated with individual quality of life. Quality of life issues from a social perspective may be ignored by professionals not used to working within family dynamics. Quality of life is also about satisfaction, but research suggests there is a natural dynamic and tension between satisfaction and new discrepancies which create new goals and opportunities (Brown, Bayer, & Brown, 1992).

Leisure

There may be little or no time for leisure activities or time to devote to personal and spiritual needs. Western society tends to see leisure as a frill and does not provide financial support to families to ensure they can become stabilized. In such situations, challenges to mental health tend to arise.

My life situation will not change. I am simply tired and run down. The level of exhaustion at the end of the day after working and keeping the kids fed, bathed, homework, sporting commitments, etc., leaves little time for other adult input.

In some cases parents (generally mothers) make contacts through volunteer work, often with organizations in the disability field. This represents both a contribution to the community and meaningful social contact.

Spiritual And Cultural Beliefs

When asked, several parents noted negligible formal spiritual or cultural beliefs and values, and frequently felt little support from spiritual and cultural organizations in their community. As one mother describes, "I have little time to put into spirituality but consider [my son] John a gift to keep me on track."

For several families, however, shared values play an important role. Within this construct the absence of involvement from churches and cultural centers is striking, for not only do these institutions possess a wealth of social capital (Bullen & Onyx, 1999), but the needs for such families also are so readily apparent. When there is a young child with multiple disabilities and other children in the family, and especially in some cases where the

father has left the home, a borderline survival mode often comes into operation as the exhausted mother becomes overly preoccupied with children's
needs and their care. "She is a happy child, but demanding, needs 24- hour
supervision and at times gets frustrated, but she's a fighter and won't give
up." The R. Brown report (2000b) recommends that far more attention be
given to meeting the needs from generic community agencies, but this will
mean a much more informed community, one that can move from a charity
to a community-based helping model.

Siblings And Social Challenges

As siblings develop skills as problem solvers and seek strategies for dealing with social issues, they frequently learn the hard way. Whether this
results in maturation or breakdown depends on many factors.

> Around new people I am meeting, I always avoid mentioning Sarah
> and her difficulties, the fact that she is not as smart. I settle for say-
> ing I have two sisters, one at university. Most people are never really
> that interested in your family so that is as far as they ask. I would
> have to know a person for quite a while before actually mentioning
> the fact she's not as smart as the rest of us.

The quality of life of each family member involves a continuum of dissatisfaction to satisfaction. Siblings, too, experience feelings along this continuum, but they sometimes express other concepts which are not readily
observed in current quality of life models.

"Sarah has enriched my life by being a part of that environment and my
sister." This sibling expresses an experience of enrichment, not just satisfaction. Although her perception was arrived at over a period of time, it was
preceded by feelings of being separate and embarrassed. Here, then, is evidence of not just acceptance, but also of recognition of life expansion. Not
all siblings experience such resolution. No doubt this may relate to their own
individual makeup, but again it is likely to develop within the overall family
value system, along with modeling and teaching within the family. It may
well also be associated with the type of behavior that the person with a disability shows, even challenging behaviors.

Parents indicated concern for their children without disabilities. Issues
relating to their development, attention, praise, and self-image arise right
from the beginning of the child's life. Older siblings are likely to face a drain-
ing away of attention as a new and lifelong focus on the child with an intellectual disability begins and is often reinforced as new challenges have to be
faced. The challenge is to ensure that quality of life is not lessened for siblings without disabilities; indeed, with some refocusing by parents, important and positive developments can be brought about.

Not placing too much responsibility on our 9-year-old. He was 5 when Ruth was born and almost immediately was required to do so much more than others his age. Not ignoring our middle child. He was almost 2 when Ruth was born. All his milestones seem to have been lost in the initial anxieties and now in the immense joy when Ruth achieves hers.

Or again . . . "We have very few photographs of the 2 younger children due to our preoccupation with our child who has a disability."

Disability, Family, And Services

Family Values And Professional Behavior—Issues Of Holism

It appears that not only personal rights but also basic and massive family needs may at times be ignored.

A particular episode in the life of Sarah and my family that stands out is the story of her heart. At one time my parents were led to believe that Sarah was born with a normal and healthy heart. It was only when she was 5 years or so, after exerting herself and turning blue that my parents realized that something was up. Querying the medical records revealed an obvious hole in the heart. I then learnt about the prejudice that the medical community felt toward the [intellectually] disabled. Sarah's heart problem was to manifest itself many times. I met the prejudice that we believed was behind the heart doctor's inability to act many times through my life, often surfacing in unlikely spots.

Thus well-being, which may be divided into domains, is in reality holistic, with one aspect influencing the other. Health issues have dramatic effects on the social performance of parents and siblings, let alone the individual with the heart defect. Further, the values held by family members should influence the judgment of professionals. The personal views of professionals have to be secondary to the family's values and this must be recognized at a professional level; an issue which comes to the fore within a quality of life model (R. Brown, 1997b).

Financial Constraints

Although quality of life may not always be dramatically influenced by financial considerations, they are more than a little relevant, both on a day-to-day and long-term basis. Many families, particularly single-parent families, face major financial difficulties that preclude attention to many of the other quality of life issues.

Basically quality of life can't compare to any normal family. We had salaries to give us expectations of security in our 50s but dollars are soaked up by need, and insecurity is always present. Life is constrained through needs of people with disabilities and their requirements—at school, finding support networks, transporting them to any activity, finding friends who understand. There is a huge financial burden which is hard to imagine many families meeting.

Planning And Support

Frequently, and probably more commonly when there is a single-parent family, parents find themselves dependent on resources outside their family. They look to disability services and social welfare offices for support. In this instance parental concern is often associated with changing personnel and changing government policy decisions. Parents come to believe that the support systems that they have managed to access will be taken away. Anxieties are present from an early stage as parents become more aware of the issues and implications, but anxieties frequently remain lifetime concerns. One parent said, "I guess we've known since she was born that she will most likely outlive us. My main worry is securing her financial future as most people plan for retirement." This is no more clear than among older parents who, thinking they have the necessary resources for their now aging children, find these may disappear because government funding and strategies change. Greater guarantees of support are critical.

Administrative Challenges

There is little doubt that administrative routines cause difficulties for parents in terms of how they are currently handled. Although illustrated in one example below, the report on the evaluation of Options Coordination (R. Brown, 2000b) is replete with examples of this kind. It is not simply that many requests for written information from parents are repeated, but that forms may simply be inappropriate.

> When Sarah turned 16 years of age, she applied for a Disability Support Pension (DSP). The DSP covers all disability types. The interminable forms were duly completed and eventually Sarah received her Disability Support Pension. Sarah has since been involved in one periodic review of her eligibility for the DSP. We were upset when the forms arrived, because we knew there was no likelihood of Sarah being "cured," and we faced a lifetime of forever filling out innumerable forms, even with Sarah's formal diagnosis. It is fortunate that Sarah now receives the DSP, as her disability has had a financial impact on family life.

Parents As Educators Of The System

Quality of life models are about changing situations, and it is inevitable, as systems such as education undergo change, that parents and families will meet these changes and their potential challenges. A key point is that many parents with children with intellectual disabilities are professionals and sometimes professionals within the field of disability. Parents who bring about change to meet their child's needs necessarily have to meet challenges in the form of misunderstanding. Sometimes the needs they see as critical for their child cannot easily be met by the existing system or the current professional personnel with whom they are working. Thus implementation for improvement is often stressful to family members and time consuming.

> I guess we are educating to a degree, the school and the teachers and the kids as well because it is all very new for them as well. And that's a fair bit of hard work. And even the parents of the other kids as well . . . you know, their attitudes and sometimes that can be a bit disheartening when you see that you are just not getting anywhere with them. So I guess they're sort of looking from a different perspective. That's the main thing, it's that constant battle.

This issue also has a lifespan quality, because changes made at any one time have effects at subsequent times throughout life. There are roll-on effects, particularly at times of transition, for example, from primary to secondary schooling, school to work, family home to separate living, partnership or marriage, and eventually retirement.

Service Changes Over The Lifespan

Quality of life is a lifespan concern, and parents are continually preoccupied with changes that have to be met by the family. Change seems to follow developmental periods. Change in the early stages of life precipitates needs and challenges at later stages. However, if changes at one stage are not followed by reciprocal changes, further family limitations tend to ensue.

> We were very worried about what Sarah would do when she left school. Would she be able to obtain some kind of work? What kinds of day options would be available to her? If she could not find anything to do during the day, one of us would have to take on the responsibility for her care. This would have meant deciding who was going to give up their job and stay at home with Sarah, and who would go to work. We were so relieved when an open employment agency called Employment Focus, working in partnership with the school, became involved with some of the students in her class during her last year at school.

Thus success at one stage sets up expectations, but if transition results in inclusion with ill-developed services or lack of opportunities, the constraints result in worries, frustration, and often failure. The development of consistently effective services throughout the lifespan is therefore critical.

Family Control

One of the concerns is that the locus of control is likely to shift from an internal parental base to external structures as services get involved. Services personnel need to find ways of enabling families to become self-sufficient on a long-term basis by concentrating on those means that enable people to empower themselves and their families. Most parents do not wish to be dependent; seeking support occurs out of desperate necessity. Also the fear that service supports will not be available when required can lead to inhibition and restriction in one's activities. For example, if effective arrangements are set up through disability services and no further help is required for the time being, parents become concerned that when they seek fresh help they will be placed on the bottom of the waiting list.

Once again there is emphasis on flexibility; services and funds need to be matched to the needs of the individual family. This is a new balance that comes into play if choices and individual funding are going to play important roles in future policy directions. It is of little benefit to the family if funding support occurs within inflexible guidelines, ones that do not allow support to be varied in the best interests of the individual or family.

Here there are issues associated with the knowledge base of personnel and the challenging lack of integration across child and adult systems, let alone between systems that provide health, education, social, and community services. The blend of services is critical. In some way it is necessary, within a quality of life model, to represent the challenges experienced by families on a lifespan and holistic basis. We are interested in what promotes and creates well-being in such families across the lifespan. Well-being includes reassurance that services will be available to allow support through major transition periods in the individual's life and that services will respond early enough to allow planning and real choices, instead of offering sometimes inappropriate support primarily at times of crisis.

Further Challenges

A fairly typical family situation is seen in the following brief vignette, which brings together a number of common elements and represents the complexity of family life.

The parent finds she has more responsibility than she wants, services are not available in her area, but members of her family engage in activities to improve family physical health, such as adequate diets and involvement in sports. Values and a sense of belonging together are important for this family. Here relatives contribute little, yet this is a family where the mother feels there is excellent support from friends and neighbors. The problem is the long wait for necessary services, and where communication with services is often unclear. The lack of local services is a concern in this and several other families. Again, though family spiritual values and beliefs are to some degree important, the family does not see the spiritual and cultural community providing any help.

Stages, Needs, And Supports

Medical concerns are not as prominent now. Even so, the last couple of visits have raised some new challenges, and there is the faint, but ever present, concern that next visit will be something serious.

The influence of the child with a disability varies at different stages, though for many families, concerns are forever present. Where the child has multiple disabilities, the initial impact is likely to be around health concerns. These may be critical, but it is important to recognize that they have an important impact on other aspects of well-being, not only at the time, but into the future. It is a serious challenge for parents to think of psychological and social impacts when a health crisis is on hand. But to ignore these other domains can have direct consequences, and professionals in the health fields need to be knowledgeable and supportive of multiple aspects of health that may appear beyond their core focus.

Parents are concerned not just about back up or emergency assistance but also about the quality of resources and personnel. They are acutely aware of their child's special vulnerability. Personnel need to be sensitive to the intensity of parental concern, attending to the perspective of its reality (i.e., the person with a disability may not have the resources to overcome certain situations, the implication being they are less able to thrive from adversity), and to the necessary watchfulness and concern that parents themselves feel. They often believe they need to watch and examine the performance of professionals much more carefully. Professionals need to recognize, understand, and support parents during such times.

I am not concerned that there will be a place (in school) for Ruth, but I do worry about the quality. Being a teacher, I know the enormous range of talent (and lack of it) amongst my colleagues. For my boys, I know they will weather the bad and thrive with the good. For Ruth, a bad year may well be the end of her time in regular schools.

Worries And Anxieties

It is important to examine the health needs and allied well-being issues of parents because of the greater stress of family involvement where there are children with disabilities. There seem good clinical reasons for supposing that parental health may be damaged because of the amount of care and changed life patterns they experience over the long term. Research into the effects of worry and anxiety on physical health is long overdue. So is a policy overdue that would allow support dollars to address immediate family needs. Such a policy would help to address long-term health well-being as well as the general function of families.

A personal account of worries comes to the fore many times. R. Brown, Bayer, and MacFarlane (1989) suggested that worries and anxieties have to be taken into account in any quality of life model. Such concerns can have a major effect on behavior. At the further end of the worry/anxiety continuum are issues of major stress, which may be chronic or acute (McConachie, 1994). Parents refer to issues of health degradation (e.g., teeth grinding while asleep, high blood pressure, sleep problems, clinical depression, and anxiety) during major times of concern. These health concerns were noted as common occurrences in the Peters (1998) study.

Family Friendships

Related to the area of necessary and appropriate supports is the issue of friends. If friendship networks develop, then a community support system begins to grow. This is a critical issue for people with intellectual disabilities (Firth & Rapley, 1990), becomes more acute when emotional disturbance is present, and has implications for all family members.

> . . . I want Jill to have friends. I know many parents who have gone to great lengths to help friendships develop ("have the best swings in town" is some advice I've heard). I also want Jill to be able to stand up for herself in the playground. She is very tiny, and I've watched kids her age, but over a head taller, push past her, or climb over her on ladders, almost as though they haven't seen her.

Individuals may find themselves becoming isolated as time moves on. The issue is holistic and lifespan-oriented for the person with a disability. Over time, height, weight, health, and growth play a role.

> . . . she's tiny. She looks about 2 even though she is 4. Even my mother-in-law insists on putting her in a highchair with a bib. Jill has trouble saying what she wants to, but she can understand. Many people don't respond to her as though she is a preschooler.

Family Values

Often issues that affect the present will be acted out in the future. Some parents are philosophical about the future, while others, or perhaps even different members of the same family, may view the weighting of the issues differently: "I don't really worry about the future as much as I've heard some do." And then there is the future role of siblings: "Although we expect our sons to look out for her, we don't expect them to become her carers." Here again variability of reaction even within the same family is considerable. However, there is little doubt that parental viewpoint, response, and guidance can directly affect and influence other members of the family through their formative years.

> Effect on our relationship is a nonissue. Perhaps it has brought us closer together, but I think we had a strong marriage before and it hasn't changed. We both took the news in the same way, sad that our daughter wouldn't have the sort of life we would have wanted, but, with God's help, we would just get on and make her life the best we could . . .

How issues are dealt with partly depends on a family's underlying value systems and personal structures, which will have been formed in the parents' own developmental years. Issues of faith and responsiveness among partners, along with issues of disability, are prevalent and now very visible in our society. They involve moral, spiritual, and ethical values that could well be addressed within the school years and that represent an important aspect of education.

Guilt And Comparison

There are issues of guilt arising from comparison.

> Dealing with guilt that I could/should/must do better is a constant battle. Early intervention has been a great support but it has its downside. Stories of those miracle children who run before they are 6 months old, read before they are born etc., etc., fill you with hope first, tinged with panic as you realize it was their parents who taught the skills to produce this impressive behavior; and then guilt that you haven't done the work that you obviously should have.

An understanding of guilt and its links with depression is an increasing theme within our society; they often appear when a family attempts to meet the challenges of having a child with an intellectual disability. Comparisons with the development of other children, both disabled and nondisabled, arise; comparisons, if frequent and preoccupying, may be associated with biochemical activity in the parents' central nervous system (James, 1996).

Reflections On Positive Outcomes

It is essential not to dwell only on the downside when looking at quality of life issues for the family. For many families, and probably increasingly, there can be pluses for parents and siblings, for the person with a disability plays an important role in the activities of all the family's members. It is often hard for others to see the pluses, and this in itself is an inhibitor to progress and a catalyst to discrimination. "Convincing others that being a parent of a child with a disability is not that bad. In fact, it's been jolly good fun at times too."

Many of the supports accessed by families come from others who face similar challenges; parent groups are an important source of knowledge and social interaction for many. For some, they become a major driving force in a family member's lifestyle. Not infrequently this is a shared and companionable role for both mother and father. As one mother describes the support they have accessed:

> . . . Parent support—service parent group and, of course, Nursing Mothers'. In both states I have lived in (South Australia and Queensland), apart from specific feeding assistance, it's wonderful to have a parent group where your child is just a baby and not a baby with a disability.

> Parent support in Queensland—weekly playgroup for children receiving services from Disability Services, but the couple of hours with the other parents was the most valuable. I am still in touch with the parents I met through this, 4 years ago.

These attributes, along with multidisciplinary and locally accessible services, are a mainstay for quality family life for many individuals. "Therapy—physio, including hydrotherapy; speech pathology; occupational therapy; visiting toy library." Newsletters that are practical and social represent support and contact. "Down Syndrome Association magazine. A very newsy journal mixing research articles with personal stories and articles by members."

The rewards, progress, and successes raise quality of life within the family. Access to generic services may further increase quality of life, but they require parental observation and judgment and need to be available and welcoming services. Indeed, helping members of the family to become knowledgeable about needs and successes and then helping them to ensure access are important roles for service providers.

> Kindergym has been a tremendous help for Jill. In directly teaching her gymnastics skills, overall benefits to her physical development have been amazing.

> Being able to seek out services available to the whole community is an important part of giving Jill the best opportunities I can. I'm fortunate to be able to find information I need and take Jill where I can access help/therapy as required. Others aren't so fortunate.

A Model For Family Quality Of Life: Implications For Services

Societal Values And Social Capital

It is apparent that, although the quality of life among families differs, there are some consistent concerns. No doubt, societal and cultural values are in varying degrees important for families. In our sample many individuals did not perceive they had support from the local spiritual and cultural community. For example, one parent reported, "Church ministers seem at a loss to know what to say or do. There is a need for education. A church youth group would accept my daughter only if a parent went along too."

Help from friends, relatives, and neighbors is often described as poor and becomes worse where there is a child with multiple disabilities and can be exacerbated as the child ages. In other families, where there is mild intellectual disability, situations often improve over time though parents are often concerned at the poor integration of transition services (e.g., school to work). Further, local disability services are frequently not present or there are long waiting periods. There is a lack of people with whom to share issues and some indication that people are expected to put a "brave face" on their situation. Many families desperately seek help and go out of their way to solve problems, for example, by obtaining social contact by volunteering for agencies working in the field of disabilities. Financial concerns often arise, particularly where it involves a single-parent family. However, individual parents are often too exhausted to do more, and their fatigue tends to cut off their social supports and reduces financial resources.

In Australia there is currently discussion concerning social capital (Bullen & Onyx, 1999). There is beginning to be some understanding that issues are not simply economic and there are noneconomic resources in the community where people have a wide range of skills and experience that could facilitate individual family members. The challenge is to ensure that these resources are tapped and directed to relevant needs. The summary of issues discussed above falls into this category.

Counseling And Support

At a community level, many of a family's initial worries and pressures might be seen as a local community responsibility, particularly if there is the application of some of the new developments in ideas, such as social capital (Bullen & Onyx, 1999). R. Brown (2000b) found that many individuals with disabilities and their carers expressed a need to talk through issues, and this they saw as an important role for service personnel. Staff, however, were so busy that a counseling role was often not met. The role required is a skilled one, involving effective listening and allied counseling expertise. "It seems I have no one to share/dump the hardship and can only be seen by others as happy and coping. There are few places to express anger, frustration, grief. I feel isolated."

Many of these issues are faced in families that do not have a child with a disability, but when such a child is present, the situation results in a severe exacerbation of the challenges. For example, in families without children with disabilities there is an intense preoccupation in the early years with bringing up and supporting very young dependent children. There is often a degree of isolation and lack of social contact associated with this time, and sometimes family breakdown and separation. Stresses can occur within any family, but when there is a child with a disability, there are powerful interactive factors that can result in much greater challenges. When asked, "To what extent does your family do things for fun and enjoyment?" one parent answered, "Hardly at all. Because of the nature of the disability, it is easier to stay home"

The situation appears cumulative and the challenge for social policy makers is to recognize what is required to support such families. At the same time providers are often constrained from employing "disability" dollars to offset problems that can normally arise in families. Perhaps such a division is arbitrary; there needs to be a much closer look at family needs and supports along with involvement of family choices to ensure greater family adaptation and higher quality of life in what has become largely an economically driven society.

The Challenge Of Disability And What It Represents To The Family

With increasing age, people with dual disabilities (emotional and physical) often present greater challenges for the family. Parents request advice on how to cope. It is not just the physical issues of disability, but also a sense of exhaustion and ongoing fatigue and isolation that affects many families. For example, whereas relatives such as grandparents were once able to help, they are now often in the workforce, and, with increasing age and weight of an individual who is physically dependent, they can no longer assist in the ways they did previously. In this day and age, it is more likely that families move interstate for employment reasons and so must exist without any help from extended family members.

Frequently parents do not feel that service staff understand the disability. Often this relates to an apparent lack of understanding of what life is like within the family. Consistent with Cummins's (2000) view, it appears that families seek equilibrium and adapt, thus perceiving their quality of life as quite satisfactory. It is when breakdown occurs that quality of life descends rapidly. Thus services should develop a preventative role. Monitoring of family situations is required, with supply of critical back-up support as necessary to ensure the family remains in homeostasis. Without this kind of proactive support, the services will become reactive to emergencies and not be able to prevent the number and severity of problems increasing. The issue for many families is that they need to talk to people who can listen and understand and then be provided with some support. Again and again as we collected our data, and in the studies quoted, parents thanked the authors for asking the questions and listening. There was a clear sense that our approach was therapeutic.

Leisure, Sport, And Recreation

Leisure, sport, and recreation are clearly seen as important as are personal value systems. But here again the community is frequently seen as unable to support these needs. It should be remembered that some of the children with intellectual disability are totally dependent and the prime carer is the mother. It is sometimes only the mother. There is a sense that they appear "left to it," and, although there are service supports for these families, both community and service systems are seen as inadequate for their needs.

The Family—A Critical Consideration

Indeed, we believe that the detailed family stories available to us demand a new look at families, with a reevaluation of needs in the context of family quality of life. Here we are not just supporting the child with a disability but also have a responsibility for the whole family's ability to function and remain in balance, thus preventing total breakdown and distress.

The data presented provide support for employing the general concepts of quality of life and intellectual disability. The same general concepts are found in a number of recent texts and articles (R. Brown 1997a; Cummins, 1997; Goode, 1994; Felce & Perry, 1995; Parmenter, 1994; Renwick, Brown, & Nagler, 1996; Schalock, 1996;) and apply within a family model of quality of life. The principles (or core concepts) represented in the following tables.

In addition, quality of life appears to have a sensitizing aspect, providing new glimpses or stimulating new ideas relevant to our understanding of families and their needs. Primarily, this information underscores the need for changing some of the directions of services, just as it reinforces some of the changes that are already being attempted.

Principles To Consider In Family Quality Of Life

Given that there are a number of generally accepted principles of quality of life (see below), these principles need to be integrated within a family context. It also is important to provide clear working definitions of the terms *family* and *quality of life*. It is then relevant to examine the domains of quality of life from a family perspective. Set out in Tables 8.1, 8.2, and 8.3 are the three essential components of a useful working model that responds to these guidelines and that clearly reflects the reports from families. The model and its components also provide important guidelines for future research, measurement, and intervention.

Table 8.1
Conceptualization Of Quality Of Life

Provide working definitions:

Family	Quality of Life

Examine quality of life domains of well-being:

Emotional	Physical
Interpersonal relations	Self-determination
Material	Social
Personal development	Rights

Investigate life satisfaction:

Short term:	transitory/immediate/present/now
Long term:	general, specific

Launch forward planning:
Links to self-image and satisfaction

There are also principles that provide focus and clarity for any family quality of life model.

Table 8.2
Principles Of Quality Of Life

HolismSelf-image
LifespanEmpowerment
ChoicesVariability
(inter- and intrafamily)
PerceptionDomains

A number of additional issues have been highlighted in this chapter.

Table 8.3
Examples of Key Family Quality of Life Indicators

Family Quality of Life Requires a Consideration of:
Cultural diversityFamily characteristics
(e.g., number, age and gender of members)
RightsSocietal factors:
    Inclusion or exclusionDiscrimination
    BarriersBoundaries
Stressors
    Acute (intensity)
    Chronic (duration)
Degree of vulnerability
    Environmental levels (see, e.g., Bronfenbrenner, 1979)
    Personal characteristics (e.g., personality constructs, health, gender)
Level of supports:
    Community (neighbors, local, extended)
    Volunteer
    Services (generic or specialized)

These discrepancies need to be addressed in formulating policy and service (i.e., what there is compared with what there could be, as shown in Table 8.4). Each of these items has been recognized by families within this study.

Table 8.4
Examples Of Critical Components In Family Quality Of Life

Critical Components Discrepancy
(what there is compared with what there could be)
Social capital
(resources from local community, local networks)Service supports (including service entitlements and self-managed financial packages, high behavioral support and respite requirements)
Finance
(personal)Interventions: Traditional or nontraditional (for parent and child)
Economy
(of country and federal, state and local governments)Urgency (short- and long-term, including crisis management)
Personal
(need for relaxation, leisure, arts, spiritual needs)Respite/Child and adult care/Emergency
Family composition
(including extended family)Relief or counseling resources
Legislation & legal
(legal services, ombudsman, rights tribunal)Advocacy/Self-advocacy

---

Some Key Recommendations

Family Focus

When working on the initial drafts of this chapter, we had the impression that the focus on disability directed a family's attention toward the child with a disability and the child's challenges. The family as an entity unto itself seemed present but remote. It seemed to be nothing more than the substrate in which the person with intellectual disability operated. It also seemed that the family's quality of life received little attention. Where there was a child with a disability, the focus for the family seemed to change, and the child with a disability became the fulcrum around which other family members revolved.

What, then, are the implications for each of the various members of the family and for their relationship within the various domains of society? (Bronfenbrenner, 1979; Mitchell & Winslade, 1997). In turn, what impact does this hyperfocus have on the child with a disability? One parent expressed that the child with a disability is likely to become "extremely self-centered with little reciprocity."

There should be a recognition of the value system held within the family about life and of the key characteristics espoused by the parents. Thus once an individual with intellectual disability enters a family, the subsequent quality of life experienced by that family is in part determined by that family's structure and value system.

This has major implications for policy makers and service personnel. Not only is it necessary to know about individual family systems and to respect them, but it is also relevant for the types of support a family may require. It therefore requires diversity of service response and, as R. Brown (1997b) has pointed out, raises the critical issue of professional versus personal values and philosophy among service personnel.

Despite our efforts to represent quality of family life from different viewpoints, in virtually every case the family was viewed by parents as a structure that rotated around the person with a disability. This centrality is frequently recognized by parents who note that other children's needs and developments may be left out or receive minimal attention. Siblings learn to adapt. Sometimes there is a cost, but in other cases hard lessons are learned and positive features emerge. Again we suggest this relates not only to each individual, but also to the family values and structure as a whole.

Variability Among Families

The issues of variability among people with disabilities and the variability among families with different economic, social, and psychological resources require a differentiated response from services. Well-being has several interconnected domains and the relationships between them are critical to an understanding of how to support a family. For example, family health may be at risk, so we recommend major studies should be directed to this health well-being, especially related to families where there is dual disability (intellectual plus emotional or physical).

It is apparent that many, and probably most, families wish to be as independent as possible, but they need both short- and long-term resources. Changes in policy should not remove, but should reinforce, the structure that parents and family members have come to rely on. So it may be necessary to deliver services in different ways, and it usually will be appropriate to assist families to become self-supporting.

Stress And The Family

Families undergo both short- and long-term stresses; these in turn promote anxieties and worries that, if not diminished by service intervention, can result in family disempowerment. On many occasions families are provided with controlling support based on the restricted availability of resources or the limited knowledge base of personnel. It is essential that provider personnel support and encourage the development of a family's internal locus of control, enabling families to resolve issues themselves. The family should be the decision makers as they seek advice, counseling, and support from many avenues. It is critical that human services support these empowerment approaches, which include parent groups and newsletters, while also offering direct service provision. Parents often know what meets their family's needs. Obviously their perceptions are limited or expanded through their knowledge base. This expansion, too, is a necessary role for human services.

But there are other activities that frustrate the development of effective family quality of life and may often detract from the resources needed for other family members. Unnecessary form filling and allied time-consuming activities fall in the unhelpful category.

Diverse value systems among services and service personnel or restrictive funding rules frustrate families even further. This frustration is often exacerbated by the lack of adequate respite, the rapid turnover of personnel, and inadequate numbers and resourcing of frontline personnel (R. Brown, 2000b). Frustrated and stressed professional personnel add to the existing problems for families.

Family-Based Care And Support

There are now major changes in our understanding of family needs, especially those needs that partly result from a move to family-based care and support, which is currently the major direction of services for those with intellectual disabilities. An enormous and ongoing burden has been placed on many families. Family employment, sibling development, family location, and local family communication in the neighborhood are among the quality of life challenges that services should respond to in a flexible manner. The consumer requires that these aspects are integrated with each other and the services provided are consistent with the families' own value systems. This is not simply a matter of government policies or services in general. There is also a major need for greater public appreciation of the issues, and to that end the intervention of the media and of other education sources is appropriate.

A Vision For The Future: Parental Viewpoint

In a more enlightened world, society having benefited from the research and education described in this chapter, it is possible to envisage the following experiences for Sarah and her family.

When Sarah attended preschool her mother, Linda, would be told: "Sarah will be fine; just come back and pick her up in 3 hours." Realistic support staff understand that Linda's presence is often a barrier to successful inclusion. Staff think the child is adequately supported because the mother is there, while children keep away because they think Sarah must be "different," with so much fuss made over her.

Of course, in this new world, special-education staff who are part of the early childhood section of the Education Department are designated a particular region and work closely with the preschool staff to show them strategies for effective inclusion of children with disabilities.

Compulsory and extensive training in special education for all teachers has led to a demystification of "disability" and greater inclusion for children with disabilities. Yet choices are available that are discussed with parents by skilled and informed counselors.

Again, this training theme has extended to health care, in particular the medical profession. In schools and preschools, specifically trained carers manage such invasive health-care interventions as tracheostomy and gastrostomy. Parents no longer have to train school personnel. Access assistants manage invasive techniques and additional support staff give intensive learning support where required. Sarah's medical specialists, now at the peak of their careers, have much improved attitudes, compared to those of 20 years ago. They have benefited from the groups with specialist knowledge about disability who have spoken to interns in their initial years following graduation from medical school. Other medical personnel have also received education about disability, and the nurses on the adult wards are more aware of caring strategies for people with disabilities. This means that Linda does not have to sit up all night in a chair besides Sarah's bedside, worrying about Sarah's care and support.

And what of Sarah's siblings, Samantha and Joe? Siblings belong to support groups, both formal and informal. Young people with disabilities and their siblings attend barbecues and other social occasions together, where they can talk freely, and share experiences without feeling under pressure.

Systems are working better. There is a guarantee of planned support being available to prevent family crisis as part of normal developmental expectations. There is no longer a need to fight for every dollar of support. The worry that previously hinged on the "unknown," and the dilemma of who would fight for services for Sarah when Linda and James were too old is no longer an issue. The concept of holistic, lifespan support is now policy.

Services for people with dual disabilities have improved. Units such as the developmental disability units operating at Monash University, Sydney University, and Brisbane University that incorporate medical consultants with expertise in disabilities are now widespread around the country and ensure instant access to advice and support.

Parents no longer have to argue for adequate funding to support their son or daughter. Government policy guaranteeing equity in access to services ensures that needs are met. The person with a disability still challenges the circle of people who constitute the family. However, society now provides sufficient support to allow each family member (disabled or not) to make personal choices without feeling his or her their own quality of life is jeopardized.

PLEASE, GOD,

ANOTHER DECADE!

> *I had no idea*
> *then,*
> *when she came—*
> *She came to stay*
> *and steal*
> *my heart away!*
> *O God!*
> *Please grant that I*
> *might live*
> *another decade more,*
> *to see*
> *what further miracles*
> *you have in*
> *Store. To see her grow,*
> *I love her so!*

Authors' Note

We appreciate the input from Rhonda Faragher, David Davey, and other parents who contributed their personal information regarding their families. Thanks also to Patricia M. Brown for her comments and editorial suggestions.

References

Andrews, F. M. (1974). Social indicators of perceived life quality. Social Indicators Research, 1, 279–299.

Anstey, T. (2001). Families of persons with head injury. Unpublished doctorial thesis, The Flinders University of South Australia, Adelaide. In progress.

Bronfenbrenner, U. (1979). The ecology of human development. Cambridge, MA: Harvard University Press.

Brown, I., Brown, R. I., & Neikrug, S. (2000). Family quality of life study: International quality of life project. Toronto: Center for Excellence for Child Welfare, School of Social Work, University of Toronto.

Brown, R. I. (1997a). Quality of life for people with disabilities: Models, research, and practice. Cheltenham, UK: Stanley Thornes.

Brown, R. I. (1997b). Quality of life and professional education. In R. I. Brown (Ed.), Quality of life for people with disabilities: Models, research, and practice (pp. 310–326). Cheltenham, UK: Stanley Thornes.

Brown, R. I. (2000a). Quality of life: Challenges and confrontation. In K. D. Keith & R. L. Schalock (Eds.), Cross-cultural perspectives on quality of life (pp. 347–362). Washington, DC: American Association on Mental Retardation.

Brown, R. I. (2000b). Evaluation of options coordination: Committee on the evaluation of quality services for people with disabilities; A report to the Minister for Disability Services: South Australia. Adelaide: Minister for Disability Services, Government of South Australia.

Brown, R. I., Bayer, M. B., & Brown, P. M. (1992). Empowerment and developmental handicaps: Choices and quality of life. Toronto: Captus University Publications; London: Chapman and Hall.

Brown, R. I., Bayer, M. B., & MacFarlane, C. (1989). Rehabilitation programmes: Performance and quality of life of adults with developmental handicaps. Toronto, Ontario: Lugus Productions.

Brown, R. I., & Brown, I. (Eds.). (1999). Exceptionality Education Canada, 9, 1–2.

Brown, R. I., & Timmons, V. (1994). Quality of life: Adults and adolescents with disabilities. Exceptionality Education Canada, 4(1), 1–11.

Brown, V. (2000). An exploratory investigation with local Aboriginal people from Adelaide/Western Region towards improving Aboriginal family health outcomes. Unpublished master's thesis: The Flinders University of South Australia, Adelaide.

Bullen, P., & Onyx, J. (1999). Social capital: Family support services and neighbourhood and community centres in NSW. Sydney, New South Wales: Paul Bullen, Management Alternatives.

Commonwealth of Australia. (1947–77). Social Services Act. Canberra: Australian Government Publishing Service.

Commonwealth of Australia. (1974). Handicapped Person's Assistance Welfare Act. Canberra: Australian Government Publishing Service.

Commonwealth of Australia. (1986). Disability Services Act. Canberra: Australian Government Publishing Service.

Commonwealth of Australia. (1986). Human Rights and Equal Opportunities Commission Act. Canberra: Australian Government Publishing Service.

Commonwealth of Australia. (1992). Disability Discrimination Act. Canberra: Australian Government Publishing Service.

Commonwealth of Australia. (1992). Commonwealth/State Disability Agreement. Canberra: Australian Government Publishing Service.

Corlett, I. (1999). Heroes. Unpublished poetry: Adelaide, South Australia.

Cummins, R. (1997). Assessing quality of life. In R. I. Brown (Ed.), Quality of life for people with disabilities: Models, research, and practice (pp. 116–150). Cheltenham, UK: Stanley Thornes.

Cummins, R. A. (2000). A homeostatic model for subjective quality of life. Proceedings of the Second International Conference of Quality of Life in Cities (pp. 51–59). Singapore: National University of Singapore.

Cummins, R. A. (2001). The subjective well-being of people caring for a family member with a severe disability at home: A review. Journal of Intellectual & Developmental Disability, 26(1), 88–100.

Davey, V. R., & Morgan, A. (1977). Supported integration of intellectually handicapped children. Whyalla, South Australia: Schools Commission Innovations Program.

Demand for Disability Support Services in Australia: Size, Cost, and Growth. (1997). Canberra: Australian Institute for Health and Welfare.

Department of Human Services. (1999). Strategic plan 1999–2000: Human services portfolio. Adelaide: South Australian Government Publishing Service.

Disability Services Queensland. (2000). Queensland government strategic framework for disability. Brisbane: Queensland Government Publishing Service.

Felce, D., & Perry, J. (1995). Quality of life: Its definition and measurement. Research in Developmental Disabilities, 16, 51–74.

Firth, H., & Rapley, M. (1990). From acquaintance to friendship: Issues for people with learning disabilities. Kidderminster, UK: BIMH Publications.

Goode, D. (1994). Quality of life for persons with disabilities: International perspectives and issues. Cambridge, MA: Brookline.

Goode, D. (1999). On quality of life for children (with disabilities). Exceptionality Education Canada, 9(1–2), 111–128.

Grimes, D. (1985). New directions: Report of the handicapped programs review. Canberra: Australian Government Publishing Service.

Helbers, D. M. (1997). An exploratory study of the perceptions and experiences of Vietnamese Australians: Mothers who have a child with a disability. Unpublished honors bachelor's thesis, The Flinders University of South Australia, Adelaide.

International Association for the Scientific Study of Intellectual Disabilities Special Interest Research Group on Quality of Life (IASSID SIRG-QOL). (2000). Quality of life: Its conceptualisation, measurement, and application: A consensus document. Geneva: World Health Organization.

James, O. (1997). Britain on the couch: Why we're unhappier compared with 1950 despite being richer: A treatment for the low-serotonin society. London: Century.

Knox, M., Parmenter, T. R., Atkinson, N., Kearney, B., Mattock, D., & Yazbeck, M., (1995). If only they would listen to us. Sydney, New South Wales: Macquarie University, School of Education, Unit for Community Integration Studies.

McConachie, H. (1994). Implications of a model of stress and coping for services to families of young disabled children. Child: Care, health, and development, 20, 37–46.

McKenzie, S. (1996). An interpretive study of quality of life for people who have young children with disabilities. Unpublished doctoral thesis, The Flinders University of South Australia, Adelaide.

McKenzie, S. (1999). Using quality of life as the focus for investigating the lives of people who have children with disabilities. International Journal of Practical Approaches to Disability, 23(2), 9–16.

McPhail, E. R. (1996). A parent's perspective: Quality of life in families with a member with disabilities. In R. Renwick, I. Brown, & M. Nagler (Eds.), Quality of life in health promotion and rehabilitation (pp. 279–289). Thousand Oaks, CA: Sage.

Mitchell, D., & Winslade, J. (1997). Developmental systems and narrative approaches to working with families of persons with disabilities. In R. I. Brown (Ed.), Quality of life for people with disabilities: Models, research, and practice (pp. 151–183). Cheltenham: UK: Stanley Thornes.

Parmenter, T. R. (1994). Quality of life as a concept and measurable entity. In D. M. Romney, R. I. Brown & P. S. Fry (Eds.), Improving the quality of life: Recommendations for people with and without disabilities (pp. 8–46). Dordrecht, Netherlands: Kluwer.

Parmenter, T. R., Cummins, R., Shaddock, A. J., & Stancliffe, F. (1994). The view from Australia: Australian legislation, service delivery, and quality of life. In D. Goode (Ed.), Quality of life for persons with disabilities: International perspectives and issues. Cambridge, MA, Brookline.

Peters, K. (1998). Review of the Family Support Services: For the Intellectual Disability Services Council. Adelaide, South Australia: Kristine Peters Project Management.

Porter, L., & McKenzie, S. (2000). Professional collaboration with parents of children with disabilities. Sydney: MacLennan & Petty.

Rasmussen, L. (1993). Quality of life for parents of a child with a developmental disability. Unpublished master's thesis: University of Calgary, Alberta, Canada.

Renwick, R., Brown, I., & Nagler, M. (1996). Quality of life in health promotion and rehabilitation. Thousand Oaks, CA: Sage.

Schalock, R. L. (1996). Quality of life: Conceptualization and measurement. Washington, DC: American Association on Mental Retardation.

Shearer, J. (2000). Aspects of the quality of life of children with a disability who are in inclusive educational settings. Unpublished master's thesis, The Flinders University of South Australia, Adelaide.

Taylor, S. J. (1994). In support of research of quality of life, but against QOL. In D. Goode (Ed.), Quality of life for persons with disabilities: International perspectives and issues (pp. 260–265). Cambridge, MA: Brookline.

Timmons, V., & Brown, R. I. (1997). Quality of life: Issues for children with handicaps. In R. I. Brown (Ed.), Quality of life for people with disabilities: Models, research, and practice (pp. 183–200). Cheltenham, UK: Stanley Thornes.

Turnbull, A., Poston, D., Park, J., & Lawson, L. (2000). A United States perspective on family quality of life: Domains and indicators. Lawrence: University of Kansas, Beach Center on Families and Disability.

Yeatman, A. (1996). Getting real: The final report of the Commonwealth/State Disability Agreement. Canberra: Australian Government Publishing Service.

Part 3

IMPLICATIONS FOR POLICIES AND PRACTICES

Part 3 concludes with two chapters on future implications of current inquiry on family quality of life related to the enhancement of policies and practices.

Chapter 9

Family Quality Of Life: Implications For Policy

Trevor R. Parmenter
University of Sydney
Ryde, New South Wales, Australia

One of the major things that has gone wrong in society is that governments have become so far removed from the average person that there is no connection between them.

Society is so complicated now, and the political process tries to reduce us by fitting us into categories. It does not work, and we cannot expect government at higher levels to respond in ways that reflect our needs, when they do not even know or understand what they are.

We have to get back to communities, and gain greater autonomy to determine the future of our own community. (Suzuki, 1991)

The lived experiences of families with a child with a disability portrayed in the chapters of this book demonstrate their resilience and indomitable spirit in the face of the additional challenges those families experience when compared to families in general. Obviously all families are faced with difficulties and challenges from time to time, but, in the case of the families with a disabled son or daughter, pressures are often unremitting throughout their lifespan.

With the exception of Nancy Breitenbach's worldview (chap. 10), the majority of the family stories and the social-cultural, economic, and political contexts described in this volume are typical of Western industrialized countries with a similar history of welfare-policy development. The following discussion concerning policy development in the context of family quality of life is, therefore, limited to those Western countries that have evolved basically within a Judeo-Christian tradition. In many countries, particularly those in Asia, the formulation of disability policy through the public participation of consumer and service delivery agencies is only slowly emerging. Miles (1989) has argued that this is because families in those countries (while families in Western developed nations) have had the sole responsibility for the support and care of their disabled children.

In the context of family quality of life, as in all discussions related to people with intellectual and other disabilities, there is great diversity within this population. There is often a tendency to homogenize people with disabilities and their families as a discrete group within the community. Attitudes and policies that have evolved over time have obviously contributed to this phenomenon.

This chapter initially will set policy development within a historical framework of service provision for people with intellectual disabilities and their families. This analysis will explore the evolution of many factors that now impact policy and service support. Next, the chapter will discuss contemporary factors that have been detailed in each of the contributions to this book. That discussion will provide a forward direction in the light of emerging societal and political developments. It will be argued that the building of social and moral capital within the framework of an "ethical community" approach may move us from the utilitarian and materialistic forces that basically underpin much of the current policy that impacts people with disabilities and their families.

Historical Developments

Braddock and Parish (2001) and Parmenter (2001) have provided a useful overview of the historical processes that in large measure have helped to shape the way services and supports to people with disabilities and their families are being delivered. In respect to people with an intellectual disability, a common historical thread has been society's continued denial of their humanity and personhood; they have been seen as disposable commodities. Happily, in more recent years we have witnessed a gradual emancipation of this group within our society.

Origins Of Discrimination

Infanticide, a common practice in antiquity, is still evident in a number of countries, especially in the case of children who are deemed to be a burden on the family and/or society generally. The tenets of natural philosophy and the social and ethical writings of both Plato and Aristotle advanced the idea that a defect of the human mind can be equated with subhuman species. In ancient Rome intellectually disabled people were kept as slaves and fools by the nobility. Similar practices were maintained throughout the medieval period, with short-statured people being employed as court jesters. The display of people with significant physical anomalies in sideshows was a feature well into the 20th century.

There were two somewhat paradoxical phenomena in the Middle Ages. On the one hand, there was the belief that a number of disabilities, including deafness, epilepsy, and mental disabilities, had demonological origins. People with these disabilities typically were persecuted as witches, or magical "cures" were prescribed to remove the condition. The linking of people with mental disabilities and satanic forces was prevalent well into the early modern period of history. Indeed, in more recent times, the guilt and shame some families experience on the birth of a child with a disability can be attributed to a belief that they have been punished for moral transgressions.

The second significant feature of this period was the development of asylums or safe havens by several monastic orders. These were places of compassion rather than of banishment. Braddock and Parish (2001) have argued that a third significant feature of this period was the acceptance of people with disabilities as a part of the natural order. The phenomena of begging and charity that have had pervasive influences on disability policies had their roots in this period of history.

Emergence Of Social Welfare And Professional Dominance

The genesis of professional dominance in the disability field can be traced, it is suggested, to the Age of Enlightenment. John Locke (1623–1704) heralded the radical belief in the value of education to counter the then deeply religious view of "man" having to bear the ineradicable stain of original sin. However, his writings still reflected the widely held view of the time that people with intellectual disabilities do not attain the same level of personhood as those of higher intelligence (Gibson, 1968).

This Age saw the origins of the scientific method and the belief that society and the environment could be manipulated to improve the life of the citizens. Both of these developments impacted people with disabilities in tangible ways. First, interventions based upon superstition and the process of supernatural forces slowly gave way to a more systematic study of illness and disease.

Second, there was a recognition that the community had a responsibility to provide for its indigent population, exemplified by the English Poor Laws as they operated from the 16th to the 19th centuries. As the welfare system of the medieval period, consisting of families, the church, and the lords of the manner, disintegrated, the various Poor Laws heralded a shift of social welfare responsibilities to the state. Cocks and Cockram (1997) suggested that this contributed to the development of a welfare infrastructure and the origins of the first modern human service system. Marcus (1981) described the Poor Law of 1834 as:

> the most important piece of social legislation passed in the 19th century. It established a new model of administration machinery—nationally centralised decision-making on substantive issues of policy, professionalised civil servants, bureaucratic rationality. In essence it was the first recognisable modern welfare system. (p. 53)

Another significant development in this period was the distinction made between those with an intellectual disability, classified as "idiots," and those with mental illness, classified as "lunatics," In the case of the former, families were expected to provide care, but people with mental illness were typically consigned to prisons and houses of corrections (Rushton, 1996). Braddock and Parish (2001) suggested that the distinction was drawn mainly by the need for the correct adjudication of property laws.

With the advent of the industrial revolution, the practice of abandonment of children noticeably increased (Malson, 1972). The celebrated case of Victor, the so called Wild Boy of Averyon who became the protégé of the French physician Jean Itard, led to the conviction of the educability of people with an intellectual disability. In 1844, the Paris Academy of Science proclaimed that Edouard Seguin, who had built on Itard's work, had solved the problem of "'idiot' education" (Baumeister, 1970).

In 1848 Seguin moved from France to the United States, where he established several institutions for people with intellectual disabilities and was instrumental in the foundation of a professional association that was to become the now named American Association on Mental Retardation. The influence of the medico-psychologists of the 19th century extended throughout much of the then-Western world and continued into the early 20th century. The rising discipline of psychology, which contributed much to the assessment and classification of intellectual disability, eventually usurped the power role formerly held by the medical professions (Crocker, 1999).

Institutionalization And Segregation

Although the motivation for the early growth of the institutionalization movement was predicated on the principle of providing an educational environment to ameliorate the effects of an intellectual impairment, the advent of the eugenics movement in the late 19th and early 20th centuries radically changed the underlying principles. The eugenics movement had a profound and lasting impact upon community attitudes toward people with intellectual disabilities and ultimately upon their families. In many countries the state legislated to enforce the sterilization of young intellectually disabled women. Significantly one of the first population groups to be annihilated in Nazi Germany in the 1930s was people with intellectual and other developmental disabilities. This issue has been comprehensively discussed in the publication of the International League of Societies for Persons With Mental Handicap[1] (1994), *Just technology? From Principles to Practice in Bio-ethical Issues.*

Segregation and the protection of society became the rallying cry and in many ways the superstitions of earlier periods were revisited. Institutions were no longer "safe havens," and gross overcrowding, understaffing, scant funding, and other factors resulted in the appalling conditions so strikingly

1   Now Inclusion International.

revealed by Burton Blatt (1981). As most of the institutions were administered by medical officers and staffed by nurses, the basis of the scientific
"medical model" that was predicated upon the curative principles of diagnosis and treatment became identified with segregation and containment. The
emergence of alternative paradigms of disability arose as a reaction to both
the impairment focus and the power dominance of the medical and allied
professions.

Although only a relatively small proportion of the total population of
people with intellectual disabilities was institutionalized, the principles
underlying segregation presented a stereotype that was to affect all individuals so diagnosed, including their families. One of the most serious effects was
the denial of an appropriate education, even in well-developed countries.
This resulted in parents forming associations that raised money to build and
staff schools outside the ambit of public schooling. These are the same parents who had to build sheltered workshops to provide a postschool facility
for their disabled sons and daughters. These are the same parents who are
now seeking alternative accommodation for their disabled sons and daughters because, owing to aging, they can no longer physically care for them.

Growth Of Parent Associations

One of the significant outcomes of these parental efforts was the development of strong parental associations that lobbied governments to assist in
the provision of basic services to their family member with a disability. The
efforts of families have positive and negative outcomes. The voluntary efforts
of families and their sharing in a common goal provided opportunities for
mutual psychological and social support. However, families, especially the
older parents, have expressed a sense of frustration and exhaustion from
what they perceive as a constant struggle to obtain sufficient resources to
support their family member with a disability (Parmenter, Atkinson, &
Yazbeck, 1996).

National parent associations were formed in many countries in the
1950s and 1960s. Of major significance was the founding in 1969 of the
International League of Societies for the Mentally Handicapped. Rosemary
Dybwad (1990), a tireless advocate and one of the architects of the League,
in an address to the Kings Fund Centre in London in 1975, commented:

> Concerned parents in India or in Brazil, in New Zealand,
> Lebanon, Mauritius, or Belgium are, of course, primarily moti-
> vated by the desire and the duty to get help for their handicapped
> children. Yet they soon learn that the help the child needs must
> come from services—educational services, vocational services, res-
> idential services, guardianship services—and to secure them, the
> parents must band together with other parents, must keep the

pressure on public officials and legislators, and must enlist the aid of professional workers and civic organizations. (p. 3)

The Normalization Principle And The Deinstitutionalization Movement

In addition to the impact of the eugenics movement upon the growth of numbers in state institutions, the severe effects of the great economic depression in the 1920s and 1930s resulted in increasing numbers of families seeking institutional care for their children, because they were unable to feed and clothe them. It was common practice for families to be advised upon the birth of a child with a disability to immediately seek institutional care as the best solution to the "problem."

Another factor leading to gross institutional overcrowding and the resultant drop in care was, ironically, advances in medical science, including the discovery of sulphonamides in 1975 and penicillin in 1944. These discoveries had substantial effects upon the morbidity and mortality of those with severe and profound levels of disability. Residents of institutions were now able to be kept alive in ways not previously possible (Judge, 1987).

There was a burgeoning of institutional populations across the world. For instance, in the United States institutional care increased continuously from the middle of the 19th century up until 1967, when it peaked at 194,650 people or 95 per 100,000 of the general population (Lakin, Bruininks, & Sigford, 1981). In 1965 the average number of residents per institution in the United States peaked at 1,500 (Lakin, Krantz, Bruininks, Clumpner, & Hill, 1982). Similar conditions were found in other developed countries (Judge, 1987). While conditions have improved for the large numbers remaining in institutions, they are still appalling in many countries, especially in a number of countries in Eastern Europe (Mutters, 1999).

In the 1960s the conditions in institutions across the world became the focus of inquiry by administrators and social advocates (Bank-Mikkelson, 1976; Nirje, 1969; President's Panel on Mental Retardation, 1962; Wolfensberger, 1969, 1972). Nirje's (1969, 1985) and Wolfensberger's (1972, 1983) formulations of the principle of normalization contributed to the growing call to move people with intellectual disabilities who were in institutions into alternative community-based accommodation. The institutional option for families with a newborn child with an intellectual disability also became limited.

The deinstitutionalization movement has sent mixed messages to families, especially those who believed they had been correct in placing their child in this form of care. Their decision was now being challenged. Many families resisted the closure of institutions, believing that the security they offered far outweighed the negative conditions. There was also a mistrust of the ability of the community to sustain the community alternatives. There was a security implicit in the "bricks and mortar" of large congregate residentials.

As government inquiries into institutional conditions gathered momentum, stimulated in part by international conventions such as the *Declaration of General and Specific Rights of the Mentally Retarded* (United Nations, 1971) and the *Declaration of the Rights of Disabled People* (United Nations, 1975), national governments enacted specific antidiscrimination and equal opportunity legislation. This legislation supported the full closure of segregated congregate care facilities.

Mansell and Ericsson (1996) argued that the pace of deinstitutionalization was sustained in the 1980s because community services were no more expensive than institutional care. In a number of countries, including the United Kingdom, the United States, Canada, and Australia, access to new central government resources certainly stimulated the pace of the development of community-based programs. However, in Britain and the United States, there are growing restrictions on access to central government resources owing to concerns about the growth in welfare expenditure. In Scandinavia, the trend toward decentralization is placing increasing demands upon local community governments (Sandvin & Söder, 1996). Despite the enthusiastic acceptance of the deinstitionalization movement by many governments in the 1980s, the 1990s have been a period in which the promised benefits of community living were yet to be fully realized. In this regard Mansell and Ericsson (1996) noted that

> Deinstitutionalization, then, is not just something that happened to people with intellectual disabilities and their families. It also happened to decision-makers and staff in services and to researchers. They have to shift their attention to new problems and issues in the community . . . But they had also to recognize that institutions were the impression of beliefs in society and that their demise may leave those beliefs and the practices that underpin them still to be tackled in the community. This is surely the greatest challenge for all societies: how to build and sustain social solidarity and mutual commitment among people with different needs, talents and aspirations, so that everyone may flourish and prosper. (pp. 252–253)

There have been equity issues apparent in these processes. First, only a relatively small proportion of the total population of people with intellectual disabilities were ever institutionalized, especially in the mid-1900s. Access to this option was generally restricted to "family crises" cases. In many cases, for families whose child with a disability stayed at home, there was little or no government support. The resources being applied to establish community-based options for those previously in congregate facilities and to upgrade those facilities for the remaining residents have severely limited resources for those families in the wider population. Many of these, as indicated above, are increasingly calling for support as they and their sons and daughters age. Just as improved health care led to population growth in the institutions, it has led to steady increases in the longevity of people with intellectual disabilities overall (World Health Organization, 2000).

In summary, the deinstitionalization movement has been both an instrument and an outcome of public policy. On both counts it can be found wanting as a major driving force in policy development for the support of family quality of life in the contemporary scene. Obviously it has been a necessary condition to the improvement of the life quality of former residents, but generally it is not a sufficient condition, in and of itself, for optimizing their overall quality of life and that of their families. However, as Emerson (1998) has asked, is it the responsibility of governments to go beyond the provision of basic life necessities?

This historical account has a number of implications for the current discussion. First, right from antiquity there has been a stereotype of "otherness" (Stainton, 1994) and the lack of full personhood for people with intellectual disabilities. Superstitions concerning this population, some of which are still evident in present-day societies, have added to their portrayal of people somewhat less than human. This has had a pervasive influence upon their care and practices over the centuries. It has also impacted more broadly upon their families, who, until relatively recent times, received little community support. Families were expected to bear this responsibility in much the same way as other marginalized groups. With the growth of modern scientific inquiry, education, health, and allied health professionals created a dominant influence over policy and practices, the result being that families were disempowered and relegated to a more passive role in the basic decision-making processes that related to the welfare of their disabled children.

Development Of Human Welfare Policies

This section will discuss the legislative developments in welfare policies, the dominance of government in leading policy and service development, the emphasis upon human rights as a driver of policy, changing paradigms in disability, and the gradual alienation of families from the service systems.

With the advent of strong economic growth in industrialized countries following World War II, governments increasingly enacted legislation that provided protection and support to people with disabilities and their families. Of course, it was not solely economic forces that stimulated this development. The growth of strong self- and family-advocacy movements, international covenants, and a growing public awareness of the needs of people with disabilities, as illustrated by the success of the International Year of

Disabled Persons in 1981, all contributed. However, strong economic growth was the engine that helped to drive and sustain the policies.

The Australian Disability Services Act (1986) and complementary state and territory disability acts, federal, states, and territory antidiscrimination legislation, and the Australian Human Rights and Equal Opportunities Commission provide a legislative basis for provisions to people with disabilities similar to those obtaining in Canada (cf. chap. 7, this volume). In the United States, the ground-breaking enactment of the Education of All Handicapped Children (Pub. L. 94–192), in 1975, together with specific legislation in the areas of developmental disabilities and rehabilitation, heralded a strong commitment by that country, especially at a federal level, to greater equity and opportunity for its citizens with disabilities. As Turnbull and colleagues point out (chap. 4, this volume), the enactment of the Americans With Disabilities Act in 1990, and the reauthorization of the Individuals With Disabilities Education Act in 1997, put an emphasis upon the achievement of outcomes. This, they suggest, is consistent with national trends that place a premium upon performance measures of outcomes, rather than upon processes. This pattern is being reflected in other countries, as noted by Schalock (1995).

Although the United Kingdom does not have a constitution, its government has also been influenced by international developments, especially the European Convention on Human Rights. The European Parliament has also made a number of initiatives that have impacted both on policy and service provision in member countries. In the United Kingdom, the Disability Discrimination Act was passed in 1995 the Disability Rights Commission was established in 2000 to oversee the implementation of this Act. The launching of the National Learning Disability Strategy (NLDS) in England, and parallel initiatives in Scotland and Wales, represents

> A fundamental program of social change narrowly understood as concerned with public sector modernization with its strong emphasis upon "top down" performance management and technocratic assumptions about evidence-based practices. More ambitiously, this programme is expressed in the commitment to reducing inequalities, promoting social inclusion . . . and delivering both these goals through renewal of local partnerships. (Towell & Hollins, 2000, p. 130)

Many of the core concepts found within current United States public policy (cf. chap. 4, this volume) can be found in public policies across the developed world. For instance, in the Australian context, the principles and associated standards that are embodied in the various federal, state, and territory Disability Acts resonate very closely with the U.S. core concepts. The standards, in particular, have been used as a benchmark against which government-provided and government-subsidized services have been evaluated. Compliance with the standards has been seen as a *sine qua non* for ongoing government support. The downside of this situation has been the practice by both the funders and providers of services to concentrate almost exclusively upon processes to the detriment of outcomes. The tyranny of rules and regulations, it is suggested, is a reflection of the way we have bureaucratized the underlying social movement of the emancipation of people with disabilities and their families.

Lack Of Entitlements

In each of the countries canvassed, there is a discrepancy between the promises of the relevant legislation and the availability of services. Although there are, in many of the countries, a number of specific legislated entitlements, such as disability pensions and substitute decision making, other entitlements, such as education and health, are part of the overall generic system applicable to all citizens. One of the policy initiatives to be influenced by the normalization principle was the right for people with disabilities to live in the community rather than in congregate care settings. A corollary at the policy level, and supported philosophically, was their right to access generic community services. However, in many areas, such as health, transport, and education, the generic services were and still are unable to provide adequately for their special needs.

It is in the area of specific social services that the lack of entitlements is felt the keenest. In all the stories in this volume, there are expressions by families of frustrations experienced in obtaining adequate services to meet the needs of their disabled sons or daughters. Special services are available in each of the countries surveyed, either by federal or state jurisdictions or by both. Usually, once eligibility for a service is determined, families are put on a waiting list until a service vacancy occurs. However, not only are services rationed, they are also fragmentary and uncoordinated. Turnbull et al. (chap. 4, this volume) argue that policies and services have dealt with only segments of families' and children's lives; a wholistic approach has been elusive. One of the reasons they suggest is that the United States has responded to *horizontal* problems by crafting vertical *semi-solutions*. Historically, this is the way services have evolved in all countries under discussion. Coordination and interagency cooperation are becoming the ideal. For instance, in several Australia states, a specific government department is charged with developing "whole of government" responses to the specific needs of people with disabilities, but there is a reluctance on the part of some government departments to accept responsibility for accommodating the needs of people with disabilities within their fiscal planning.

New Directions In Resource Allocation

Traditionally, government support for service delivery has been in the form of block grants to nongovernmental agencies to provide a service for an agreed number of clients. There are moves in several countries to make payments directly to individuals who are then able to purchase specific services from community groups. Such approaches have been described as "brokerage," "case-based funding," or "direct funding." These approaches represent a shift toward flexibility for families or individuals to design their own service package according to need. They also support the policy of fostering the empowerment of families or individuals and the encouragement of self-determination.

Parmenter (2000) has raised a number of concerns that have not as yet been adequately explored in the context of direct funding. Among these are the difficulties some individuals or families may experience in having to manage their own services. Direct funding is also contingent upon appropriate services being available within a person's accessible locality, particularly in semiremote areas. Governments are also concerned about accountability for expenditure given directly to families.

A good example of how service systems can be stimulated to evolve into being more responsive to families' needs comes from Western Australia. This state has initiated a comprehensive statewide program called Local Area Coordination (LAC). Under this program, people can access individualized funding as one of a number of more personal support strategies. Within LAC, people have access to direct consumer funding. Currently the program supports about 7,000 individuals throughout the 2.5 million square kilometres of that state. The director of services coordination, Eddie Bartnik, has indicated that the amount of the total system dollars under individualized funding is increasing substantially and will soon overtake the amount of block funds. Bartnik (personal communication, 2000) suggested that

> Our experience is all about evolution, with a clear vision and set of values with a pilot/phasing approach. Providers have certainly adjusted to the new systems and people seem to appreciate that when individuals and families really get what they want it works better for everyone . . . We have been successful in demonstrating that the use of a more individual approach, with direct funding and emphasis on natural and local community supports, is a very sound preventative strategy. We are trying to load more resources into the family support end of the service spectrum rather than just the high cost accommodation support end of the service.[2]

A parent's view of her needs (expressed to the direct-funding e-mail list), suggests caution, but also indicates that not all is well with current systems.

2   See http://www.dsc.wa.gov for further details of the Western Australian system.

My vision of a future for my son includes being able to purchase services from an agency. I do not want to carry a beeper around 24/7. I do not want to have to fill in when someone's car dies, I do not want to have to learn about finger-printing and how to file unemployment compensation claims. I want a strong agency that will hear my vision of quality. I want an agency that will be up on the latest regs, and opportunities for grants, an agency that will know how to meet the paperwork requirements and who the contact person in the state is for whatever we need. I want the agency to do well.

I haven't figured out how to do that though. The agency we are using now is supposed to be the best in the country. But it is spreading itself too thin, it is meeting minimum standards, and it just announced that it is looking into a really innovative idea of buying a farm and selling candles. (I couldn't make this up.) Also the staff makes about $8.00 an hour, which explains why we have been without a home manager since December 11, and the new director brought in two abused homeless men with labels and reputations to stay in my son's house when he went away for the weekend. (I still have not gotten over that. I do know parents who took the money directly from the state/county to hire staff, but the money was so inadequate (i.e., $8,000, year to do supported employment) that after a few months, they gave up. I really do not know if an agency is the answer. Is there another solution besides me doing it all?

To meet the principle of equity in the distribution of what always seems to be limited resources, direct funding, as well as block grants, must rely upon the adequate classification of support needs of each individual. The historical approach was to concentrate upon an assessment of the level of impairment of the individual. Contemporary approaches to classification, such as the American Association on Mental Retardation definition and classification of mental retardation (Luckasson et al., 1992) and the World Health Organization (2000) revision of the *International Classification of Disability and Health* reflect a paradigmatic shift to a recognition of the importance of the interaction of the individual with his or her environment when determining support needs. At present we lack adequate classification instruments that capture the environmental variables that either facilitate or restrict a person's ability to participate effectively in his or her community.

Political And Economic Forces

As noted earlier there is a worldwide trend, stimulated by the impact of neoclassical economic theories and the globalization of the world economy, to devolve government rights and services from central to local government levels. In those countries with federal and state jurisdictions, this develop-ment has become known as the "new federalism." The industrialized nations have embarked upon policies of macro- and microeconomic reform. The role of macroeconomic reform is to reduce the dependence upon overseas capital and hence reduce current account deficits. The implication of micro-economic reform is to enhance competition as a means to efficiency and thus reduce the cost of production. The neoclassical economic engine driving this approach is basically about "utility-maximization," given limited resources. The mantra of this approach is that individuals must be free to choose how they will use their resources, unfettered by undue government interference. This approach is in direct opposition to the concept of the "welfare state" that influenced policies in many countries, especially the United Kingdom, Israel, Australia, and New Zealand. de Carvalho (1996) has summed up the position as follows:

> It is not hard to see why economic rationalism is associated with a political ideology that emphasises individual freedom, plays down negative distributional impact of greater economic freedom, and abhors intervention by collective institutions like governments in the affairs of individuals. (p. 4)

A popular economic argument, advanced during the President Reagan era in the United States and that of Prime Minister Thatcher in the United Kingdom, was the "trickle down" theory that suggested that a strong national economy was an essential ingredient for the provision of adequate social services to disadvantaged populations. The evidence would indicate that worldwide there has been an increasing economic gap between the "haves" and the "have nots," even in periods of strong economic growth. Indeed, Schalock (1999) has warned that "human services organizations are being challenged to provide quality services within the context of two pow-erful, potentially conflicting forces: person-centered values and economic-based restructured services" (p. 55). There is a seductive similarity, nevertheless, between these forces, for both appear to concentrate upon indi-vidualism. But have we gone too far in emphasizing individualism, where we should be concentrating more upon the concept of communality? de Carvalho (1996) has suggested that "the challenges of responding to the new era of marketization require that many more creative responses be discussed and tried if the community sector(s) . . . are to remain true to their mission to promote social justice and the common good" (p. 62).

Changing Paradigm Of Disability

Historically, the concept of disability has been defined in a variety of dif-ferent ways, within specific societies and, in particular, within social con-texts. A common feature, however, is an emphasis upon the degree to which a person with a disability differs from the "norm." In the case of people with intellectual disabilities, this principle became manifested in the assessment of intelligence. For other disability conditions variations in physical impairments defined their status. The development in 1980 by the World Health Organization (WHO) of the *International Classification of Impairment, Disability, and Handicap (ICIDH)* acknowledged that environmental barriers had the potential to further handicap a person who had a disabling condition. This was a recognition that disability was not solely intrinsic to the person (WHO, 1980). The recent revision by WHO of the *ICIDH–2* (WHO, 2000) goes further in its emphasis upon the interaction between environmental contexts and impairments restricting a person's participation in society. Another significant development is the principle that the classification system is universal, hence relating to all people.

It can be argued, especially from a sociological perspective, that disability can be only properly understood as a social construction. Albrecht and Levy (1981) have contended that

> disability definitions are not rationally determined but socially constructed. Despite the objective reality, what becomes a disability is determined by the social meanings individuals attach to particular physical and mental impairments. Certain disabilities become defined as social problems through the successful efforts of powerful groups to market their own self-interests. Consequently the so called "objective" criteria of disability reflects the biases, self-interests, and moral evaluations of those in a position to influence policy. (p. 14)

Michael Oliver (1989), one of the United Kingdom's staunchest disability advocates, has proposed that the process of social construction is not solely dependent on individual meanings or the activities of powerful groups and vested interests for "the category disability is itself produced in part by policy responses to it" (p. 6). Harlan Hahn (1985), an equally articulate American advocate, has supported this perspective.

> Fundamentally, disability is defined by public policy. In other words, disability is whatever policy says it is . . . The fact that disability is basically determined by public policy moreover seems to demonstrate the need for careful investigations of definitions that are embedded in existing policies. (p. 294)

One may ask, what are the underlying factors or assumptions that influence public disability policy? An implicit ideology is that disability is a personal tragedy for individuals so "afflicted" and their families. In the current debate concerning the benefits and possible negative implications of the human genome project, there is a widespread expectation developing that eventually science will have the facility to prevent all disability. Society generally has the belief that it is common sense that disability is always an undesirable condition. This ideology is portrayed by the media, but it is also entrenched in the scientific community.

Oliver (1989) has suggested that the central idea underpinning the social construction of disability as a particular kind of social problem has been that of dependency. Dependency, he has argued, can have a variety of economical, political, and professional bases. Given the economic imperatives that are currently driving government policies, recent changes in the structure of the welfare state have been driven by the need to reduce this dependency. In the Australian context, this is embodied in the notion of "mutual obligation," wherein people receiving welfare support have an obligation to return something to society. For instance, people in receipt of a disability pension are expected wherever possible to seek work. Likewise, the corporate world is being asked to contribute more readily to supporting charitable bodies that provide support to disadvantaged groups in society.

Rather than seeking to remove dependency because it is a threat to state economies through short-term solutions, Oliver has suggested that the creation of an infrastructure of state services that facilitate user choice and control is the only way in which dependency can be permanently removed. While Oliver's approach to the definition of disability has been warmly embraced, especially among advocacy groups such as Disabled Persons International, Mercer's (1992) analysis of changing paradigms in disability supports the view that the field has moved from a single dominant paradigm, often characterized as the "medical model," to multiple paradigms that "better explain the natural and social world" (p. 16).

Limitations Of Formal Human Services And Legislation

Recurrent themes in the data presented in this volume are the continual struggle that families experience in not only accessing services, but also in having a say in their nature and delivery. Too often families are treated indifferently by government agencies and are not accepted as partners in the delivery processes (Knox et al., 1995). Bowman and Virtue (1993) have contended that the focus of family support and service provision must move beyond merely acting as a "prop to help families keep going" (p. 184). Services should be provided in a manner that enhances families' integrity and sense of control over their lives. Indeed, the empowerment of families may be seen as an essential ingredient of a family's quality of life (Knox, Parmenter, Atkinson, & Yazbeck, 2000).

But one has to go beyond the professional arrogance of the frontline bureaucracy to detect where the essential malaise lies. Cocks and Cockram

(1997) have argued that formal human services now represent powerful social institutions whose power

> has been enhanced through the adoption of bureaucratic profes-
> sional and technological means, and a union with judicial sources of
> legitimacy. These purposes are a far cry from a conception of human
> services as looking after the well being of vulnerable people and
> facilitating their empowerment and self determination. (pp.
> 222–223)

They suggest further that since World War II the acceleration in the growth of service systems is such that there is major economic reliance upon them to the extent that their primary concern can be considered to be the production of goods and services and the allocation of resources (Hoggett, 1990).

Both Cocks (1994), an Australian policy analyst, and Howe (2000), a former Australian deputy prime minister and federal minister for commu-nity services, have alluded to the current level of social conflict and societal turbulences experienced in Western cultures and have attributed those con-flicts and disruptions in part to the "shaking of the foundations" of the old post-World War II social order. Modern Western society can be described as "transitional" and "turbulent" as a result of rapid social change (Sztompka, 1993). Change occurs, Cocks (1994) has suggested,

> in patterns of living and in fundamental social institutions such as
> the family . . . critical changes occur within the ethical and moral
> fabric exemplified by the dilemmas in the area of socio-biology . . .
> where technological advances which assume an imperative to imple-
> mentation, outstrip the capacity of people and social institutions
> such as the law to cope. (pp. 18–19)

Howe's (2000) argument is that the community continually needs to rebuild its foundations and the interconnecting structures of the welfare state. In particular, the nexus between economic and social welfare policy requires careful examination. The effects of marketization, competition pol-icy, and the overall emphasis on utilitarian policies have significant and sometimes quite subtle effects upon the ways the frontline professionals interact with families. There is little doubt that the power balance is cur-rently biased in favor of the bureaucracy. The growing drift toward increased professionalization, bureaucratization, and technological solutions consis-tently alienates the users of the services. Despite the various legal underpin-nings of equity policies, there will never be sufficient resources to meet the needs of all families. Hence, as Cocks and Cockram (1997) have suggested, some will wait and others will never receive them.

Unfortunately, so often this result is seen as a resource issue rather than a problem inherent in the ways social welfare policies are conceptualized and delivered. There is an urgent need to move away from the behemothian structures of the welfare "industry" that disempowers the users to a redistribution of the power structures where the redistribution will facilitate the building of social and moral capital within communities. The earlier discussion about direct funding represents one approach that is attempting to "shake the foundation" of the current delivery systems.

Limitations Of The Rights Discourse

Undoubtedly, one of the most significant forces that has supported the emancipation to full citizenship of people with disabilities, and those with intellectual disabilities in particular, has been the principle of human rights. In the United States a catalyst was the civil rights movement. Internationally, as indicated above, various United Nations declarations and conventions have underpinned the advocacy efforts of bodies such as Inclusion International and organizations representing other disability groups. The most recent development was the proclamation by the United Nations in 1993 of *The Standard Rules on the Equalization of Opportunities for Persons With Disabilities*. Throughout the subsequent period, there have been concerted efforts by a special United Nations task force to encourage member countries to implement the provisions of the *Standard Rules* that touch upon those areas of a person's life where discrimination on the grounds of disability can be evident.

There is no gainsaying that the human rights movement in the disability field has been a potent force for change, yet rights legislation enacted by individual countries has been a necessary, but not sufficient, condition, for people with intellectual disabilities to enjoy the acceptance of the community. Reinders (1999) has argued that the moral language of rights is neither sufficient nor necessary to ground moral responsibility for disabled people. He suggested that "to claim equal rights for the disabled makes sense only on the basis of commitments that draw on other moral sources than the sources that are intrinsic to the morality of rights" (p. 2). In the case of people with intellectual disability, Reinders's essential argument is that the contemporary rights discourse is deficient in accounting for the moral features of caring practices, practices that are committed to the well-being of people who are dependent upon the support of others. His concluding comments are quite apposite. "Without people who have sufficient moral character to care, rights can do little to sustain the mentally disabled and their families. People can be forced to comply, but they cannot be forced to care" (p. 23).

In a subsequent paper Reinders (2000) again draws attention to the possible limitations of the strategies and policies that have helped to secure the new vision of a "good life" for citizens with intellectual disabilities. In particular, he has drawn a distinction between, on the one hand, the forces of public morality in a liberal society that have achieved much of the emancipatory goals of self-determination, individual choice, and the benefits of full citizenship, and, on the other, the more personal domain of the informal social world. In terms of ethics Reinders has suggested that

> inclusion in formalized societal structures is valuable because it enabled people to participate as a member of society. Participation in society is definitely an important aspect of the good life. But it is not identical with the good life, because the good life for human beings includes the personal sphere of social bonds and friendships . . . we are beginning to discover more and more that the success of inclusion for individual persons with intellectual disabilities in the long run depends on the strength of their informal networks. (p. 7)

For Nirje (1985), one of the major architects of the principle of normalization, a key ingredient of the "good life" for people with an intellectual disability is their opportunity "to be themselves among others." He, too, recognized the transcendent importance of social networks and interpersonal relationships. In his most recent elaboration of the principle, Nirje (1985) noted that

> Laws and legislative work cannot provide total answers to problem solving and proper actions with regards to realization of human rights. These can only come into existence in the full cultural and human context. Such problems are not only practical, but also ethical. (p. 65)

To return to the theme of the dominance of professionalization and bureaucratization, there is a need to balance the standards of *judicial security* with a strong respect for the ideal of *antipaternalism* (Tännsjö, 1999). The ultimate test of the success of social policies for people with intellectual disabilities and their families, particularly in the context of quality of life, is the extent to which they have

> met their needs to create their own meanings so they can establish and sustain a viable self in the social world . . . there is a need for consensuality whereby humans help each other unfold and establish contact and unity in their social existence. (Parmenter, 1992, p. 267)

The above discussion indicates that there are basic deficiencies in current human welfare policies, deficiencies that essentially exclude people with intellectual disabilities and their families from genuine participation in the processes of policy development. There is a rhetoric of consultation and collaboration but in essence the power structures in the "welfare industry" are biased toward the bureaucracy that is intrinsically oppressive, controlling, and disempowering.

Family Empowerment

Having examined a number of the historical, social, political, and economic forces that have impacted people with intellectual disabilities and their families, this final section will look to the future, suggesting directions toward which disability policy needs to move. This analysis, in part, draws upon the life experience of families revealed in this volume. A leading Australian bioethicist, Christopher Newell (2000), confirms the need for policy developers to listen more attentively to these voices. "It is the lived experience of people on the margins of society which constitutes the rejected knowledge found in contemporary dominant debates regarding social policy and the evaluation of economic justice" (p. 11).

As Suzuki (1991) admonishes, "we have to get back to communities" in order to capture the spirit of cooperativeness that will help to empower families to seek solutions that more adequately meet their needs. To do this, a more direct "bottom up" approach is required—one that recognizes the need to build community capacity and social capital.

Family Identity And Quality Of Life

As Todd and colleagues (chap. 5, this volume) have indicated, in "accounts of dissatisfaction with professionals . . . reflect a sense that one's identity is under threat." It is suggested that a family's identity is influenced by a wider range of factors, including those described under the historical and welfare policies sections above. The denial of personhood of a person with an intellectual disability and the portrayal of the welfare image of a highly dependent individual send overt and covert messages to families that their family member is a liability and even a threat to society. The family in turn develops the concept that it, too, is a burden to society. In many cases, it turns inward and isolates itself from the wider family and community network. The pathologization of parental experiences manifests itself a culture of dependence.

Doyal and Gough (1991) have identified autonomy as one of two basic human needs of all people, the other being physical health. Autonomy, they suggested, has three components: the ability of a person to undertake by him- or herself, his or her culture, and the expectations of him- or herself as an individual within that culture; the psychological capacity to formulate options for him- or herself; and the objective opportunities enabling him or her to act on those options. For a family with a member with an intellectual disability, the development of an "intact" positive identity and its capacity to develop autonomy is closely related, it is suggested, to its ultimate quality of life. However, Dokecki (1992) has warned that ethical thinking based on the notion of individual civil rights, personal autonomy, and the autonomous individual is not adequate for policy decisions concerning intellectual disability. It must be noted that families with a member with an intellectual disability are members of a community, and individual rights and personal autonomy must be understood in relation to that community. This issue will be taken up later.

In his discussion of a conceptual base for quality of life, Parmenter (1992) has included a positive identity as a necessary component. In discussing quality of life of individuals with disabilities, he pointed out that

> In addressing . . . what it means to be disabled they are confronted by two messages. One comes from the outside and proceeds from the social order. The other, however, comes from within and relates to what they know they can or cannot do. Thus, they have to deal with the negative aspects of their personal condition and at the same time cope with the negative effects of stigmatization and stereotyping. From a philosophical point of view there is a conflict between the existential nature of a person and the social nature of human experience. In trying to establish a coherent meaning for life as well as creating and maintaining self-esteem, the conflict between the messages the person with a disability receives often presents insuperable problems. (pp. 266–267)

For families to feel empowered, they need to start with a sense of confidence that they can make a difference to the life situation of their family members and, in so doing, emerge as a stronger family unit.

Interdependence Versus Independence

Reaction to dependence as a guiding principle in the decision-making process in the provision of services was especially challenged by people with physical disabilities in the 1970s, leading to the development of the independent living movement (Parmenter, 1980). Social welfare agencies still apply classification procedures that assign people to a "dependency category," although, as indicated above, this process is moving toward the notion of classification on the basis of "support needs." At the same time, agencies espouse individualism, treating every service user as an individual with the achievement of independence as a desired outcome. In the field of intellectual disabilities, a driving force for the goal of independence was the evidence that these people could learn given appropriate pedagogical techniques (Tizard, 1974). But have we gone too far in embracing the independence mantra? The alternative "support needs" approach embodies the concept of achieving successful interdependence, "which recognizes what people contribute to each other's sense of self and ability to act within the world, rather than independence which asserts the separation of individuals from each other" (Barnes, 1997, p. 73).

Barnes has further indicated that interdependence, being a universal feature of human existence, is not necessarily antithetical to independence. They are not dichotomous, with one positive and the other negative. Individuals and families shift from one position or condition depending upon resources and the situation they are facing. "Empowerment," Barnes asserted, "needs to be understood as relating to the nature and quality of people's relationships with others, rather than a feature of unconnected individualism" (p. 73).

Conflict Or Partnership

Jones (1998) has described five parent-partnership models that have developed over the past 20 years: the "input model," the "transplant model," the "consumer model," the "empowerment model," and, finally, the "negotiating model." Despite the evidence that many professionals and bureaucracies still exert control over the parent-professional relationship, it is apparent that there is a healthier approach being attempted, especially by professionals who have been exposed to more enlightened training programs. There is a shift in the perspective from that of the professional giving knowledge and the parent being a passive receptacle, to one where a process of negotiation takes place between parent and professional (Murray, 2000). However, as Jones (1998) has warned, the definition of need is still essentially conditioned by what is perceived as an individual problem. The rhetoric of partnership may not challenge underlying value judgments. The concept of "otherness" and the perception that to be disabled means to be "lesser than" has to be recognized as part of the "problem," before an effective partnership can be established.

It needs to be recognized, too, that the parent-professional roles do not ignore the role of the child with a disability in the negotiation process. Just as service providers, including professionals, may take an overly paternalistic approach to parents, so, too, parents may give insufficient attention to allowing their child to develop as a relatively autonomous human being. In a United Kingdom study of parental dissatisfaction with professional attitudes, coping, therapy, support, aesthetics, the child's body, and concerns for the future, Case (2000) found that parents were deeply concerned about their child's future, especially in terms of age, exaggerating the child's disability, and the child's future level of independence. Both professionals and parents are capable of overpathologizing the child's disability.

A particular area where there has been an imbalance in the professional-parent partnership is research. This is equally true in the researcher–disabled-person relationship. Seldom have families or the disabled family member been involved in either the selection of research questions or in the planning or execution process. Carpenter (1997) reported three examples of the "parent as researcher" paradigm that is premised on the action research approach. In each of the studies, there was evidence of parents investigating, inquiring, and discovering information, planning, and delivery services, as well as monitoring, and evaluating. Involving families as researchers in their own right is a potent means of empowerment. At the same time it allows families to stand back and look at issues from a different perspective.

The voice of a parent more adequately illuminates the question: conflict or partnership?

> Our experience was that it was only possible for partnerships to be formed when professionals, whilst simultaneously doing their best for my son, were able to enjoy him without wanting him to change in order that he fit into the current education system. From this perspective, it is first necessary to concentrate upon the value placed upon the life of a disabled child . . . in order to establish 'partnership'. It appears that a necessary precursor to valuing an individual's life is simply enjoying being with that individual. (Murray, 2000, p. 696)

Building An Ethical Community

Community can mean a group of people in an area or it can relate to a community of interests in which members feel a sense of common identity. In the latter sense, people may belong to more than one community or to none at all. The two meanings can lead to confusion. Most publicly funded services are organized on "place," whereas communities of interest focus on social relationships. In the United States, suggested Clegg (1998), some social scientists and politicians have united under the banner of communitarianism, which expands the social interdependency aspects of community. However, the extreme reactionary element of this movement has been criticized, as has its nostalgic view of progress (Lasch, 1994). Nevertheless, in sociological terms, families are looking to "conceived" communities for a spirit of *gemeinschaft,* rather than *gesellschaft* that characterizes more economically driven relationships being found in the way policies have been currently developed.

Dokecki (1992) has suggested that while we have moved away from the often dehumanizing paternalistic approach to intellectual disabilities, to an emphasis on individual civil rights and personal autonomy, we are left with an ethical framework "that is insufficient for confronting many of the ethical issues that will arise in the future" (p. 40). One such example is the implications of the discoveries of the human genome project. An alternative approach is to work toward an ethical conception of community "which convincingly establishes that all persons are fundamentally equal as human beings" (p. 40).

How can we foster an ethical community, as suggested by Dokecki, one in which the primary support roles are taken by family, friends, and extended support networks, rather than exclusively by professionals? Turnbull (1998) asserted that each member of a community must recognize that all are vulnerable in some aspects of our lives. As a first step, therefore, the ethical community must recognize "a mutuality of need and reciprocity of vulnerability" (H. R. Turnbull, 1988). The ethical community would also recognize that all people are dependent upon others in a metaphysically deep way (Edwards, 1997). A basic feature of being human, a feature that constitutes the basis of ethics, "is that we are all subject to undeserved discriminations that produce inequalities at birth" (Dokecki, 1992, p. 44).

As early as 1983 Dokecki suggested practical ways to envisage the notion of an ethical community. The ethics of community in intellectual disability, he asserted, is to promote interrelated community and human development values, expressed as two sides of the same ethical coin:

1. The aim of intervention should be *to enhance community . . .* so that individuals and their families have a legitimate claim on community resources and support in the performance of their developmental tasks.

2. The aim of intervention should be *to enhance human development* so that individuals and their families might be effective participants in the community. (pp. 115–116).

As we move from an era classified as modernism, epitomized by the penetration of market forces into every aspect of life, into a society characterized as postmodern, we need to recognize, as Toulmin (1990) has suggested, that the way ahead lies less on power and force and more upon moral influence. Moral influence, it is suggested, rests in part on the strengthening of human relationships that produce social rather than a physical capital. Coleman (1988) has suggested that "social capital . . . comes about through changes in the relations among people that facilitate action" (p. 100). The development of social capital may prove to be an antidote to the social policy agenda of most nations that are contributing in large measure to social fragmentation and growing alienation on the part of marginalized groups.

The Development Of Social Capital

In the Boyer lectures, social commentator Eva Cox (1995) identified four major capital measures: financial capital, physical capital, human capital, and social capital. She suggested that too little attention has been paid to social capital, which she saw, drawing on Putman (1993), as the processes among people that establish networks, norms, and social trust and that facilitate coordination and cooperation for mutual benefit.

In their study of social capital, Bullen and Onyx (1999) examined family support services and neighborhood and community centers in five communities in the state of New South Wales, Australia. Principal findings from the study were that it is possible to measure social capital in local communities. Within the general social capital factor, they found eight elements that formed two broad groups. The first group, arenas, consisted of participation in local community, neighborhood connections, family and friend connections, and work connections. The second group, capacity-building blocks, comprised proactivity in a social context, feelings of trust and safety, tolerance of diversity, and value of life. Bullen and Onyx (1999) have schematized these elements into a dynamic model of social capital (Figure 9.1).

Of special interest for the present discussion are their findings for the sample of family support services clients compared with the typical commu-

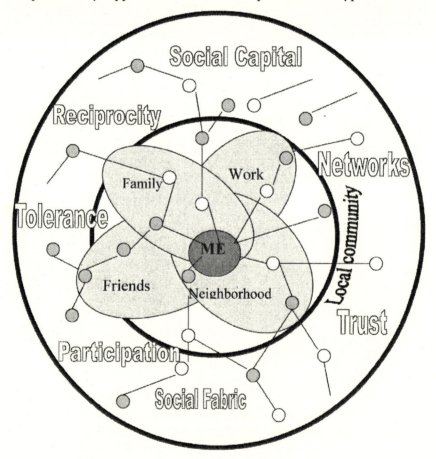

Figure 9.1 **A Dynamic Model Of Social Capital.**

nity members in the five communities studied. On average the family support clients had

- the lowest average score on the social capital general factor;
- the lowest scores on four of the social capital elements (family and friends, value of life, trust and safety, and proactivity);
- relatively low scores on two further elements (community participation and neighborhood connections);
- midrange scores on tolerance and diversity;
- the lowest education and income levels.

The study (Bullen & Onyx, 1999) concluded that families in crisis and stress do not have access to the social capital in their community.

Implications for the way support services assist families with a disabled family member include an examination of ways families can develop connections with the community's social capital. Support services need to also make explicit the social capital issues in the way they develop individual service goals and plans in collaboration with families and the disabled family member. They also need to link families with the wider community services.

Again within the state of New South Wales, there are three initiatives worthy of comment. The first is the Families First program, which is a supported network for families raising children. The broad aims and objectives of Families First are to support parents and carers raising children through a coordinated network of services, and help them to solve problems before those problems become entrenched. The project, an initiative of the state government, commenced in 1999 in three areas of the state, and is planned to be implemented statewide over the subsequent 4 years. A number of government departments and government-funded nongovernmental agencies already provide a range of support services to families. The goal of Families First is to better link these services and help them to expand and remodel themselves into a coordinated service delivery network centered around the following fields of activity:

- supporting parents who are expecting or caring for a new baby;
- supporting parents who are caring for infants and young children;
- assisting families who need extra support;
- linking families to communities and communities to families.

The second initiative that grew out of the study by Knox et al. (1995) is more of a "bottom up" approach. In the rapidly expanding Macarthur region of Sydney, a group of families formed Families in Partnership to give families with children with disabilities the opportunity to work together to provide better outcomes for their child by sharing their experiences and drawing on the hurdles they have faced. Families are promoting a family-centered "whole of life" concept of care with the guidance of university researchers, local services, and professionals.

Although the group has identified serious resource gaps in their area, there are other priorities it seeks to address that can be achieved with little additional cost. These include:

- incorporating disability issues into staff training;
- challenging existing policies;
- training medical staff in communication;
- developing parent friendly information on available services.

In the group's "whole of life planning" proposal, it asserts that things need to be done differently as families are still expressing the same needs after many years with little response or inappropriate responses from government. Under the heading "what do we need?" they indicate a different way of thinking, a new vision, and a paradigm shift. This shift would include the building of a community development model that is based on community building and sharing of expertise, coordinated through community development officers, and developed from the bottom up. The dreams of families, including the here and now and the future, need to be recognized. The group's vision is for a community developed by the community that is seen as a "broad church," including families, service providers, and tertiary (postsecondary) education. In essence the group's mission resonates very much with the development of the social capital concept.

The third initiative, the development of family coordinated microboards, is an excellent example of a new way of thinking in the way services are delivered. It also represents a good example of family empowerment. Life Activities is a nongovernmental support service, funded by the New South Wales government, that conducts a wide range of support initiatives, including staff development. Life Activities' essential goal is to build community capacity so that people with disabilities and their families can receive more sensitively delivered services in their own community. The microboard project is but one example of the range of community-building activities the organization has developed.

A microboard is formed when a small group of committed family and friends joins together with person with a disability to form a board. This board addresses the person's planning and support needs in an empowering and individually customized fashion. Microboard members can be family, friends, and acquaintances who are committed to knowing and having a relationship with the person. Relationships are the most important part of microboards. Microboard members do not need to have qualifications or expertise, because these valuable skills can be purchased from others. The members bring to the board their relationship with, commitment to, and knowledge of the individual.

A microboard establishes itself as a nonprofit incorporated body and functions to identify and address an individual's support and personal skills development needs, along with that individual, as a team. Members do this by establishing a relationship or friendship with the individual, acting as a sponsor the community, ensuring the individual is supported to both give to and receive from the community, taking control of funding, and completing a person-centered planning process. The primary purpose of a microboard is to enable a disabled person to become or remain part of the fabric of the community. A secondary but no less important purpose of a microboard is to share the responsibility for support for a disabled person among a group of relatives and friends so that this responsibility will not fall on the shoulders of one or two close relatives.

The empowerment of families with a disabled family member is increasingly being recognized as a way to respond to their unique needs. In terms of family quality of life, we may need to broaden our understanding of "ordinary lives," an important ethic developed by Enlightenment thinkers to challenge the power of kings and priests. In his development of a moral ontology, Taylor (1989) has suggested that respect is the dominant ethic in contemporary Western societies. This concerns the ethics of obligation, a duty deriving from the Enlightenment to treat others as autonomous and as living ordinary lives that are valuable. Demographic changes are leading to an increasing proportion of families having a member who has a disability, be it intellectual, the effects of old age, physical, or a mental health problem, living with them for much of their lives. This is part of the ordinary experience of that already variable social group we call "the family." However, Barnes (1997) has urged us to explore more fully the nature of relationships within families with an intellectually disabled member in order for policies to be developed in a way that supports the empowering strategies that families wish to adopt. Finally, we also need to recognize that we must help people with intellectual disabilities to participate in relationships and social activities beyond their families.

Conclusions

This chapter has attempted to analyze a number of policy issues that are relevant to the development of the quality life of families with a child with an intellectual disability. In particular, it has explored the historical, social, political, and economic contents that have impacted on the ways families have received support in the caring processes. The historical contexts have had a profound impact upon the ways families have perceived themselves as parents of a child with an intellectual disability. The negative messages of the centuries have portrayed their child as something less than a full person.

These values have influenced the family's identity and the subsequent development of their perceived life quality.

Families have also been portrayed in a dependent role along with their disabled family member, especially as social welfare policies developed in Western countries. Although we have witnessed in recent years a distinctive paradigm shift in the way disability has been defined and perceived, the underlying values of dependency have not changed. Service systems are still trying to remedy dependencies and to resolve problems in a typical top-down fashion. However, there are positive trends emerging, especially in the tentative steps to empower families and to enrich community capacity through the building of ethical communities. The notion of developing social capital is a promising direction, especially if a bottom-up approach is adopted where families are helped to solve problems in unique ways.

As Brown and Brown indicate in the introductory chapter, family quality of life deals with the goodness of family life. The uniqueness of every family must be recognized if the ideal is to be achieved. While not wishing to close on a negative note, a warning concerning the need to empower families to achieve the "good life" is that policy planners should not see the paradigm shift to ethical community building as a way to reduce or to stagnate the share of a country's wealth that its disabled citizens deserve.

References

Albrecht, G., & Levy, J. (1981). Constructing disabilities as social problems. In G. Albrecht (Ed.), *Cross national rehabilitation policies: A sociological perspective*. London: Sage.

Americans With Disabilities Act of 1990, 42 U.S.C.A. § 12101 *et seq.* (West 1993).

Bank-Mikkelson, N. (1976). The principle of normalization. In B. Nielsen (Ed.), *Flash—On the Danish National Service for the mentally retarded*. Copenhagen: Personal Training School.

Barnes, M. (1997). Families and empowerment. In P. Ramcharan, G. Roberts, G. Grant, & J. Borland (Eds.), *Empowerment in everyday life* (pp. 70–87). London: Jessica Kingsley.

Baumeister, A. A. (1970). The American residential institute: Its history and character. In A. A. Baumeister & E. Butterfield (Eds.), *Residential facilities for the mentally retarded* (pp. 1–28). Chicago: Aldine.

Blatt, B. (1981). *In and out of mental retardation. Essays on educability, disability, and human policy.* Austin, TX: Pro-Ed.

Bowman, D., & Virtue, M. (1993). *Public policy. Private lives.* Canberra: Australian Institute on Intellectual Disability.

Braddock, D. L., & Parish, S. L. (2001). An institutional history of disability. In G. L. Albrecht, K. D. Seelman, & M. Bury (Eds.), *Handbook of disability studies*. New York: Sage.

Bullen, P., & Onyx, J. (1999). *Social capital: Family support services and neighbourhood and community centres in New South Wales.* Sydney: Local Community Services Association. See also www.mapl.com.au/A12.Ltm

Carpenter, B. (1997). Moving forward together: Collaborative research with families, In B. Carpenter (Ed.), *Families in context. Emerging trends in family support and early intervention* (pp. 164–175). London: David Fulton.

Case, S. (2000). Refocussing on the parent: What are the social issues of concern for parents of disabled children? *Disability & Society, 15,* 271–292.

Clegg, J. (1998). *Critical issues in clinical practice.* London: Sage.

Cocks, E. (1994). *Encouraging a paradigm shift in services for people with disabilities.* Perth, Australia: Edith Cowan University, Centre for the Development of Human Resources.

Cocks, E., & Cockram, J. (1997). Empowerment and the limitations of formal human services and legislation. In P. Ramcharan, G. Roberts, G. Grant, & J. Borland (Eds.), *Empowerment in everyday life: Learning disability* (pp. 222–240). London: Jessica Kingsley.

Coleman, J. S. (1988). Social capital in the creation of human capital. *American Journal of Sociology, 94,* 100–106.

Commonwealth of Australia. (1986). Disability Services Act. Canberra: Australian Government Publishing Service.

Cox, E. (1995). *The Boyer lectures*. Sydney: Australian Broadcasting Commission.

Crocker, A. C. (1999). The medical model. A mostly historical discussion. In H. Bersani (Ed.), *Responding to the challenge: Current trends and international issues in developmental disabilities* (pp. 3–9). Cambridge, MA: Brookline.

de Carvalho, D. (1996). *Competitive care: Understanding the implications of national competitive policy and the COAG agenda for the community services sector.* Canberra: Australian Catholic Social Welfare Commission.

Dokecki, P. R. (1983). The place of values in the world of psychology and public policy. *Peabody Journal of Education, 60,* 108–125.

Dokecki, P. R. (1992). Ethics and mental retardation: Steps toward the ethics of community. In L. Rowitz (Ed.), *Mental retardation in the year 2000* (pp. 39–51). New York: Springer-Verlag.

Doyal, L., & Gough, I. (1991). *A theory of human need.* Basingstoke, UK: Macmillan.

Dybwad, R. (1990). Mental handicap: The world scene. In R. Dybwad (Ed.), *Perspectives on a parent movement: The revolt of parents of children with intellectual limitations* (pp. 3–16). Cambridge, MA: Brookline.

Education for All Handicapped Children Act of 1975, Pub. L. No. 94-142. (August 23, 1977). Title 20, U.S.C. 1401 *et seq.* Stat. 100. 1145-1177.

Edwards, S. D. (1997). The moral status of intellectually disabled individuals. *Journal of Medicine & Philosophy, 22,* 29–42.

Emerson, E. (1998). Keynote address to annual conference of the Australian Society for the Study of Intellectual Disability. *Quarterly services and economic rationalism.* Adelaide.

Gibson, J. (1968). *Locke's theory of knowledge and its historical relations.* Cambridge: The University Press.

Hahn, H. (1985). Disability policy and the problem of discrimination. *American Behavioral Scientist, 28,* 291–298.

Hanssen, J. I., Sandvin, J. T., & Söder, M. (1999). The Nordic welfare states in transition. In J. Tøssebro, A. Gustavsson, & G. Dyrendahl (Eds.), *Intellectual disabilities in the Nordic welfare state: Policies and everyday life* (pp. 24–44). Drunningengst: Norwegian Academic Press.

Hoggett, P. (1990). *Modernisation, political strategy and the welfare state: An organizational perspective. Studies in decentralisation and quasi-markets No.2.* Bristol, UK: School for Advanced Urban Studies.

Howe, B. (2000). Shaking the foundations. In L. Davies & F. Sullivan (Eds.), *Civilising community for us all* (pp. 73–90). Adelaide: Australian Theological Forum.

Individuals With Disabilities Education Act Amendments of 1997, Pub. L. No. 105-17, 111 Stat. 37 (1997).

International League of Societies for Persons With Mental Handicap. (1994). *Just technology? From principles to practice in bioethical issues.* Toronto: Roeher Institute.

Jones, C. (1998). Early intervention: The eternal triangle? Issues relating to parents, professionals, and children. In C. Robinson & K. Stalker (Eds.), *Growing up with disability* (pp. 43–55). London: Jessica Kingsley.

Judge, C. (1987). *Civilization and mental retardation: A history of the care and treatment of intellectually disabled people.* Mulgrave, Victoria: Magenta Press.

Knox, M., Parment,er T. R., Atkinson, N., Kearney, B., Mattock, D., & Yazbeck, M. (1995). *"If only they would listen to us": The needs of families living in the Macarthur Area who have a child with a disability—The viewpoints of family members.* Sydney: Macquarie University.

Knox, M., Parmenter, T. R., Atkinson, N., & Yazbeck, M. (2000). Family control: The views of families who have a child with an intellectual disability. *Journal of Applied Research in Intellectual Disabilities, 13,* 17–28.

Lakin, K. C., Bruininks, R. H., & Sigford, B. B. (1981). Introduction. In R. H. Bruininks, C. E. Meyers, N. B. Sigford, & K. C. Lakin (Eds.), *Deinstitutionalization and community adjustment of mentally retarded people, Monograph No. 4* (pp. vii–xvi). Washington, DC: American Association on Mental Deficiency.

Lakin, K. C., Krantz, G. C., Bruininks, R. H., Clumpner, J. L. & Hill, B. K. (1982). One hundred years of data on populations of public residential facilities for mentally retarded people. *American Journal of Mental Deficiency, 82,* 1–8.

Lasch, C. (1994). *The revolt of the elites and the betrayal of democracy.* New York: Norton.

Luckasson, R., Coulter, D., Polloway, E., Reiss, S., Schalock, R., Snell, M., Spitalnik, D., & Stark, J. (1992). *Mental retardation. Definition, classification, and systems of supports* (9th ed.). Washington, DC: American Association on Mental Retardation.

Malson, L. (1972). *The wolf children.* Middlesex, UK: Penguin.

Mansell, J., & Ericsson, K. (1996). Conclusion: Integrating diverse experience. In J. Mansell & K. Ericsson (Eds.), *Deinstitutionalization and community living: Intellectual disability services in Britain, Scandinavia, and the USA* (pp. 241–253). London: Chapman & Hall.

Marcus, S. (1981). Their brothers' keepers: An episode from English history. In W. Gaylin, J. Glasser, S. Marcus, & D. Rothman (Eds.), *Doing good: The limits of benevolence* (pp. 29–66). New York: Pantheon Books.

Mercer, J. R. (1992). The impact of changing paradigms of disability on mental retardation in the Year 2000. In L. Rowitz (Ed.), *Mental retardation in the year 2000* (pp. 15–38). New York: Springer-Verlag.

Miles, M. (1989). Rehabilitation development in South West Asia: Conflicts and potentials. In L. Barton (Ed.), *Disability and dependency*. London: Falmer Press.

Murray, P. (2000). Disabled children, parents and professionals: Partnerships on whose terms? *Disability & Society, 15*, 683–698.

Mutters, T. (1999). The situation of mentally handicapped persons and their families in Eastern Europe. In H. Bersani (Ed.), *Responding to the challenge. Current trends and international issues in developmental disabilities* (pp. 133–142). Cambridge, MA: Brookline.

Newell, C. (2000). Whose community? Which values? In L. Davies & F. Sullivan (Eds.), *Civilising community for us all* (pp. 3–23). Adelaide: Australian Theological Forum.

Nirje, B. (1969). The normalization principle and its human implications. In R. Kugel & W. Wolfensberger (Eds.), *Changing patterns in residential services for the mentally retarded* (pp. 179–195). Washington, DC: President's Committee on Mental Retardation.

Nirje, B. (1985). The basis and logic of the normalization principle. *Australia and New Zealand Journal of Developmental Disabilities, 11*, 65–68.

Oliver, M. (1989). Disability and dependency: A creation of industrial societies? In L. Barton (Ed.), *Disability and dependency* (pp. 6–22). London: Falmer Press.

. Parmenter, T. R. (1980). *Vocational training for independent living*. New York: World Rehabilitation Fund.

Parmenter, T. R. (1992). Quality of life for people with developmental disabilities. *International Review of Research in Mental Retardation, 18*, 247–287.

Parmenter, T. R. (2000, July). *A public policy priority: Balancing the use of individualized funding and traditional block funding*. Paper presented to Funding, Freedom, Citizenship. First International Conference on Self-Determination and Individualized Funding. Seattle, WA.

Parmenter, T. R. (2001). Intellectual disabilities—Quo vadis? In G. L. Albrecht, K. D. Seelman, & M. Bury (Eds.), *Handbook of disability studies* (pp. 267–296). New York: Sage.

Parmenter, T. R., Atkinson, N., & Yazbeck, M. (1996). *The needs of aging families and their relatives*. Sydney: Macquarie University, Unit for Community Integration Studies.

Putman, R. (1993). *Making democracy work: Civic traditions in modern Italy*. Princeton, NJ: Princeton University Press.

President's Panel on Mental Retardation. (1962). *A proposed program for national action to combat mental retardation*. Washington, DC: Superintendent of Documents.

Reinders, H. S. (1999, April). *The limits of the rights discourse.* Paper presented to the Roundtable of the Special Interest Research Group on Ethics, International Association for the Scientific Study of Intellectual Disabilities. Doorn, The Netherlands.

Reinders, H. S. (2000, August). *The good life for citizens with intellectual disabilities.* Paper presented to the 11th World Congress of the International Association for the Scientific Study of Intellectual Disabilities, Seattle, WA.

Rushton, P. (1996). Idiocy, the family, and the community in early modern northeast England. In D. Wright & A. Digby (Eds.), *From idiocy to mental deficiency: Historical perspectives on people with learning disabilities* (pp. 44–64). London: Routledge.

Sandvin, J. T., & Söder, M. (1996). Welfare state reconstruction. In J. Tøssebro, A. Gustavsson, & G. Dyrendahl (Eds.), *Intellectual disabilities in the Nordic welfare states* (pp. 107–139). Drunningengst: Norwegian Academic Press.

Schalock, R. A. (1995). *Outcome-based evaluation.* New York: Plenum.

Schalock, R. A. (1999). A quest for quality. In J. F. Gardner & S. Nudler (Eds.), *Quality performance in human services: Leadership, values, and vision* (pp. 55–80). Baltimore: Paul H. Brookes.

Stainton, T. (1994). *Autonomy and social policy: Rights, mental handicap, and community care.* Aldershot, UK: Avebury.

Suzuki, D. (1991, February 2). *Sydney Morning Herald,* p. 35.

Sztompka, P. (1993). *The sociology of social change.* Oxford: Blackwell.

Tänssjö, T (1999). *Coercive care: The ethics of choice in health and medicine.* London: Routledge.

Taylor, C. (1989). *Sources of the self: The making of modern identity.* Cambridge: Cambridge University Press.

Tizard, J. (1974). Longitudinal studies: Problems and findings. In A. M. Clarke & A. D. B. Clarke (Eds.), *Mental deficiency: The changing outlook* (3rd ed., pp. 223–256). London: Methuen.

Toulmin, S. (1990). *Cosmopolis: The hidden agenda of modernity.* New York: The Free Press.

Towell, D., & Hollins, S. (2000). Achieving positive change in people's lives through the National Learning Disability Strategy: An invitation to partnership between higher education and the world of practice. *British Journal of Learning Disabilities, 28,* 129–136.

Turnbull, H. R. (1998, June). *Are we gaining ground in the pursuit of life, liberty, and happiness?* Keynote address to 122nd Annual Conference of the American Association on Mental Retardation, San Diego, CA.

United Nations. (1971). *Declaration of general and specific rights of the mentally retarded.* New York: Author.

United Nations. (1975). *Declaration of the rights of disabled people.* New York: Author.

United Nations. (1993). *The standard rules on the equalization of opportunities for persons with disabilities.* New York: Author.

Wolfensberger, W. (1969). The principle of normalization and its implications to psychiatric services. *American Journal of Psychiatry, 27,* 291–297.

Wolfensberger, W. (1972). *The principle of normalization in human services.* Toronto: National Institute on Mental Retardation.

Wolfensberger, W. (1983). Social role valorization: A proposed new term for the principle of normalization. *Mental Retardation, 21,* 234–239.

World Health Organization. (1980). *International classification of impairments, disabilities, and handicaps (ICIDH).* Geneva: Author.

World Health Organization. (2000a). *Ageing and intellectual disabilities—Improving longevity and promoting healthy ageing: Summative report.* Geneva: Author.

World Health Organization. (2000b). *International classification of disability and health (ICIDH-2)* Prefinal draft. Geneva: Author.

Chapter 10

Family Quality of Life: Implications For Family Support

Nancy Breitenbach
Formerly of Inclusion International
Paris, France

Research into the quality of life of entire families is a monumental task. Just as scientists took years to crack the basic building block of our physical world (the atom) and the basic recipe of our physical being (the human genome), so it will probably require years before we fully understand the components and the dynamics of the basic building block of human society.

It is intriguing that one of the starting points of this research appears to be a group which normally remains in the shadows of quality of life research: families with children who have an intellectual disability.

There are reasons for this innovation. It reflects a general and very positive trend toward goal-oriented services for people with disabilities (as opposed to older models that aimed more at maintenance or custodial care) and an evaluation of outcomes: What is achieved by the services provided and are these results truly beneficial for the people involved? It may also be an unexpected offshoot of the 1993 *United Nations Standard Rules on Equal Opportunities for Persons with Disabilities,* which noted that not individuals with disabilities but their families as well should have equal opportunities for fulfillment.

These reasons more than justify the effort deployed. As such, family quality of life research is a welcome addition to the range of investigative techniques that clarify the legitimate needs of family caregivers, and the work furthered by the Beach Center is exemplary. Not only because families are strongly present in the research, but because they represent a variety of countries.

But Haven't Parents Always Been Involved?

Taking families into account when planning service provision, giving them a real role in the evaluation process, taking their feedback seriously— all this is relatively new to social scientists though it is not new to Inclusion International (formerly known as the International League of Societies for Persons With Mental Handicap [ILSMH]) which has been defending and promoting the parental viewpoint for 40 years. It reflects significant method-ological changes in the field of disability research: the growing acceptance of a qualitative approach and the introduction of participatory research (which could be linked to the larger movement in favor of self-advocacy and self-determination for people with disabilities).

For many years parents' opinions and feelings were discounted, their life goals perceived as irrelevant (if not opposed) to the best interests of the disabled child. Fortunately, parental voices are now acknowledged as valid, especially when they take on a particular shape: when confirmed academics collect and process the data, or when the parents themselves conform to academic stan-dards. This has resulted in the publication of ground-breaking testimony, for instance the work first published in 1988 by Kaufman, who used the tech-niques she was studying in anthropology to analyze her experience as the mother of a young woman with intellectual disability. Ingstad (1995), a trained social anthropologist, drew on her perceptions as mother of a disabled son to analyse attitudes towards families of children with disabilities not only in her native land, Norway, but in Botswana. This project concerning family quality of life research, to which parents pursuing disability studies at the university level have contributed throughout, is another excellent example.

Should One Consider The Participating Parents Representative Of Families Everywhere?

To a certain extent, no. First, a significant number of them have children with severe or multiple disabilities and serious behavior disorders. The nature of these disabilities probably accentuates these parents' vision of what is pres-ent compared to what is lacking in their lives. It may also influence readers' impressions of what it is like to raise a child with intellectual disability:

> My first two years I felt my life was finished. My smile left me for-ever . . . My life was full of horror (mother of a child with self-inju-rious behavior). (Family Saleh, from Jordan, quoted in H. Mittler, 1995, p. 18)

The majority of families do not have to contend with such levels of disability.

Second, many of the children described are relatively young or close to adolescence,[1] whereas more and more, as time goes on, the problems of older family caregivers with adult children are coming to the fore.

Third, many of the participating parents belong to the prosperous strata of relatively mobile, industrialized nations. In contrast to the situation in most regions of the world, formal supports exist in their respective countries.

---

1   Adolescence can be a stressful period for all families, whether or not the child in ques-tion has a disability. Prolonged states of adolescence can be particularly difficult for all concerned.

These parents know how to access them, and they qualify for the services available. Their sophisticated backgrounds also distinguish them from what typifies the vast majority of parents of children with intellectual disabilities: their involvement in university-level disability studies, and their enthusiasm for this research project in particular, set them clearly apart.

Thus these families may appear quite special, even privileged, compared to others. But distress does not depend solely on economic resources or social standing, as witness the recent case in the United States of America of a couple who, despite their wealth and public commitment to the cause of disability, suddenly felt themselves incapable of caring for their severely disabled child and left him with his toys and medical supplies on the doorstep of a hospital (Copeland, 1999). Who knows, who will ever truly understand, what hardship this couple felt unable to face alone.[2]

We must not disregard the families participating in this study on the grounds that they are too well off to know what the "real" problems are. On the contrary, we need to acknowledge that which, in their testimony, relates to families everywhere. As will be seen by the complementary quotations in this chapter, collected during the International Year of the Family, these exceptionally eloquent parents are representative in many ways because their words echo those voiced by families in equally developed countries but with differing cultural backgrounds, by families coming from less privileged social strata in the same countries, and by families in developing nations around the globe.

What Quality Of Life Domains Are Truly Universal?

In his chapter discussing this research, Bob Schalock identified eight fundamental domains of individual quality of life. This is an excellent framework. But once one attempts to judge the respective importance of these domains, it is essential to maintain the notion of overall balance. Living conditions and value systems vary greatly from one part of the world to another. What appears a weighty issue in one setting may be of negligible significance elsewhere. Entire domains may, to the uninitiated observer, appear absent; the division between work and play may not be clear; advocacy may be hesitant in certain nations; formal supports and services may not exist.

Should this imply that families living in economically impoverished environments cannot conceivably attain a good quality of life? Such an assumption should be avoided at all cost, as recent anthropological studies of disability in different cultures have made evident (e.g., Holzer, Vreede & Weigt, 1999; Ingstad, 1995; Kalyanpur & Harry, 1999). This being said, we can, and must, point out obvious shortcomings that, regardless of the country, can make families' lives extremely difficult: negative attitudes,

2   Every year we hear of desperate cases like this one. Although they are the exception rather than the rule, they must nevertheless be heeded as cries for help from the many.

inadequate or nonexistent supports, services that undermine the family's as well as the individual's best interests.

What Are The Challenges To Achieving Family Quality Of Life?

Given the variety of situations they embrace, organizations like Inclusion International (200 local, national, and regional parent-driven associations, 115 countries, a global population of 60 million children and adults with intellectual disability) are constantly forced to go back to basics. An ecological definition of quality of life, based on the overall interaction of mankind and "his" environment, suits our purposes. According to Marika Bakonyi (1997) of the Centre Universitaire d'Ecologie Humaine et des Sciences de l'Environnement in Geneva,

> satisfaction of physical and physiological needs alone, often dependent on the quality of the physical environment in which the individual (or population) lives, are not enough to fulfill a person's expectations with regard to personal existence. The need for security, for social contact, for respect, self-realization and aesthetics, all of which depend on the social environment, must also be satisfied. (author's translation, p. 59)

Regardless of the wealth of a nation and the way this wealth is distributed among its citizens, what appears to be most lacking in quality of life for families of children with intellectual disabilities is Bakonyi's second category, covering social needs. Throughout the world, the way parents feel about their lives as they bring up a child with an intellectual disability seems to be just as important as the tangible circumstances with which they cope.

Scars From The Initial Impact

From the beginning, family confidence is shaken. The birth of a child diagnosed as having an intellectual disability immediately transforms any life plans the parents may have made.

> It was so unexpected. It was a tremendous shock, just as if our happiness was going to be taken away from us, as if our life would change as a whole, entirely. (Family Oleffe, from Belgium, quoted in H. Mittler, 1995, p. 19)

Some parents appear to have experienced a fracture in time: seeing their lives flash in front of their eyes, some dreams never to return. They are forced to reconstruct their own future while caring for a child who may be more difficult than an ordinary child would be. All the while they must cope with social messages that are a far cry from the welcome signs usually given an ordinary child.

The majority of neighbors and local people see the whole issue as a curse from God. (Family Marandu, from Tanzania, quoted in H. Mittler, 1995, p. 23)

The early years are particularly hard, especially for mothers (Redmond, 1996, Roeher Institute, 2000). Both parents must learn their task from day to day. Young couples may feel themselves "institutionalized" within the confines of their own home.

A Jordanian mother explained her problems by speaking of the exhaustion, tension, and sleepless nights she and her husband endured because of the demands of caring for their daughter. So great was this mother's difficulty that she compared her situation to a prisoner's, and wished that she had been one of the prisoners pardoned by the late King Hussein (H. Mittler, 1995, p.58)

Many children experience health problems, are slow to acquire social and mental skills, have only a shaky relationship with the community. All of these challenges can contribute to a sense that, no matter what they plan from there on, everything will be a question mark.

Fortunately many families of children with intellectual disabilities are quite resilient. Once they are familiar with their child and the environment in which they must function, they snap back. They learn to track down those who can truly help where help is needed, and to work the system.

A member of a Belgian family who consulted a psychologist found answers to questions that medical doctors and books did not provide (H. Mittler, 1995, p. 81)

Their knowledge and coping skills increase as time goes on. Their sense of balance returns.

Uncertainty

Unfortunately this balance can be upset at any time by a variety of factors. In the modern societies presented in the study, one of the fundamental expectations is that people should plan ahead and be able to see their plans fulfilled. Many families of children with intellectual disabilities have greater difficulty maintaining this level of "quality" in their lives than do others because the pattern of their lives must be continually reshaped.

Their children do not follow the usual course, but who can really tell them what course their children *will* follow? Sometimes the short-term predictions come true; sometimes they are belied. Many families have the strong impression that nobody knows, or that nobody will tell them. Some choose not to believe what they are told because their child already contradicts what the experts say. All in all, there are few sound truths on which they can rely anymore.

Within minutes we were told that Jo-Ann had Down's Syndrome. They thought that she had a hole in the heart and that there was a chance that she would not live. If she did live she would not sit up until she was 2, would not walk until she was 7 and would have a severe speech problem (if she talked at all).

The only thing that they were right about was the speech. . .

In February 1993 Jo-Ann was 18 so we decided to have a party . . . It was a great evening . . .

Not too bad for a child they said would not live, is it? (Margaret Crutch, quoted in Fairbrother, 1994)

When the strains of adolescence hit, families often have great difficulties coping with the situation.

Life in a family where there is an adolescent member can be worrying and frustrating. Life in a family where there is an adolescent member who also has (an intellectual disability) can be intolerable. (Fairbrother, 1994)

Balanced family dynamics? If supports are insufficient, family energy turns inward in order to sustain the disabled child. Relations between spouses can shift. Siblings may lose out because there are not enough mental, physical, and financial resources within the family circle to fulfill everyone's needs, and because of stigmatization encountered outside.

His younger brother loved Lee Eun when he was little, and Lee Eun has always got on well with his younger brother, but as he has gotten older Sin Myong thinks that her younger son has suffered through having a disabled brother. He has expressed resentment that his parents did not have another healthy child to share the tasks and to help care for Lee Eun. He was upset and hurt because of the teasing and verbal abuse that Lee Eun was exposed to . . . He was also reluctant to bring friends home. (Family Yang, from Korea, quoted in H. Mittler, 1995, p. 48)

Todd and Shearn (1996) have described vividly the changing quality of time for families that bring up an intellectually disabled child. "Free" time often becomes a thing of the past. To ensure the care their child requires, parents may forego personal leisure activities, even holidays. Their days are often marked by tight organization:

It is difficult to go out on the spur of the moment, and everything has to be planned before any leisure activity can be pursued. (Family Ghareb, from Lebanon, quoted in H. Mittler, 1995, p. 57)

At the same time, such plans can be upset at any given moment if the child with intellectual disability has unanticipated needs or erratic patterns of behavior. Planning ahead, even through to the end of the week? Preparing the child's future as well as their own? Pious wishes. Living from one day to the next, often told that their child has no tomorrow, it may appear pointless for them to imagine the future, knowing that the projections they make can be demolished within seconds.

Financial Insecurity

Family life is more or less the same (with a disabled child) except that we have less money. (Family Leung, from Hong Kong, quoted in H. Mittler, 1995, p. 31)

Referring to a study in the United Kingdom by the Office of Populations Censuses and Surveys (1988), P. Mittler & H. Mittler (1994) write that, despite disability allotments, families of children with disabilities have incomes that are on average 22% lower than those of equivalent families in the population as a whole. How can this be?

As a result of care-giving responsibilities, careers sometimes take unexpected, often irreversible directions. Parents may find it very difficult to reconcile their family responsibilities with employers' demands, restricting their opportunities for choice of position and promotion. Professional couples may find one or the other spouse moving to part-time work or giving up any prospect of gainful employment.

Professor Chowdhury turned down offers of banking jobs because of the pressure this would involve, and also refused work that might involve transfers which would dislocate the family. (Family Chowdhury, from Bangladesh, quoted in H. Mittler, 1995, p. 31)

Single parents may find it difficult to find adequate employment at all. This has long-term effects on financial status. Carers whose careers have been compromised lose pension credits in those states where there is a social security plan. In societies where parents count on their offspring for care during their twilight years, life-long care giving for a child who cannot work, in turn, means loss for the parent(s) of their own future support.

Women are typically struck harder than men. They may find themselves divorced or abandoned by their spouses due to the presence of disabled children. Single working mothers can find themselves living close to the poverty line, since a woman's salary is likely to be far lower than what the father of her child would have brought home for performing the same job.[3]

---

3   This is where the nuclear family shows itself to be most vulnerable, because support depends on a single individual whose means for sustenance are restricted by social mores. In societies where the extended family remains intact and mutualization of resources is a given, the possibilities for informal support are greater, balancing out to some extent the lack of social services.

Families that do obtain "entitlements" may be wary of them because these are not, in fact, guaranteed. Allotments may be sufficient to cover the child's needs today but will not be enough to cover them tomorrow. The supports received can be withdrawn, depending on the whims of a social worker who decides that the family no longer qualifies, service provision criteria that reduce supports at a given point in time, or the changing policies of governments.

> The local council home help carers are very good, but the administration has been most unsatisfactory in recent years. They have tried very hard to limit their service. (David's Family, from Australia, quoted in H. Mittler, 1995, p. 80)

Personal Insecurity

The sense of personal security may be shaken when one has a child with an intellectual disability. Some parents, living with a child with difficult behavior, are physically vulnerable. All know they can be subjected to socialized forms of aggression as soon as they leave the home: public criticism coming from other parents, bullying of the child by other children on the playground. The presence of an intellectually disabled child in a family's midst can draw the entire family into the public eye, inviting people from all walks of life to pass judgment.

It takes years for some families to develop a skin thick enough to resist such slings and arrows, and it can wear thin again as time goes by since levels of social tolerance tend to drop as the child grows older (especially if the adolescent or adult does not bear visible signs of disability).

Unreliable Networks

Formal supports change regularly. The new speech therapist on Thursday follows the physiotherapist on Wednesday. His schedule conflicts with that of the psychotherapist, whose philosophy and techniques differ from those of the psychiatrist who was reassigned the case a few weeks before, and who is never on time for appointments anyway.

Informal support networks, too, change with time. In the mobile urban societies described, parents of children with intellectual disabilities see friends drift away, professional circles shrink, and opportunities for involvement outside the home rise like mist, evaporating with the dawn.

> For example, H. Mittler (1995) describes an Israeli family in a Tel Aviv apartment building, whose members are isolated and seldom interact with neighbors or family (p. 54).

In more traditional societies there appears to be more stability in relationships, but, given the world we live in, networks can dissipate as quickly as neighborhoods shift in color and composition.

In our old neighborhood the neighbors were nice. They would take Akrima into their homes. The present neighbors don't interact much. They are upset if we leave him outside. (Family Sorayra, from Jordan, quoted in H. Mittler, 1995, p. 52)

Discrimination

Those who use service groups have been defined as clients rather than people. Moreover, service group users are thought to lack the confidence and other positive qualities that would help them be autonomous (National Institute for Social Work, 1993).

Parents perceived as seeking help too early are sometimes called over-anxious, while those who opt out of respite care are called overprotective. Families find it difficult to avoid being labelled abnormal (P. Mittler, H. Mittler, & McConachie, 1986).

Like people with disabilities themselves, parents of children with intellectual disabilities often face discriminatory attitudes. The fact that they have produced such a child reflects upon them (after all, there is no smoke without fire).[4] Their ability to raise the child in an adequate manner may be put into doubt. Despite the fact that financial supports seldom compensate for the real, long-term costs of raising and sustaining children with intellectual disability throughout their lifetime, such allotments are perceived as "benefits." When a report comes in about the rare family which appears to be exploiting the welfare system, the entire group of supported families may be tarred with disrepute.

Siblings of children with intellectual disabilities are judged as well. If they stand up for their brother or sister who is being abused, some people will label them defensive. In industrial societies, those who provide care may be looked upon as "surrogate parents." If, however, they distance themselves from their sibling, they may be criticized for "rejecting" the disabled member of their family.

Those who, later, throw themselves into social work may be perceived as compensating. But if they throw themselves into other lines of work and succeed, they can still be viewed as compensating through overachievement. In other words, no matter what they do, brothers and sisters of children with intellectual disability may find it hard to win.

The "core" of disability in their family may even mean that some of them will have difficulty finding spouses.

4   It is important to remember that for centuries, the birth of an intellectually disabled child implied that the parents were either morally or genetically at fault. Today in Western society it is understood that the first no longer applies, but the second, more than ever.

Frustration And A Sense of Injustice

Many parents appear exasperated. Supports are in insufficient supply, they are not adapted to the child's needs or the family's lifestyle, and they cost too much. Coherent information is hard to find. Services must be fought for and even those obtained are not truly free. If one does not apply when the child is young, it is even more difficult to obtain supports later on. The overall impression is that of an endless struggle with the system, as if everything must be paid for in the currency of strife and humiliation.

Viewed from the outside, one has the impression that parents of children with intellectual disability have been charged overnight with a crime, found guilty, and condemned for life with no one coming to their defense. They are quickly shunned, shunted into a gray zone whose very existence they hadn't suspected, and subjected to the dictates of this new world's guardians: doctors and nurses, case workers, psychologists, special educators.

How many families must fill out endless forms to prove that they qualify, subject their lives to endless scrutiny, stand in long queues and put their names on long waiting lists, listen to experts pontificate and accept services that are not what they want (because they are better than nothing)? Beyond the pure waste in energy which many welfare services appear to demand, there is something vaguely punitive about all this.

Can The Caring Relationship Contribute To Family Quality Of Life?

How then do families maintain their sense of personal identity and self-respect? They draw upon their own strengths as well as those of peers, and they develop networks of support where all have the same goals. They learn to rise above superstition, ignore negative images, and manage on their own. They do whatever they can to regain control of their lives. And they change their scale of values.

To many, the effort expended in raising and sustaining a child with intellectual disability may be considered a throwaway, without any return. But if it is so unrewarding, why do parents take on this task, much less persist in their care-giving role for years and years?

The answers are not new. Parents have been telling us for years that their children have brought something exceptional into their lives, something which they would never have encountered otherwise. (H. Mittler, 1995).

Why does the literature not transmit this information? Admittedly, parental testimony is rarely expressed in terms suited to scientific accountability. Poetry often appears the only way to express the powerful feelings families find themselves caught up in and lyrical phrases are, of course, easily discounted as not objective. But how else does one convey the electric charge of validation when one's eyes finally meet those of one's child, or the intense joy of seeing him or her master an essential task? The problem, how-ever, lies beyond issues of scientific method and style. It's more a question of deep-seated prejudice.

In modern, industrialized societies, people who are not intimately involved in raising a child with intellectual disability find it difficult to imag-ine that the child is anything more than a millstone. Children and adults alike are so devalued that it is almost impossible for outsiders to imbue them with anything positive and to give credit to what parents say about the qual-ity of their lives with these children. Parents who insist they find personal value in loyalty and love are seldom believed.

Can people who have not gone through such an experience suspend their disbelief? I once asked a parent from Eastern Europe if this were possi-ble. He answered, "With the mind, yes; but with the heart, no. Only those who have been there can truly understand."

One *can* make the conscious choice to believe these committed parents. Once this is done, raising a child with intellectual disability can be seen as potentially fulfilling. But we quickly find ourselves in a paradoxical situa-tion: If families present themselves as finding value in what lies beyond most people's imaginations, if they present their lives in a positive light, can they expect anything from the community?

The answer is troubling. When seeking support, families must insist on the burden of care (as opposed to the satisfactions), demonstrate without a doubt that they are unequal to the task and that they need help. Doing one's duty in difficult circumstances is seldom enough to merit aid. Parents may have to present an image of defeat if they wish to gain anything.

> Parents are partners in the care of their child—they deserve respect, sensitivity. No one chooses to have a disabled child . . . you should-n't have to break down in order to get services. (parent, quoted in Russell, 1994)

Where Do Families Find The Support They Need?

If society expects families with children who are intellectually disabled to be victims (if not sinners) and perpetuates age-old mechanisms that keep them exhausted and downtrodden, who is there to help them regain a posi-tive image of themselves and their sense of self-respect? Who exonerates par-ents and siblings, telling them that intellectual disability is not a tragic flaw in their essential background, that they are not to blame for what has befallen them, and that regardless of how they are judged by others, they can, and will, cope? Peers who have gone through the same trials.

Families have been supporting each other since time began. Parents of children with intellectual disability have always spoken to other parents, because in doing so they realize that they are neither alone in what they are facing, nor are they alone to face it.

> The parents of several such disabled children have formed a self-help group, and we are trying to help each other in a small way. (Family Murthy, from India, quoted in H. Mittler, 1995, p. 71)

Parent-driven groups encourage and glorify amateurism in the fullest sense of the word: They are composed of self-made people who truly love their children. Self-help groups provide precious information, a space to express one's feelings about raising a child with intellectual disability, practical and moral support, a remedy for the social isolation encountered elsewhere. They also encourage pride and a real sense of accomplishment, given that the older members of such groups are living proof of what can be achieved within the space of a single lifetime.

Many descriptions of parents of children with intellectual disabilities, written by professionals, leave the impression that these parents are (to paraphrase Winnicott) "never good-enough." But unlike professionals who have opted for this vocation and received the training necessary for fulfilling the job's demands, parents of children with a disability have not chosen this trail, nor have they been prepared for it. They very seldom benefit from any advance warning and, as one Welsh mother has described, they "hit the ground running." Despite the element of surprise, within a short time many develop an exceptional sense of direction as well as the capacities required. All this is done without the benefit of formal training.

As a whole, they are ordinary people who find themselves in exceptional situations, forced to go far beyond what is normally expected of a parent. To do so, they tap unsuspected resources within themselves and reach out to strangers as well, setting themselves goals they would never have considered otherwise.

Some parents attain levels of competence that equal, and even surpass, those of professionals. Obliged to function within complicated welfare systems, they often find themselves knowing the rules of the game better than those who manage the game.

Some take up professional studies in order to provide, themselves, the care their child needs:

> I learned how to drive a car so that I could bring her to the private class. I started a degree in psychology and speech therapy so that I could help my daughter. (Helen's mother, from Belgium, quoted in H. Mittler, 1995, p. 40)

Others invent special techniques and equipment; create services out of nothing; learn to manage major not-for-profit enterprises; organize events on the local, regional, national, even international level. A number of them develop skills as political and social advocates, communicate with academics and philosophers, even find themselves dealing with government and elected officials as familiars. For a handful, the scale of achievement in the defense of their children goes far beyond anything anyone could have ever have dreamed: making the leap from a small-town existence to addressing the United Nations Commission for Social Development.

For any other parent, such accomplishments would be considered exceptional careers. Are the parents of children with intellectual disability granted equal recognition?

What Will Be The Situation 25 Years From Now?

If we continue to track the same families that shared their experiences at the turn of the 21st century, we will find the children much older in 2025. Some will be in prime adulthood; others will have reached middle age; a few will even be approaching old age.[5] Among them will be severely disabled adults whom no one expected to see survive. The needs and expectations of these adults with regard to health, housing, employment, social life, and recreation will have evolved, consistent with the advance of time. One hopes society will have been able to respond to these new needs, in particular appropriate health care and supports at the moment of retirement.

What is important to retain regarding family quality of life is the fact that their parents will be even older. Most of the families contributing to this book are middle-aged professionals: In 2025 they will probably be reducing their commitments as they themselves reach retirement age. Given the increased life expectancy of their children, their responsibilities as caregivers will not necessarily have ceased with time (as was often the case in the past). As a result, they may find themselves bound to the care-giving role for years on end.

Concurrently those parents who are elderly may be experiencing increasing problems with regard to health and physical strength. Many will suddenly find themselves single caregivers because their spouses have passed on.

The critical situation of aging caregivers will become more and more visible as the current tendency gathers speed, of elderly parents and grandparents continuing to act as primary caregivers. Will the "children" still be living with these (grand)parents in 2025, as the policies of 2000 would appear to encourage?

The idea of adult children remaining in the family home throughout their lifetimes may appear an absurdity to some, but it is not. Even in countries where residential care was (or still is) the official norm, a significant proportion of adults with intellectual disabilities continue to live with their

5   In the not-so-distant past, care for a child with an intellectual disability lasted a relatively short time: In the 1960s children with Down syndrome, for instance, barely survived adolescence. Now they commonly live 60 to 65 years.

parents. In those countries that have made significant efforts to downsize long-stay institutions and to resettle people with intellectual disabilities in the community, hundreds of thousands of adults have remained outside this movement, having never left their parents' homes in the first place. And in countries where service provision is close to nil, there never has been any place for them to live other than with their family.

In such cases, will the relationships between parents and offspring remain the same? How will the generation gap affect the quality of their shared lives? In dealing with family quality of life, we must look carefully at the implications of family care as time draws on.

Three fundamental situations sum up the amount and type of care older families may be called upon to provide: weekend parenting, part-time parenting, and full-time parenting (Breitenbach, 1999).

Weekend Parenting

Weekend parenting complements some form of residential provision, more or less distant from the family home. Parents who are relieved of daily care giving may nonetheless feel responsible for weekends and holidays, because these signify that the parents continue to "care."

Unfortunately, parental aging and fatigue can lead to discordant recreational needs. Younger people with intellectual disability may be tempted by sports and other outdoor occupations, whereas their parents may have developed less energetic tastes such as reading or watching television. How will they deal with this?

New supports may be required, such as that of accompanied travel. If parents cease to drive their personal vehicle and public transportation is unavailable or unreliable, the adult child with intellectual disability will likely have difficulty reaching the family home on his or her own. How can the family relationship, embodied by regular visits, be maintained?

Part-Time Parenting

Part-time parenting implies some form of daycare occupying the adult with a disability, who returns to the parental home evenings as well as weekends and holidays. The issue of recreation is just as important here, although distance may not be an issue. But there are new factors producing stress and anxiety.

If no housing separate from the family home has been arranged for, planning for the day when the "child" can no longer depend on his or her parents for family care will slowly but surely become a concern. Moreover, if the adult child is dependent, parents may find themselves incapable of providing the physical effort required to move, lift, bathe the person, and so forth.

Full-Time Parenting

Full-time parenting signifies day-in and day-out care, 365 days of the year. Voluntarily or involuntarily distanced from social services, these parents maintain full responsibility for their child, whose physical and social universe is the replica of their own. Often only one parent remains, resulting in high levels of interdependence: Neither member of the dyad knows how to function without the other close by.

The physical and mental effort of providing care every day is telling, at an age when peers are supposedly entitled to devote their time to travel, to grandchildren, or to peaceful occupations like quiet gardening. However, providing care appears to keep elderly caregivers going. Krauss and Seltzer (1993) have observed that, despite health problems, mothers who continue to provide care for an adult with intellectual disability consider themselves healthier than do mothers who no longer have children at home. Nevertheless, health becomes a real preoccupation since any fragility in the caregiver puts the whole family unit at risk.

More important is the constant stress of wondering what will happen to the adult child when the parent is no longer there to watch over him or her, given that there is no obvious relay in sight. Can the elderly parent(s) call on siblings to fill in for them? There may be no siblings, or siblings may choose not to fulfill such parental expectations. Others may not be prepared to take on the full task assumed by the parent, because as families grow smaller, the possibility of shared responsibility shrinks accordingly. And even if some are devoted to their brother or sister, siblings may have personal concerns that can make replacing the parent caregiver rather difficult: their own families to raise; crowded housing (as a result of the worldwide exodus to cities); and dual careers (when both spouses work, there is no carer at home in the daytime, as was the case for previous generations).

Without the prospect of an immediate surrogate within the family circle, parental anxiety can increase with each new sign of approaching mortality. Every day they wonder at what point in time the dreadful break will occur, whether or not they will have any warning at all, and what will happen after they are gone. For some parents, this stress is harder to bear than the actual task of providing care, and quality of life is irrevocably compromised.

Such families exist today, even in nations with highly developed and extensive service systems. A recent study in France, where the population approaches 60 million, projected the figure of 10,000 to 20,000 older families caring full-time for an adult child with a disability (Breitenbach, 1997). The majority had offspring with moderate-severe intellectual disabilities. The same phenomenon has been observed in other developed nations, and the problem is now emerging in less prosperous nations as well (Breitenbach, 2000).

Instances in industrialized countries of long-term, full-time care are likely to diminish with the passing of this generation of parents. But in other countries, in particular developing countries where life expectancy for both parents and offspring is increasing just as elsewhere, there will still be, undoubtedly, numerous full-time caregiver families in 2025.

Worldwide, parallel aging of parents and offspring will bring new pressures on social services. At present, only a handful among the 60 million people with intellectual disability have reached the standard age at which individuals are counted as "older": 60 years or more. Only now are they are beginning to be noticed among the 580 million people in the world today who have reached the same age marker.

The vast majority of the parents of the young people with intellectual disability who are involved in this study on family quality of life will, by 2025, have joined this age group. In the meantime the global number of persons 60 years and older will probably have increased by 75% (World Health Organization, 1999). Because of age-related diseases and impairments, the parents will have their own needs, in particular those who develop Alzheimer-type dementia (a disease that affects 20% of people aged 80 or more and has long-term effects not only on the individual but on the support system). Thus intellectual impairment, regardless of whether it occurred at birth or is acquired, will affect growing numbers of people worldwide.

Given that there will be only so much money to go around and that the demands for support will be so great, aging adults with life-long intellectual disability may find themselves in competition with their own parents for services. To respond, there may well be a shift from specialized provision for identified groups (e.g., older people with intellectual disability) toward generic provision based on compensation of particular functions.

What About Future Generations?

One hopes that attitudes will have softened with time, that the birth of a child with intellectual disability will not be perceived as negatively as it is now. But to achieve this softening, we must counter the age-old idea that such people should not be. Unfortunately this idea appears stronger every day.

Genetic research is extremely attractive and raises huge hopes for reducing certain kinds of disability. The problem is that the only "treatment" currently proposed for fetuses in whom intellectual disability is detected, is definitive. Parents who learn as a result of prenatal diagnosis that they are likely to produce a disabled child encounter pressure to terminate the pregnancy. Such pressures are likely to increase in time, despite efforts from groups like Inclusion International to ensure free choice. Parents who persist in desiring a child who has been announced in advance as being "different" may see their medical insurance coverage threatened (such cases have already occurred). Social supports may also come under threat if the idea spreads that such parents must take the full consequences of their decision.

There is also the risk that society will develop the illusion that, thanks to biotechnology, all forms of intellectual disability can be prevented. What will this mean for the many children in whom the presence of intellectual disability cannot be attributed to genes? Will the families of such children, who had no choice in the matter, be treated like those who could (should?) have decided against their child's life?

Despite the popular dream that certain disabilities will soon be a thing of the past, families with disabled offspring may actually be more numerous than they are at present, because medical technology is already saving children who "normally" would not have survived. What quality of life can be expected for parents who find themselves bound by love as well as by obligation to offspring who will remain heavily dependent for 35 to 40 years and more, if society does not lend a helping hand?

What Supports Will Fulfill Families' Needs?

Generally speaking, one hopes society will have acknowledged by 2025 both the right for such children to exist and the right of such families to be supported. Specifically, we will need an unbiased view of what is involved in caring for a child with an intellectual disability, one that registers not only the burden involved but the positive benefits and achievements.

Family quality of life research will help us achieve this view. For some of the domains discussed in earlier chapters, the distribution appears fairly clear. Families of children with intellectual disability appear to find positive value in interpersonal social and "political" relationships (i.e., the domains of emotional well-being, family relations or functioning, and community involvement and advocacy). On the other hand, they frequently lose out or score negatively on financial prosperity and free time (i.e., the domains of financial well-being and recreation and leisure).

The remaining domains of health, productivity, and supports all are somewhat harder to position in the scale.

Physical and mental health can tip either way, depending on biological as well as psychological factors.

Evaluating productivity depends a great deal on what a given society perceives as value-adding effort. Just like any other job, providing care requires physical and emotional energy as well as time. But if care giving is considered nonproductive, this domain will continue to be problematic for families of children with special needs.

What about supports? The temptation here is to equate "supports" with "services." Supports are invaluable, and they can come from any source. But they are not necessarily professional or even organized by welfare services. In fact, many economically disadvantaged countries are learning to use local resources to support the families of children with disabilities, rather than call for formal, specialized services that, beyond the issue of whether or not the community can afford them, tend to cut families off from others. Although it is not a panacea (see O'Toole, 1991), community-based rehabilitation (CBR) appears to offer great potential for both the children and the families involved and for the community as a whole.

Even in countries where formal, institutionalized services are available, it would be unwise to suggest which kinds of services are needed by all families. Lifestyles and expectations vary so much from one nation to another, from one culture to another, even from one family to another.

Do families need *more* services? Family quality of life will not necessarily be ensured by increased service provision. To be perfectly truthful, this author has met families that have chosen to do without the welfare services in their country in order to *preserve* their family quality of life.

The only answer to "what supports will fulfill families' needs?" is to put the question to those most intimately involved, the individual families themselves. They know what they need, and what they don't need. They are competent advisors, and their words must be considered credible both by the people charged with making overall policy decisions, and by those implementing the policies in the field.

Basing their findings on the results of the work performed by ILSMH Task Force for the International Year of the Family, Peter Mittler and Helle Mittler (1994) have summed up what parents seek, regardless of the country in which they live: access to information, practical advice, advocacy in situations of conflict, protection from abuse for their children. Desired supports range from more positive attitudes, shared care, financial assistance, and counseling to family-to-family and self-help groups.

In the same document published by the United Nations to celebrate the International Year of the Family, Mittler and Mittler (1994) discussed some general guidelines for supports. Their priorities for support included: (a) respecting the rights of the person with disabilities, (b) listening to and working with families to identify needs, (c) ensuring that support is tailored to individual families, (d) maintaining flexibility of support in response to changes over time, (e) identifying those needs among people with disabilities and their families that are similar to the needs of other people, (f) empowering people with disabilities and their families to exert as much control as possible, and (g) fostering community integration for the person with disability and his or her family.

The sum of these considerations is clearly related to the need for supportive attitudes and respect. To parents of children with intellectual disabilities, the exact number and type of services available may be far less important than the spirit in which they are offered.

Conclusion

The legitimate and necessary role of families as carers must be better recognized. Families raise the citizens of tomorrow, nurture those who came before, and ensure the well-being of those who can (as well as those who cannot) work today. We need to accept that caring for others is a real occupation, worthy of compensation and supports. This means sufficient resources must be available to families so that they can fulfill this task, either by themselves or with the aid of others.

In the long-term we need a life-span approach to family care so that older carers can continue to ensure that which society counts on them to provide, without their quality of life being irrevocably compromised. To do this requires a real sense of partnership with families and a family-centred approach as opposed to one that targets only the individual with a disability.

It will be a great boon to all if service provision, whatever form it takes, can be perceived and organized as a whole rather than as a succession of multiple bits, and if workers in the field of social services can pull themselves out of certain charity-based models of behavior. The greatest coverage in the world will be worth nothing if families that come asking for support are not treated with consideration.

A Word Of Caution

Will family quality of life research lead to improvements in the quality of the lives of care-giving families? That is the intention of the people who have initiated this project and the objective we have all worked for.

If family quality of life research leads to concrete measures designed to ensure and enhance quality of life for families caring for a child with intellectual disability, then we are on positive ground and the initial purpose of this research will have been fulfilled.

But a potential skid is already laid out. The chapter from Wales describes how, as government shifts more and more of the responsibility for care back onto families, policy makers are realizing that care-giving families must be kept operational if they are to continue relieving society of this charge. To "prevent any breakdown of the caring relationship," the essential needs of these families must be understood and addressed.

Thus family quality of life research interests policy makers. But their interests are not necessarily in the best interest of families. If, for instance, in this era where everything must be quantified and costs must be reduced wherever possible, family quality of life research leads to refinement of "minimum daily requirements for family survival" and governments align their service provision to ensure only these minima, then a number of desperate families may obtain even less than they have now. The original objective of this research will have been perverted. [6]

Can such deviations be prevented? Perhaps not. Can they be tempered? Yes, by insisting on qualitative analysis (as opposed to quantitative) and by ensuring that the voices of those most intimately involved is always heard loud and clear: *the voices of the families themselves.*

Author Note

The author respectfully thanks the families and friends of Inclusion International who assisted her in preparing this text: Maarit Aalto, Cristina Braun, Moussa Charafeddine, Françoise Jan, Ronit Jana-Kashmon, Elaine Johansson, Peter Mittler, Peter Müller, and Maria Amélia Vampré Xavier.

6   A similar trap was noted recently when, appalled by the conditions prevalent in a number of Eastern and Central European institutions housing children with disabilities, some well-meaning nongovernmental organizations wanted to establish international standards for such institutions. Organizations of people with disabilities were quick to advise caution, given that establishment of norms implicitly condoned warehousing of children with disabilities and could authorize service providers to reduce quality wherever institutions were superior to what the norms required.

References

Bakonyi, M. (1997). La qualité de vie en écologie humaine: quelques définitions [The quality of life in human ecology: Some definitions]. *Prévenir, 33,* 59.

Breitenbach, N. (1997). *Fortes et fragiles: Les familles vieillissantes qui gardent en leur sein un descendant handicapé [Strong and fragile: The aging families who provide home care for handicapped relatives and children].* Paris: Fondation de France.

Breitenbach, N. (1999). *Une saison de plus: Handicap mental et vieillissements [One more season: Mental handicap and aging].* Paris: Desclée de Brouwer.

Breitenbach, N. (2000). Aging: Achieving a broader view. In M. Janicki & E. Ansello (Eds.), *Community supports for aging adults with lifelong disabilities.* Baltimore: Paul H. Brookes.

Breitenbach, N. (in press). Growing old with disability, discovering disability with old age: Same or different? In M. Priestly (Ed.), *Disability and the life course.* Leeds, UK: Leeds University.

Copeland, L. (1999, December 30). Disabled and abandoned: A Pennsylvania mystery. *The Washington Post,* p. A1.

Fairbrother, P. (Ed.). (1994). *Adolescence in the family.* Brussels: International League of Societies for Persons With Mental Handicap.

Ingstad, B. (1995). Mpho ya Modimo—A gift from God: Perspectives on "attitudes" toward disabled persons. In B. Ingstad & S. R. Whyte (Eds.), *Disability and culture.* Los Angeles: University of California Press.

Kalyanpur, M., & Harry, B. (1999). *Culture in special education: Building reciprocal family-professional relationships.* Baltimore: Paul H. Brookes.

Kaufman, S. Z. (1999). *Retarded isn't stupid, Mom!* (2nd ed.). Baltimore: Paul H. Brookes.

Krauss, M. W., & Seltzer, M. M. (1993). Current well-being and future plans of older caregiving mothers. *Irish Journal of Psychology, 14*(1), 48–63.

Mittler, H. (1995). *Families speak out: International perspectives on families' experiences of disability.* Boston: Brookline.

Mittler, P., Mittler, H., & McConachie, H. (1986). *Working together: Guidelines for partnership between professionals and parents of children and young people with disabilities,* Guides for Special Education No. 2. Paris: UNESCO.

Mittler, P., & Mittler, H. (1994). *Families and disability.* Occasional Papers Series, No. 10, Vienna, Italy: United Nations.

National Institute for Social Work. (1993). *Building bridges between people who use and people who provide services.* London: NISW.

Nolan, M., Grant, G., & Keady, J. (1996). *Understanding family care: A multidimensional model of caring and coping.* Buckingham, UK: Open University Press.

Office of Populations Censuses and Surveys. (1988). *Survey of disability in Great Britain: Part 5. Financial circumstances of families.* London: Her Majesty's Stationery Office.

O'Toole, B. (1991). *Guide to community-based rehabilitation services.* Guides for Special Education No. 8. Paris: UNESCO.

Redmond, B. (1996). *Listening to parents: The aspirations, expectations, and anxieties of parents about their teenager with learning disability.* Dublin, Ireland: University College, Family Studies Centre.

Roeher Institute (2000). *Beyond the limits: Mothers caring for children with disabilities.* North York, Ontario, Canada: L'Institut Roeher Institute.

Russell, P. (1994). Access to the system: Support services, financial assistance, and practical help for parents of children with disabilities. In P. Mittler & H. Mittler (Eds.), *Innovations in family support for people with learning disabilities,* (pp. 33–54). Lancashire, UK: Brothers of Charity (U.S. distributor Paul H. Brookes).

Todd, S., & Shearn, J. (1996a). Struggles with time: The careers of parents with adult sons and daughters with learning disabilities. *Disability & Society, 11,* 379–401.

Todd, S., & Shearn, J. (1996b). Time and the person: The impact of support services on the lives of parents of adults with intellectual disabilities. *Journal of Applied Research in Intellectual Disabilities, 9*(1), 40–60.

United Nations. (1993). *The standard rules on the equalization of opportunities for persons with disabilities.* New York: Author.

Winnicott, D. W. (1971). *Playing and reality.* London: Tavistock.

World Health Organization. (1999). *Ageing: Exploding the myths.* Geneva: Author, Ageing and Health Programme.

Epilogue

For many people, life is a panorama of shadings, of hues that do not change radically and that blend comfortably, of common expectations and predictabilities, of usualness. There are few jarring intrusions, infrequent colorings that dramatically change one's worldviews.

For families who have children with disabilities, however, there are no panoramas of shadings, of compatible hues, of commonness and usualness. From the very beginning, all is different. For Margaret and Tony Jones, of Adelaide, Australia, pregnancy with Ryan was the first jarring intrusion, the first recoloring of their world:

When my amniocentesis tests revealed that my baby had chromosomal abnormalities and Down syndrome, I broke down and cried . . . It was a very stressful pregnancy, because they give you all the negatives and none of the positives in whatever was going on . . . Look, there are a lot of people who think I'm stupid and self-centered because I've gone and had him, [when I was] too old. You know, I'm not sorry. You know, he's special. I don't know whether it is because he is my last . . . We've got a tough road ahead. We'll take whatever comes . . . I reckon the problems [with his health] will come later on, when he goes to school. That's not going to make much difference; he's just another human being, really . . . I'm not sorry we had him because he's so much love, and everything else he's brought to our family . . . It's very negative, [the perspective of some physicians]. It really shouldn't be, because, [speaking about Ryan], they're a life, they're human . . . I think [friends and service providers] cannot be bothered with [Ryan's] kind in society; that's what it is . . . It's like getting a kick in the tummy and bouncing back up again. I mean, I'd do it again. It's hard sometimes . . . I hope 25 years down the track things will be different for Down syndrome children . . . Yes, I'd like to see him achieve what most other children achieve . . . I want to see [children with disabilities] get in this society *more of a fair go*.

And just what is "more of a fair go"? It's a fair question, answerable only if one entertains still other inquiries. How shall one know a "fair go" when one sees it? Who will determine what is fair? By what standards and processes will societies and countries measure "a fair go"? What role can the tripartite combination of families, researchers, and policy leaders play?

This much we ourselves know: Less able does not mean less worthy. This moral assertion—this Judeo-Christian or Kantian creed—is true of people who have disabilities, and it is no less true of their families.

Indeed, it may well be, as the authors in this book individually and collectively assert, that less able means more worthy. More worthy of systemic inquiry, more worthy of the benefits of research, more worthy of policy and programs, and more worthy of social and moral capital.

That is an end much to be desired, and perhaps it is one that is attainable through the international effort evidenced by the Eloisa de Lorenzo Symposium (described in chap. 1).

Family quality of life inquiries, however, have more than their instrumental, their utilitarian values. They have their existential values, too, for they illuminate the complexities of life and ask us all—whether or not we are affected by disability—to embrace those complexities.

And then to act, for to embrace is but the first step toward enhancing the quality of life of all the Margarets, all the Tonys, and all the Ryans.

The second step is best summed up in a maxim from the chapter we wrote with our colleagues: Knowledge is power only if the knowledgeable act powerfully.

And this is equally true: Knowledge is power only if the powerful are knowledgeable.

If this book contributes anything of lasting value, it will be to inform—to make more knowledgeable; to stimulate—to make more powerful; and to illuminate—to express the poetry of life affected inescapably and most existentially by disability.

Rud Turnbull

Ann Turnbull

Ivan Brown